Lecture Notes in Computer Science 15379

Founding Editors

Gerhard Goos
Juris Hartmanis

The series Lecture Notes in Computer Science (LNCS), including its subseries Lecture Notes in Artificial Intelligence (LNAI) and Lecture Notes in Bioinformatics (LNBI), has established itself as a medium for the publication of new developments in computer science and information technology research, teaching, and education.

LNCS enjoys close cooperation with the computer science R & D community, the series counts many renowned academics among its volume editors and paper authors, and collaborates with prestigious societies. Its mission is to serve this international community by providing an invaluable service, mainly focused on the publication of conference and workshop proceedings and postproceedings. LNCS commenced publication in 1973.

Margherita Antona · Constantine Stephanidis ·
Qin Gao · Jia Zhou
Editors

HCI International 2024 – Late Breaking Papers

26th International Conference on
Human-Computer Interaction, HCII 2024
Washington, DC, USA, June 29 – July 4, 2024
Proceedings, Part VI

 Springer

Editors
Margherita Antona
Foundation for Research and Technology -
Hellas (FORTH)
Heraklion, Crete, Greece

Constantine Stephanidis
University of Crete and Foundation for
Research and Technology – Hellas (FORTH)
Heraklion, Crete, Greece

Qin Gao
Tsinghua University
Beijing, China

Jia Zhou
Chongqing University
Chongqing, China

ISSN 0302-9743 ISSN 1611-3349 (electronic)
Lecture Notes in Computer Science
ISBN 978-3-031-76817-0 ISBN 978-3-031-76818-7 (eBook)
https://doi.org/10.1007/978-3-031-76818-7

Foreword

This year we celebrate 40 years since the establishment of the HCI International (HCII) Conference, which has been a hub for presenting groundbreaking research and novel ideas and collaboration for people from all over the world.

The HCII conference was founded in 1984 by Prof. Gavriel Salvendy (Purdue University, USA, Tsinghua University, P.R. China, and University of Central Florida, USA) and the first event of the series, "1st USA-Japan Conference on Human-Computer Interaction", was held in Honolulu, Hawaii, USA, 18–20 August. Since then, HCI International is held jointly with several Thematic Areas and Affiliated Conferences, with each one under the auspices of a distinguished international Program Board and under one management and one registration. Twenty-six HCI International Conferences have been organized so far (every two years until 2013, and annually thereafter).

Over the years, this conference has served as a platform for scholars, researchers, industry experts and students to exchange ideas, connect, and address challenges in the ever-evolving HCI field. Throughout these 40 years, the conference has evolved itself, adapting to new technologies and emerging trends, while staying committed to its core mission of advancing knowledge and driving change.

As we celebrate this milestone anniversary, we reflect on the contributions of its founding members and appreciate the commitment of its current and past Affiliated Conference Program Board Chairs and members. We are also thankful to all past conference attendees who have shaped this community into what it is today.

The 26th International Conference on Human-Computer Interaction, HCI International 2024 (HCII 2024), was held as a 'hybrid' event at the Washington Hilton Hotel, Washington, DC, USA, during 29 June – 4 July 2024. It incorporated the 21 thematic areas and affiliated conferences listed below.

A total of 5108 individuals from academia, research institutes, industry, and government agencies from 85 countries submitted contributions, and 1271 papers and 309 posters were included in the volumes of the proceedings that were published just before the start of the conference. Additionally, 222 papers and 104 posters were included in the volumes of the proceedings published after the conference, as "Late Breaking Work". The contributions thoroughly cover the entire field of human-computer interaction, addressing major advances in knowledge and effective use of computers in a variety of application areas. These papers provide academics, researchers, engineers, scientists, practitioners and students with state-of-the-art information on the most recent advances in HCI. The volumes constituting the full set of the HCII 2024 conference proceedings are listed on the following pages.

I would like to thank the Program Board Chairs and the members of the Program Boards of all thematic areas and affiliated conferences for their contribution towards the high scientific quality and overall success of the HCI International 2024 conference. Their manifold support in terms of paper reviewing (single-blind review process, with a minimum of two reviews per submission), session organization and their willingness to act as goodwill ambassadors for the conference is most highly appreciated.

This conference would not have been possible without the continuous and unwavering support and advice of Gavriel Salvendy, founder, General Chair Emeritus, and Scientific Advisor. For his outstanding efforts, I would like to express my sincere appreciation to Abbas Moallem, Communications Chair and Editor of HCI International News.

September 2024   Constantine Stephanidis

HCI International 2024 Thematic Areas
and Affiliated Conferences

- HCI: Human-Computer Interaction Thematic Area
- HIMI: Human Interface and the Management of Information Thematic Area
- EPCE: 21st International Conference on Engineering Psychology and Cognitive Ergonomics
- AC: 18th International Conference on Augmented Cognition
- UAHCI: 18th International Conference on Universal Access in Human-Computer Interaction
- CCD: 16th International Conference on Cross-Cultural Design
- SCSM: 16th International Conference on Social Computing and Social Media
- VAMR: 16th International Conference on Virtual, Augmented and Mixed Reality
- DHM: 15th International Conference on Digital Human Modeling & Applications in Health, Safety, Ergonomics & Risk Management
- DUXU: 13th International Conference on Design, User Experience and Usability
- C&C: 12th International Conference on Culture and Computing
- DAPI: 12th International Conference on Distributed, Ambient and Pervasive Interactions
- HCIBGO: 11th International Conference on HCI in Business, Government and Organizations
- LCT: 11th International Conference on Learning and Collaboration Technologies
- ITAP: 10th International Conference on Human Aspects of IT for the Aged Population
- AIS: 6th International Conference on Adaptive Instructional Systems
- HCI-CPT: 6th International Conference on HCI for Cybersecurity, Privacy and Trust
- HCI-Games: 6th International Conference on HCI in Games
- MobiTAS: 6th International Conference on HCI in Mobility, Transport and Automotive Systems
- AI-HCI: 5th International Conference on Artificial Intelligence in HCI
- MOBILE: 5th International Conference on Human-Centered Design, Operation and Evaluation of Mobile Communications

Conference Proceedings – Full List of Volumes

1. LNCS 14684, Human-Computer Interaction: Part I, edited by Masaaki Kurosu and Ayako Hashizume
2. LNCS 14685, Human-Computer Interaction: Part II, edited by Masaaki Kurosu and Ayako Hashizume
3. LNCS 14686, Human-Computer Interaction: Part III, edited by Masaaki Kurosu and Ayako Hashizume
4. LNCS 14687, Human-Computer Interaction: Part IV, edited by Masaaki Kurosu and Ayako Hashizume
5. LNCS 14688, Human-Computer Interaction: Part V, edited by Masaaki Kurosu and Ayako Hashizume
6. LNCS 14689, Human Interface and the Management of Information: Part I, edited by Hirohiko Mori and Yumi Asahi
7. LNCS 14690, Human Interface and the Management of Information: Part II, edited by Hirohiko Mori and Yumi Asahi
8. LNCS 14691, Human Interface and the Management of Information: Part III, edited by Hirohiko Mori and Yumi Asahi
9. LNAI 14692, Engineering Psychology and Cognitive Ergonomics: Part I, edited by Don Harris and Wen-Chin Li
10. LNAI 14693, Engineering Psychology and Cognitive Ergonomics: Part II, edited by Don Harris and Wen-Chin Li
11. LNAI 14694, Augmented Cognition: Part I, edited by Dylan D. Schmorrow and Cali M. Fidopiastis
12. LNAI 14695, Augmented Cognition: Part II, edited by Dylan D. Schmorrow and Cali M. Fidopiastis
13. LNCS 14696, Universal Access in Human-Computer Interaction: Part I, edited by Margherita Antona and Constantine Stephanidis
14. LNCS 14697, Universal Access in Human-Computer Interaction: Part II, edited by Margherita Antona and Constantine Stephanidis
15. LNCS 14698, Universal Access in Human-Computer Interaction: Part III, edited by Margherita Antona and Constantine Stephanidis
16. LNCS 14699, Cross-Cultural Design: Part I, edited by Pei-Luen Patrick Rau
17. LNCS 14700, Cross-Cultural Design: Part II, edited by Pei-Luen Patrick Rau
18. LNCS 14701, Cross-Cultural Design: Part III, edited by Pei-Luen Patrick Rau
19. LNCS 14702, Cross-Cultural Design: Part IV, edited by Pei-Luen Patrick Rau
20. LNCS 14703, Social Computing and Social Media: Part I, edited by Adela Coman and Simona Vasilache
21. LNCS 14704, Social Computing and Social Media: Part II, edited by Adela Coman and Simona Vasilache
22. LNCS 14705, Social Computing and Social Media: Part III, edited by Adela Coman and Simona Vasilache

https://2024.hci.international/proceedings

26th International Conference on Human-Computer Interaction (HCII 2024)

The full list with the Program Board Chairs and the members of the Program Boards of all thematic areas and affiliated conferences of HCII2024 is available online at:

http://www.hci.international/board-members-2024.php

HCI International 2025 Conference

The 27th International Conference on Human-Computer Interaction, HCI International 2025, will be held jointly with the affiliated conferences at the Swedish Exhibition & Congress Centre and Gothia Towers Hotel, Gothenburg, Sweden, June 22–27, 2025. It will cover a broad spectrum of themes related to Human-Computer Interaction, including theoretical issues, methods, tools, processes, and case studies in HCI design, as well as novel interaction techniques, interfaces, and applications. The proceedings will be published by Springer. More information is available on the conference website: https://2025.hci.international/.

General Chair
Prof. Constantine Stephanidis
University of Crete and ICS-FORTH
Heraklion, Crete, Greece
Email: general_chair@2025.hci.international

https://2025.hci.international/

Contents – Part VI

Design for Older Adults

Accessibility and Design for All

Playing Games with NAO: Gamified Training for Mild Cognitive Impairment with Socially Assisted Robots

Xiao Dou and Li Yan[✉]

College of Fine Arts, Guangdong Polytechnic Normal University, Guangzhou, China
xiaodou@gpnu.edu.cn

Abstract. The social assistant robot (SAR) has a more human like interaction mode. It can effectively encourage MCI patients to actively participate in repeated cognitive training and enhance their social confidence by displaying a series of human like, multimodal emotional expressions and body language. This study constructed a research framework for SAR based intervention in MIC patients, designed a more persuasive and interventional cognitive training program, and implemented it on NAO robot, a representative model of SAR. By comparing the effectiveness of this training cognitive program before and after use in MIC patients, we can verify whether NAO robot based cognitive training interactive games have application value. The results show that SRA is reasonable and effective in cognitive training intervention for MIC patients, which is expected to provide different levels of cognitive intervention services for mild cognitive impairment patients.

Keyword: NAO; MIC; cognitive training; intervene

1 Introduction

With the increase of aging population in major industrialized countries, the number of mild cognitive impairment (MCI) has increased significantly [1]. It is becoming more and more important to provide them with support to avoid or at least slow down their cognitive decline, and participation in cognitive training can effectively prolong the progress of mild cognitive impairment (MCI) to dementia [2, 3]. Compared with traditional computer supported cognitive training, social assistant robot (SAR) has a more human like interaction mode. They can effectively motivate people by displaying a series of human like, multimodal emotional expressions and body language [2]. This makes it possible for them to encourage patients with MCI to actively participate in repeated cognitive training and enhance their social confidence.

Recent research shows that SAR intervention provides substantial cognitive benefits for individuals with social disability, autism and dementia. (Huijnen, Lexis,&de Witte, 2016) (Esteban et al., 2017; Marino et al., 2020) emphasized the positive impact of SAR assisted training on cognitive function [4–6]. Famous SAR models include PARO, NAO and Pepper robots. (Pino, Palestra, Trevino,&De Carolis, 2020) [7] Use NAO robot

M. Antona et al. (Eds.): HCII 2024, LNCS 15379, pp. 3–13, 2025.
https://doi.org/10.1007/978-3-031-76818-7_1

to carry out memory training for the elderly, focusing on slowing down the cognitive decline of patients with mild cognitive impairment (MCI).

Their research shows that NAO enhanced memory training can improve visual attention and treatment participation, and provide potential cognitive enhancement for the elderly. Gamification is now crucial in non-drug intervention. Serious play (SG) enables patients to participate in long-term through customized play mechanisms. Previous studies have shown that SAR plays the role of director and demonstrator in sports training, while serious games play content games to improve interest and effectiveness.

This study introduces a SAR based MCI cognitive training interactive game, which optimizes the role of SAR as a training instructor, and establishes a more dependent cognitive training program. Therefore, the main purposes are:

1. Design a cognitive training program that is more persuasive and interventionist.
2. It is implemented on the representative SAR model NAO robot.
3. The effectiveness of the training cognitive scheme is explored by comparing it with that of the MIC patients before and after use, so as to verify whether the NAO robot based cognitive training interactive game has application value.

2   Literature Review

2.1   SAR

In the field of assisted medicine, family use, support for the elderly and disabled or help with children in various activities, the demand for social assistant robots (SARs) with various environments, functions and users is growing SAR can be defined as the intersection of auxiliary robot (AR) and social interactive robot (SIR), because they provide help through social interaction [8]. Manca M et al. Therefore, SAR's participation in the field of auxiliary medicine is more advantageous and easier for patients to accept.

Since SAR can be classified in many ways according to the tasks and environments they perform, their autonomy [10] or their initiative and mobility [11], SAR design must consider these functional differences, as well as users, expected user experience and environment [12]. It is believed that social robots have been and are currently being used in many projects, research plans and experiments, but as many as one third of auxiliary technologies are abandoned within one year after use (Gurley&Norcio, 2009) [13]. Ferna´ Ndez Llamas et al. (2018) believed that in order to avoid this situation, it is necessary to propose a mechanism to understand users' views and attitudes towards technology, especially their views on robot platforms [14]. The development of SAR based on medically assisted treatment first gives priority to the needs of patients, then the needs of clinicians and nurses. Therefore, priority tasks need to be evaluated to determine the gaps in service provision, affordable prototyping opportunities, and design requirements for development [15].

2.2   Cognitive Training for MIC

Mild cognitive impairment (MCI) is an initial stage of cognitive decline, which does not affect the function of daily life, but may develop into more serious cognitive degradation, especially dementia [16]. Prevent MIC from further deterioration by inhibiting cognitive function through preventive measures.Christos Karapapas (2021) Propose a user-defined method of MCI detection capability combining serious games and machine learning, which includes a series of steps to train and evaluate the classification model. The model can distinguish healthy and cognitive disabled individuals according to game performance and other subjective data, This indicates that the combination of serious games and machine learning methods may become a supplement or alternative tool to the traditional cognitive screening process [17]. Chien Hsiang Chang et al., the results show that the new ISGR has aroused the interest of the elderly and improved their willingness to continue rehabilitation [18]. Research has confirmed that emerging training methods using new technologies such as virtual reality (VR) and mobile phones can be effectively used for cognitive training. Ruhong Ge et al. Sum-Yuet Joyce Lau&Harry Agius (2021) proposed the MCI-GATE (MCI-GAME Therapy Experience) framework for developing serious games as an effective cognitive and physical rehabilitation tool. The framework includes four parts, which can be used to guide game design and development: MCI players' brief introduction, representing the ability of MCI players; Core game elements, supporting games and game activities; Therapeutic element, which supports cognitive and physical rehabilitation through tasks and scenes according to the player's ability; Motivating elements to improve players' attitude towards serious tasks [16].

From this point of view, compared with other carriers, SAR is more suitable for cognitive training of MIC patients and easier to accept. The high-quality cognitive training mode should not only meet the needs of the MIC patients themselves, but also meet

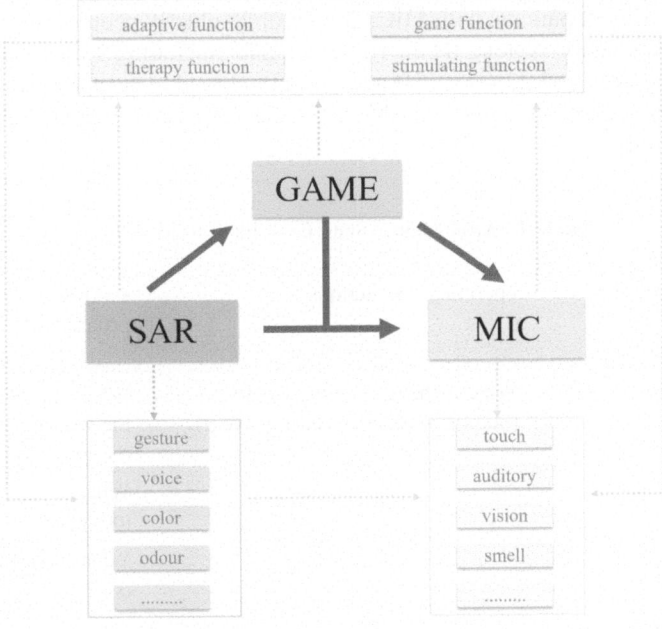

Fig. 1. The framework of the study

the play style while treating, so as to promote patients to accept more easily, and at the same time, it also needs to have incentive function to improve patients' enthusiasm. The way of SAR carrying cognitive training can be presented through voice, light, gesture and other ways that are consistent with the patient's sense of vision, hearing and touch. Therefore, according to this concept, we propose a research framework for SAR based intervention in MIC patients, as shown in Fig. 1.

3 Methodology

In this study, NAO robot, a typical model of SAR, is selected as the carrier for testing. The research route is: experiment task (cognitive training game) Input robot - select appropriate experimental objects - test their cognitive level before cognitive training - conduct cognitive training - test their cognitive level after training - compare their cognitive level before and after training - judge the effectiveness of task design and implementation according to the comparison data.

3.1 User Groups

The study selected an elderly community in Shandong Province, China, and the data were collected from February to March 2024. Participants are selected by convenient sampling. The initial screening included the management of the Mini Mental State Examination (MMSE) scale (Table 1) [20, 21]. The registration criteria were set as individuals with scores between 17 and 26, and this interval score represented mild cognitive impairment patients with MIC. A total of 25 elderly people were recruited to participate in the study. Among them, 16 participants, including 7 men and 9 women, with an average age of 63.22 years (SD age = 7.43), proved to meet the requirements of this experiment after being tested by the MMSE scale. Lock these patients for appropriate cognitive training.

Table 1. Mini Mental State Examination (MMSE)

Inspection program	operating instructions	scoring program	Correct score keeping
Orientation Orientation	What is the (day of the week) (number) (month) (season) (year)?	What day of the week is today?	1
		What's today's date?	1
		What month is it?	1

(*continued*)

Table 1. (*continued*)

Inspection program	operating instructions	scoring program	Correct score keeping
		What season is it?	1
		This year's vintage?	1
	Where are we now: (province or city) (district or county) (street or township) (what place) (what floor)	Where are we now (province, city)?	1
		Where are we now (district, county)?	1
		What street (township, village) are we in now?	1
		What is this place (address name)?	1
		What floor are we on now?	1
Memory Registration	Now I'm going to say the names of three things, and when I'm done, I'd like you to repeat them. (Please repeat them carefully for one second each). **"Balls," "flags," "trees."**Could you please say all three of these things again (mark for the first answer)	Repeat: Pickleball	1
		Repeat: Pickleball	1
		Repeat: trees	1
Attention and calculation	Please calculate 100 minus 7, then subtract 7 from the number you get, and so on, and tell me the answer after subtracting each 7 until I say stop. (If one answer is wrong, but the next answer is correct, only one error will be recorded.)	$100-7 = 93$	1
		$93-7 = 86$	1
		$86-7 = 79$	1
		$79-7 = 72$	1
		$72-7 = 65$	1

(*continued*)

Table 1. (*continued*)

Inspection program		operating instructions	scoring program	Correct score keeping
Recall		Now would you please name the three things I just asked you to remember? **"Balls," "flags," "trees."**	Memories: Balls	1
			Memories: The Flag	1
			Memories: Trees	1
language skills (6 sub-capacities) Language	naming capabilities	(Show the watch.) What is this thing called?	Identification: watch	1
		(Show the pen.) What is this thing called?	Identification: fountain pen	1
	the ability to restate	Now I'm going to say one thing, and I'm going to ask you to repeat it clearly after me." "Forty-four stone lions."	Repeat: forty-four stone lions	1
	reading skills	Please read the words and do what they say.**Close your eyes**	Follow the instructions on the paper: Close your eyes	1
	the ability to carry out orders	I'm going to give you a piece of paper and ask you to do what I tell you to do, now **"Take this piece of paper in your right hand, fold it in half with both hands and place it on your lap."** (Do not repeat instructions and do not demonstrate)	Follow verbal instructions: Hold the paper in your right hand	1
			Follow verbal instructions: Fold the paper in half	1
			Move on verbal instructions: place the paper on your lap	1

(*continued*)

Table 1. (*continued*)

Inspection program		operating instructions	scoring program	Correct score keeping
	writing skills	You write me a complete sentence	Be able to write a complete sentence (with subject, predicate, object)	1
	structural capacity	Here's a diagram. Draw it on a piece of paper, please	Drawing by example	1
Full marks				**30**

Results Interpretation	The mini mental state examination (MMSE), also known as the mini mental state examination, is simple, widely used at home and abroad, and is the first choice for dementia screening. There are 30 questions in total, 1 point for each correct answer, 0 point for wrong or unknown answer, and the total score range of the scale is 0–30 points
	Scoring reference
	27–30 points: normal cognitive functioning
	<27 points: cognitive dysfunction
	21–26 points: mild cognitive impairment
	10–20 points: moderate cognitive dysfunction
	Score 0–9: Severe cognitive dysfunction

3.2 Experimental Tasks and Implementation

In this study, the NAO robot's posture and trapper functions are used to program the task content into the robot, and experiments are carried out according to the task. MIC patient task is to continuously write a multiple of 3. The patient writes a number himself (he thinks it is a multiple of 3), gets the position of the visual capture device above the robot's eyes, and the robot will judge whether the number is a multiple of 3. If yes, it will nod, if not, it will shake its head. As shown in Fig. 2.

The experiment lasted for six weeks. During this period, participants were asked to play this designated game with NAO robot, at least 15 min a day, three days a week. Six weeks later, that is, after the cognitive training, the 16 MIC patients were tested again with the MMSE scale, and the corresponding test data were obtained. The standard of this test is that each MIC patient must have received at least 6 training sessions, otherwise, it

Fig. 2. Experimental scenario

means that the experimental requirements were not met, and the 16 patients all met the requirements. The data before and after cognitive training intervention (Table 2) were compared and discussed.

Table 2. Pre- and post-experimental data of the subjects

No	Sex (1 = male; 2 = female)	Age	First test MMSE	Last test MMSE	Whether or not the full six training sessions
1	1	68	21	24	Yes
2	2	72	22	24	Yes
3	2	77	21	25	Yes
4	1	73	23	25	Yes
5	2	84	22	26	Yes
6	1	81	22	25	Yes
7	2	81	22	24	Yes
8	2	69	24	24	Yes
9	1	70	23	26	Yes
10	2	78	22	27	Yes
11	2	77	21	26	Yes
12	1	77	24	26	Yes
13	2	64	22	25	Yes
14	2	79	24	25	Yes
15	2	76	23	24	Yes
16	2	77	22	27	Yes

Table 3. Comparative analysis of group test results

	Grouping	N	Mean	standard deviation	standard error of the mean
Test results	First mmse	16	22.3750	1.02470	.25617
	Last mmse	16	25.1875	1.04682	.26171

4 Experimental Results and Discussion

4.1 User Demand for Nao Robot

The experimental data were analyzed by SPSS, and the cognitive function was significantly improved when comparing the scores before and after the test after the cognitive training intervention. As shown in Table 3, specifically, 16 MIC patients were divided into one group, and the cognitive training effect was tested in groups. Before the cognitive training intervention, the mean MMSE for the first time was 22.3750, while the mean MMSE after the intervention was 25.1875, which fully showed that the cognitive training intervention was effective and significant.

In addition, in the average equivalence T test results (Table 4), it is assumed that the isovariance value is -7.680, the degree of freedom is 30, and the bilateral P value in the significance is <0.001. From this, the cognitive training intervention has achieved remarkable results.

Table 4. Test Results of Independent Sample T

		Levin variance equality test		T-test of mean equivalence					
		F	Significance	t	freedom	Significance		Average difference	Standard error difference
						One side P	Bilateral P		
Test results	Assumed equal variance	.007	.936	$-$7.680	30	$< .001$	$< .001$	-2.81250	.36622
	Do not assume equal variance			$-$7.680	29.986	$< .001$	$< .001$	-2.81250	.36622

The results of this study show that it is reasonable and effective to use NAO robots to intervene in cognitive training for MIC patients. NAO robots are expected to provide different levels of cognitive intervention services for people with mild cognitive impairment. MIC patients have a welcoming attitude towards social assistance robots, which may be accompanied by NAO robots, common game interaction Timely feedback and other functions can give MIC patients psychological texture function, which can not only provide emotional comfort when they are lonely, but also provide cognitive repair during the game, playing a different role than tablet computers [9]. Therefore, there is great potential to use SAR for cognitive intervention in MIC patients, and further exploration can be made in the intervention mode and degree.

4.2 Limitations and Further Research

There are some limitations in this study. First, the task of cognitive training is mainly to focus on the understanding of multiples of 3, and the requirements of response speed and accuracy are not mentioned. Sensitivity and accuracy testing are two important standards [17]. If the required results can be written within 3 s, will there be better auxiliary effects? If the auxiliary is blessed with both contents, whether it will help to repair the cognitive level remains to be further explored and may have better effects; Secondly, the cognitive training in this study is too simple, and it is impossible to know whether more complicated training tasks [22] or training combined with patients' body movements [23] will have better effects. It is possible that more complicated tasks will be beneficial to scientific intervention in cognitive repair, and it is possible that body movements will have more obvious effects on cognitive repair. Future research can be further expanded in these two aspects.

5 Conclusion

This study verified that SAR game cognitive training has a good effect on the cognitive impairment repair of MIC patients, which provides a certain reference for research in this field.

Acknowledgments. This study was funded by the Guangdong Social Science Association (grant number GD20XYS22) and Guangdong Polytechnic Normal University (grant number 2021SDKYB026).

References

1. Dou, X., Wu, C.-F.: Are We ready for "them" now? The Relationship between Human and Humanoid Robots. In: Rezaei, N. (eds.) Integrated Science: Science without Borders, vol. 1, pp. 377–394. Springer, Cham (2021). https://doi.org/10.1007/978-3-030-65273-9_18
2. Isernia, S., et al.: Diagnostic validity of the smart aging serious game: an innovative tool for digital phenotyping of mild neurocognitive disorder. J. Alzheimer's Dis. **83**, 1789–1801 (2021)
3. Xue, B., Xiao, A., Luo, X., Li, R.: The effect of a game training intervention on cognitive functioning and depression symptoms in the elderly with mild cognitive impairment: a randomized controlled trial. Int. J. Methods Psychiatr. Res. **30**, e1887 (2021)
4. Huijnen, C.A., Lexis, M.A., de Witte, L.P.: Matching robot Kaspar to autism spectrum disorder (ASD) therapy and educational goals. Int. J. Soc. Robot. **8**, 445–455 (2016)

5. Esteban, P.G., et al.: How to build a supervised autonomous system for robot-enhanced therapy for children with autism spectrum disorder Paladyn. J. Behav. Robot. **8**, 18–38 (2017)
6. Marino, F., et al.: Outcomes of a robot-assisted social-emotional understanding intervention for young children with autism spectrum disorders. J. Autism Dev. Disord. **50**, 1973–1987 (2020)
7. Pino, O., Palestra, G., Trevino, R., De Carolis, B.: The humanoid robot NAO as trainer in a memory program for elderly people with mild cognitive impairment. Int. J. Soc. Robot. **12**(1), 21–33 (2020)
8. Broekens, J., Heerink, M., Rosendal, H.: Assistive social robots in elderly care: a review. Gerontechnology **8**, 94–103 (2009)
9. Manca, M., et al.: The impact of serious games with humanoid robots on mild cognitive impairment older adults. Int. J. Hum. Comput. Stud. **145**, 102509 (2021)
10. Feil-Seifer, D., Mataric, M.J.: In: Defining Socially Assistive Robotics, 9th International Conference on Rehabilitation Robotics, IEEE: 2005, pp 465–468 (2005)
11. Schulz, T.W., Herstad, J., Tørresen, J.: Classifying human and robot movement at home and implementing robot movement using the slow in, slow out animation principle. Int. J. Adv. Intell. Syst. **11**, 234–244 (2018)
12. Liberman-Pincu, E., Parmet, Y., Oron-Gilad, T. Judging a socially assistive robot by its cover: the effect of body structure, outline, and color on users' perception. ACM Trans. Hum. Robot Int. **12**(2), 1–26 (2023)
13. Gurley, K., Norcio, A.F. In: Nuray Aykin, N. (eds.) A Systematic Review of Technologies Designed to Improve and Assist Cognitive Decline for Both the Current and Future Aging Populations, Internationalization, Design and Global Development: Third International Conference, IDGD 2009, Held as Part of HCI International 2009, San Diego, CA, USA, July 19–24, 2009. Proceedings 3, Springer, pp 156–163 (2009). https://doi.org/10.1007/978-3-642-02767-3
14. Fernández-Llamas, C., Conde, M.A., Rodríguez-Lera, F.J., Rodríguez-Sedano, F.J., García, F.: May i teach you? Students' behavior when lectured by robotic vs human teachers. Comput. Hum. Behav. **80**, 460–469 (2018)
15. Johnson, M.J., et al.: Task and design requirements for an affordable mobile service robot for elder care in an all-inclusive care for elders assisted-living setting. Int. J. Soc. Robot. **12**, 989–1008 (2020)
16. Lau, S.-Y.J., Agius, H.: A framework and immersive serious game for mild cognitive impairment. Multimedia Tools Appl. **80**, 31183–31237 (2021)
17. Karapapas, C., Goumopoulos, C.: Mild cognitive impairment detection using machine learning models trained on data collected from serious games. Appl. Sci. **11**, 8184 (2021)
18. Chang, C.-H., Yeh, C.-H., Chang, C.-C., Lin, Y.-C.: Interactive somatosensory games in rehabilitation training for older adults with mild cognitive impairment: usability study. JMIR Serious Games **10**, e38465 (2022)
19. Ge, R., et al.: The effects of two game interaction modes on cortical activation in subjects of different ages: a functional near-infrared spectroscopy study. IEEE Access **9**, 11405–11415 (2021)
20. Folstein, M.F., Folstein, S.E., McHugh, P.R.: "Mini-mental state": a practical method for grading the cognitive state of patients for the clinician. J. Psychiatr. Res. **12**, 189–198 (1975)
21. Wu, J.: Neurology. In: People's Medical Publishing House(eds.) (2005)
22. Jirayucharoensak, S., Israsena, P., Pan-Ngum, S., Hemrungrojn, S., Maes, M.: A game-based neurofeedback training system to enhance cognitive performance in healthy elderly subjects and in patients with amnestic mild cognitive impairment. Clin. Interv. Aging **14**, 347–360 (2019)
23. Lin, Y.F., et al.: Pilot study of interactive-video games in people with mild cognitive impairment. Int. J. Environ. Res. Public Health **19**(6), 3536 (2022)

Simplified Modelling Based on an Ontology of Users with Cerebral Palsy Interacting with People or Systems: Case Study of an Assistive System Used in Mobility

Yohan Guerrier[1] , Siegrid Bosquet[2], Octave Valadier[2], Nicolas Cauchois[1] ,
Véronique Delcroix[2] , Káthia Marçal de Oliveira[1] , and Christophe Kolski[1(✉)]

[1] LAMIH, CNRS, UMR 8201, University Polytechnique Haut-de-France, 59313 Valenciennes,
France
{Yohan.Guerrier,Nicolas.Cauchois,Christophe.Kolski}@uphf.fr
[2] Master TNSID, University Polytechnique Haut-de-France, 59313 Valenciennes, France
{Siegrid.Bosquet,Octave.Valadier}@uphf.fr

Abstract. Cerebral palsy is a domain not trivial when one should developed interactive systems. Based on that, an ontology describing different elements of cerebral palsy disability is proposed in order to support designers of interactive applications dedicated to users with this profile. This paper presents the iterative process used for the creation of this ontology, developed using Protégé software. The results of an initial evaluation based on a questionnaire are explained. A proof of concept for communication aid software usable in mobility illustrates its use by designers. Various perspectives arising from this ongoing research are then listed.

Keywords: Cerebral palsy · User model · Ontology · Communication aid · Mobility · Protégé · ComMob · Disability

1 Introduction

The World Health Organization (WHO) has classified the various types of disability into different categories [2]. We argue that, it is important for designers of interactive systems to at least be aware of the characteristics of users with disabilities who are likely to use the systems in question, and then to develop their knowledge on this subject.

This paper focuses on the category of physical disability, and more specifically on athetoid cerebral palsy (CP) [5]. This disability is often due to a lack of oxygen either during pregnancy, during delivery or a few hours after delivery [37]. This lack of oxygen can be caused by cardiac arrest or placement of the umbilical cord around the neck. There are two categories of cerebral palsy disability: athetoid and spastic. The athetoid category causes involuntary movements of the upper and lower limbs [43]. These movements are amplified during moments of stress, and disappear during sleep. The spastic category is symbolised by stiffness in the upper and lower limbs [4].

M. Antona et al. (Eds.): HCII 2024, LNCS 15379, pp. 14–29, 2025.
https://doi.org/10.1007/978-3-031-76818-7_2

In addition, people with CP have varying degrees of difficulty in speaking; this is known as dysarthria [9]. This speech problem causes a distortion of the sounds coming out of the person's mouth, but the person usually has no problem formulating correct sentences. It is important to note that people with athetoid CP often do not have intellectual or cognitive disabilities.

To compensate for speech difficulties, there are various communication aids [19]. The best known is the virtual keyboard. It is present on all computer devices. The virtual keyboard comes in several categories, meeting different needs [29]. Then one can find pictograms either in physical form in a communication notebook, or in computerised form in a communication aid application [13]. In both cases, the pictograms are organised into categories and themes. Finally, there are physical communication aids. This category includes the finger guide, the unicorn, eye tracking and voice recognition [12].

Designers (or more generally engineering specialists) are often unaware of such information. Therefore, modelling can be very usefull to support the development of interactive applications for people with cerebral palsy. To do this, we used an ontology. In computing, an ontology is a structured set of themes and concepts representing a field of information [42]. The ontology constitutes a data model representing a set of concepts in a domain, as well as the relationships between these concepts. It is used to reason about the objects in the domain concerned. An ontology makes it possible to organise and structure a body of shared knowledge and to establish a common vocabulary.

In this paper, we explain the approach taken to arrive at the first version of an ontology for modelling various elements related to the athetosis-type PC disability, without seeking to be exhaustive. The aim of this ontology is to help designers gain a better understanding of this disability, and consequently to help make their applications accessible to them.

This user modelling contributes to a traditional stage in the design of interactive systems in human-computer interaction [10, 25, 28]. This stage contributes to the identification of the user's needs in relation to the interactive system in question. The starting point for all modelling is the collection of data, which can come from a variety of sources (field observations, study of the literature, knowledge extraction from experts in the field, etc.). Next comes the structuring of this data. Finally, the modelling stage can begin.

This paper is organised as follows. Section 2 presents a brief state of the art in user modelling. Section 3 proposes a simplified ontology, focusing on cerebral palsy disability. Based on this proposal, Sect. 4 provides the results of an initial evaluation of the ontology. Section 5 describes a proof of concept of the use of this ontology using a communication assistive application. The paper ends with a conclusion and research prospects.

2   State of the Art in User Modelling

User modelling supports the design of interactive products and software, and user interfaces [10, 39]. It can be considered as one of the pillars of the field of human-computer interaction. Generally speaking, it enables us to understand end users, while helping to identify their characteristics, needs, behaviours and/or preferences, etc., in order to create solutions that are tailored to them.

The objectives of user modelling can in fact be varied [40], but can also be combined:

- Understanding users - User modelling aims to gain a more or less in-depth understanding of end users, their characteristics, skills, objectives and motivations. A better understanding can also be used to train designers. This is the objective of this paper.
- User-centred design [27] - By placing users at the centre of the design process and analysing them in detail, user modelling can help create products and services that effectively meet their needs and expectations.
- Optimising the User eXperience (UX) - By analysing user behaviour and preferences, user modelling helps to improve the user experience, by improving the quality of human-machine interactions.
- Personalisation and adaptation - By developing user models, it is possible to personalise interactions according to individual preferences, context of use and/or past behaviour, for example. This is part of the vast field of intelligent interaction.

Upstream of user modeling, there are various methods that can be combined [30, 35], for instance:

- User research - this includes qualitative methods (interviews, observations, focus groups, brainstorming) and quantitative methods (questionnaires, usage analyses) to gather information about users and their needs.
- Personas and scenarios - The creation of personas [7, 26] and usage scenarios (both textual and diagram-based, e.g. using UML activity diagrams) makes it possible to represent different types (or profiles) of current or future users and their possible interactions with the system.
- Cognitive modelling - this involves analysing the mental processes involved in using the system, including perception, attention, memory and decision-making. Frameworks on this subject have existed for many years, see for example the decision ladder proposed in [36].
- Analysis of usage (or interaction) traces - this involves exploiting real usage data (e.g. website usage) to understand user behaviour and identify areas for improvement (e.g. by noticing human errors and/or that pages are being ignored by users).
- It is also possible to identify and formalise a set of characteristics that will serve as criteria for customising or adapting both the user interface and the recommendations to be provided.

A user model is a data structure that is used to capture certain characteristics of an individual user, and a user profile is the actual representation in a given user model [40]. For example, an entity-association model, a class diagram or an ontology can be used. The data structure used in our research is the ontological structure (see Sect. 3), following on from our previous work [16]. The data included in the model depends on the purpose of the application. The model can include personal information such as users' names and ages, job types, interests, skills and knowledge, goals and plans, likes and dislikes, or data about their behaviour and interactions with the system [38].

In the case of people with disabilities, it can be difficult to identify certain needs or characteristics (for instance interaction skills) that need to be reflected in the user model, particularly in the case of communication disorders. Various case studies can be found in the literature. For example, in [21] and [23], the authors highlight the contribution of members of the disabled person's social environment in human-centered approaches. In

[1], proposals are made for adapting needs capture methods. In [8], the authors show how difficult it is to capture the needs of users who are deprived of speech, in the context of designing an eye-tracking system for computer control. Many other examples of studies can be found, such as [24] or [41].

3 Towards Ontological Modelling for Cerebral Palsy Disability: Approach and First Version

3.1 Objectives

The aim of our work on ontological modelling of cerebral palsy disability is to produce an initial version that presents, in simplified form, elements to support the training of interactive system designers. The aim is to identify a set of characteristics that can help them in their work, by giving them initial ideas about these potential target users.

Such support for this initial familiarisation is only proposed as a preliminary training stage. In the context of real projects, it will of course be essential for the designers who have been made aware to then interact directly with the target users, if possible, throughout a user-centred design process [27].

3.2 Work Process

Two Master's level designers in computer science were involved in the process. As part of their training, they had taken several teaching modules in software engineering and human-computer interaction, and had already had the opportunity to work on projects and/or training periods involving the design of interactive systems. Their objective was to propose an ontology focusing on cerebral palsy, aimed at designers of interactive systems intended for users with this profile. The aim was to raise designers' awareness of essential (representative) characteristics to be taken into account in projects.

Figure 1 summarizes the work process.

These designers began by reading various scientific papers on cerebral palsy in general, as well as papers describing work on designing systems for people with cerebral palsy (for example [16–18] ou [20]). It was also possible to consult web sites dealing with disability in general, and cerebral palsy in particular (including [11]).

Throughout the project, they were able to interact with two experts in the field of designing and evaluating systems for users with disabilities. These systems concerned users with disabilities directly (Parkinson's disease [34], cerebral palsy [17], intellectual disability [14]) or indirectly (disability awareness in companies [32]). It is important to note that one of these two experts is a person with cerebral palsy, and has a deep understanding of the needs and characteristics of the field. Interaction with the experts took the form of weekly meetings, and e-mail exchanges for additional information, particularly on cerebral palsy disability and the modeling of features related to it. During the meetings, the experts were able to study the ontology under construction and provide advice on how to improve it. The experts were also consulted on the procedures to be used to evaluate the ontology (importance of a pre-evaluation, versions of the questionnaire, types of participants, data analysis).

Several versions of the ontology have been produced, as illustrated in Fig. 1, all of which have been presented and evaluated at meetings, with the aim of improving the ontology.

The various versions of the ontology were produced using the Protégé software [33]. Protégé is an ontology editor. It is an open-source knowledge management system. It was created at Stanford University by Marc Musen. It is very popular in the semantic web field and in computer science research.

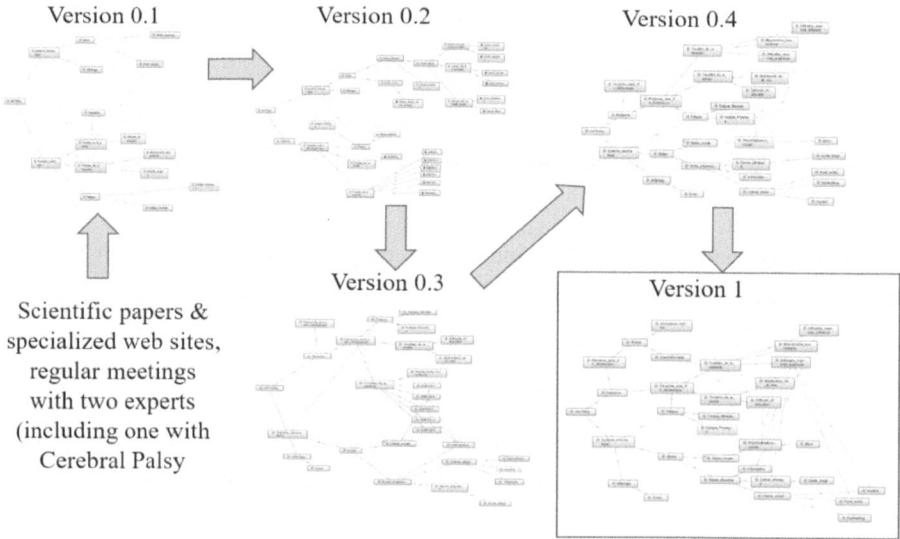

Fig. 1. Global approach

Figure 1 is not intended to show and explain each version of the ontology. Its aim is merely to give an overview of the various stages (versions) involved in arriving at the final version of our ontology. It is essentially this final version (called Version 1) that is explained in this paper (see Sect. 3.3, Fig. 2.

The first version (Version 0.1) only used the class and link functionalities (as defined by Protégé). Very general, it was considered too incomplete to be useful for a developer's understanding of cerebral palsy disability. This version did not cover enough aspects and lacked nuance about the different profiles of people with cerebral palsy. Indeed, it is important to specify that individual differences (which can be significant) exist and that each individual has their own preferences and abilities. It was also proposed to establish several models for several situations, and to add documentation via the annotation system of the Protégé software. In addition, the class names were not explicit enough to be clearly understood.

In the second version (Version 0.2), the designers decided to use individuals (in the sense of Protégé). Individuals are classes that can be instantiated only once. However, during the development of the ontology, the use of individuals quickly showed its limitations, as in order to model the cerebral palsy disability, they realised that the number of individuals would be too large, and therefore that the ontology would be incomprehensible. In addition, the terms used were too scientific and, as a result, application designers might have difficulty understanding the ontology. For example, the terms based on the acronym GMFCS (Gross Motor Function Classification System) designate different levels of limb mobility but are not explicit enough. In addition, the decision to develop the different types of virtual keyboard in this version was too specific and could not take into account all the existing virtual keyboards. This second version did not show how individuals interact with each other, or how people with disabilities interact with the system. Finally, it was also relevant to add clarifications regarding existing laws on certain classes. For example, specifying that the display is via a screen and that Fitts' law [31] must be taken into account. This law specifies that the larger the target to be reached on a screen, the easier it will be to reach it.

In the third version (Version 0.3), the designers decided to return to using classes for the ontology in order to make it more comprehensible. However, even when documented, the class names were still too precise. The decision was taken at a meeting to generalise the themes, using words that everyone could understand.

The third version was pre-evaluated on the basis of a questionnaire (the questionnaire used is described in Sect. 4.1) with a limited number of evaluators (6 evaluators). The initial comments (see Sect. 4.2) collected with the questionnaire were used to improve the ontology (in a fourth version, called Version 0.4) by simplifying the scientific themes and overly general concepts.

A final version (called Version 1) was then produced. It is described in the following section.

3.3   Description of the Latest Version of the Ontology (Version 1)

For the latest version of the ontology (Fig. 2), a person without cerebral palsy has been added. This person is part of the social environment of the person with a disability, also called the ecosystem by [22, 23]. We have chosen to mention only the caregivers because they are the ones who will have an impact on the behaviour and use of the system by the person with cerebral palsy.

This final version is the result of the combination of all the meetings and discussions. In particular, the experts provided a range of explanations on disability and its main characteristics, on the various technical means of compensating for disability in human-machine interaction, and on the importance of interaction between the disabled person and their caregiver(s). This final version takes also into account the feedback from the pre-evaluation carried out with 6 evaluators), see Sect. 3.2. This ontology is made up of two parts. The first represents the disabled person and the able-bodied person; the characteristics of these people and their interactions are summarised. The second part lists the different systems that enable people with cerebral palsy to communicate.

An overall description of this ontology, visible in Fig. 2, is as follows. The ontology, in its current simplified version, aims to express that we consider two types of people: those with cerebral palsy and those without cerebral palsy. The person with cerebral palsy may be characterised by motor disorders, speech disorders, as well as fatigue, which may be mental or physical. Speech problems can lead to elocution difficulties and a change in voice. Motor disorders can lead to difficulties with the lower limbs, as well as the upper limbs, and involuntary movements. The person without cerebral palsy may be a caregiver, able to provide assistance with motor skills; this person may have problems understanding the person with cerebral palsy.

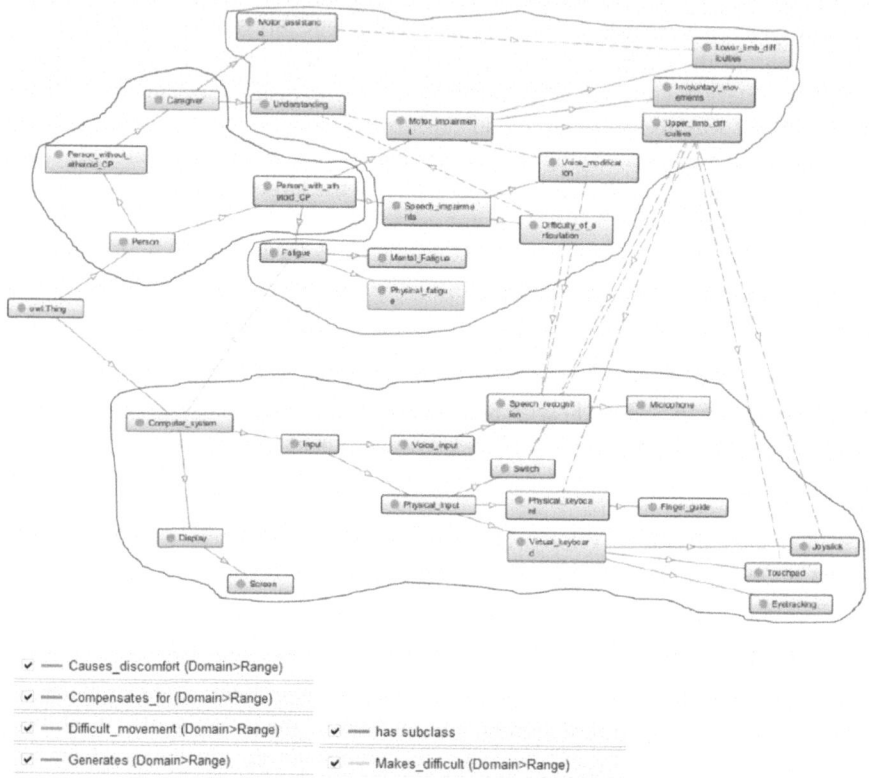

Fig. 2. Latest version of the ontology, obtained at the end of the process (called Version 1). The zone highlighted in blue corresponds to the field of IT and assistive technology; the red zone considers people; the green zone is specific to the field of disability.

The ontology also considers a computer system with a screen-type display. Using the system can cause fatigue. Input can be vocal, with voice recognition, requiring a microphone. Input can also be physical, with a switch, a physical keyboard (which may require a finger guide) or a virtual keyboard. The virtual keyboard can be combined with a joystick, touchpad or eyetracking.

Blue arrows correspond to subclasses (classical is-a relation in ontology). Green, gray and orange arrows represent relationship between concepts expressing possibilities of compensation (for instance by using *speech_recognition*).

The definition of each ontology theme is provided below.

Person: Represents a person.

Person_without_athetoid_CP: Represents a person without athetosis cerebral palsy.

Caregiver: Entity representing a person without cerebral palsy providing assistance to the person with cerebral palsy.

Motor assistance: Entity representing any motor-related assistance that can be provided (movement in space, limb guidance, etc.).

Understanding: Entity representing the caregiver's ability to understand when interacting with a person with cerebral palsy.

Person_with_Athetoid_CP: Represents a person with athetoid cerebral palsy.

Motor_Impairment: Entity grouping together the various motor disorders linked to athetoid cerebral palsy.

Involuntary_movements: Involuntary movements of the limbs of a person with athetoid cerebral palsy. These movements are more or less important depending on the person.

Upper_limbs_difficulties: Includes all the difficulties linked to the motor skills of the upper limbs, for example slight, partial or total paralysis of the upper limbs.

Lower_limb_difficulties: These include all difficulties related to lower-limb motor skills, for example the use of a cane to get around, or a manual or electric wheelchair.

Speech_Impairments: This entity covers the various speech disorders associated with athetoid cerebral palsy.

Voice_modification: Also known as dysarthria, this entity represents a change in voice tone and articulation linked to athetoid cerebral palsy.

Difficulty_of_articulation: This entity represents speech difficulties linked to athetoid cerebral palsy, more specifically the symptoms of athetosis on language, i.e. uncontrolled and involuntary movements of the tongue muscle.

Fatigue: Entity grouping together the different types of fatigue experienced by people with athetoid cerebral palsy.

Physical_fatigue: Fatigue felt physically by the person.

Mental_fatigue: Fatigue felt mentally by the person.

Computer_system: Represents any computer system.

Display: Entity representing the types of display of the computer system

Screen: Display screen of a computer system. Note that it is often preferable for the user to have a large enough screen to make it easier to use the computer system, particularly when using a virtual keyboard.

Input: Entity grouping together the different types of information input, whatever their nature.

Voice_input: Entity covering the different types of voice input.

Voice_recognition: Type of voice input. Entity grouping together the different voice recognition tools.

Microphone: Tool used for voice recognition.

Physical_input: Entity grouping together the different types of physical entry.

Physical_keyboard: Type of physical input. Entity grouping together the different physical keyboards.

Finger_guide: Type of equipment linked to the classic keyboard. This is a piece of equipment or a keyboard equipped so that the user cannot press two keys at the same time or change trajectory. It generally consists of a plastic plate with holes for each key placed on the keyboard.

Virtual_keyboard: Type of physical input, generally displayed on a screen. Entity grouping together the various tools for using a virtual keyboard.

Touch_pad: Tactile tool for using a virtual keyboard.

Joystick: Equipment connected to the computer system enabling a cursor and/or virtual keyboard to be used.

Eye_tracking: Input method for a virtual keyboard. Using a camera, it follows the user's eye in order to direct a cursor and/or use a virtual keyboard.

Switch: Type of physical input. Switches can be placed on an appliance or in a house in the case of a home automation system. They require movement of the user's upper limbs, and may also require movement of the lower limbs.

4 Initial Evaluation of the Ontology, Based on a Questionnaire

4.1 Questionnaire Adapted from the System Usability Scale (SUS)

To evaluate the ontology, we used a questionnaire adapted from the System Usability Scale (SUS) [6]. This questionnaire consists of 10 questions, scored from 0 to 4, ranging from "Strongly disagree" to "Strongly agree" (using a Likert scale). Each question alternates between positive and negative wording. A SUS score above 70 is considered, according to some studies, to be a favorable score [3].

In the initial SUS questionnaire (translated in French), we replaced the word 'system' with 'model'. The questions are as follows:

1. I think that I would like to use this model frequently
2. I found this model unnecessarily complex
3. I think the model is easy to use
4. I think I would need the support of a technical person to be able to use this model
5. I found the various functions in this model were well integrated
6. I thought there was too much inconsistency in this model
7. I would imagine that most people would learn to use this model very quickly
8. I found this model very cumbersome to use
9. I feel very confident using the model
10. I needed to learn a lot of things before I could get going with this model

Using these 10 questions, combined with a free-response question, we were able to evaluate and identify aspects of the ontology that needed to be adjusted.

The questionnaires were administered using Google Forms, an online platform for creating questionnaires and analysing responses.

4.2 Results

Initially, a small-scale evaluation of version 0.3 of the model was undertaken with the aim of refining our latest modifications and taking a step back, as well as allowing an evaluation of the questionnaire itself. On a panel of 6 users (average age 23; 5 men and 1 woman, field of activity: 5 in IT and 1 in health), the average score attributed to our ontology was 54.58. Feedback from users focused mainly on two points:

- The visibility of the arrows, which were considered difficult to discern.
- Clarification of certain terms, in particular the meaning of the finger guide.
- This analysis also highlighted a lack of clarity in the question "I think that I would like to use this model frequently". In fact, users did not take into account the context of the development of systems dedicated to people with cerebral palsy. In order to clarify this point, a contextual information was provided.

Following the application of these adjustments to the ontology and questionnaire, a larger-scale evaluation was carried out, this time on Version 1 of the model. From a sample of 23 participants (average age 31; 12 men and 11 women), the average score obtained was 70.80. The breakdown of the evaluators' field of study or activity is as follows: the majority study or work in the IT field (12 participants). For the others, the fields are: healthcare (2), engineering (other than IT) (2), human sciences / teaching (3), management (3), not mentioned (1).

The diagram visible in Fig. 3 illustrates the normalized average scores for each question. Normalization was achieved by considering the two types (odd/even) of questions (items) in the S.U.S. questionnaire and the method used to calculate the score of an item (for odd items: subtract one from the user response; for even-numbered items: subtract the user responses from 5). The average for each question (from 0 to 4) was then divided by four to obtain a value between 0 and 1.

Two questions received the lowest averages: Question 1 ("I think that I would like to use this model frequently"), and Question 4 ("I think I would need the support of a technical person to be able to use this model"). These averages show that the context would have benefited from even greater clarification. The average SUS score for these 23 participants was 70.54 (from 100, that can can be considered as *good*).

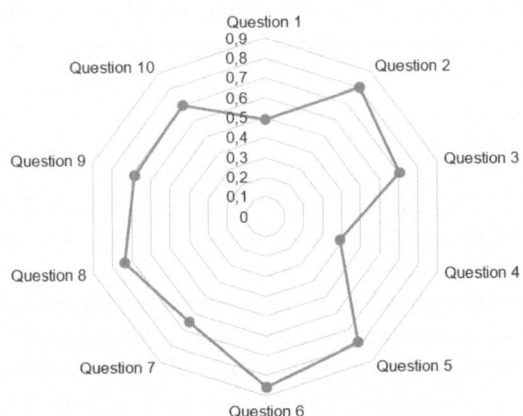

Fig. 3. Normalized scores of each question for all the answers

Restricting ourselves to the responses of people working in the fields of IT and health, the score stands at 68.03, slightly below a value considered favorable, but generally consistent with the overall score. We still notice a low average for Question 1. However, the drop in value for Question 4 is no longer apparent (see Fig. 4).

The evaluation of the model gives promising first results. It also gave us the opportunity to identify areas for improvement by studying the verbatims provided by the
participants.

Fig. 4. Normalized scores for each question for people in IT and healthcare domains

In the following section, a proof of concept gives an illustration of the exploitation of
the elements of the ontology. The framework used is that of a communication assistive
system for people with cerebral palsy, usable in mobility.

5   Proof of Concept on Using the Ontology for the Development of a Communication Assistive System Usable in Mobility

This section describes through a proof of concept the design of *ComMob Web* based
on the proposed ontology. *ComMob Web* is an application whose first version (called
ComMob) was proposed and developed by the first author of this paper, during his
PhD [17]. The aim of this assistive system is to help people with motor disabilities and
speech problems to communicate in mobile situations. One profile targeted in particular
concerns people with athetoid cerebral palsy.

ComMob stands for Communication and Mobility. Initially in software form, it was
transformed into a web application for easier access. *ComMob Web* offers the user a
set of pictograms grouped by theme and category. All the user has to do is select them
to formulate sentences. Users can prepare dialogues in advance to make discussions
more fluid. Finally, pictograms, categories and themes can be managed (added, deleted…). Figure 6 shows examples of *ComMob Web* screen pages (in french). For more
information, see [15] (Fig. 5).

From now on, let us imagine that *ComMob Web* has not yet been developed, and that
our objective is to develop a communication assistive system for people with cerebral
palsy. Let us assume that the client has provided us with the ontology presented in this
paper to understand initial elements relating to cerebral palsy.

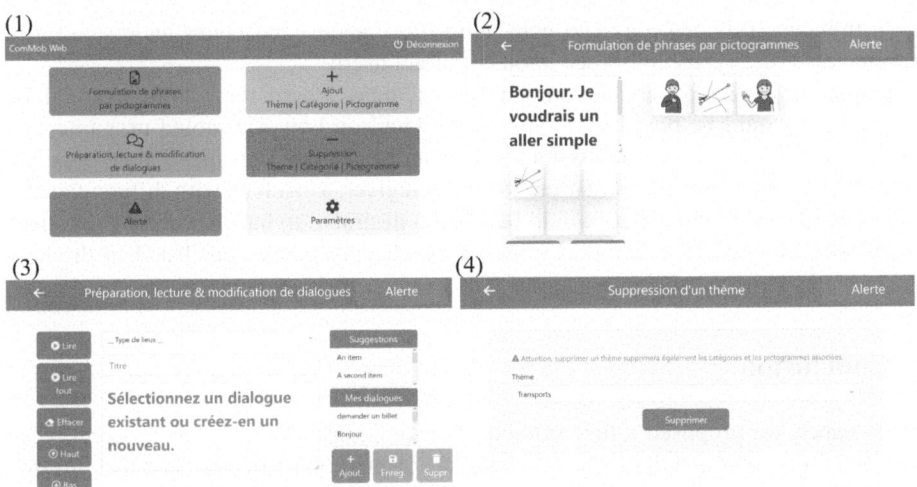

Fig. 5. (1) ComMob Web homepage. (2) Sentence formulation page with pictograms. (3) Dialogue preparation page. (4) Topic deletion page.

By studying the ontology, we can see that we have information on the people who will be using our future application, i.e. the disabled person and their caregiver. Then, we have explanations of the cerebral palsy disability. Finally, we can see a list of IT tools that can be used by the disabled person.

This ontology enables us to better understand certain needs and constraints of target users. For example, the fact that people easily experience mental fatigue tells us that we need to make the application as easy to use as possible. The use of icons to represent dialogues makes it easier to orientate oneself than would be the case with full texts. Another way of reducing the mental workload is to integrate a system that detects your surroundings and automatically suggests appropriate dialogues. To better understand this, let us take the following example: if the user is in an airport, the application could suggest prepared airport-related dialogues.

The ontology also points out that it is not easy for certain people with cerebral palsy to be precise in their movements. For this reason, the buttons used to interact with the application need to be large.

We also note that not all users have the same configuration (phone, tablet, with keyboard, voice recognition, etc.). This can encourage us to create a tool that can respond to as many cases as possible. That is why ComMob has been exported to the web, to be as compatible as possible. Of course, we have to make the tool responsive and ensure that it works on multiple devices and with all major web browsers.

The fact that caregivers are present in the ontology is also valuable for us. Indeed, they are important actors in the lives of the target users, and it is essential to take them into account. That is why, for example, an alert button can be integrated into the system to broadcast aloud the fact that you re in difficulty, to draw the attention of those around you. It may also be useful to allow you to notify a relative or help center via SMS or e-mail that you need assistance.

In this way, this ontology can help us to think about, and better understand to a certain extent, the needs and expectations of target users.

However, we have identified a number of areas where the ontology could be improved. It would be possible to have more detail on how a disabled user interacts with a smartphone, tablet and computer. It would have been useful to have concrete examples of communication situations with a caregiver, as well as with different actors in the outside world. Finally, it would have been desirable to have specific recommendations for user interface design. Further research perspectives are listed in the next section.

6 Conclusion

In this paper, we proposed a first version of an ontology related to the cerebral palsy disability. This version will evolve following the evaluation carried out and then following other uses and evaluations to be implemented. The approach was followed by two junior designers in regular interaction with two experts in the field of human-machine interaction applied to disabilities, including one with cerebral palsy (integrated into a team participating in numerous projects linked to disability domain). The aim of this ontology was to offer a simplified representation of different elements linked to cerebral palsy. This representation aimed to be easily understandable by designers of interactive applications so that they can adapt their analysis to this type of disability. Our ontology allows us to provide a first level of knowledge (before going deeper into it).

Several versions of this ontology were produced before arriving at a final version (called Version 1). Subsequently, we evaluated this version of the ontology with a panel of people who did not necessarily have knowledge in the IT field or in the field of disability. This evaluation was done through an online questionnaire and then the data was analyzed. Overall, the results are promising, with the ontology being generally understandable by the participants.

From this first version of the ontology, several research perspectives can be highlighted. First of all, it would be possible to improve this version by (1) continuing to test it with people without specific knowledge concerning cerebral palsy, then (2) by testing it with several cerebral palsy disability specialists, and also with caregivers. In addition, we can also ask for additional opinions from people who have cerebral palsy themselves to make improvements or additions. These complementary evaluations could be done in the form of a questionnaire as we did for the evaluation of this version and/or during interviews. Note that other ontology evaluation methods may be considered following a state of the art on ontology evaluation in general. To find specialists and people with cerebral palsy, it would be possible to contact specialized centers welcoming people with disabilities. The ideal would be to go on site to ensure that the assessments or interviews go smoothly.

Following the new data collected, a new version of the ontology could be produced and again evaluated with another panel of people in order to further improve this ontology (approach to be repeated if necessary).

In Sect. 5, a proof of concept was presented by using a concerned a communication assistive system, usable in mobility, called *ComMob Web*. This approach aimed to give an example of designing an application based on the first version of the ontology. It would be interesting if it were used in the case of other projects targeting different systems aimed at the users targeted in this paper.

A longer-term perspective would be to transpose this ontology to other disabilities, using the same approach. Finally, the creation of a general ontology which could be valid for a wide spectrum of disabilities would be very interesting to allow designers to adapt their product more easily.

Ackowledgments. The authors thank their funders for the experiences acquired during various projects such as ParkinsonCom (European Regional Development Fund (Interreg V France-Wallonie-Vlaanderen) and the Agency for quality life AVIQ (l'Agence pour une Vie de Qualité) from Wallonia), PIA3 Valmobile (Département du Nord and the National Agency for Urban Renovation (ANRU)), SG-HANDI (Agefiph), SAMDI (Hauts-de-France Region). The project that inspired this idea of ontology is the ARI Model'mobile (LAMIH). The authors also thank all of the ontology evaluators.

References

1. Antona, M., Ntoa, S., Adami, I., Stephanidis, C.: Chapter 15 - User Requirements Elicitation for Universal Access. In: The Universal Access Handbook, C. Stephanidis (ed.), pp. 15.1–15.14, CRC Press (2009)
2. Bornman, J.: The world health organisation's terminology and classification: application to severe disability. Disabil. Rehabil. **26**(3), 182–188 (2004)
3. Bangore, A., Kortum, P., Miller, J.: Determining what individual SUS scores mean: adding an adjective rating scale. J. User Experience **4**(3), 114–123 (2009)
4. Barrett, R.S., Lichtwark, G.A.: Gross muscle morphology and structure in spastic cerebral palsy: a systematic review. Dev. Med. Child Neurol. **52**(9), 794–804 (2010)
5. Bax, M., Goldstein, M., Rosenbaum, P., et al.: Proposed definition and classification of cerebral palsy. Dev. Med. Child Neurol. **47**(8), 571–576 (2005)
6. Brooke, J.: SUS: a "quick and dirty" usability scale. In: Jordan, P.W., Thomas, B., Weerdmeester, B.A., McClelland, A.L. (eds.), Usability Evaluation in Industry, London: Taylor and Francis (1996)
7. Cooper, A.: The Inmates Are Running the Asylum: Why Hi-tech Products Drive Us Crazy and How to Restore the Sanity. Macmillan Publishing Co. Inc, Indianapolis (1999)
8. Donegan, M., et al.: Understanding users and their needs. Univ. Access Inf. Soc. **8**, 259–275 (2009)
9. Enderby, P.: Disorders of communication: dysarthria. In: Handbook of Clinical Neurology, vol. 110, pp. 273–281 (2013)
10. Fischer, G.: User modeling in human-computer interaction. User Model. User-Adap. Inter. **11**(1–1), 65–86 (2001)
11. Fondation paralysie cérébrale. https://www.fondationparalysiecerebrale.org/
12. Fossett, B., Mirenda, P.: Augmentative and alternative communication. In: Handbook on Developmental Disabilities, The Guilford Press, pp. 330–348 (2007)
13. Garcia, L.F., de Oliveira, L.C., de Matos, D.M.: Evaluating pictogram prediction in a location-aware augmentative and alternative communication system. Assist. Technol. **28**(2), 83–92 (2016)

14. Guedira, Y., et al.: Démarche de Conception Centrée Utilisateur de Systèmes d'Aide numériques à la Mobilité pour Personnes avec Déficience Intellectuelle. Adjunct Proceedings of the 34th Conference on l'Interaction Humain-Machine, IHM 2023, Troyes, France, April 3–6. ACM, pp. 3:1–3:6 (2023)
15. Guerrier, Y., Kolski, C.: Du système ComMob à ComMob Web pour l'aide à la communication pour des personnes en situation de handicap. Poster, Journée IHM et Santé, Metz, France, may (2019)
16. Guerrier, Y., Kolski, C., Delcroix, V.: Vers une modélisation d'utilisateur avec paralysie cérébrale pour la conception de système interactif. IHM 2021, Proceedings of the 31st Conference on l'Interaction Homme-Machine: Adjunct, ACM, Metz, France, pp. 1–6, April (2021)
17. Guerrier, Y.: Proposition d'une aide logicielle pour la saisie d'information en situation dégradée: application à des utilisateurs IMC athétosiques dans des contextes liés au transport et aux activités journalières. PhD Thesis, Université de Valenciennes et du Hainaut-Cambrésis, France (2015)
18. Guerrier, Y., Kolski, C., Poirier, F.: Towards a communication system for people with athetoid cerebral palsy. In: Kotzé, P., Marsden, G., Lindgaard, G., Wesson, J., Winckler, M. (eds.) Human-Computer Interaction–INTERACT 2013: 14th IFIP TC 13 International Conference, Cape Town, South Africa, September 2–6, 2013, Proceedings, Part IV 14, vol. 8120, pp. 681–688. Springer, Heidelberg (2013). https://doi.org/10.1007/978-3-642-40498-6_61
19. Guerrier, Y., Kolski, C., Poirier, F.: État de l'art sur les systèmes d'aide à la communication envisageables pour des utilisateurs de profil IMC athétosique. J. d'Interaction Personne-Système 6(1), 1–45 (2018)
20. Guerrier, Y., Naveteur, J., Kolski, C., Anceaux, F.: Discount evaluation of preliminary versions of systems dedicated to users with cerebral palsy: simulation of involuntary movements in non-disabled participants. In: HCII 2021: Universal Access in Human-Computer Interaction. Design Methods and User Experience, Washington DC, pp. 71–88 (2021)
21. Guerrier, Y., Vigouroux, N., Kolski, C., Vella, F., Guffroy, M., Teutsch, P.: Conception centrée utilisateur d'aides techniques pour des utilisateurs en situation de handicap avec troubles de la communication : retour d'expérience pour une participation systématique de leur écosystème. Revue des Interactions Humaines Médiatisées 21(1), 29–56 (2020)
22. Guffroy, M., Guerrier, Y., Kolski, C., Vigouroux, N., Vella, F., Teutsch, P.: Adaptation of user-centered design approaches to abilities of people with disabilities. In: Miesenberger, K., Kouroupetroglou, G. (eds.) The 16th biennial International Conference on Computers Helping People with Special Needs (ICCHP), LNCS 10896, Springer, Linz, Austria, June, 462–465 (2018). https://doi.org/10.1007/978-3-319-94277-3_71
23. Guffroy, M., Vigouroux, N., Kolski, C., Vella, F., Teutsch, P.: From human-centered design to disabled user & ecosystem centered design in case of assistive interactive systems. Int. J. Sociotechnol. Knowl. Dev. (IJSKD) 9(4), 28–42 (2017)
24. Hannukainen, P., Holtta-Otto, K.: Identifying customer needs: disabled persons as lead users. In: International Design Engineering Technical Conferences and Computers and Information in Engineering Conference, vol. 42584, 243–251 (2006)
25. Hewett, T., et al.: Curricula for human-computer interaction. Technical report, ACM, New-York (1996)
26. Idoughi, D., Seffah, A., Kolski, C.: Adding user experience into the interactive service design loop: a persona-based approach. Behav. Inform. Technol. 31(3), 287–303 (2012)
27. ISO: Ergonomics of human-system interaction - Part 210: Human-centred design for interactive systems. ISO 9241-210:2019, ISO, Geneva (2019)
28. Johnson, A., Taatgen, N.: User modeling. In: Handbook of Human Factors in Web Design, Lawrence Erlbaum Associates, pp. 424–439 (2005)

29. Koester, H.H., Arthanat, S.: Text entry rate of access interfaces used by people with physical disabilities: a systematic review. Assist. Technol. **30**(3), 151–163 (2018)
30. Lallemand, C., Gronier, G.: Méthodes de design UX: 30 méthodes fondamentales pour concevoir et évaluer les systèmes interactifs. Editions Eyrolles, Paris (2015)
31. MacKenzie, I.S.: Fitts' law. InL The Wiley Handbook of Human Computer Interaction, vol. 1, pp. 347–370 (2018)
32. Mourali, Y., et al.: Design and prototyping of a serious game on interactive tabletop with tangible objects for disability awareness in companies. AAATE: Assistive Technology: Shaping a sustainable and inclusive world (2023)
33. Musen, M.A.: Domain ontologies in software engineering: use of Protege with the EON architecture. Methods Inf. Med. **37**(04/05), 540–550 (1998)
34. Oliveira, K., et al.: ParkinsonCom Project: Towards a Software Communication Tool for People with Parkinson's Disease. In: Antona, M., Stephanidis, C. (eds.) HCII 2021: Universal Access in Human-Computer Interaction. Design Methods and User Experience, Springer, Washington DC, 418–428 (2021). https://doi.org/10.1007/978-3-030-78092-0_28
35. Pruitt, J., Grudin, J.J.: Personas: practice and theory. In: Proceedings of the Designing for User Experiences, DUX 2003, ACM Press, pp. 1–15 (2003)
36. Rasmussen, J.: Information Processing and Human-Machine Interaction, an Approach to Cognitive Engineering. Elsevier Science Publishing (1986)
37. Reddihough, D.S., Collins, K.J.: The epidemiology and causes of cerebral palsy. Aust. J. Physiotherapy **49**(1), 7–12 (2003)
38. Robert, J.M.: Que faut-il savoir sur les utilisateurs pour réaliser des interfaces de qualité ? In: Boy, G. (ed.) Ingénierie cognitive, pp. 249–283. IHM et cognition, Editions Hermes-Lavoisier, Paris (2003)
39. Seta, K., Ikeda, M., Kakusho, O., Mizoguchi, R.: Capturing a conceptual model for end-user programming: Task ontology as a static user model. In: Jameson, A., Paris, C., Tasso, C. (eds.) User Modeling, vol. 383, pp. 203–214, Springer, Vienna (1997). https://doi.org/10.1007/978-3-7091-2670-7_22
40. Skillen, K.L., Chen, L., Nugent, C.D., Donnelly, M.P., Burns, W., Solheim, I.: Ontological user profile modeling for context-aware application personalization. In: Bravo, J., López-de-Ipiña, D., Moya, F. (eds.) International Conference on Ubiquitous Computing and Ambient Intelligence, pp. 261–268, Springer, Berlin, Heidelberg (2012). https://doi.org/10.1007/978-3-642-35377-2_36
41. Slegers, K., Hendriks, N., Duysburgh, P., Maldonado Branco, R., Vandenberghe, B., Brandt, E.: Sharing methods for involving people with impairments in design: exploring the method story approach. In Proceedings of the 2016 CHI Conference Extended Abstracts on Human Factors in Computing Systems (CHI EA 2016), San Jose, California, USA, May, pp. 3331–3338, AC (2016)
42. Velardi, P., Fabriani, P., Missikoff, M.: Using text processing techniques to automatically enrich a domain ontology. In: Proceedings of the International Conference on Formal Ontology in Information Systems, pp. 270–284 (2001)
43. Yokochi, K., Shimabukuro, S., Kodama, M., Kodama, K., Hosoe, A.: Motor function of infants with athetoid cerebral palsy. Dev. Med. Child Neurol. **35**(10), 909–916 (1993)

Enhancing the Smart User Experience of Green Spaces: A Study of Accessible Map for the Visually Impaired Persons

Bo Yan Lin[1], Jia Xin Xiao[1]([✉]), Ming Jun Luo[2,3], Mickey Mengting Zhang[4], Wenhua Li[5], and Ze Li[6]

[1] School of Art and Design, Guangdong University of Technology, 729 Dongfengdong Road, Guangzhou 510000, China
cynthia.xiao@gdut.edu.cn
[2] Guangdong Industry Polytechnic, Guangzhou 510000, China
[3] City University of Macau, Macau, China
[4] Faculty of Humanities and Arts, Macau University of Science and Technology, Cotai, China
mtzhang@must.edu.mo
[5] Guangzhou Academy of Fine Arts, Guangzhou, China
[6] Central South University of Forestry and Technology, Changsha, China

Abstract. This study examines the efficacy of accessible maps in enhancing the user experience of visually impaired persons (VIPs) within park and green space settings. Conventional navigation systems frequently overlook the unique requirements of VIPs in these environments. Our field observations reveal a predominant focus on accessibility designs catering to individuals with mobility impairments, with limited attention dedicated to optimizing accessibility for VIPs. The proposed accessibility map endeavors to provide VIPs with an alternative means of perceiving park landscapes through the utilization of technology, including audio cues. By addressing this gap, this study contributes to advancing the inclusivity and spatial equity of VIPs within green spaces.

Keywords: Accessible map · Green space · Visually impaired persons · User experience

1 Introduction

Since the mid-nineteenth century, parks have served as a response to urban challenges stemming from the industrial revolution in the Western world. In contemporary times, as urbanization progresses and living standards improve, parks have emerged as vital spaces for urban dwellers to engage in recreation and reconnect with nature. Recognizing the pivotal role of parks and green spaces in urban development, governments have increasingly prioritized their establishment and enhancement. In China, the government has notably escalated investments in park construction. As per data from the Ministry of Housing and Construction, by the close of 2022, there were 24,841 parks covering 868,500 hectares, with the majority accessible to the public at no cost, underscoring

M. Antona et al. (Eds.): HCII 2024, LNCS 15379, pp. 30–43, 2025.
https://doi.org/10.1007/978-3-031-76818-7_3

their availability to visitors. However, for individuals with disabilities, many parks and green spaces are predominantly designed without their needs in consideration, rendering them inaccessible. As integral components of a city's development, parks and green spaces have not been fully inclusive of individuals with disabilities. In recent years, governmental recognition of the significance of including individuals with disabilities in urban spaces has prompted initiatives to prioritize accessibility and inclusive design in park and green space planning (Siu, 2013).

The World Vision Report, published by the World Health Organization, highlights a staggering global statistic: over 2.2 billion individuals suffer from visual impairment or blindness, with nearly half attributed to conditions such as myopia, hyperopia, glaucoma, and cataracts, among others. Regrettably, many cases of impaired vision or blindness stem from untreated minor issues. Given the unique challenges faced by visually impaired individuals, they are unable to access visual information, further compounded by the absence of accessibility features tailored specifically for them in existing map navigation software. Additionally, the inadequate optimization of parks and green spaces for accessibility further impedes visually impaired individuals from enjoying their rights and privileges as integral members of urban communities.

With the rapid advancement of modern science and technology, increasing attention has been directed towards addressing the challenges faced by visually impaired individuals and leveraging technology to enhance their daily lives. Nair et al. (2018) introduced a novel hybrid localization and navigation approach integrating low-power Bluetooth (BLE) beacons with Google Tango technology. Similarly, S.A. Cheraghi et al. (2017) proposed the GuideBeacon system, enabling visually impaired individuals to interact with Bluetooth-based beacons deployed in indoor environments for smartphone-assisted navigation. Additionally, the Indriya device, developed by Kallara (2017), offers handheld functionality capable of providing voice-assisted navigation, obstacle detection, and integration with Android and Internet of Things (IoT) devices. However, a common limitation observed in these technological solutions is the requirement for additional attachments or devices to enable navigation for VIPs. This dependency poses challenges and burdens for VIPs in accessing and utilizing these devices effectively.

Given the precedence of barrier-free construction initiatives, particularly in Guangzhou city, it is imperative to conduct an investigation into the current state of barrier-free facility development within park green spaces. Taking a typical park in Guangzhou as an example, this paper aims to elucidate strategies for furnishing accessibility maps tailored to the needs of VIPs within park and green space environments. Through this examination, the paper endeavors to enhance the user experience of VIPs navigating parks and green spaces in Guangzhou.

2 Method

2.1 A Case Study of Tianhe Park, Guangzhou

In 2003, Guangzhou initiated a comprehensive barrier-free reconstruction program targeting the city's major parks. Subsequently, in 2004, the Guangzhou Barrier-Free Facilities Construction Management Regulations were enacted, followed by the city being conferred the prestigious title of 'National Barrier-Free Construction Demonstration

City' in 2005. Notably, Guangzhou Tianhe Park, situated in the Tianhe District, was designated by the Guangzhou Municipal Government as the earliest 'Love Park' in China in 2012. Public records indicate that this designation encompassed provisions for barrier-free facilities catering to VIPs. Concurrently, various experiential venues within the park, such as Love Square, Love Stage, and Love Pavilion, have commenced offering services tailored to the needs of the visually impaired. These initiatives are pivotal in enhancing the user experience of VIPs during park visits.

2.2 Research Method

This paper employs the field research method to conduct a comprehensive investigation of parks in Guangzhou. This method underscores direct observation and hands-on exploration, entailing visits to the research sites to observe, engage in communication, and document findings to acquire detailed firsthand information. The study primarily focuses on green spaces within parks, encompassing pathways, restroom facilities, seats, barriers, and advancements in landscape science and technology. The objective is to assess the extent to which these park facilities are optimized for VIPs. Additionally, interviews were conducted with park management personnel to obtain insights into the implementation of accessibility measures within the parks. Subsequently, data collected through field observations were analyzed to ascertain the prevailing status of accessibility within the parks.

3 Results

3.1 Accessibility Challenges

Previous research has illuminated the challenges faced by many VIPs when navigating unfamiliar environments, often leading to reluctance in exploring new places to avoid inconveniencing family and friends. However, our interviews with VIPs revealed a keen desire to explore new locales, with many expressing a preference for, or even undertaking, longer journeys.

According to available public information, Guangzhou Tianhe Park implemented Braille signage and a guided path for VIPs in 2015. VIPs could utilize either a remote control provided by the park or download corresponding software onto their mobile devices to access the park's voice guidance system seamlessly. However, our field research at Guangzhou Tianhe Park unveiled the absence of Braille signage, as depicted in Fig. 1, and the discontinuation of the voice guidance system for the visually impaired. Subsequently, we conducted interviews with park management, revealing that the voice guidance systems ceased to be operational a few years ago. However, they were temporarily decommissioned due to insufficient funds to sustain equipment maintenance. The prohibitive costs associated with equipment procurement and upkeep rendered the program financially unsustainable for the park, posing challenges for visually impaired individuals in affording access to such services. In light of these findings, it becomes imperative to devise cost-effective measures to render park amenities accessible to VIPs.

Fig. 1. The Signage in Tianhe Park

3.2 Pathways, Restroom Facilities, Resting Areas, and Educational Information

Based on our observations and interviews, the needs of visually impaired individuals to engage in park green spaces can be categorized into four primary areas: pathways, restroom facilities, resting areas, and educational information regarding the park's features. This paper will analyze these needs based on these four categories.

Pathways serve as crucial conduits for navigating within the park's green spaces, constituting a significant portion of the park's landscape. Taking Guangzhou Tianhe Park as a case study, pathway conditions can be classified into four categories: main pathways, secondary pathways, steps, and pathways obstructed by immovable obstacles. The main pathway within Tianhe Park features the Guangdong Greenway, composed of asphalt (Fig. 2). Unlike secondary pathways, the main pathway does not feature steps. Portions of the main pathway are designed with barrier-free accessibility features, facilitating mobility for individuals with physical disabilities and visually impaired persons. Handrails positioned along both sides of the barrier-free pathway aid VIPs in navigation. However, it is noteworthy that these barrier-free designs do not span the entire park, and their design includes gradual slopes to regulate wheelchair speed, although resulting in a longer distance to traverse compared to standard pathways (Fig. 3).

The total size of Tianhe Park is large as the characteristic of comprehensive park. Numerous small areas are connected by branching pathways. These pathways, however, are often intricate and irregular, deviating from a flat terrain (Fig. 4). Moreover, certain areas within the park require access via steps due to variations in elevation, posing challenges for VIPs to navigate independently (Fig. 5). Additionally, some pathways are obstructed by immovable obstacles, including trees growing in the middle of the pathway, even on the main pathways. Such obstacles pose safety hazards for VIPs. For instance, Liuhua Lake Park has implemented visual sign reminders for these hazardous pathway conditions (Fig. 6). However, such visual reminders are inaccessible to VIPs, resulting in a poor user experience.

Fig. 2. Main section in Tianhe Park

Accessible restroom facilities have become increasingly prevalent in various settings, including tourist destinations. However, VIPs often encounter difficulties in locating these facilities when visiting such places. This issue was observed in Tianhe Park, where despite the presence of eight accessible restrooms, signage along park pathways intended to assist visually impaired individuals failed to effectively communicate the locations of these facilities. As illustrated in Fig. 7, the signage primarily relied on visual cues,

Fig. 3. Barrier-free path in Tianhe Park

Fig. 4. Branching pathway in Tianhe Park

rendering it inaccessible to VIPs and hindering their ability to access and utilize the restroom facilities. This highlights the need for inclusive design strategies to ensure that essential amenities, such as accessible restrooms, are readily accessible to all park visitors, regardless of visual impairment.

Seating arrangements constitute a prominent feature within resting areas of Tianhe Park. Numerous seats line both sides of park pathways; however, observations reveal a disparity in accessibility. Some seats are positioned on a step, while others are seamlessly integrated with the ground level, facilitating ease of access without necessitating traversal of steps (Figs. 8 and 9). Regrettably, seats with accompanying steps pose safety hazards for VIPs, compounded by the absence of signage delineating seating areas. Unlike the general public, VIPs lack the ability to discern the location of seating areas and their proximity within the park.

Fig. 5. Steps in Tianhe Park

Fig. 6. Tree trunks on the side of the road sticking out into the road

Natural science popularization is one of the most essential parts of the user experience the dissemination of natural science knowledge stands as a pivotal component of the user experience within green spaces of parks. Most comprehensive parks offer an array of natural landscapes, comprising trees and flowers, for visitors' exploration and enjoyment. These parks often feature science introduction boards accompanying various plants, furnishing brief insights into their botanical taxonomy, characteristics, and related information. Additionally, these boards typically incorporate QR codes enabling visitors to access more detailed plant information (Fig. 10).

Furthermore, the park incorporates informative boards detailing the historical significance of renowned landmarks, such as the Deng Shichang Clothes Crown Mound and Liao Bing Brother Square, alongside commemorative tributes such as the statue honoring Huang Nai, the father of Chinese Braille. However, all such informational content is exclusively presented in textual form (Fig. 11). Regrettably, no provisions for Braille or

Fig. 7. Barrier-free restroom signposts

Fig. 8. Seats with steps in front

voice-based introductions have been implemented, thus impeding VIPs from accessing the aforementioned information. Consequently, VIPs are prevented from acquiring relevant insights from the textual content displayed during their park visitation, highlighting the necessity for inclusive design initiatives to augment accessibility for all park patrons.

3.3 The Usage of Navigation Software

The research team utilized a widely used navigation software 'Gaode Map' within Tianhe Park. Through observations, it was noted that the current navigation functionality within the park necessitates input of both starting and ending points to generate a route (Fig. 12). Furthermore, only select areas within the park, such as Yuehui Garden, Deng Shichang Clothes Mound, and Ice Brothers Art Plaza, are searchable within the navigation software, potentially leading to routes that traverse challenging terrain, such as side roads or

Fig. 9. Seats without steps in front

Fig. 10. Botanical introduction board

steps, for visually impaired individuals. Additionally, it was observed that when searching for nearby restroom facilities within the navigation map software, only a single restroom within the park could be identified, as shown in Fig. 12. This limitation creates a discrepancy between the available information in the software and the actual restroom locations within the park.

The findings highlight a gradual improvement in the accessibility features within parks and green spaces. Most areas have completed fundamental accessibility modifications, primarily catering to individuals with mobility impairments, such as those reliant on wheelchairs. However, these modifications are predominantly visual in nature, potentially excluding VIPs and detracting from their user experience. In effect, aside from the inability to perceive visual stimuli, VIPs possess similar capabilities to those without

Fig. 11. Huang Nai, the father of Braille in China, sculpted a introduction plate

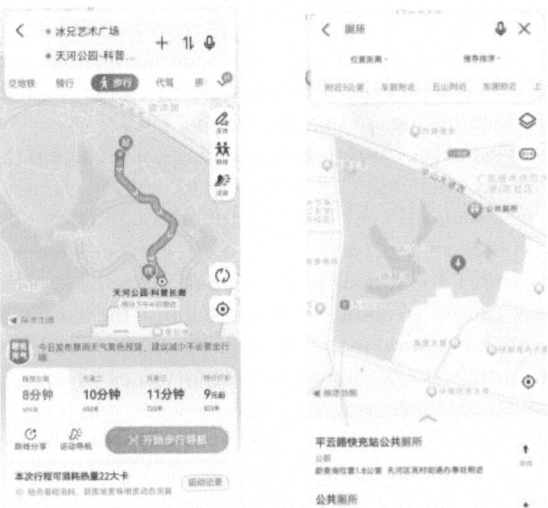

Fig. 12. Navigating the way inside the park via 'Gaode Map' App (left) and the results of Searching Bathroom within the Park (right)

visual impairments. Thus, the current emphasis on visual accessibility designs overlooks the unique needs of this demographic, resulting in a unsatisfactory user experience.

This entails a shift from visual-centric accessibility designs to ones prioritizing auditory and tactile elements, thereby fostering a more inclusive environment for all visitors. This transformation represents a pivotal step towards ensuring equitable access and enhancing the overall user experience within green spaces.

4   Discussions

To explore the multifaceted needs of diverse user groups in park green space construction, this paper centers on the user experience of VIPs and the imperative for inclusive design in park green spaces tailored to their needs. While many parks and green spaces have made strides in accommodating various disabilities to enhance user experience, VIPs continue to face challenges in accessing and utilizing these facilities. This disparity arises from the inherent differences in how users perceive their surroundings, with visually impaired individuals lacking the ability to visually discern existing barrier-free designs within parks and green spaces.

In light of these challenges, this paper aims to provide VIPs with an alternative means to 'perceive' these designs through technological support, thereby enhancing their user experience. By ensuring that the majority of VIPs can access and utilize park facilities while also reducing maintenance costs, this study propose design strategies across four key categories: pathways, restroom facilities, resting areas, and educational resources on natural science.

Taking into account the needs of both VIPs and park authorities, cell phone map navigation software emerges as a particularly fitting solution. Presently, the majority of VIPs possess smartphones, which offer distinct advantages such as computational power and a range of sensors including accelerometers, gyroscopes, and magnetometers. These sensors contribute to enhancing the accuracy of map navigation software. Leveraging cell phones as user terminals presents an advantageous option, as it eliminates the need for either VIPs or park authorities to incur additional costs.

Based on the analysis of previous research findings, it is evident that certain types of road surfaces pose safety challenges for VIPs due to their unevenness and complexity. Therefore, it is advised that VIPs avoid navigating through these areas independently. Instead, navigation routes should be planned to circumvent such road sections. Conversely, main roads with flat surfaces and minimal obstacles are deemed suitable for visually impaired navigation. To address obstacles within the park roads, the integration of IoT technology with navigation map software is recommended. By equipping obstacles with audio transmitters, VIPs can receive auditory cues when nearing obstructions, enabling timely avoidance. Furthermore, access to accessible toilets and seating areas within rest zones is essential for VIPs. However, caution must be exercised regarding seating areas with steps to ensure safety. Hence, reminders should be provided to alert VIPs of potential hazards. To optimize park accessibility, real-time information including road conditions, accessible toilets, and rest areas can be provided by the park and integrated into cell phone map navigation software. This collaborative effort between the park and navigation software providers facilitates seamless navigation within the park environment.

Regarding science popularization, converting visualized text into audio formats enhances user experience. Near Field Communication (NFC) technology can enable smartphone users to access science-related information via contactless interaction. Alternatively, science popularization content can be embedded within navigation maps, allowing users to engage with the material audibly.

As shown in Fig. 13, this paper proposes a collaborative model involving VIPs, park management, and navigation software providers. This model comprises three key stakeholders: VIPs, park management, and navigation map software providers, who collaborate to enhance accessibility within the park environment. Park management enhance auditory design elements for the visually impaired, building upon existing visual accessibility features within the park infrastructure. Additionally, park management can furnish the navigation map software provider with a high-fidelity park map, incorporating comprehensive details such as road networks, area locations, and scientific information. Leveraging the technical expertise of the navigation map software provider, VIPs can utilize their smartphones as platforms to access and contribute to the development of an accessible park map, facilitating navigation and search functionalities within the park. Through the accessibility map, VIPs can fully immerse themselves in the park's open spaces, while the park management endeavors to enhance the overall user experience for visually impaired individuals. Furthermore, this collaborative effort presents opportunities for the navigation map software provider to expand its user base and refine the precision of park map data.

The development, maintenance, and operation of the accessibility map necessitate the collective efforts of multiple stakeholders to meet the needs of VIPs in parks and green spaces. By ensuring their access to the conveniences of urban environments, we strive to provide them with a positive user experience. This collaborative endeavor underscores our commitment to inclusivity and accessibility within our communities.

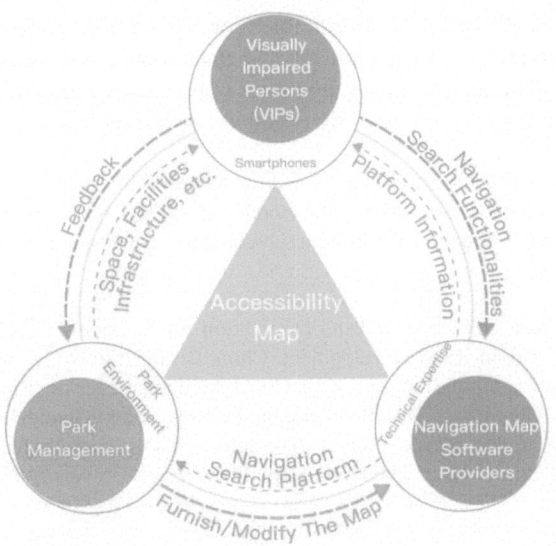

Fig. 13. Cooperation Model Chart.

5 Discussions

In this paper, the accessibility design within comprehensive parks in Guangzhou is analyzed, focusing on strategies to enhance the user experience of VIPs in park and green space settings. Using Tianhe Park, China's pioneering caring park, as a case study, we observed a predominant emphasis on barrier-free design catering to individuals with mobility impairments. However, earlier initiatives targeting the VIPs have been suspended due to challenges such as aging equipment and financial constraints. Consequently, there is a noticeable dearth of barrier-free designs tailored specifically for the visually impaired, mirroring challenges observed in other comprehensive parks. Upon analyzing the unique needs of VIPs, it becomes evident that current accessibility measures must be optimized to prioritize non-visual senses such as hearing or touch. By adapting to these needs, we can better accommodate VIPs within park and green space environments.

In response to these identified needs, this paper systematically categorizes and observes the existing accessibility facilities within parks and green spaces, subsequently proposing a comprehensive design strategy. Considering factors such as popularity and cost-effectiveness, this study advocates for an accessible map design approach that involves collaboration among visually impaired users, park management, and navigation map software providers. This strategy aims to balance the interests of all stakeholders while fostering a sustainable closed loop of accessibility design through collaborative efforts. Embracing inclusive design principles for VIPs within parks and green spaces not only enhances their user experience but also encourages them to engage with nature and outdoor environments. Moreover, it creates opportunities for socialization, thereby fostering a virtuous cycle of community engagement and inclusion.

Acknowledgments. The authors would like to acknowledge Philosophy and Social Sciences Fund of Guangdong Province (GD24CYS04), Philosophy and Social Sciences Fund of Guangdong Province (GD22XYS17), Guangdong Province higher vocational colleges art design specialty education and teaching reform project (2023YSSJ20), Research on the development-oriented city of youth in Foshan (2024-QNFZ34) and the National Natural Science Foundation of China (52008114) for the data collection and the preparation of the paper. The authors thank Ministry of Housing and Urban-Rural Development, China Disabled Persons' Federation, Office of Guangzhou Municipal Commission on Aging, China Association for the Blind, China Disabled Persons' Federation, Guangzhou Disabled Persons' Federation and Guangzhou Volunteer Association for providing support for the research. The authors also acknowledge Prof. Siu, the Chair professor of Public Design Lab of The Hong Kong Polytechnic University for providing a lot of useful information.

References

Berka, J., Balata, J., Jonker, C.M., Mikovec, Z., van Riemsdijk, M.B., Tielman, M.L.: Misalignment in semantic user model elicitation via conversational agents: a case study in navigation support for visually impaired people. Int. J. Hum. Comput. Interact. **38**(18–20), 1909–1925 (2022)

Cheraghi, S.A., Namboodiri, V., Walker, L.: GuideBeacon: beacon-based indoor wayfinding for the blind, visually impaired, and disoriented. In: 2017 IEEE International Conference on Pervasive Computing and Communications (PerCom), pp. 121–130. IEEE (2017)

Gibson, J.J.: The Ecological Approach to Visual Perception: Classic Edition (1979)

Hassenzahl, M.: Experience Design: Technology for All The Right Reasons. Morgan & Claypool Publishers (2010)

Hassenzahl, M.: The Thing and I: Understanding the Relationship Between User and Product. In: Funology (2005)

Hartson, R.: Cognitive, physical, sensory, and functional affordances in interaction design. Behav. Inform. Technol. 22(5), 315–338 (2003)

Kallara, S.B., Raj, M., Raju, R., Mathew, N.J., Padmaprabha, V.R., Divya, D.S.: Indriya—a smart guidance system for the visually impaired. In: 2017 International Conference on Inventive Computing and Informatics (ICICI), pp. 26–29. IEEE (2017)

Long, Y.L., Xiao, J.X., Luo, M.J., Chen, Y., Huang, W.W.: Inclusive design and the user experience in green spaces: a case in Guangzhou, China. In: Duffy, V.G., Krömker, H., A. Streitz, N., Konomi, S. (eds.) International Conference on Human-Computer Interaction, pp. 568–582. Cham: Springer Nature Switzerland. (2023). https://doi.org/10.1007/978-3-031-48047-8_38

Ma, Y., et al.: Evaluating the effectiveness of accessibility features for roadway users with visual impairment: a case study for Nanjing, China. Transport. Res. F: Traffic Psychol. Behav. 97, 301–313 (2023)

Mediastika, C.E., Sudarsono, A.S., Kristanto, L., Tanuwidjaja, G., Sunaryo, R.G., Damayanti, R.: Appraising the sonic environment of urban parks using the soundscape dimension of visually impaired people. Int. J. Urban Sci. 24(2), 216–241 (2023)

Nair, V., Tsangouri, C., Xiao, B., Olmschenk, G., Seiple, W.H., Zhu, Z.: A hybrid indoor positioning system for blind and visually impaired using Bluetooth and Google tango. J. Technol. Persons Disabil. 6, 61–81 (2018)

Siu, KWM.: Pleasurable products: public space furniture with userfitness. J. Eng. Des. 16(6), 545–555 (2005)

Siu KWM.: Accessible park environments and facilities for the visually impaired. Facilities 31(13/14), 590–609 (2013)

Wu, K.C., Song, L.Y.: A case for inclusive design: analyzing the needs of those who frequent Taiwan's urban parks. Appl. Ergon. 58, 254–264 (2017)

Measurement and Analysis on Effects of Peripheral Vision Training on Human Body

Yasuyuki Matsuura[1,2], Kiminori Sorimachi[2], Hiroshi Tahara[3], and Hiroki Takada[2(✉)]

[1] Gifu City Women's College, 7-1 Hitoichiba Kitamachi, Gifu 5010192, Japan
[2] University of Fukui, 3-9-1 Bunko, Fukui 9108507, Japan
takada@u-fukui.ac.jp
[3] REMEDIA Co., Ltd., 904 Nitto Building 6-15-11 Sotokanda Chiyodaku, Tokyo 1010021, Japan

Abstract. Generally, healthy people obtain approximately 80% of their sensory information from their vision. However, the amount of time spent using smartphones has been increasing in recent years. In particular, there are concerns about an increase in the number of young people suffering from acute esotropia and a decline in their visual acuity. Therefore, training to improve visual acuity using stereoscopic images has been attracting attention. It is necessary to conduct studies on whether young people can see stereoscopic images. In this study, a stress test was conducted on healthy young subjects to determine whether they can see stereoscopic images. Additionally, the effectiveness of visual training (VIT) to improve visual acuity using stereoscopic images was measured in healthy young men. The results showed that 45% of the subjects were unable to see stereoscopic images within 3 min, highlighting a serious concern. Furthermore, immediately after our original training to improve visual acuity, there was a temporary improvement in the visual acuity of the subject in their peripheral vision fields (VAPFs). However, this improvement was not sustained until the next day's pre-measurement. As a future perspective, it is necessary to confirm whether the change in visual acuity and the persistence of the improvement can be maintained by increasing the time and frequency of the VIT.

Keywords: Vision · Stereo Test · Visual Acuity · Visual Acuity in their Peripheral Vision Fields (VAPFs) · Stereoscopic Images · Visual Training (VIT)

1 Introduction

In recent years, the number of users of social networking services (SNS) has been increasing due to the widespread use of smartphones and portable game consoles. The number of SNS users is particularly high among those in their 20s, with their average daily smartphone usage exceeding 3 h. Smartphone usage time has been rising over the past few years [1]. This increase in smartphone use has led to two major problems: the first is the increase in the number of people, especially young people, suffering from acute entropion [2]. The second problem is the decline in average visual acuity among

M. Antona et al. (Eds.): HCII 2024, LNCS 15379, pp. 44–53, 2025.
https://doi.org/10.1007/978-3-031-76818-7_4

the younger generation. In response to these issues, tools for visual training (VIT) have been developed. It is said that VIT can improve naked-eye vision without significant costs in terms of time and money [3]. Furthermore, with the recent development of stereoscopic imaging technology, VIT using stereoscopic images has gained attention [4].

Vision plays an important role in facilitating the input of approximately 80% of ambient information into our central nervous system [5]. In the central visual field, the main task is tracking vision, while in the peripheral visual field, the main task is peripheral vision. Visual information in the human visual field, consisting of the central and peripheral visual fields, is processed in separate pathways in the brain, particularly in the dorsal visual pathway for the central visual field [6]. Pyramidal cells are densely distributed in the central fovea, contributing to high-definition vision in the central visual field, while rod cells relate visual information in the peripheral visual field and play a role in light/dark discrimination [7]. Additionally, visual acuity includes near and far vision, with cognitive processing of visual information mainly depending on near vision in the central visual field and on far vision in the peripheral visual field. Techniques to detect cognitive impairment from eye movements have attracted much attention, as Zola et al. (2013) and Oyama et al. (2019) have been working on developing such techniques [8, 9]. Many children with learning disabilities, dementia, and mild cognitive impairment (MCI) tend to suppress information-rich cognitive processing in peripheral vision, supporting the hypothesis that higher-order functions in the cerebrum are impaired [10, 11].

In this study, we conducted stereo testing (Experiment 1) and our VIT on young adults (Experiment 2). In Experiment 1, a stereo test was conducted on 58 healthy young subjects to assess the effects of prolonged smartphone use and other factors. In Experiment 2, nine healthy young male subjects performed the VIT to gather knowledge on the effects of VIT using stereoscopic images on their visual function and organism.

2 Methods

2.1 Experiment 1

In Experiment 1, 58 healthy young adults aged 18–22 yr (mean age ± standard deviation: 19.91 ± 1.10 yr) were tested. Subjects were fully informed about the study and were also told that they could discontinue the experiment at any time of their own free will. Their consent to participate in the experiment was obtained. In the experiment, a stereo test was conducted for 3 min (Figs. 1 and 2a). The test images (Fig. 2a) were displayed on SONY's XPERIA Ace III, and the subjects wore 3D glasses made by Blinky. Subjects indicated during the stereo test when they were able to recognize the composite image as shown in Fig. 2b. We recorded the time required for binocular vision. Subjects who could not see stereoscopic images within 3 min of the start of the experiment were judged to be non-visualizers of stereoscopic images. Subjects also filled out a medical questionnaire before the stereo test, which included questions such as the total time spent looking at the LCD screen on the previous day and the degree of eye fatigue at the time of the experiment.

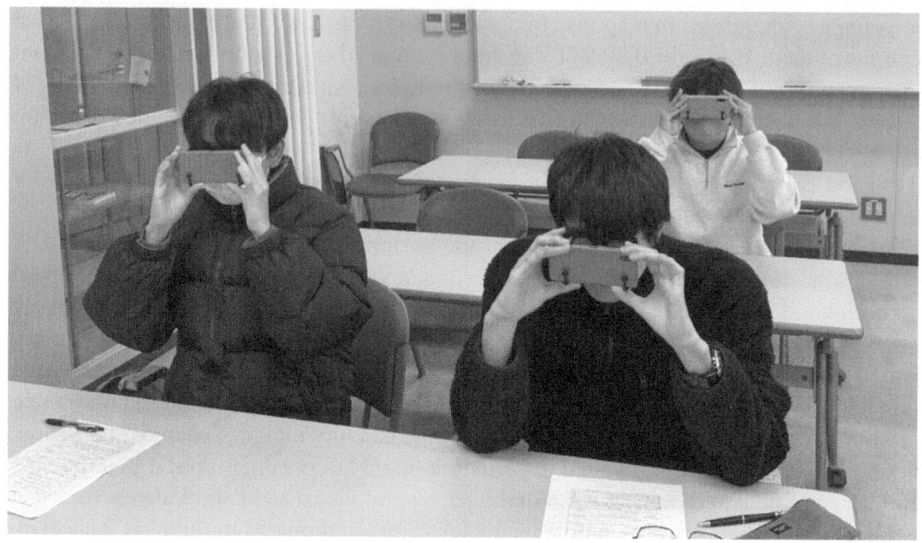

Fig. 1. Schematic of Experiment 1.

(a)   (b)

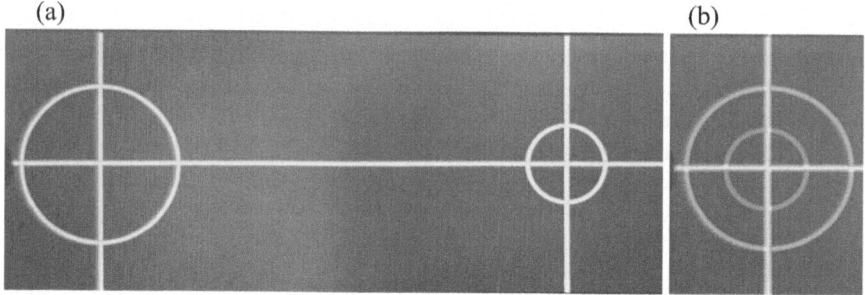

Fig. 2. Images used for our stereo test. Image presented to each eye (a), recognized composite image in which image for right eye (right image in Fig. 2a) is fully encompassed by that for left eye (b).

2.2 Experiment 2

In Experiment 2, nine healthy young males aged 21–24 yr (mean age ± standard deviation: 22.89 ± 0.89 yr) were tested (Fig. 3). Subjects were fully informed about the study and were told that they could stop the experiment at any time of their own free will. Their consent to participate in the experiment was obtained. We conducted stereo tests, Kraepelin tests, and tests for visual acuity in the peripheral visual fields (VAPFs) before and after the VIT to examine the effects of VIT using stereoscopic image recognition on visual function and the organism. Subjects performed the VIT for 5 consecutive days. The stereo test, Kraepelin test, and tests for the VAPFs were performed daily before and after training. The experimental protocol is shown in Fig. 4. The Kraepelin test involves simple single-digit addition to determine the behavioral characteristics of the examinee. In Japan, the Kraepelin test is widely used in companies, government offices, and educational institutions such as universities, high schools, and vocational schools. The stereo test was conducted using the same procedure as in Experiment 1. We compared the percentage of correct responses in the stereo test and the Kraepelin test. We also measured the electroencephalogram (EEG) during the Kraepelin test for those who showed improvement in the VAPF after the VIT and for those who did not show improvement.

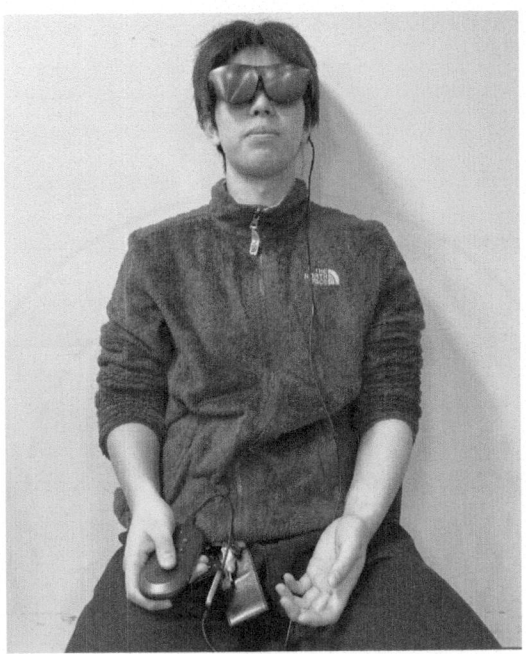

Fig. 3. Schematic of Experiment 2.

Pre-measurement		Vision Improvement Training	Post-measurement	
Kraepelin test (3 min)	Eye test		Eye test	Kraepelin test (3 min)

Fig. 4. Experimental protocol for Experiment 2.

The Kraepelin test also included 2-electrode EEG measurements of Fp1 and Fp2 using a banded telemetry 2-electrode simple electroencephalograph manufactured by NeuroSky (Fig. 5). The sampling frequency was 600 Hz. In the EEG analysis, the EEG was processed by a bandpass filter with a cutoff frequency of 1–49 Hz. The power spectral density of Fp1 and Fp2 was calculated, and the percentage of each frequency component in the EEG signal was determined. The following frequency bands were distinguished in the EEG analysis:

- δ wave: 0.1–4 Hz
- θ wave: 4–8 Hz
- α wave: 8–12 Hz
- low β wave: 12–15 Hz
- mid β wave: 16–20 Hz
- high β wave: 21–30 Hz
- γ wave: 30–100 Hz

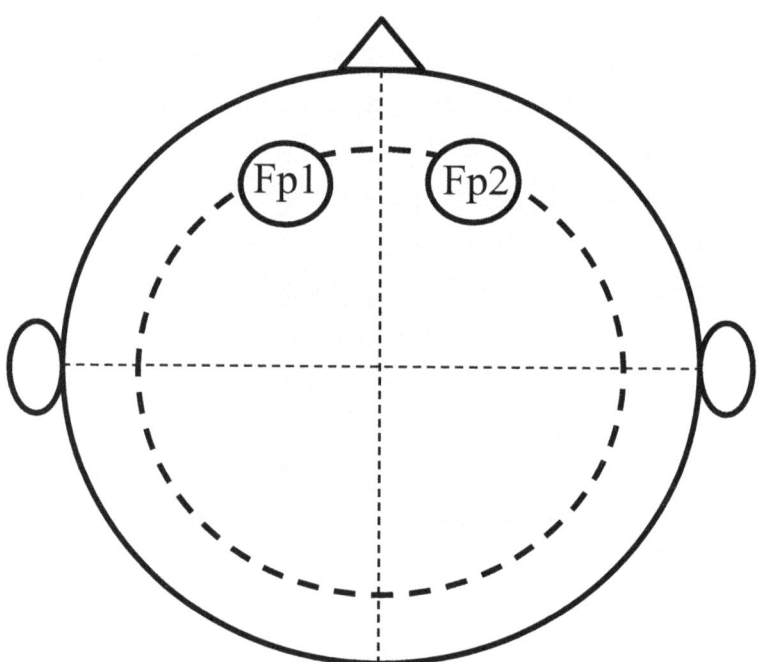

Fig. 5. EEG electrode position.

For the VIT and tests for the VAPFs, subjects wore VR goggles manufactured by Rokid. In the VIT, subjects watched stereoscopic video content (Fig. 6) in which a sphere moves in the proximal and distal directions for 3 min and 10 s. In the test for the VAPF, the subjects were asked to identify an optotype (E-chart) (Fig. 7) that appeared in the peripheral visual field, and the percentage of correct responses was recorded. The VIT lasted approximately 8 min, and the VA before and after the VIT was statistically processed using a paired t-test. The significance level was set at 0.05.

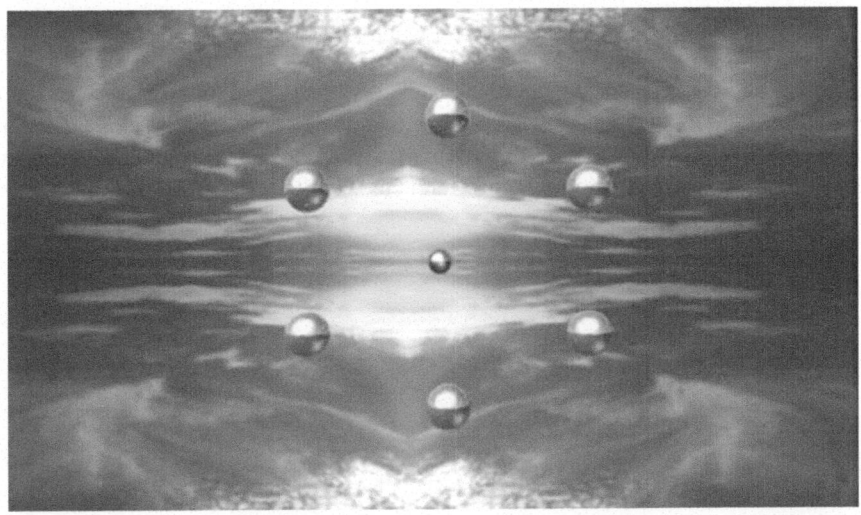

Fig. 6. Schematic of our contents of VIT.

Fig. 7. E-chart of VIT.

3   Results and Discussion

3.1   Experiment 1

Of the 58 subjects, 32 were able to visualize stereoscopic images, while the remaining 26 could not. More than 80% of those who were able to visualize stereoscopic images did so within 2 min, and nine of them managed to visualize the images within 10 s after looking through the 3D glasses. A histogram showing the time it took to visualize the stereoscopic image is shown in Fig. 8.

Compared to the non-visualizers, the visualizers of stereoscopic images spent more time looking at the LCD display on the previous day. Statistical comparisons were made between visualizers and non-visualizers using Mann-Whitney's U test (significance level of 0.05), but no statistically significant differences were found.

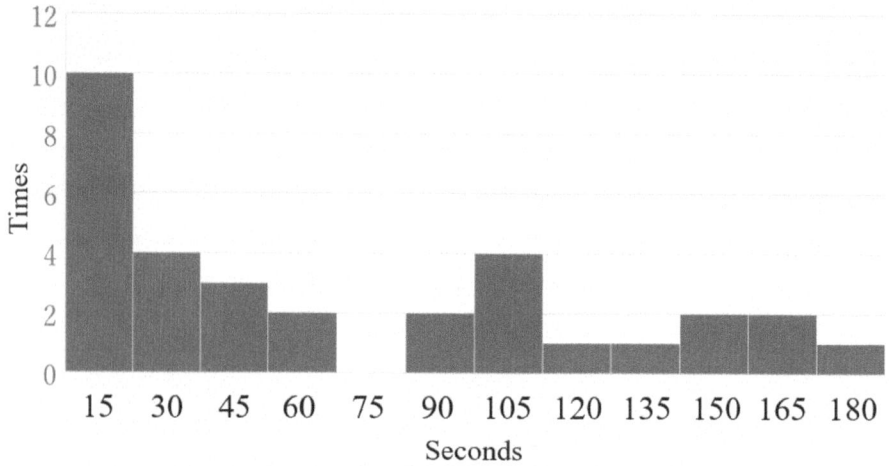

Fig. 8. Distribution of time required for binocular vision.

3.2 Experiment 2

A comparison of the subjects' VAPF before and after the VIT showed an increase in their visual acuity after the VIT, with a significant difference ($p < 0.05$) (Fig. 9). Immediately after the VIT, there was a temporary improvement in the subjects' VAPF. However, this improvement was not sustained until the next day's pre-measurement. Additionally, a comparison of the VAPF between the pre-measurement on the first day of the VIT and the post-measurement on the fifth day, using a paired t-test at a significance level of 0.05, showed no statistical difference. This suggests that the VIT in this study did not improve long-term visual acuity.

No significant difference ($p < 0.05$) was found when comparing the percentage of correct responses in the Kraepelin test with and without the improvement in the VAPF after the VIT, using a paired t-test. The percentage of correct responses in the Kraepelin test represents the ability to concentrate before and after the VIT. Figure 10 shows the percentage of correct responses in the Kraepelin test for those who did and did not show improvement in their VAPF after the VIT.

Using a paired t-test, values of each frequency band of the EEG during the Kraepelin test were compared before and after the VIT. Regardless of the improvement in the VAPF, the values in the δ and θ bands decreased after the VIT, but the differences were not significant. These findings suggest that concentration could not be enhanced by the VIT.

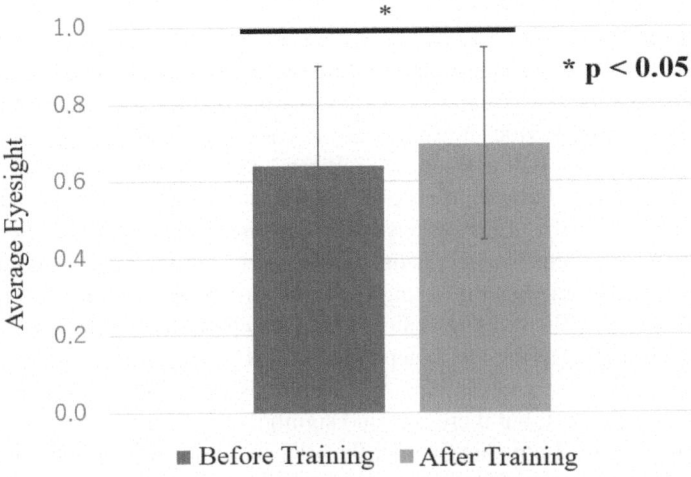

Fig. 9. Average of VAPF before and after VIT.

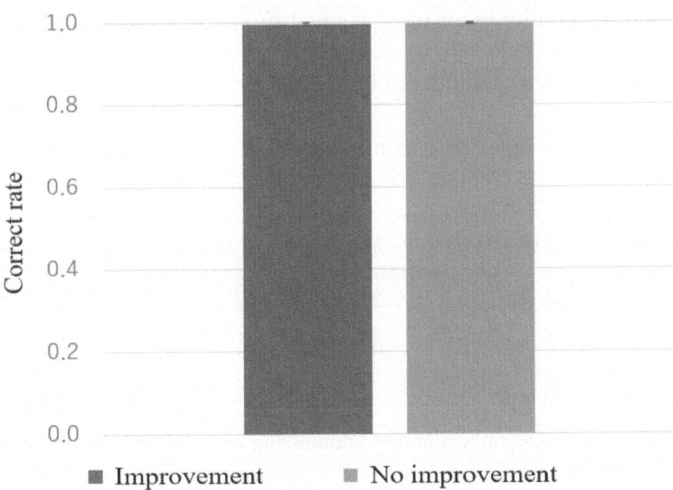

Fig. 10. Percentage of correct rates in Kraepelin test after VIT.

4 Conclusion

In this paper, two empirical studies were conducted to obtain public health data on stereoscopic image visibility and to accumulate knowledge on the effects of VIT using stereoscopic images on visual function.

In Experiment 1, 58 healthy young adults were subjected to a stereo test. Of these, 32 could visualize stereoscopic images, while the remaining 26 could not. Compared to the non-visualizers, the visualizers of stereoscopic images spent more time looking at the LCD screen the previous day, but there was no statistically significant difference. As a future prospect, we will measure the subjects' daily time spent looking at the LCD screen and the distance between their eyes and the screen, to confirm whether there is a correlation between the ability to visualize stereoscopic images and the time spent looking at the LCD screen, as well as the distance between their eyes and the screen.

In Experiment 2, nine healthy young males underwent the VIT for five consecutive days. Before and after the training, a stereo test, Kraepelin test, and tests for the VAPF were performed daily. During the Kraepelin test, EEG measurements were taken along with performance measurements. The δ and θ bands of the subjects' EEG decreased during the Kraepelin test, but there were no significant differences in the values of the other frequency bands. Immediately after the VIT, there was a temporary improvement in the subjects' vision, but this recovery trend was not sustained until the next day's pre-measurement. Additionally, no change in the VAPF was observed between the pre-measurement on the first day of the VIT and the post-measurement on the fifth day of training. Therefore, as a future perspective, it is necessary to confirm whether changes in the VAPF and the continuity of improvement in visual acuity can be maintained by increasing the time and frequency of the VIT. In addition, the VIT using stereoscopic images can be expected to have certain benefits for MCI and children with learning disabilities.

Note that portions of this paper contain revised versions of the co-author's thesis [12].

Acknowledgments. This work was supported in part by the Kayamori Foundation of Informational Science Advancement and the Japan Society for the Promotion of Science, and Grant-in-Aid for Scientific Research (B) (Grant number 23K28367) and (C) (Grant numbers 20K12528 and 22K12141).

Disclosure of Interests. The authors have no competing interests to declare that are relevant to the content of this article.

References

1. Hirata, A., Ito, A., Funakoshi, M.: Media use activities of today from the perspective of usage of smartphones, television, and other devices - from the 2021 time use survey on media use. NHK Monthly Report Broadcast Res. **72**(7), 88–111 (2022)
2. Akatsuka, M., Nakagawa, M., Usui, C., Hayashi, T.: Acute onset esotropia in two sets of brothers. Jpn. Orthoptic J. **49**, 45–49 (2020)

3. Kawamoto, K.: Smartphone Blindness. Kanki Publishing, Tokyo (2023)
4. Sugiura, A., Miyao, M., Yamamoto, T., Takada, H.: Effect of strategic accommodation training by wide stereoscopic movie presentation on myopic young people of visual acuity and asthenopia. Displays **32**(4), 219–224 (2011)
5. Kato, Z., Okubo, T.: Methods to Measure Bio Functions for Beginners. Nihon Shuppan Service Co. Ltd, Tokyo (1999)
6. Hirayama, K., Takeda, K.: What is the dorsal visual stream doing? High. Brain Funct. Res. **35**(2), 197–198 (2015)
7. Tachibanaki, S., Kawamura, S.: Molecular bases of the difference between rod- and cone-mediated vision. Comp. Physiol. Biochem. **34**(3), 70–79 (2017)
8. Zola, S.M., Manzanares, C.M., Clopton, P., Lah, J.J., Levey, A.I.: A behavioral task predicts conversion to mild cognitive impairment and Alzheimer's disease. Am. J. Alzheimer's Dis. Other Dementias **28**(2), 179–184 (2013)
9. Oyama, A., et al.: Novel method for rapid assessment of cognitive impairment using high-performance eye-tracking technology. Sci. Rep. **9**(1), 12932 (2019)
10. Ono, R., Matsuura, Y., Miyao, M., Takada, H.: Pattern of body sway while viewing 3D video clips in various age groups. Jpn. J. Hyg. **77**, 20009 (2022)
11. Itatsu, Y., Takada, H.: Discrimination of components in radial motions using deep learning. Image Lab **2022**(5), 61–66 (2022)
12. Sorimachi, K.: A study on the influence of stereoscopic video viewing on visual function, Senior thesis in department of mechanical and system engineering, School of Engineering, University of Fukui (2024)

Inclusive IT Design in Higher Education

Christian Meske[1]($\boxtimes$), Florian Brachten[1], Ayseguel Doganguen[2], and Julia Hermann[2]

[1] Ruhr University Bochum, 44799 Bochum, Germany
sski-research@ruhr-uni-bochum.de
[2] Hochschule Ruhr West, 46236 Bottrop, Germany

Abstract. Inclusive Design in Information Technology (IT) focuses on creating digital solutions accessible to all users, including those with disabilities, driven by demographic shifts and legal standards. This paper aims to highlight the benefits of inclusive IT design, emphasizing its importance in higher education. By examining how inclusive design fosters an equitable learning environment, enhances accessibility, and promotes diversity, the paper underscores the necessity of integrating these principles into educational curricula. Key results demonstrate that inclusive IT design improves user experiences and accessibility, expands market reach, and increases employee productivity and job satisfaction. In higher education, inclusive design ensures equal access to learning resources, fostering a culture of diversity and inclusion. The paper concludes that incorporating inclusive design principles into IT curricula is essential for preparing students to create accessible and innovative technology, ultimately benefiting both society and industry.

Keywords: Inclusion · IT Design · Higher Education · Disabilities

1 Introduction

Inclusive Design in Information Technology (IT) signifies a fundamental shift in acknowledging and embracing user diversity within the digital sphere. By prioritizing inclusivity, this approach ensures that individuals with disabilities have access while also improving usability for a broader audience that mirrors the diverse fabric of global society. There is a growing consensus underscoring the importance of IT design that caters to all human abilities and preferences, transcending the limitations of catering solely to the majority [1]. This inclusive perspective integrates the needs of marginalized groups into mainstream technology solutions, fostering a more equitable digital landscape. In this paper, we delve into the details of the benefits of inclusive IT design, exploring how it enriches user experiences and drives innovation [2].

Recognizing global demographic shifts, projections from the World Health Organization indicate a significant increase in the aging population, with an estimated 1.5 billion people aged 60 or older by 2050 [3]. This demographic transition underscores the pressing need for accessible technologies that support productive living and independence among older adults [4]. Concurrently, an increased awareness of diverse user needs is driving the establishment of stricter legal and ethical standards for inclusive

M. Antona et al. (Eds.): HCII 2024, LNCS 15379, pp. 54–65, 2025.
https://doi.org/10.1007/978-3-031-76818-7_5

IT design [5]. This highlights a growing demand for products and services thoughtfully designed to accommodate the full spectrum of users, necessitating the integration of robust inclusive design principles into digital solutions [6].

Hence, the relevance of inclusive IT design in higher education cannot be overstated. As educational institutions increasingly rely on digital platforms for teaching and learning, ensuring accessibility becomes paramount to provide equal educational opportunities for all students [7]. Inclusive IT design not only aligns with legal and ethical imperatives but also enriches the learning experience for a diverse student body [8], preparing them for an increasingly heterogeneous world. By integrating inclusive design principles into higher education curricula, institutions can create more engaging and effective educational experiences tailored to the needs of every student [9].

This paper aims to highlight the benefits of inclusive IT design in general, explore its relevance in higher education and describe important aspects for integrating inclusive IT design in higher education curricula.

The paper is hence structured as follows. First, an examination of the advantages stemming from inclusive IT design is presented. Following this, emphasis is placed on elucidating the significance of inclusive IT design within the realm of higher education, highlighting how it fosters an equitable learning environment, enhances accessibility for all students, and promotes a culture of diversity and inclusion that is essential for preparing students for a diverse and technologically advanced world. Subsequently, we explore practical methods and strategies for integrating inclusive IT design principles into higher education curricula. Finally, the discourse culminates with a concluding segment that encapsulates key insights and highlights the overarching importance of embracing inclusive IT design principles in educational contexts.

2   Benefits of Inclusive IT Design

In the context of modern information technology, inclusive design significantly enhances user experience and accessibility, facilitating interface adaptability and integrating user-centric features. This broadens access for all users, making technology more accessible and interactions more seamless. [10] underscores this point by showing that combining user trials with exclusion calculations effectively tailors' products to meet diverse needs, thereby maximizing the potential of inclusive design to enhance user experience across various demographic groups.

Furthermore, integrating accessibility features in software not only assists users with disabilities but also elevates the overall user experience, aligning with the principles of universal design. This approach ensures that software is usable by the widest possible audience without necessitating adaptations, which [11] finds leads to higher user satisfaction and more extensive usability. This inclusive approach fosters an environment where all users, regardless of ability, can interact efficiently and comfortably with technology.

The strategic business advantages of inclusive design are significant, tapping into new market segments and fostering enhanced brand loyalty. [12] and [13] highlight that companies embracing inclusive design and prioritizing accessible technology gain access to a broader customer base, including aging populations and people with disabilities, thus expanding market reach and enhancing customer relationships. This broader inclusivity not only captures a wider audience but also strengthens brand loyalty among existing customers and cultivates greater overall satisfaction. Such outcomes underscore the direct link between accessible technology and enhanced business performance, as a more satisfied customer base often leads to increased profitability and brand strength.

Voice-controlled smart assistants significantly empower individuals with physical impairments, improving their autonomy and ease of use. [14] explore how these devices enable users with limited mobility or dexterity to interact with their environment via simple voice commands, thereby fostering greater independence and interaction with the technological world. This technology not only supports individual users but also has broader implications for the accessibility of smart home technologies and interactive devices.

The optimization of smart home ecosystems with adaptive algorithms further illustrates the potential of inclusive IT design to enhance accessibility for users with disabilities. According to [15], these systems adapt to the user's preferences and needs, which increases the functionality and accessibility of the home environment, making daily tasks more manageable and enhancing the quality of life for individuals with various disabilities.

Customizable user interfaces that accommodate visual and cognitive impairments promote inclusivity and improve the user experience. [16] note that these interfaces can be tailored to meet individual needs, thereby enhancing the accessibility and usability of digital content. Such customization ensures that all users, regardless of their specific impairments, can effectively engage with technology, highlighting the critical role of adaptive design in promoting inclusivity.

Real-time captioning and automated translation play crucial roles in making digital content accessible to a global audience, including those with hearing impairments and non-native speakers. [17] points out that these technologies provide text alternatives to spoken content and translate it into various languages, broadening the reach and inclusivity of digital platforms. This not only enhances accessibility but also ensures that content is available to a diverse global audience, thereby reducing linguistic barriers.

Educational software incorporating assistive technologies and adaptive learning systems show the extensive benefits of inclusive IT design in educational settings. [18] discuss how these technologies provide customized learning experiences that cater to diverse learning styles and needs, ensuring that all students, including those with disabilities, have equal opportunities to succeed academically. This inclusive approach in education is essential for fostering an equitable learning environment where all students can thrive.

Overall, inclusive technologies enhance usability for everyone, embodying the principles of universal design. [19] emphasize that making products and services accessible to the broadest user base not only meets regulatory compliance but also enhances user retention and satisfaction. This comprehensive approach to design not only addresses the needs of those with specific disabilities but also improves the user experience for the general population, underscoring the universal benefits of inclusivity in technology.

Inclusive IT design in workplace environments significantly boosts employee productivity and job satisfaction by fostering a supportive and accessible work environment. This positive impact stems from employees feeling valued and able to contribute effectively, regardless of their abilities or disabilities. The inclusive nature of these environments encourages a culture of respect and equality, which has been shown to lead directly to higher levels of overall workplace satisfaction and productivity [20].

Organizations that implement inclusive IT practices report higher levels of employee engagement and organizational commitment. This enhancement is particularly evident when inclusive practices are aligned with overall business strategies, creating a work environment that values diversity and inclusion. Such alignment not only boosts morale but also solidifies a sense of belonging among employees, which is essential for sustaining long-term commitment and reducing turnover rates [21].

Inclusive IT design helps businesses reach and serve global markets more effectively. By considering a wide range of user needs, companies can cater to diverse consumer bases, enhancing their international reach and competitiveness. This global approach not only expands market potential but also builds a more resilient business model capable of adapting to varied consumer preferences and regulatory environments across different regions [22].

By incorporating inclusive design principles, IT products and services can bridge the gap between users with varying degrees of access and ability, thus reducing the risk of a digital divide. This approach promotes equality in technology access, ensuring that all users can benefit from digital advancements. Ensuring equitable access is vital for fostering social and economic inclusion, as it enables all segments of society to participate fully in the digital age [23].

Inclusive IT design increases the adaptability of technology products across various cultural and environmental contexts, so we argue. Such adaptability is crucial for technologies that are used in diverse geographical locations, ensuring that they meet the localized needs of users in different parts of the world. This flexibility not only improves user satisfaction but also ensures compliance with international standards and local regulations, which is key to successful global operations [24].

In summary, modern information technology has seen a significant shift towards inclusive design, which not only enhances user experience and accessibility but also broadens market reach and fosters brand loyalty. Through a combination of tailored products, inclusive workplace environments, and strategic alignment with business goals, companies can capitalize on the benefits of inclusive IT design, ranging from increased productivity and customer satisfaction to better access to global markets and reduced digital divides. Moreover, inclusive design promotes adaptability across diverse cultures and environments, ensuring technology's effectiveness and relevance on a global scale. Ultimately, embracing inclusive IT practices not only promotes social equity but also drives innovation and business success in the digital age.

3   The Relevance of Inclusive IT Design in Higher Education

Inclusive design principles can enhance the learning experiences for all students, not just those with disabilities, by providing multiple means of engagement, representation, and expression [25]. By incorporating UDL into educational practices, instructors can create diverse learning opportunities that cater to various learning styles and preferences. For instance, offering multimedia materials alongside traditional lectures accommodates visual and auditory learners, while interactive activities allow for hands-on engagement. This approach not only ensures that every student can access and engage with the content but also promotes deeper understanding and retention of information. Moreover, by acknowledging and embracing the diversity of learners, inclusive design fosters a sense of belonging and inclusivity within the classroom, encouraging active participation and collaboration among students from different backgrounds and abilities.

By implementing inclusive design, higher education can better support the diverse learning needs and backgrounds of its students, contributing to more equitable learning outcomes [26]. Inclusive design recognizes that students come to the classroom with varying levels of prior knowledge, skills, and experiences. Therefore, instructional materials and activities can be intentionally designed to accommodate this diversity and provide multiple entry points for learning. For example, offering alternative assessments such as project-based assignments or oral presentations alongside traditional exams caters to students with different strengths and preferences. Additionally, providing supplementary resources, such as study guides or tutoring services, ensures that students have access to additional support when needed. By embracing inclusive design, higher education institutions can create an environment where every student feels valued, respected, and empowered to succeed academically.

Inclusive design in higher education ensures that all learning environments, both physical and digital, are accessible to all students, which is essential for creating equitable educational opportunities [27]. Accessibility encompasses not only physical accommodations, such as wheelchair ramps and accessible seating, but also digital accessibility, including screen readers and captioned videos. By proactively addressing barriers to access, higher education institutions can ensure that students with disabilities may fully participate in all aspects of academic life. Moreover, accessible design benefits not only students with disabilities but also those with temporary impairments, such as injuries or illnesses, and those with situational impairments, such as noisy environments or limited internet connectivity. By prioritizing accessibility, higher education institutions demonstrate their commitment to diversity, equity, and inclusion, fostering a supportive and inclusive learning environment for all students.

Adopting inclusive design in higher education settings promotes social inclusion and helps to integrate students with special educational needs, enhancing their academic and social experiences [28]. Social inclusion goes beyond mere accessibility to encompass meaningful participation and belonging within the academic community. Inclusive design fosters a culture of acceptance and respect for individual differences, challenging stereotypes and promoting positive interactions among students. By creating opportunities for collaboration, teamwork, and peer support, inclusive design facilitates the formation of diverse social networks and friendships. Moreover, inclusive design encourages the celebration of diversity and the recognition of the unique contributions that each student brings to the community. As a result, higher education institutions become more vibrant, inclusive, and welcoming spaces where every student feels valued and accepted for who they are.

Inclusive design can increase the competitiveness of higher education institutions by attracting a broader range of students and meeting global educational standards [29]. In today's interconnected world, students have a multitude of options when choosing where to pursue their higher education. Institutions that prioritize inclusive design differentiate themselves by demonstrating a commitment to equity, diversity, and inclusion. By offering accessible and inclusive learning environments, institutions signal to prospective students that they value diversity and are dedicated to ensuring that every student can thrive academically and socially. Moreover, by meeting global educational standards for accessibility and inclusivity, institutions enhance their reputation and standing within the international academic community. As a result, they attract a diverse student body from around the world, enriching the educational experience for all students and positioning themselves as leaders in inclusive education.

The principles of inclusive design encourage institutions to continuously improve their teaching strategies and curriculum to meet the evolving needs of their student population [30]. Inclusive design is not a one-time effort but rather an ongoing commitment to diversity, equity, and inclusion. Institutions that embrace inclusive design actively solicit feedback from students, faculty, and staff to identify areas for improvement and implement changes accordingly. For example, they may conduct regular accessibility audits of their physical and digital infrastructure to ensure compliance with accessibility standards and guidelines. Additionally, they may offer professional development opportunities for faculty and staff to enhance their knowledge and skills in inclusive pedagogy. By fostering a culture of continuous improvement, institutions create learning environments that are responsive to the diverse needs of their students and reflective of best practices in inclusive education.

Inclusive design fosters an academic culture that values diversity, encourages participation, and respects the contributions of all students, which is vital for nurturing a sense of belonging and community within educational institutions [31]. An inclusive academic culture goes beyond mere compliance with accessibility standards to encompass a commitment to equity, diversity, and inclusion in all aspects of academic life. Inclusive design ensures that every member of the academic community, regardless of background, identity, or ability, feels valued, respected, and supported in their pursuit of knowledge and learning. By creating a welcoming and inclusive environment, institutions foster a sense of belonging and connectedness among students, faculty, and staff, promoting collaboration, creativity, and academic excellence. Moreover, an inclusive academic culture prepares students to thrive in diverse and multicultural environments, equipping them with the skills and perspectives needed to succeed in an increasingly globalized world.

Without teaching inclusive design in higher education, graduates may not consider inclusive practices in their later organizational roles. Considering e.g. the example of computer science graduates, this lack of awareness can lead to the development of software and technologies that do not consider the diverse needs of all users, perpetuating accessibility barriers and exclusionary practices. Embedding inclusive design in the curriculum, for instance for computer science, ensures that graduates become inclusive software designers, capable of creating technology that is accessible and beneficial to a broad audience [32]. By integrating inclusive design principles into computer science education, institutions prepare students to become agents of change in the technology industry, advocating for accessibility and inclusion in all aspects of software development. Through hands-on projects, collaborative learning experiences, and real-world applications, students become aware and sensitive to this topic, learn how to design, develop, and evaluate technology with a focus on accessibility and usability for diverse user populations. This holistic approach not only equips students with technical skills but also instills in them a deep understanding of the social, ethical, and legal implications of technology design, empowering them to create technology that is inclusive, equitable, and impactful.

4 How to Integrate Inclusive IT Design in Higher Education Curricula: 10 Recommendations

In the following, we provide recommendations on integrating inclusive IT design into higher education curricula, drawing from existing literature.

Early Integration in Curriculum: Introducing inclusive design principles early in the curriculum, such as in computer science, is crucial. Embedding these principles in introductory courses helps students understand the importance of considering diverse user needs from the beginning of their education [33]. By incorporating inclusive design concepts into foundational courses, students develop a solid understanding of accessibility and inclusivity as fundamental aspects of software development. This early exposure sets the stage for students to integrate inclusive design thinking into their future projects and coursework, laying a strong foundation for their professional careers. Additionally, early integration fosters a mindset of empathy and consideration for diverse user perspectives, preparing students to create technology that is truly inclusive and accessible to all.

Project-Based Learning: Implementing project-based learning that incorporates inclusive design can provide practical experiences for students [34]. Through hands-on projects, students have the opportunity to apply inclusive design principles in real-world scenarios, bridging the gap between theory and practice. Engaging in project-based learning encourages students to think critically about accessibility challenges and develop innovative solutions that address the diverse needs of users. Moreover, collaborative projects allow students to work in teams, promoting communication, teamwork, and problem-solving skills essential for their future careers in technology.

Interdisciplinary Collaboration: Encouraging collaboration between different disciplines like computer science, psychology, and social sciences can enrich students' understanding of inclusive design [35]. Interdisciplinary collaboration exposes students to diverse perspectives and methodologies, broadening their understanding of accessibility and inclusivity. By working with experts from various fields, students gain insights into the social, psychological, and cultural factors that influence user interactions with technology. This holistic approach encourages students to consider the broader societal impact of their designs and develop solutions that address complex human needs and experiences.

Faculty Training and Development: Providing ongoing training and professional development for faculty on inclusive design is essential [36]. Faculty members play a crucial role in shaping the educational experiences of students and integrating inclusive design principles into the curriculum. Continuous training ensures that educators stay informed about the latest advancements and best practices in accessibility and inclusivity. Additionally, faculty development programs provide opportunities for educators to collaborate, share resources, and exchange ideas for integrating inclusive design into their teaching practices effectively.

Inclusion of Accessibility Topics: Specific courses on accessibility and universal design should be integral to the computer science curriculum [37]. These courses provide students with specialized knowledge and skills for designing software and systems that are accessible to users with diverse abilities. Topics may include accessibility standards, assistive technologies, user testing methodologies, and inclusive design frameworks. By offering dedicated courses on accessibility, institutions demonstrate their commitment to preparing students to create technology that is usable and beneficial for all users, regardless of their abilities.

User-Centered Design: Incorporating the topic of user-centered design that require students to consider a range of abilities and backgrounds can foster empathy and a deeper understanding of diverse user needs [38]. By placing users at the center of the design process, students learn to empathize with individuals with different abilities and experiences. These projects challenge students to think creatively and innovatively to address the unique needs and preferences of diverse user groups. Moreover, user-centered design projects encourage students to engage in user research, usability testing, and iterative design processes, honing their skills as empathetic and user-focused designers.

Leverage Technology and Tools: Incorporating technology and tools that facilitate inclusive design is essential [39]. The curriculum should include training on software and tools specifically designed to improve accessibility, such as screen readers, accessibility testing tools, and inclusive design frameworks. This practical knowledge prepares students to integrate these tools into their development processes effectively. Moreover, staying abreast of the latest advancements in assistive technologies equips students with the skills to leverage emerging tools and platforms to create more inclusive and accessible software solutions. By integrating hands-on training with these technologies, students gain valuable experience in applying inclusive design principles in real-world settings, enhancing their readiness for future professional roles in technology.

Case Studies and Real-World Examples: Integrating case studies of successful inclusive software designs can provide students with clear examples of good practices [40]. Discussing both successes and failures in real-world applications helps students understand the implications of design decisions and learn from existing solutions. Analyzing case studies allows students to explore the design choices made by industry leaders, understand their impact on user experience, and identify strategies for improving inclusivity in their own projects. Additionally, exposure to diverse case studies from various domains and user demographics broadens students' perspectives and fosters critical thinking skills essential for designing inclusive technology solutions.

Student-Led Research and Innovation: Encouraging student-led research projects on topics related to inclusive design can foster innovation and deeper learning [41]. By engaging in research, students can explore new areas of inclusive technology, develop their solutions, and contribute to the field's body of knowledge. Student-led research projects empower students to tackle real-world challenges, experiment with innovative solutions, and drive meaningful change in the field of inclusive design. Moreover, engaging in research encourages students to collaborate, communicate their findings, and present their work to peers and industry professionals, honing their research and communication skills essential for success in academia and industry.

Assessment of Inclusive Design Integration: Regular assessment of how well inclusive design principles are integrated into the computer science curriculum can help institutions continuously improve their educational offerings. By collecting feedback from students, faculty, and external stakeholders, institutions can evaluate the effectiveness of their inclusive design initiatives and identify areas for enhancement [31]. Assessment methods may include surveys, focus groups, student portfolios, and course evaluations. By prioritizing ongoing assessment and feedback, institutions ensure that their curriculum remains responsive to the evolving needs of students and reflects best practices in inclusive education.

5 Conclusion

Inclusive IT design stands as an imperative for the future of technology development and deployment. However, its realization hinges not only on industry adaptation but also on the integration of inclusive design principles into higher education curricula. The essence of inclusive design lies not merely in meeting legal requirements but in fostering a mindset of empathy, understanding, and creativity among future generations of computer scientists and software engineers. Without adequate education on inclusive design principles, there is a risk of perpetuating a cycle where the concept of inclusion remains foreign to developers, resulting in digital products and services that inadvertently exclude marginalized users.

The necessity of inclusive design in IT is underscored by the growing recognition that technology should cater to the entire spectrum of human abilities and preferences. Yet, for this vision to materialize, it is imperative that higher education institutions take proactive steps to incorporate inclusive design into their computer science and engineering programs. By integrating inclusive design principles into coursework and providing hands-on experience with designing accessible technologies, universities can equip students with the knowledge and skills needed to champion inclusivity in their future careers.

Failure to prioritize inclusive design education in higher education not only risks leaving a significant gap in the skill set of future IT professionals but also perpetuates a cycle of exclusion within the tech industry. Without a foundational understanding of inclusive design principles, developers may inadvertently perpetuate biases and inequalities in their creations, ultimately hindering progress towards a more equitable and inclusive digital landscape.

In summary, inclusive design in IT is not just a matter of compliance or market strategy; it is a moral imperative and a prerequisite for building a more inclusive society. Higher education institutions play a crucial role in shaping the attitudes and practices of future technology professionals. By prioritizing inclusive design education, universities can empower students to become catalysts for change, driving innovation that not only meets the needs of all users but also fosters a more equitable and inclusive technological future.

Acknowledgments. This work was supported by funding from the Foundation for Innovation in Higher Education (Stiftung Innovation in der Hochschullehre), project "Integration of Design Science and Positive Computing (DESCPOS) for an Inclusive World".

Disclosure of Interests. The authors have no competing interests to declare that are relevant to the content of this article.

Declaration. Generative AI was utilized to assist in the research and composition of this manuscript.

References

1. Heylighen, A., Van der Linden, V., Van Steenwinkel, I.: Ten questions concerning inclusive design of the built environment. Build. Environ. **114**, 507–517 (2017)
2. Wilson, N., Thomson, A., Thomson, A., Holliman, A.F.: Understanding inclusive design education. In: Proceedings of the Design Society: International Conference on Engineering Design (2019)
3. World Health Organization: Global Health and Aging (2019). https://www.nia.nih.gov/sites/default/files/2017-06/global_health_aging.pdf
4. Czaja, S.J.: Technology and older adults: designing for accessibility and usability. In: Proceedings of the 8th International ACM SIGACCESS Conference on Computers and Accessibility (2006)
5. Abascal, J., Nicolle, C.: Moving towards inclusive design guidelines for socially and ethically aware HCI. Interact. Comput. **17**(5), 484–505 (2005)
6. Roland Buß: Inclusive Design - Go Beyond Accessibility. HCI (3), pp. 400–407 Springer (2020)
7. Lisboa, I., Barroso, J., Rocha, T.: Digital accessibility of online educational platforms: identifying barriers for blind student's interaction. In: Proceedings of the International Conference on Innovative Technologies and Learning, vol. 12396, pp. 441–450. Springer, Cham (2020)
8. Brooks, R., Grady, S.D.: Course design considerations for inclusion and representation. Quality Matters White Paper (2022)
9. Silver, P., Bourke, A., Strehorn, K.C.: Universal instructional design in higher education: an approach for inclusion. Equity Excellence Educ. **31**(2), 47–51 (1998) . Taylor & Francis
10. Goodman-Deane, J., Bradley, M., Waller, S., Clarkson, P.J.: Quantifying exclusion for digital products and interfaces. In: Designing for Inclusion, pp. 140–149. Springer, Cham (2020)
11. Sapp, W.: Universal design: online educational media for students with disabilities. J. Visual Impairment Blindness 495–500 (2007).
12. Goodman, A., Langdon, P., Clarkson, P.J.: Providing strategic user information for designers: methods and initial findings. Des. Stud. **27**(6), 657–683 (2006)
13. Waller, S.D., Bradley, M.D., Hosking, I.M., Clarkson, P.J.: Making the case for inclusive design. Appl. Ergon. **46**, 297–303 (2015)
14. Pradhan, A., Mehta, K., & Findlater, L.: "Accessibility Came by Accident": use of voice-controlled intelligent personal assistants by people with disabilities. In: Proceedings of the 2018 CHI Conference on Human Factors in Computing Systems (2018)
15. Reinisch, C., Kofler, M.J., Kastner, W.: ThinkHome: a smart home as digital ecosystem. In: Proceedings of the Conference on Digital Ecosystems and Technologies (2010)

16. Bilek, P., Macik, M., Mikovec, Z.: Supporting personalized care of older adults with vision and cognitive impairments by user modeling. In: Federated Conference on Computer Science and Information Systems (2019)

17. Kawas, S., Karalis, G., Wen, T., Ladner, R.E.: Improving real-time captioning experiences for deaf and hard of hearing students. In: Proceedings of the ACM Conference on Computers and Accessibility (2016)

18. Grönlund, Å., Lim, N., Larsson, H.: Effective use of assistive technologies for inclusive education in developing countries: Issues and challenges from two case studies. Int. J. Educ. Dev. Inform. Commun. Technol. (2010)

19. Moon, N.W., Baker, P.M.A., et al.: Designing wearable technologies for users with disabilities: accessibility, usability, and connectivity factors. J. Enabling Technol. (2019)

20. Narenthiran, O.P., Torero, J., Woodrow, M.: Inclusive design of workspaces: Mixed methods approach to understanding users. Sustainability (2022)

21. Choi, S.B., Tran, T.B.H., Park, B.I.: Inclusive leadership and work engagement: mediating roles of affective organizational commitment and creativity. Soc. Behav. Personal. Int. J. **43**(6), 931–944 (2015)

22. Ivanova, N.: People-centred business continuity: a case for inclusive design. Des. Manag. J. (2022)

23. Warschauer, M.: Technology and Social Inclusion: Rethinking the Digital Divide. MIT Press, p. 235 (2003)

24. Tuominen, M., Rajala, A., Möller, K.: How does adaptability drive firm innovativeness? J. Bus. Res. **2004**, 495–506 (2004)

25. McGuire, J.M., Scott, S.S.: Universal design for instruction: extending the universal design paradigm to college instruction. J. Postsecondary Educ. Disabil. **19**(2), 124–134 (2006)

26. Rossi, V.: Inclusive Learning Design in Higher Education: A Practical Guide to Creating Equitable Learning Experiences. Routledge (2023)

27. Lee, Y., Cassim, J.: How the inclusive design process enables social inclusion. Inter. Assoc. Soc. Des. Res. (2009)

28. Njui, H.W.: Building and sustaining globally competitive higher education institutions: transforming education through inclusive classrooms. Eur. J. Educ. Stud. (2017).

29. Moriña, A.: Inclusive education in higher education: challenges and opportunities. Eur. J. Spec. Needs Educ. **32**(1), 3–17 (2017)

30. Navarro, S., Zervas, P., Gesa, R., Sampson, D.: Developing teachers' competences for designing inclusive learning experiences. Educ. Technol. Soc. **19**(1), 17–27 (2016)

31. Patel, P., Chu, J., Kumar, Y., Kwak, D., Morreale, P.: Implementing inclusive software design in the CS Curriculum. In: Presented at the ACM Conference on Innovation and Technology in Computer Science Education 2022 (2022)

32. Dong, H.: Strategies for teaching inclusive design. J. Eng. Des. **21**, 237–251 (2010)

33. Worsley, M., Bar-El, D.: Inclusive making: designing tools and experiences to promote accessibility and redefine making. Comput. Sci. Educ. (2022). Taylor & Francis

34. Jorgenson, S.: Bridges and boundaries to power: how teachers used project-based learning to design a radically inclusive STEM high school. Crit. Educ. **9**(16), 17–39 (2018)

35. Hedegaard-Soerensen, L., Jensen, C.R., Tofteng, D.M.B.: Interdisciplinary collaboration as a prerequisite for inclusive education. Eur. J. Spec. Needs Educ. **33**(3), 382–395 (2018)

36. Lombardi, A.R., Murray, C., Gerdes, H.: College faculty and inclusive instruction: self-reported attitudes and actions pertaining to universal design. J. Divers. High. Educ. **4**(4), 250–261 (2011)

37. Ribu, K., Nes, M.: Introducing usability engineering and universal design in the computer science curriculum. international conference on engineering education (2007).

38. Kross, S., Guo, P.: Five pedagogical principles of a user-centered design course that prepares computing undergraduates for industry jobs. In: ACM Technical Symposium on Computer Science Education, pp. 168–174 (2022)..
39. McMahon, D.D., Walker, Z.: Leveraging emerging technology to design an inclusive future with universal design for learning. CEPS J. **9**(3), 167–186 (2019)
40. Dong, H., Cassim, J., Coleman, R.: Addressing the challenges of inclusive design: a case study approach. In: Universal Access in Ambient Intelligence Environments, pp. 273–292. Springer, Berlin, Heidelberg (2007)
41. Lister, K., McPherson, E., Coughlan, T.: Towards inclusive language: exploring student-led approaches to talking about disability-related study needs. In: ICERI2019 Proceedings, IATED (2019)

Pathways to Make Biochemistry Accessible by Applying Universal Design to the Creation of Novel Educational Materials

Cristina Gehibie Reynaga-Peña[1]([⊠]) [iD], Carolina del Carmen López-Suero[2] [iD], Jonathan Ely Arévalo-Arguijo[1], Lilia Gómez-Flores[1] [iD], Eduardo Magaña-Cruz[1] [iD], Luis Fernando Garza-Vera[1], and Daniel Alejandro Cuellar-Reynaga[1] [iD]

[1] Tecnologico de Monterrey, Av. Eugenio Garza Sada 2501, Monterrey, N.L., Mexico
cristina.reynaga@tec.mx
[2] Universidad Iberoamericana, Prol. Paseo de Reforma 880, Ciudad de México, Mexico

Abstract. Undergraduate students who need to understand metabolic pathways to apply it in their professional field, usually choose to learn them by heart. However, not achieving a meaningful knowledge of the system could lead to failure and frustration. That is why it is important to have educational materials in this area, but even more important to have it accessible to all learners, regardless of whether they have a disability or not. With the goal of making metabolic pathways concepts, and specifically the Krebs cycle, accessible for all users, our team of experts in chemistry, education, design and engineering joined efforts to create a novel educational product that can be used in Biochemistry classroom. This product was conceived applying the principles of universal design, so it can be used by blind and visually impaired learners or sighted students, helping the generation of inclusive teaching spaces. This work describes the whole creative process, the considerations for their design, the technologies used, and the novel educational materials constructed.

Keywords: Educational Innovation · Inclusive Education · Higher Education · Biochemical Education

1 Introduction

1.1 Equitable Education of Chemistry and Biochemistry

Since the right to equitable education for students with disabilities was recognized in international statements [1], education agencies worldwide were pressed to provide access to education to all individuals. In terms of STEM education, in the last decades it is also recognized the need of making those fields accessible to individuals with disabilities [2–4], with global increased efforts as the world demands more inclusive societies and more individuals with disabilities in fields such as Health Sciences [3, 5, 6]. Some efforts to support inclusive STEM education have created full libraries of accessible tactile diagrams for chemistry in secondary and tertiary education, such as

M. Antona et al. (Eds.): HCII 2024, LNCS 15379, pp. 66–82, 2025.
https://doi.org/10.1007/978-3-031-76818-7_6

the Tactile Reading Dedicon [7], where interactive molecular diagrams are available for teachers and blind learners. Examples of current projects to create tactile 3D printed objects and diagrams especially accessible for the blind is the Diagram Center [8] in the US, Accessible Graphics in Australia [9] or the Tactiles project in Europe [10], where one of the subjects is Chemistry.

Within the areas of Chemistry, Biochemistry is a challenging one, because it implies the understanding of the chemical reactions that occur in living beings [11]. In the Biochemistry courses, the students must learn about different metabolic pathways. For example, learning about metabolism in the human body means having to learn thousands of reactions happening simultaneously or in chain. Memorizing these metabolic pathways is not the most recommended, since it is difficult for the students to understand how a substrate is transformed into a product through a series of intermediate metabolites, and how this knowledge is applied in their professional career. Also, researchers have recognized that "Students are often confused when faced with the complex structures and paths of physical and chemical data, since biochemistry textbooks rely on visualization in the form of 2-dimensional (2D) diagrams consisting of many arrows and figures" [12].

For students with visual disabilities, understanding of Biochemistry as a subject, including the metabolic reactions that take place in the body, can be much more complex, and accessible ways to learn the subject have to be available to support blind and visually impaired learners [13]. Studying metabolism through the lenses of organic chemistry could help the learners to truly understand the chemical transformations that occur, because it is easy to identify the bonds that are breaking and those forming. Once a student understands the basic principles that govern the chemical reactions of the biochemical processes, it is possible to achieve meaningful learning that conducts to deeper knowledge acquisition. This knowledge is important for professionals that need a thorough understanding of biochemistry and deep comprehension of biochemical concepts, regardless of whether they have a disability or not. Thus, meaningful learning must also be accessible to everyone.

To study the structure and the transformation of chemical molecules in two dimensions (2D), chemists use three classical drawings: structural, semi-structural and bond-line; the last ones are the most common and easy to use. Once the student understands the bond-line drawing, the teacher can use them to explain how molecules transform. A further step to support a higher level of understanding is to later migrate or complement with the use of three-dimensional (3D) representations of molecules; the bond-line drawing can also be visualized in 3D as a first approach and later on the other representations can follow. These can range from molecule building kits to construct models of simple molecules (for example, those from Fisher Scientific), to more complex ones, such as those showing protein structures. Nowadays, full 3D representations and models of molecules and other bioscientific and medical models are available from the National Institutes of Health of the US, and they can be freely accessed in formats to be 3D printed [14].

1.2 Accessible Educational Materials for Biochemistry Topics

In the last 10 to 15 years, there have been multiple efforts to find best practices for teaching chemistry concepts to students with visual impairments and finding ways to represent chemical molecules [15–17] among them some have been proposed by groups in which blind Chemists take part [18–20].

For Biochemistry, to the best of our knowledge, there are few examples of attempts to make inclusive educational materials accessible to blind students. Nevertheless, our group has been working on the development of educational resources with technology to level up education for blind and visually impaired (BVI) students at different school levels. The materials designed by EduMakers seek to provide BVI students with tactile 3D representations enriched with audio information that aim to supply them with the same quality and variety of information as their sighted peers [21–23]. These means of representations can support access to any subject.

Within Biochemistry topics, the Krebs cycle is one that teachers identify as a complex metabolic pathway to teach and learn by students in general [24, 25]. Nevertheless, it is one of the most important biochemical processes for the generation of energy of multicellular organisms, and therefore, is fundamental that students learn it. Therefore, the project we describe in this report is focused on how to make Biochemistry and the Krebs cycle accessible to BVI learners, while enhancing engagement for the majority of learners by applying the principles of Universal Design for Learning [26]. This work is innovative, as there are no learning materials on this topic accessible to blind students neither designed with Universal Design principles.

The research question driving this work is: How can we create an optimal form of representation of chemical molecules, and their transformation during biochemical processes, intended for universal access to understand Biochemistry topics? Thus, this work describes how we designed and prototyped educational materials that can be used in any biochemistry class and by any student as a tool to study the molecules and their transformations.

2 Methods

2.1 Conceptual Considerations for the Design

For the design of educational materials, it was decided to create tactile representations of the molecules involved in metabolic processes. As previously reported, the design methodology was a mix of design thinking, user-centered design and universal design for learning [21]. To define what type of representation was useful, previous research was considered; in this case, researchers from the US Shaw's lab [19, 20] previously reported that blind students can read 3D printed tactile representations of formulas of simple chemical molecules. They produced those representations using a program available online, where any image can be converted into a lithophane, and then 3D printed in resin of grey color that would be observed by sighted people using back illumination [19, 20].

Our group decided to take a different approach, so the tactile molecular representations could also be 3D printed in contrasting colors to make them accessible to low-vision students and also engaging for sighted students. Finally, a most important consideration in educational materials is scientific accuracy; thus, we followed a strict protocol of revisions for the designs as they were developed following the processes described below. The decisions that were taken along the process for pedagogical reasons are described in the Results section.

2.2 Tools for CAD Design and Manufacture of Prototypes

When designing the digital layouts and other components for the project, several crucial points had to be considered, including available tools, the team's skills, and the need for the resulting designs to meet specific criteria, such as:

- Measurability: Digital Designs (DD) needed to have predetermined and clear measurements, providing an initial size reference for manufacturing or scaling.
- Customizability: DD had to include customizable variables or parameters, making them easier to modify or edit.
- UDL Approach: The resulting designs should be inclusive and adaptable to different needs and learning styles.

As a result, SolidWorks, a widely recognized computer-aided design (CAD) software, was chosen as the main tool for the elaboration of the designs. SolidWorks stood out for its ability to define precise dimensions in millimeters and establish positional relationships. Additionally, as a software provided by the university for the collaborators and engineering students, which offers a wide range of parametric modeling functions and tools, and given the team's prior experience with it, as well as its compatibility with various file formats, it facilitates collaboration and design sharing within the team. In this particular design process, those were key aspects to assure advances and adjustments throughout itself.

In terms of 3D printing techniques, two main options were evaluated: resin printing (SLA) and filament printing (FDM). While resin printing offers high precision and fine detail, as well as excellent surface quality, it is often more expensive and requires a more delicate post-processing process; also, resin printers available in the lab allowed printing in one color only. On the other hand, filament printing is cheaper, faster and easier to handle, which makes it ideal for projects where production of parts with specific characteristics is required, as in our case.

When choosing filament 3D printing over resin printing, the ease of achieving multi-colored parts was prioritized, as well as the more accessible price and speed of printing. In addition, filament printing allows for a greater variety of materials, expanding the finish options and functionality of the parts. Then, to achieve the goal or producing objects printed in more than one color, the selection was to use 3D printers equipped with a system that allows printing in multiple colors simultaneously. This is possible by using a pair of BambuLabs X1 Carbon printers due to their capacity to use up to 8 different colors at the same time, providing greater versatility in the design and production of multi-color parts, while the resolution was enough to produce high-quality prototypes.

2.3 Iterations and Validation Cycles

a. With users. To validate the materials, tests were conducted with users in the Civil Association "Vemos con el Corazón", (roughly translated is "We see with our hearts"), located in the city of Toluca, Mexico. The criterion for selecting the sample was the following: people over 18 years of age, with visual disability, and a minimum of high school education who had taken at least one course related to science, preferably chemistry. Sixteen people at the association met the criteria and voluntarily agreed to be part of the sample, which was made up of 12 women and 4 men, the ages ranged from 19 to 88 years old; they hold different levels of study, 4 of them completed high school, 11 have bachelor or engineering degrees, and 1 has a master's degree. Because almost all of them had coursed Chemistry at some point, it was informally asked to them if they liked it, and if so, what did they liked the most, to that, they answered that they liked the lab experiments and chemical formulas composed of elements.

The tools used were semi-structured interviews and non-participant observation of users' interaction with the materials. All participants were shown the same pieces that for easy of understanding they were called slats (see figures below) of the first prototypes of tactile molecular representations of the Krebs Cycle, and they were given instructions only on how to take the first tablet to read it properly (with the wedge pointing to the upper right), and then proceeded to ask the questions regarding what they were touching, what they understood with the tactile representations and what were the challenging features. After gathering all the data, the team iterated the designs to create a new set of prototypes integrating the suggestions we got from our sample of users.

b. With scientists and other experts. Within the iterative design cycle, it took place also a constant validation with scientists, in this case, a PhD. Professor in Chemistry who revised each digital design proposal to make sure the concepts were clearly shown in the tactile representations of molecules, but also that they were adequate to reach the learning objectives. Also, each design was verified to assure the educational prototypes comply with the global conventions of representations of chemical molecules. A second validation with two possible users who were experts in Chemistry was performed; one was a sighted student who was in his last year of chemistry degree, one was a blind professor with a doctorate degree in Chemistry. The educational aspect was also validated on each step by team members experts in science education for visually impaired learners. All of them are part of our collaborative team.

2.4 Technology and Electronics

To provide engaging educational experiences, the 3D objects were complemented with a display of audible information using low-cost technology which was also developed by the engineering team using available materials such as electronic board, microcontroller (Arduino), sensors, audio output and voltage regulators. In this manner, this audio display, which complements the 3D models, aims to enable user interaction with the pieces without the need for an accompanying teacher to facilitate understanding. This is achieved through the implementation of Hall effect sensors in the electronic box for piece detection, which are responsible for detecting the presence of a magnetic field generated by the 3D pieces when a neodymium magnet is placed inside them, activating a relay on the sensor, and sending a signal to the electronic board. It is worth noting that this design and implementation are based on prior work by the team of EduMakers [22], which identified both the Hall effect sensors and neodymium magnets as the most optimal components for this purpose, considering the following features:

- The Hall effect sensors, when used as electronic switches, are less prone to mechanical failure since there is no wear on physical parts.
- The neodymium magnets produce a stronger magnetic field in comparison with other magnets, that allows the sensor to detect the presence of the pieces even if they were in wrong positions or not perfectly aligned.

Therefore, it is not needed as much precision for placing objects, making easier to lift and return the objects by people with visual impairments. Lifting the objects from their box triggers the display of auditory information corresponding to each of the pieces containing a sensor (a magnet). Then, after the physical objects were fabricated, the team selected the proper scientific information that would be displayed when the objects were lifted. The group decided that the audio should contain the essential scientific information of the reaction step that the learner is studying. All the information that was recorded was previously revised by chemistry experts, according to the pedagogical purpose of the object and the subject matter. Audios were stored in an SD card and read by the Arduino system inside the electronics, so they can be replaced according to specific goals by each course and audience (chemistry students, medical students, etc.).

2.5 How the Electronic Board Works

For the integration of interactive elements to the prototype, an electronic circuit board was used so that each individual formula and overall biochemical reaction can be identified and subsequently play a previously recorded auditory information. Since the Krebs cycle is too complex for a single audio file containing information explaining each step, an approach to split the information into these steps helps improve reactiveness of the interaction with the material. Following this logic, the electronic component therefore should be able to identify the physical objects relative of each reaction of the cycle and provide information about the substrates, enzymes, products or reaction type details. To achieve this, the use of Hall effect sensors was added (see previous section), so that attaching a magnet to the 3D printed piece triggers the information for the user.

The proposed use case is that the person will first assemble all reactions of the Krebs cycle to get an overall idea of the reactions involved before dwelling into detail of each equation. Afterwards, the user will place each step of the cycle on top of a base where the electronics will be contained, then the microcontroller identifies which reaction is being placed either by magnets or notches on the edge of the rectangle in which the 3D pieces are placed. Once the reaction is identified the user can place and remove the substrate and products at will, to trigger the auditory information that provides in-depth information of each component. For the auditory information it is essential to pause, play and switch between layers of information in a responsive manner to make listening explanations repetitively as part of the learning process as smooth as possible to avoid added frustration. These audio manipulation features are integrated on the casing or base on which the reaction will be placed.

Another feature that is planned for future improvements is that the device could explain each component individually but also describe the interaction between them when more than one is placed at a time. This is especially interesting for users since information on the interaction between substrates and by products or between the products themselves, or even the characteristics of the type of reactions that are taking place is possible to provide more complete explanations.

3   Results

The collaboration of a multidisciplinary team was mandatory to generate functional prototypes of inclusive educational materials that were accessible to blind learners but useful attractive to all students. Although several other researchers and educators have proposed quick and efficient ways of translating two-dimensional diagrams into tactile graphics for accessibility of Chemistry topics to the blind [18–20], there was an area of opportunity for including an inclusive pedagogical approach incorporating Universal Design.

A major aspect to consider in the design of educational materials is the learning objectives, and the didactic sequence to reach those objectives supported by the educational materials. This means the overall design included a careful and deep-thought process, tightly adhered to the pedagogical purpose, in which we need to assure that all students obtain all the information needed to make accurate mental maps of the concepts or processes depicted in the educational materials. In other words, it is not only converting an image into 3D, but it also implies selecting and organizing the information parting from pedagogical approaches relative to the field.

In the case of the topic presented in this work, the Krebs Cycle, the pedagogical approach was to "dissect" the eight main biochemical reactions taking place during the Krebs cycle in eight corresponding steps. The idea was that separating the reactions of each step would support a better understanding of the modification of the molecules on each step and also identify general characteristics that the reactions share. Furthermore, learners can begin recognizing simple concepts and then move on to more complex ones, including relationships with other metabolic pathways of the cell. Both the design of the approach and the design of the educational materials strictly adhered to the scientific information to convey.

3.1   Finding Optimal Ways of Representation of Concepts by UDL Design

A most important step in the design process was to identify how to best represent the molecules and the changes in the molecules involved in the Krebs Cycle throughout the pathway, taking into consideration not only Universal Design/UDL but also conventions for representations in Chemistry.

Taking as departing point previous work of Shaw's lab [19, 20], where they successfully used 3D printed lithophanes as a form to make tactile representations of electropherograms, micrographs, mass spectra and textbook illustrations [19] and later on also chemical formulas [20] available to blind students, the design process of the Krebs Cycle began by creating a series of 3D-printed pieces representing the formulas of the molecules involved on each of the steps of the Krebs cycle. The process was, however, different from lithophane production, as described in the Methods section, in order to make the products engaging for more students with the use of colors, rather than being only gray as the lithophanes previously reported [20].

Formulae representations had to be printed on a base, also generated by a 3D printing process. The base shown in the case of lithophanes was geometrical, either square or rectangular, evoking the visual representations of formulas; then, the first design of the base of the molecule formulas in the Krebs cycle was geometrical as well (Fig. 1).

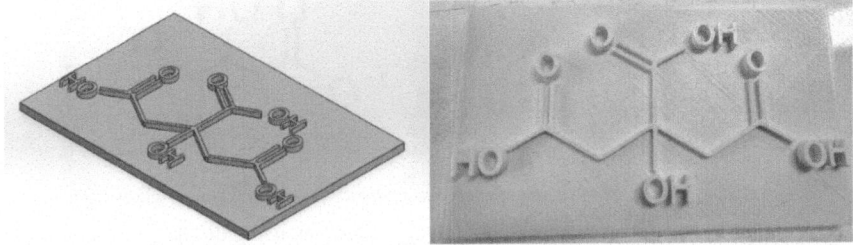

Fig. 1. First digital design of the citrate molecule on a rectangular base and its 3D printed piece.

However, the Krebs cycle is of complex nature, and it involves a great number of compounds, as it consists of at least eight steps (eight reactions) in its simplified form for learning purposes. So, it was necessary to find ways to facilitate the organization and positioning of the pieces, and this led to the design of non-geometric bases, with similar features among them, but at the same time with small differences between them (Fig. 2).

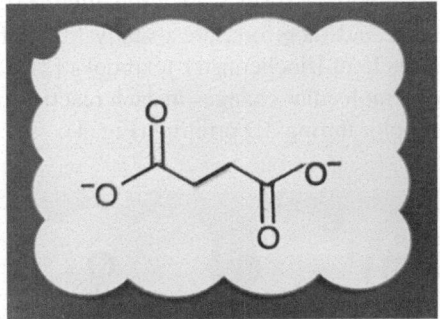

Fig. 2. A succinate ion representation in a non-geometrical base.

User validation tests carried out early in the design informed that 100% of participating adult individuals with different degrees of blindness preferred non-geometrical bases, and 88% of them also expressed that those were more engaging and interesting for them to explore, making them curious about their use. They explained that usually, they use materials with basic rectangular shapes, therefore when they first touch non-geometrical bases, they find them intriguing and out of curiosity, they want to find out what is inside of them or what they are about.

Representation's formulae involve letters and lines, thus, the next feature to determine was the thickness of the lines and the font size. Thus, designs were 3D printed in at least two different sizes, to determine the minimum size of all elements involved in a formula that was recognized by touch for individuals with limited sight (Fig. 3).

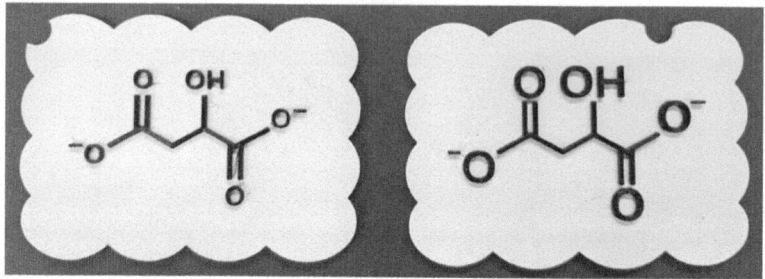

Fig. 3. Examples of two forms of representation of malate ion, using different sizes of lines and font in the chemical formulae.

The validation tests informed that all participants indicated that thickness was appropriate within the range presented to them. Data collected with a different group of users suggested to increase the size of the letters within the formulas.

The use of color was a relevant feature added to the designs for the Krebs cycle with the intention of helping learners to show details of how participating molecules are modified during the cycle and to identify the specific changes in the molecules, as they take place by the action of enzymes along the cycle. Those changes are key to understand the generation of crucial compounds for the cell's functioning, such as carbon dioxide and guanosine triphosphate, and therefore, are usually highlighted within the visual descriptions of the Krebs cycle in Biochemistry textbooks [27]. In an emulation to the visual color cues to identify molecular changes in each reaction of the cycle, the digital designs added changes of color during 3D printing (Fig. 4).

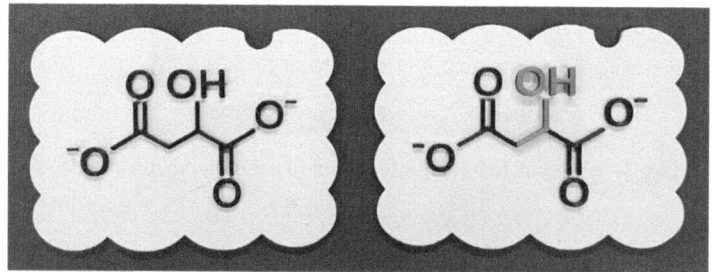

Fig. 4. Tactile molecular representations of the malate ion, the one to the right shows the changes that will take place in the next biochemical reaction.

Furthermore, differences in height where the colors changed (Fig. 5) were also added, so they could be perceived by touch also. Again, prototypes were made using two different heights for tactile differentiation, and validation tests with users helped to identify the optimal difference in height within a line that was perceived by blind learners on the representations of formulas. In those tests, 94% of participants indicated that they can feel a difference and when they were shown various height measurements, the majority agreed that the ideal ones are 2 and 3 mm (about 0.12 in) of difference.

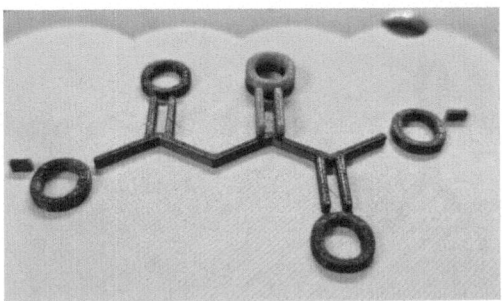

Fig. 5. Molecular representation of the oxalacetate ion, showing the change in color and height of the part of the molecule that will undergo changes in the next biochemical reaction.

Adjustments also had to be made to provide these tactile features smoothly, that will not cause aggression to the highly sensitive perception by touch. All users found the smooth texture of the letters and lines pleasant to the touch and suitable for easy understanding of the formulas. However, when a base texture was proposed in the background (Fig. 6), to create a contrast that will help identify the "R" group of the formulas (the group of atoms and bonds that don't change but are attached to the ones that do change), all of the users responded that they found it scratchy, aggressive, and difficult to understand. They commented that it distracts them from the information, that it would hurt them after a while, and that does not help the tactile sensitivity of the fingers. Thus, the idea of representing the "R" group was discarded.

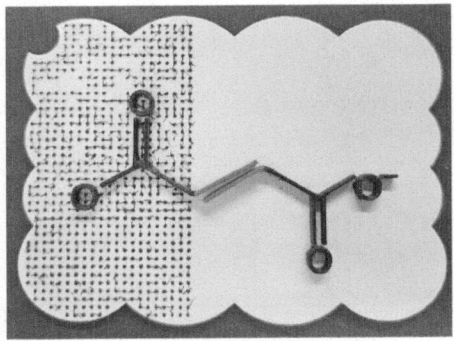

Fig. 6. Attempt to represent the "R" group within the chemical formula of fumarate ion.

Finally, it was necessary to add a slot where the magnet would be placed to the pieces containing the formulae. Given that the thickness of the base was 3 mm, round neodymium magnets with a thickness of 1 mm and a diameter of 0.8 mm were used. Figure 7 shows the position of the magnet within the base of the slat where formulae were printed.

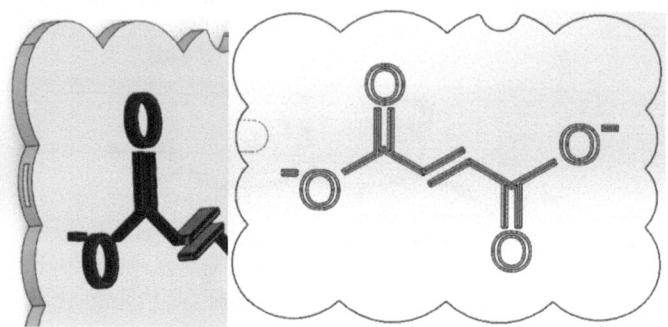

Fig. 7. Representation of the slot for the magnet in the base of the fumarate molecule.

3.2   Tactile Representations of Other Molecules Involved in the Cycle

In the Krebs cycle there are many molecules involved, and finding the best form for representing them was another step in the design process taking parallel to the design of the representations of the main metabolites involved. In the case of enzymes, the proteins which activity produce the changes in the molecules, their structure is quite complex and almost impossible to represent in a tactile diagram. Then, an arbitrary decision was made to give them unique shapes that gave teachers an opportunity to explain the nature of their function, but also, the features had to allow physically fitting the representations of the molecules that interacted with them (Fig. 8).

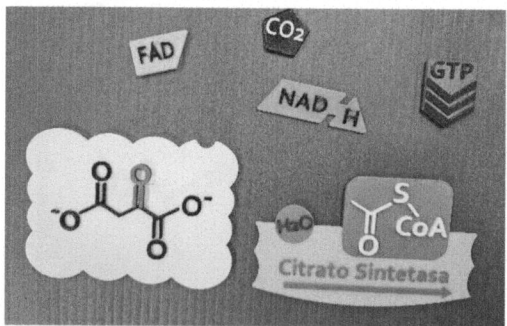

Fig. 8. First representations of other metabolites and the enzymes involved in the Krebs cycle.

As found in Fig. 8, other molecules were also given arbitrary shapes to facilitate showing interactions and to describe processes. In the case of pairs such as Guanosine di-phosphate (GDP) and Guanosine triphosphate (GTP), of NAD and NADH, their representation was designed to make easy to explain the changes occurring during the biochemical reactions.

3.3   Other Pedagogical Decisions

Because we all learn differently, and one of the objectives of this work was to find the best way to engage all learners, a parallel design was developed for tactile molecular representations. Testing other forms of representation agreeable with chemical conventions led to design of the molecules using semi-spheres to represent the atoms of the molecule (Fig. 9) instead of the skeletal line and letter type of representation of molecules, as an effort to accompany the learner in the natural migration for 2D to 3D representations of molecules.

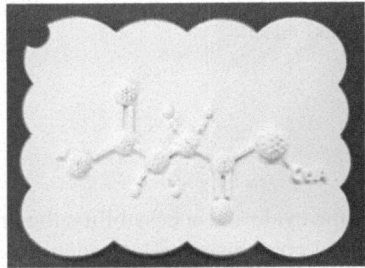

Fig. 9. First prototypes of representations of molecules using spheres for testing, with no color.

In the first validation with users, they were asked if they could distinguish the semi spherical representations of molecules and 88% answered yes; however, only 75% could feel the difference in size in the semi-spheres, which indicated to us that although that shape works, it had to be iterated and improved. Among the 16 participants in the validation, there are different degrees of blindness in one or both eyes and, in some cases, they have total blindness. We did a first test of representations incorporating random, bright, contrasting colors and found that for users who can distinguish colors, black and green were the most clearly identified. For the individuals that could see colors, they prefer dark backgrounds and bright colors on top. This preference most likely depends on the type of visual disability they have. Then, for scientific reasons, it was decided the representation of atoms on the molecules would have to follow chemical conventions.

Thus, the next step was to design tactile molecular representations adhering to chemical conventions of molecular representations such as 1) an international color coding for the semi spheres that represent the atoms; for example, carbon is represented in black color, oxygen in red color, hydrogen in white color, and so on and 2) the bond angles of the molecule of each central atom involved. However, they had to be perceived without sight; thus, a major challenge here was to create spheres of atoms of very close atomic radius, such as carbon and oxygen distinguishable by touch.

After testing multiple texturizing ideas with users, we realized the spheres were too small to introduce textures, as differences in the details were difficult to perceive by touch, so the spherical representation of the carbon atom was modified to have a flat top surface. Figure 10 shows how atoms within a molecule were distinguished by color and tactile features on each molecular representation produced to explain the Krebs cycle.

Fig. 10. Details of tactile molecular representation of the oxalacetate molecule using spheres and colors adhering to chemical conventions.

3.4 Final Assembly

To facilitate understanding of the cycle and accessibility, the information was distributed in three "panels". The first panel contains a guide to identify each representation of the molecules participating; for example, to identify the main molecules involved, how is the representation of the enzymes, the substrate, the intermediate metabolites, and the product, like those shown in Fig. 8. Iterations with users supported the need of a "guide" containing information before presenting the reactions of the cycle per se.

The second panel contains each biochemical reaction that is part of the Krebs cycle, as previously described, so the cycle is dissected in eight steps. An example of how the tactile components are assembled to present the entire reaction is shown in Fig. 11. In this representation, made with letters instead of semi spheres, the red color within the formula highlights the parts of the molecule that undergo changes during the reaction. Finally, the third panel (not shown) will show the whole cycle as a continuum, just as it occurs in the cells.

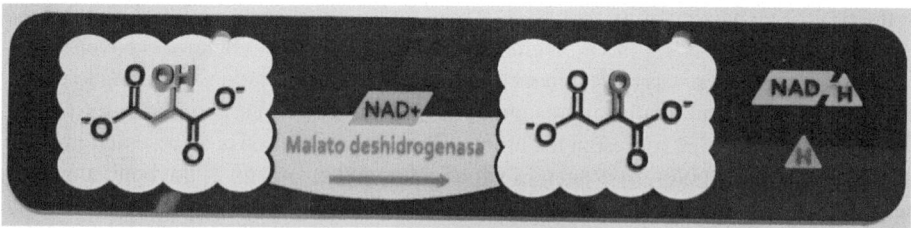

Fig. 11. First prototype of the biochemical reaction where malate is transformed in oxalacetate in a reaction catalyzed by the enzyme malate dehydrogenase, where NAD+receives a hydrogen and NADH is formed.

It is necessary to mention that the three panels are presented in a puzzle-like organization, so each piece fits only in one place, to make it easy for learners to know that each molecule plays a specific role in the cycle. This form or representation can serve different purposes, such as engaging learners (given that a piece fits only in one place), it can also serve for evaluation, and to create curiosity due to the challenge of finding the correct place.

3.5   A Work in Progress

Innovation is a constant and iterative process. At the moment, and after rounds of iteration, we were able to obtain functional prototypes of tactile molecular representations of the Krebs cycle in two formats. The next step is to make further validation rounds with a diversity of users, including sighted students in regular classrooms. In the first validations performed, we found that the tactile representations were accessible and engaging to blind and visually impaired users, and that the interpretation of the information was in the right direction. For example, to the question "What do you think you are feeling?" The response of the majority of participants was: a slat with letters, balls, and lines that interconnect, waves, sequences" and in two cases, they responded "a formula of elements".

It was also recognized the use or application of the tactile molecular diagrams. To the question "What do you think the object you are feeling can be used for?" The answers were: "to explain something visually through touch, to understand the composition of something, to understand structures such as atomic models, formulas, diagrams, products, equations, body parts, to represent things with Braille", while only two of the sixteen interviewees answered that they did not know.

We acknowledge that BVI students might have difficulties to recognize some of the letters due to their size, for example, those printed on top of the enzymes, so we will include braille to facilitate reading, even if participants in the first validation phase mentioned that having audible information would be better for most of them.

The next step in this research is to see if the complete set of the Krebs cycle tactile molecules comply with the objectives of helping BVI and other students with and without disabilities form accurate mental models of the scientific processes taking place in this metabolic pathway.

4   Discussion

Universal Design for Learning (UDL) is a conceptual framework that proposes to provide multiple forms of representation of concepts of the subject matter, so diverse learners can choose the most suitable form of representation for their learning. UDL also suggests the incorporation of educational resources that make use of multiple senses to present the information. In this paper, we describe the design and creation of various tactile representations of molecules, enzymes and other metabolites involved in the Krebs cycle, a topic of Biochemistry that is complex to learn for a great majority of students.

What did we do differently from previously proposed chemistry materials? Following UDL principles, we generated educational materials rich in visual, tactile and auditory cues associated to the objects that aim to facilitate reaching the educational objectives they were built for, in a format that can be inclusive and accessible to students with and without visual disabilities.

Mainly, we generated at least two forms of tactile representation of the atoms that form the molecules, the changes that the molecules undergo in every step of the cycle were highlighted with colors and a change of height, and other participating metabolites were given distinct shape, color and form. Also, these tactile representations make use of inexpensive technology to provide multi-sensory possibilities for learning. We also added multiplicity to the representations, given that the information in three panels that complement each other. Each panel serves a different purpose and complement the information contained in them but can be explored independently.

The products presented in this work are unique, and they focus in the subject of Biochemistry and a complex topic, the Krebs cycle, that is not commonly accessible to blind and visually impaired users. Even for sighted students, this topic poses important challenges, and this is the reason why several innovative approaches for teaching the topic have been proposed; among them, role playing [25], virtual reality visualizations [12], and use of imagery mnemonics [24], among other, suitable for sighted students.

It is fair to also notice that the products that we designed have integrated not only the criteria for UDL, but also pedagogical considerations that allows the learner to understand the different reactions that occur in the Krebs cycle, individually, and as a whole. Likewise, this approach will help the user (students) to identify the common characteristics they have, and then transfer this form of analyzing a metabolic route to other metabolic pathways that they will study in the future.

Because our design was based on universal design i.e. to provide universal access, we can predict the products resulting from this work will be useful in regular classrooms and we are currently carrying on pilot tests to analyze their impact in real classrooms.

Acknowledgments. This work was financed by the Challenge Based Research Funding Program of Tecnológico de Monterrey, project number E115-EHE-GI01-D-T2-E. We thank the support of the *Innovaction Gym* at Tecnologico de Monterrey, Monterrey campus for providing a space for innovation. We deeply thank all social service students who have participated in EduMakers and helped in this project, specially to Angel de Jesús Pérez Armendáriz. A key element for obtaining great results is the feedback of users and experts, so we thank Mona Minkara and Gael Chávez for their comments to the designs. We also thank the openness of the association "Vemos con el Corazón" and its members, they were generous in providing feedback on the first prototypes.

Disclosure of Interests. The authors have no competing interests to declare that are relevant to the content of this article.

References

1. UNESCO: World Declaration on Education for All and Framework for Action to Meet Basic Learning Needs. UNESCO, Paris (1990)
2. Cawley, J.F.: Science for students with disabilities. Remedial Spec. Educ. **15**, 67–71 (1994). https://doi.org/10.1177/074193259401500202

3. Brown, E.: Disability awareness: the fight for accessibility. Nature **532**, 137–139 (2016)
4. Kizilaslan, A., Zorluoglu, S.L., Sozbilir, M.: Improve learning with hands-on classroom activities: science instruction for students with visual impairments. Eur. J. Spec. Needs. Edu. **36**, 371–392 (2020)
5. National science foundation: women, minorities, and persons with disabilities in science and engineering. National Science Foundation (2015)
6. Swenor, B., Meeks, L.M.: Disability inclusion—Moving beyond mission statements. N. Engl. J. Med. **380**, 2089–2091 (2019)
7. Good knowledge from dedicon. https://goedekennis.dedicon.nl/
8. DIAGRAM Center: Building new paths to accessibility. http://diagramcenter.org/
9. Accessible graphics: home of accessible graphics resources. https://accessiblegraphics.org/
10. Tactiles.eu: Designed to support the education of learners with a vision impairment. https://tactiles.eu/
11. Wood, E.J.: Biochemistry is a difficult subject for both student and teacher. Biochem. Educ. **18**, 170–172 (1990)
12. Kim, S., Heo, R., Chung, Y., et al.: Virtual Reality Visualization Model (VRVM) of the Tricarboxylic Acid (TCA) cycle of carbohydrate metabolism for medical biochemistry education. J. Sci. Educ. Technol. **28**, 602–612 (2019). https://doi.org/10.1007/s10956-019-09790-y
13. De Oliveira, F.S., Nascimento, A.S.d., Bianconi, M.L.: Teaching enzyme activity to the visual impaired and blind students. Technologies **5**, 52 (2017). https://doi.org/10.3390/technologies 5030052
14. NIH 3D: An open, community-driven portal for bioscientific and medical 3D models. https://3d.nih.gov/
15. Miner, D.L., Nieman, R., Swanson, A.B. & Woods, M. (eds): Teaching Chemistry to Students with Disabilities 4th edn. American Chemical Society (2001)
16. in't Veld, D., Sorge, V.: The dutch best practice for teaching chemistry diagrams to the visually impaired. In: Miesenberger, K., Kouroupetroglou, G. (eds.) Computers Helping People with Special Needs. ICCHP 2018. LNCS(), vol. 10896. Springer, Cham. https://doi.org/10.1007/978-3-319-94277-3_99
17. Mukhiddinov, M., Kim, S.Y.: A systematic literature review on the automatic creation of tactile graphics for the blind and visually impaired. Processes **9**, 1726 (2021)
18. Supalo, C.A., Kennedy, S.H.: Using commercially available techniques to make organic chemistry representations tactile and more accessible to students with blindness or low vision. J. Chem. Educ. **91**, 1745–1747 (2014)
19. Koone, J. C. et al.: Data for all: tactile graphics that light up with picture-perfect resolution. Sci. Adv. **8**(33), eabq2640 (2022). https://doi.org/10.1126/sciadv.abq2640
20. Alonzo, E.A. et al.: Universal pictures: a lithophane codex helps teenagers with blindness visualize nanoscopic systems. Sci. Adv.**10**, eadj8099 (2024). https://doi.org/10.1126/sciadv.adj8099
21. Senties Maqueda, A., et al.: Application of RFID technology to create inclusive educational resources. In: Antona, M., Stephanidis, C. (eds.) Universal Access in Human-Computer Interaction. HCII 2023. LNCS, vol. 14021, pp. 405–416. Springer, Cham. https://doi.org/10.1007/978-3-031-35897-5_29
22. Magaña-Cruz, E., Garza Vera, L.F., Arévalo Arguijo, J.E., Treviño Peña, A., Gómez Flores, L., Reynaga-Peña, C.G.: Engineering for UDL-based education: translating book images into interactive 3D educational materials for Health Sciences subject. In: press 2023 International Conference on Inclusive Technologies and Education (CONTIE)

23. Pérez Armendáriz, A. de J., Rodríguez Quintanilla, M., Lozano Herrejón, A.A., Oyervides Ramírez, G.E., Santillán-Rosas, I. M., Reynaga-Peña, C.G.: Use of a tactile talking tablet to make inclusive educational resources for health sciences topics based on Universal Design for Learning. In: press 2023 International Conference on Inclusive Technologies and Education (CONTIE)
24. Morisaki, R., Bon, C., Levitt, J.O.: The use of an imagery mnemonic to teach the Krebs cycle. Biochem. Mol. Biol. Educ. **44**(3), 224–229 (2016)
25. Saab, M., Shaaban, E.: The impact of modeling and role play on grade eleven students' achievement and motivation while teaching Krebs cycle in biology. Int. J. Res. Educ. Sci. **8**(2), 219–242 (2022)
26. Meyer, D.A., Rose, D.H., Gordon, D.: Universal Design for Learning: Theory and Practice. CAST Professional Publishing, Wakefield, MA (2014)
27. Nelson, D.L., Cox, M.M.: Lehninger Principles of Biochemistry, 7th edn. W.H. Freeman, New York (2017)

A Developer-Oriented Framework Proposal for Evaluating the Accessibility of Video Games

José Shimabukuro[1] , Arturo Moquillaza[1,2] , and Johan Baldeón[1,2,3](✉)

[1] Pontificia Universidad Católica del Perú, Facultad de Ciencias e Ingeniería, Ingeniería Informática, Av. Universitaria 1801, Lima, Peru
{jkshimabukuro,johan.baldeon}@pucp.edu.pe, amoquillaza@pucp.pe
[2] Pontificia Universidad Católica del Perú, Informatic Section, Engineering Department, Lima, Peru
[3] Pontificia Universidad Católica del Perú, Avatar Group, Lima, Peru
https://www.pucp.edu.pe/

Abstract. Despite advancements, the gaming industry often overlooks accessibility, excluding individuals with disabilities. This paper proposes a novel framework to address this gap. The framework empowers developers through a categorized accessibility guideline catalog validated by experts, providing clear guidance for various disabilities (motor, visual, auditory, and cognitive) with real-world examples. Validated evaluation tools and techniques: These tools address scenarios where developers use non-configurable default values, potentially creating accessibility barriers. A well-defined evaluation process: This process, outlined using established methods, ensures a structured and efficient evaluation. In addition, this proposal allows for the acquisition of a quantitative value that allows comparisons between designs and between different video games, as well as the establishment of KPIs in improvement projects. The framework was rigorously validated by HCI and gaming experts and successfully applied to assess the accessibility of action-based third-person games. This application yielded valuable insights, enabling comparisons between games and identifying accessibility strengths and weaknesses for different disabilities. This framework empowers developers to integrate accessibility throughout development, fostering a more inclusive gaming environment for all.

Keywords: Accessibility evaluation · video games · accessibility guidelines · accessibility framework · accessibility tools · accessibility assessment · game accessibility · developer-oriented framework

1 Introduction

The video game industry has experienced phenomenal growth in recent years, attracting players from diverse backgrounds and abilities [6]. This diverse audience encompasses individuals with disabilities, who often face significant barriers

M. Antona et al. (Eds.): HCII 2024, LNCS 15379, pp. 83–102, 2025.
https://doi.org/10.1007/978-3-031-76818-7_7

to enjoying video games due to a lack of accessibility features [1]. Individuals with disabilities encounter significant challenges due to the current limitations in accessibility within gaming environments [21]. These limitations, ranging from auditory and visual impairments to cognitive and motor disabilities, not only restrict access to gaming content but also have a detrimental impact on the overall gaming experience of these individuals.

Addressing accessibility in video games is crucial for several reasons. Firstly, it promotes social inclusion and ensures that individuals with disabilities have the opportunity to participate in and enjoy the cultural and social aspects of gaming alongside others [16]. Secondly, accessible games contribute to positive mental health and well-being for individuals with disabilities by providing opportunities for entertainment, relaxation, and social connection [4]. Finally, fostering accessibility in video games aligns with universal design principles, aiming to create products and environments usable by all individuals, regardless of their abilities [8]. By prioritizing accessibility, the video game industry can create a more inclusive and equitable gaming experience for all.

Despite the growing importance of accessibility, developers face several challenges in integrating accessibility features into video games. These challenges include: (1) Existing guidelines are often scattered across various sources, leading to confusion and inconsistency in implementation [15]. (2) The absence of established frameworks makes it difficult for developers to systematically assess the accessibility of their games throughout development [5,23]. (3) Developers often lack readily available resources and case studies showcasing effective accessibility implementations, hindering their ability to incorporate best practices [20]. (4) Some developers may hold misconceptions regarding the impact of accessibility features, believing they might negatively affect the overall gameplay experience for non-disabled players [26]. Additionally, concerns about the perceived cost and complexity of implementing accessibility features can further discourage developers from prioritizing them [19].

The combined effect of these challenges is evident in the widespread presence of insufficient accessibility features in many commercially available video games. This results in the exclusion of a significant portion of the gaming population and hinders the industry's potential to create a truly inclusive and equitable gaming environment [8]. By addressing these challenges and fostering a culture of accessibility in game development, the industry can positively impact the lives of individuals with disabilities, promoting social inclusion, well-being, and, ultimately, the enjoyment of video games for all [1].

In light of these challenges, there is a pressing need for a developer-oriented framework that provides clear guidelines, standardized evaluation processes, and practical resources to support developers in creating more accessible video games. By addressing these challenges and offering a comprehensive framework for evaluating accessibility, developers can enhance the inclusivity of their games and ensure that individuals with disabilities can fully participate in and enjoy the gaming experience.

This work addresses the lack of accessibility features in games due to developer challenges. It proposes a novel framework for evaluating accessibility, featuring clear guidelines, validated tools, and a structured process. The framework was successfully applied to action games, highlighting its strengths and validating its effectiveness. The paper concludes by discussing its impact and potential for future improvements.

2   Related Work

Despite the growing recognition of accessibility in video games, significant challenges remain in its consistent and effective implementation. This section reviews existing research on accessibility guidelines, evaluation methods, and frameworks, highlighting their limitations and the need for improved developer-oriented solutions.

2.1   Accessibility Guidelines and Their Limitations

Several organizations are responsible for providing guidelines to evaluate the accessibility of video games for individuals with disabilities. These include the World Wide Web Consortium (W3C) and the Web Content Accessibility Guidelines (WCAG) [24,25], which offer standards and recommendations for web accessibility. Additionally, AbleGamers works towards creating inclusive gaming experiences [3], the International Game Developers Association (IGDA) promotes developers' interests globally [12], and the Game Accessibility Guidelines (GAG) [7] categorize guidelines into different levels to enhance the accessibility of video games for individuals with disabilities.

These guidelines offer valuable resources outlining best practices for creating inclusive gaming experiences. However, they face several limitations: (1) Accessibility guidelines are often scattered across various bodies, creating confusion for developers who struggle to identify the most relevant and comprehensive resources [15]. Additionally, inconsistencies and overlapping recommendations across different guidelines can lead to difficulties in prioritization and implementation. (2) Some guidelines lack clear and specific instructions, leaving room for interpretation and inconsistent application across games [11]. This ambiguity can hinder developers' ability to translate guidelines into actionable design decisions. (3) Existing guidelines often primarily focus on specific disability types, such as visual and motor impairments [2,13,14], overlooking the needs of individuals with cognitive, auditory, or other disabilities [10]. This narrow scope limits the potential for creating truly inclusive gaming experiences that cater to diverse user needs.

2.2   Existing Evaluation Methods and Frameworks

While some studies have explored specific accessibility evaluation methods for video games [1], these methods often lack consistency and widespread adoption [11]. Existing frameworks often suffer from the following limitations: (1) Implementing certain frameworks can require significant effort and expertise, making them infeasible for small development studios or projects with tight resources [5]. (2) Many existing frameworks focus on evaluating accessibility after a game is already developed, limiting opportunities for early identification and correction of accessibility issues [20]. This approach can be costly and inefficient, as fixing accessibility problems later in the development process is more time-consuming and expensive. (3) Existing frameworks may not be specifically designed with the needs and workflows of developers in mind, potentially hindering their usability and adoption within the development community [15].

2.3   The Need for Improved Developer-Oriented Solutions

The limitations of existing guidelines, evaluation methods, and frameworks highlight the need for improved solutions that are: 1) comprehensive and unified, offering a single framework encompassing best practices for various disabilities, 2) clear and actionable, providing practical recommendations for seamless integration throughout development, and 3) time-efficient and cost-effective, fitting within typical development constraints, and 4) tailored for developers, catering to their needs and workflows for smooth integration into existing processes.

This work aims to address these critical gaps by proposing a novel developer-oriented framework for evaluating the accessibility of video games. This framework seeks to be comprehensive, user-friendly, and efficient, empowering developers to create more inclusive and accessible gaming experiences.

3   Proposed Framework

This section introduces a novel, developer-oriented framework for evaluating the accessibility of video games. This framework aims to address the limitations of existing approaches by providing comprehensive, user-friendly, and efficient tools for developers to assess and improve the accessibility of their games throughout the development lifecycle.

3.1   Components of the Framework

The framework consists of three key components designed to support developers in evaluating accessibility:

A. Categorized Catalog of Accessibility Guidelines:

Method: Developed through a systematic review of existing accessibility guidelines and semi-structured interviews with accessibility experts and game developers. The guidelines were filtered by type of disability, the associated level of accessibility and which area of the game it belongs to. Furthermore, the repeated lineaments were grouped and placed in the lineament source cell.

Description: This component provides a comprehensive catalog of accessibility guidelines categorized by disability type (e.g., vision, motor, cognitive, auditory) and specific game elements (e.g., menus, controls, audio, and visuals). Each guideline includes clear descriptions, specific recommendations, and practical implementation examples to facilitate understanding and application. After the systematic review, it was found that the most used sources were AbleGamers, GAG, IGDA and MediaLT, with IGDA being a set of guidelines from other sources. Table 1 shows a small excerpt of guidelines categorized by visual impairment. The complete list is detailed in [22].

As shown in Table 1, the guidelines in some sources are related to each other, and some guidelines are not mentioned in other sources. In addition, it has been possible to determine the respective game area such as the interface, sound and text that each guideline refers to and its level of accessibility. In the expected result, the details of each guideline will be specified, specifying the problem it wants to solve and examples that will allow you to see how some games have implemented the guideline.

The list of guidelines was validated through an interview with an HCI expert. The expert made several adjustments to the list, including: Adding a new tab for guidelines that can be used to evaluate multiple types of disabilities at once. Three new guidelines were added: (1) Provide descriptive subtitles during dialogue for hearing impairments. (2) Compatibility with medicated hearing devices for hearing impairments. (3) Use tactile feedback for visual impairments.

B. Validated Evaluation Tools and Techniques

Method: Identified and reviewed through a systematic review of existing evaluation methods and semi-structured interviews with accessibility experts and game developers. Subsequently, these tools and techniques were validated through practical application and expert feedback.

Description: This component offers a collection of validated and practical tools and techniques for developers to assess whether their games comply with the accessibility guidelines outlined in the catalog. These tools and techniques may include automated testing tools, checklists, and manual testing procedures tailored to different aspects of accessibility (e.g., color contrast checkers and text-to-speech conversion testing). Table 2 presents the tools and techniques used in the proposed framework.

Each of the tools and techniques are described below.

General Flow for Accessibility Evaluation: This flow generally describes how the accessibility evaluation will be carried out in a video game, where three phases are established: planning, evaluation and reporting. Each section of the flow is detailed in [22]. Figure 1 shows the general flow for accessibility evaluation.

Accessibility Insights for Windows [17]*:* This tool in Fig. 2 allows you to check the contrast as well as the font size of an application. It will be used for guidelines where contrast and text for visual and cognitive disabilities are evaluated.

Table 1. Example of a list of visual impairment guidelines.

Source	Guideline	Description	Game Element	Accessibility Level
GAG	Use legible font size	Visually impaired players have difficulty reading the text on the screen	Text (Size)	Basic
GAG	Ensure that no essential information is communicated through colors alone	Players with color blindness have difficulty recognizing certain colors such as red or green	Interface (Objects)	Basic
MediaLT	Use recognizable auditory feedback for rewards	Visually impaired players need sound feedback to know that what they have done was correct	Sound	Intermediate
GAG	Use surround sound technologies	Visually impaired players require sound to be able to identify where enemies or items are coming from	Sound	Intermediate
GAG AbleGamers MediaLT	Allow font size to be adjusted	Players cannot read default game text	Text (Size)	Advanced
GAG MediaLT	Provide audio descriptions	Audio description seeks to provide as much information as possible through audio, sound, actions, facial expressions, player appearance, environment, etc.	Sound	Advanced

The tool has the option to automatically detect contrast where the mouse is located or select the two colors to evaluate to determine the contrast ratio. Additionally, it displays the font size of the text which is useful for evaluating whether the font size is appropriate based on the screen resolution.

Table 2. Framework tools and techniques.

Tool/Technique	Use
General evaluation flow	General flow of the accessibility evaluation process
Accessibility Insights for Windows	Tool that allows you to review the contrast and font size of a screen or application
Template in MS Excel to carry out the accessibility evaluation in a video game	Tool that allows you to calculate the "accessibility level" of a video game based on questions that refer to each selected guideline.
Evaluate surround sound and binaural recording	Technique to evaluate whether a video game uses surround sound or simulates binaural recording
Evaluate dependence on game sound	Technique to evaluate if a video game highly depends on sound to provide information to the player
Evaluate dependence on game colors	Technique to evaluate if a video game is highly dependent on colors for game elements
Evaluate simplicity of controls	Technique to evaluate the simplicity of game controls

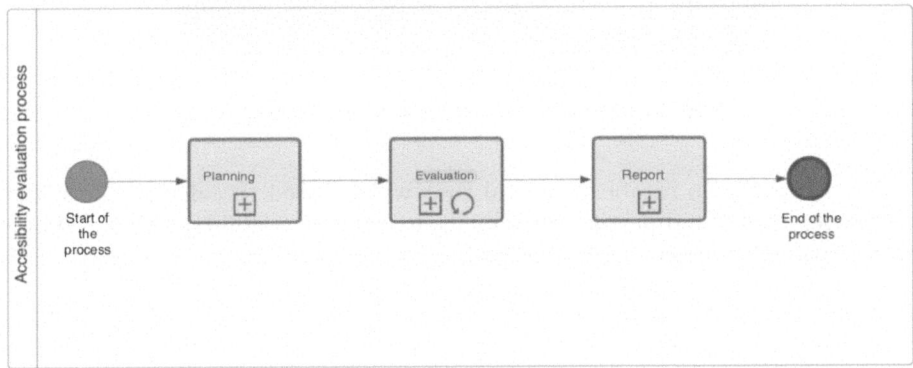

Fig. 1. General process flow.

Template in MS Excel to Carry out the Accessibility Evaluation in a Video Game: The template takes inspiration from Granollers' "Usability Evaluation with Heuristics, Beyond Nielsen's List" document [9], adapting its principles for accessibility evaluation and allowing evaluators to score each guideline after interacting with the game. This approach generates a numerical value that establishes an "accessibility level" for the game. The complete template can be found in [22]. An example of the template is presented in Table 3. The evaluation consists of 100 questions corresponding to the 100 accessibility guidelines identified and detailed in the previous section. Each question has four predetermined answer options: (a) Yes (1 point): The guideline is fully implemented in the game. (b) No (0 points): The game does not implement the guideline. (c) Neither Yes nor No (0.5 points): The guideline is partially implemented in the game. (d) Not Applicable - Not an Issue (-): The guideline does not apply to the game or is not a significant accessibility issue.

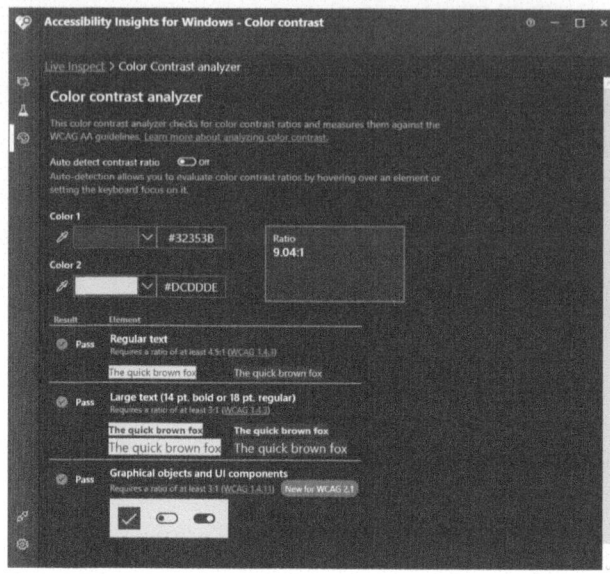

Fig. 2. Accessibility Insights tool for Windows.

These scores help establish a total that will be used to calculate both the percentage of total and partial accessibility by type of disability. Figure 8 shows how the evaluation results are displayed.

Technique Au1: Evaluating Sound Envelopment and Binaural Recording: Binaural recording is a technique that aims to capture and simulate the human ear's perception of sound directionality. This is achieved by creating an artificial head with microphones placed in the positions of the ears, preserving the sound direction and enhancing immersion (Symposium, 2015).

To evaluate guidelines related to sound direction in a game, the following steps can be taken: (1) Place the character in any scene or event and close the eyes. (2) Identify whether the sound direction can be recognized as front, back, left, or right. (3) If the evaluator can identify not only cardinal directions but also the altitude of the sound (above or below), the guideline is considered to be met.

Technique Au2: Evaluating Game Progression Reliance on Sound: To evaluate guidelines that consider whether a game heavily relies on sound for progression, the following steps should be taken: (1) Play the game completely in silence, muting all audio channels. (2) Identify any instances where progress is impeded due to information conveyed solely through sounds, such as audio cues: Footsteps, environmental sounds, enemy noises; background dialogue: NPC conversations, critical story information; and event direction: Sound effects indicating key moments or hazards. (3) If the lack of visual representation for these sounds creates barriers to progression, the guideline is considered to be unmet.

Table 3. Example of the template to evaluate accessibility.

Guideline	Game Element	Question	Answer	Comments
Provide subtitles for all important speech	Audio/ Sound	Does the game provide subtitles for all important speeches	No	
Ensure no essential information is conveyed by sounds alone	Audio/ Sound	Does the game ensure no essential information is conveyed by sounds alone?	Yes	
Provide separate volume controls or mutes for effects, speech and background/ music	Audio/ Sound	Does the game provide separate volume controls or mutes for effects, speech and background/music?	Neither	
Offer choices for speed, duration, voices and volume for different auditory information etc.	Audio/ Sound	Does the game offer speed, duration, voices and volume choices for different auditory information, etc.?	Not applicable- It is not a problem	

A deaf player attempts a new zombie game but is unable to progress. The developers have designed the game such that zombie sounds indicate an attack from a player's blind spot (AbleGamers, 2012). Without this audio information, the player cannot effectively defend themselves and progress in the game.

Technique Vi1: Evaluate Guidelines with Reference to the Colors of the Game: One way to evaluate the color accessibility of a game is to imagine playing it in grayscale or black and white (AbleGamers, 2012). If a player cannot differentiate between key game elements in grayscale, then the game is likely not meeting color accessibility guidelines. Pilestone's color blindness simulator [18] is a user-friendly tool that allows users to preview a website or image with different types of CVD. This can help designers and developers identify potential color accessibility issues and make necessary adjustments. Figure 3a shows an example of how a game looks to different types of color blindness. It also allows you to upload any image, so to evaluate you only have to take a screenshot of the game and simulate it. As can be observed, despite the game utilizing different colors for objects, their distinct shapes aid in differentiation should one be unable to recognize the colors. Another desktop tool that comes by default with the Windows operating system is the Color filters tool (See Fig. 3b). This tool allows you to change the colors of the entire system and can be used to test games in grayscale or with different filters.

Technique Mo1: Evaluate Guidelines with Reference to the Simplicity of Controls: Control simplicity and the ability to customize controls are critical factors in ensuring game accessibility for players with motor disabilities. Evaluating these aspects is an essential step in HCI research and game development. One simple method for evaluating control simplicity is to attempt playing the game

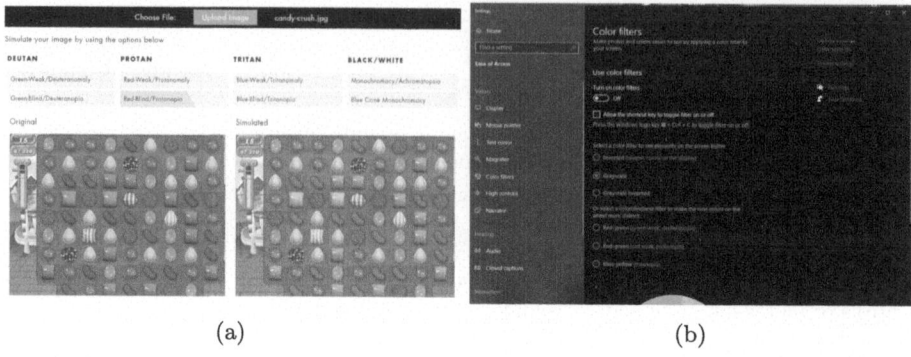

(a)   (b)

Fig. 3. Tools to evaluate guidelines with reference to the colors of the game. (a) Candy Crush game color blindness simulation using Pilestone color blindness simulator. (b) Windows Color Filter.

with one hand without configuring the controls [3]. If actions or buttons are impossible to perform or reach, the controls are likely not simple enough for a player with motor disabilities. In PC games, attempting to play with a controller instead of a keyboard and mouse can provide insights into control customization. If the game does not allow controller use or the process is overly complicated, it does not meet the guideline of providing simple controls or facilitating the use of assistive technologies like switches.

C. Well-Defined Accessibility Evaluation Process

Method: Designed using Business Process Model and Notation (BPMN) and visualized using Lucidchart software, incorporating feedback from accessibility experts and game developers.

Description: This component outlines a step-by-step process for conducting accessibility evaluations throughout the development lifecycle. It defines specific activities, roles, and deliverables for each stage, guiding developers through the evaluation process in a structured and efficient manner. The process emphasizes early and iterative integration of accessibility considerations, facilitating early identification and resolution of accessibility issues. Figure 1 presents the general flow and its phases:

1. **Planning**: This phase defines the initial stage related to the preparation of the accessibility evaluation. In this phase, the following are defined and prepared: Evaluator(s), Game(s) to be evaluated, Tools to be used, and Evaluation template. Once the above has been defined, the accessibility evaluation can begin. Additionally, it must be specified whether one or multiple disabilities will be evaluated, or all of them (See Fig. 4).
2. **Evaluation**: This phase defines the execution phase of the accessibility evaluation using the evaluation template. In this phase, the evaluator(s) will use

the template and, according to the decisions made in the planning phase, will
proceed to evaluate the selected disabilities by answering the questions one
by one and using the tools listed for the guidelines that require them (See
Fig. 5).

3. **Reporting**: This phase defines the analysis of the results of the accessibility
   evaluation. In this phase, the results of the evaluators are consolidated and
   the level of accessibility obtained for each disability is discussed with the
   objective of determining which guidelines are not being met or in which areas
   the game can be improved (See Fig. 6).

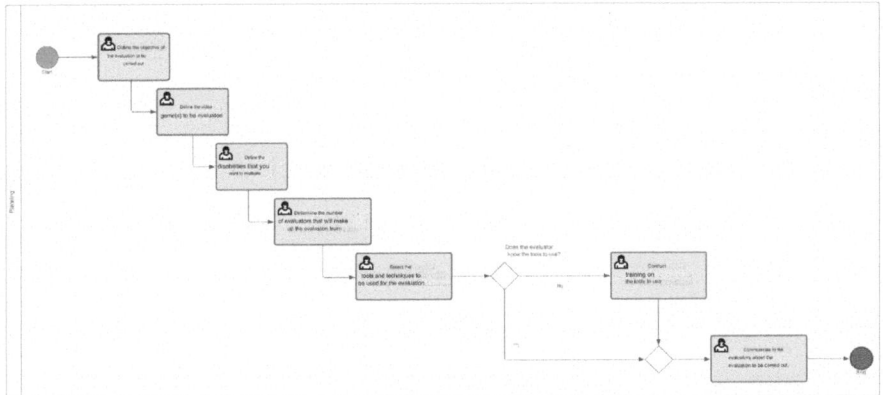

Fig. 4. Planning phase flow.

3.2 Additional Considerations

The framework is designed to be modular and adaptable, allowing developers to
tailor the evaluation process and tools to their specific needs and project constraints. The framework promotes the integration of accessibility considerations
throughout the development lifecycle, not just as a post-development assessment. The framework encourages collaboration between developers, accessibility
experts, and players with disabilities for comprehensive and iterative evaluation.
By providing a comprehensive catalog of accessibility guidelines, validated evaluation tools and techniques, and a well-defined process, this framework empowers
developers to create more inclusive and accessible video games, fostering a more
equitable gaming environment for all.

4 Framework Validation and Application

4.1 Validation Process

To ensure the effectiveness and usability of the proposed framework, a two-
phased validation process was conducted:

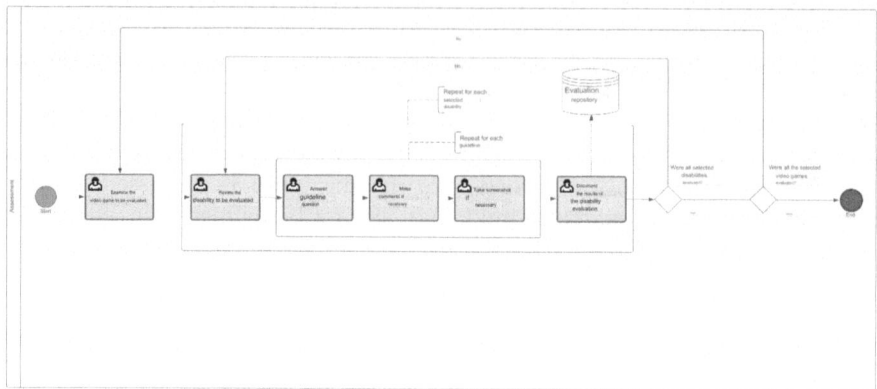

Fig. 5. Evaluation phase flow.

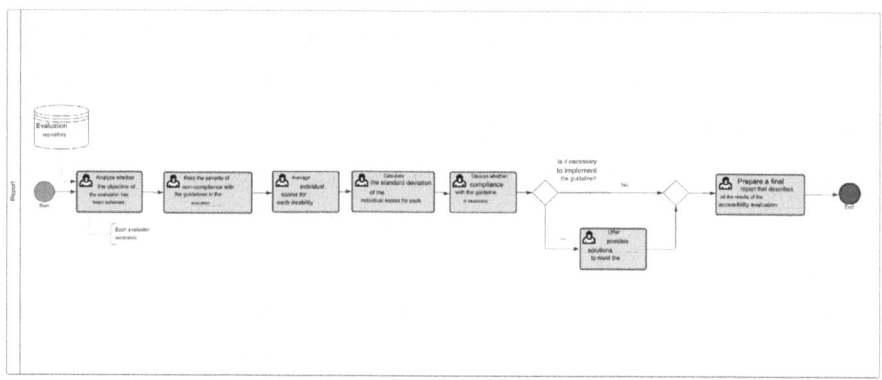

Fig. 6. Reporting phase flow.

Expert Review: The framework components were presented to a panel of HCI and gaming experts, including researchers, accessibility specialists, and game developers. Experts evaluated the framework's comprehensiveness, clarity, and appropriateness for its intended audience. Their feedback informed iterative refinements to the catalog of accessibility guidelines, selection of evaluation tools and techniques, and clarity of the evaluation process.

Pilot Testing: The framework was then piloted on a small scale by applying it to evaluate the accessibility of four commercially available video games. This provided valuable insights into the framework's practicality, ease of use, and ability to identify accessibility issues in real-world game contexts.

4.2 Framework Application

To demonstrate the framework's application and gather data on its effectiveness, it was used to evaluate the accessibility of a selection of four action-based third-person games. This genre was chosen due to its prevalence, diverse gameplay mechanics, and potential accessibility challenges (e.g., fast-paced action, complex controls, spatial navigation).

We developed a plan for applying the framework to evaluate the accessibility of four video games. The plan includes defining the evaluation objectives, selecting the video games to assess, identifying the disabilities to consider, determining the tools and techniques to use, assembling the evaluation team, and establishing the documentation storage location for screenshots and evaluation templates.

The selection of video games for evaluation was based on recent awards and nominations in the third-person action category. The plan was validated through an interview with an HCI specialist, who approved both the selected video games and the application plan. This validation process ensured that the evaluation plan was comprehensive and aligned with the objectives of assessing accessibility in video games. Table 4 lists the video games and additional information about them. The evaluation was conducted on a personal computer running Windows 10 with an Intel i7 7700k processor, Nvidia RTX 2060 graphics card, and 16 GB of RAM. The evaluator fulfilled multiple roles during the evaluation, also acting as evaluation manager and results analyst. By detailing the steps involved in the planning phase, we set the foundation for a systematic and structured approach to evaluating the accessibility of video games. The collaboration with HCI experts ensures that the evaluation process is rigorous and well-defined, laying the groundwork for the subsequent application of the framework in assessing the accessibility of entertainment video games.

The document containing the evaluation comments, screenshots and the proposed framework template allowed for the accessibility evaluation of the video games. It also enabled a comparison between them, identifying the strengths and weaknesses of each game to propose improvements.

The evaluation was conducted using a two-monitor setup. The game being evaluated was displayed on the right monitor, while the document with the comments and template was displayed on the left monitor (See Fig. 7). This setup allowed the evaluator to easily compare the game to the accessibility criteria while playing. The evaluator played the game and recorded their observations and comments in the document. They also took screenshots of the game to illustrate their comments.

For example, the game Tales of Arise had a lower percentage for visual impairment, while it had a higher score for cognitive impairment, resulting in a final accessibility level of 65.4%. Figure 8 show the accessibility percentages of the game. Table 5 presents an example of a guideline with its comment and Fig. 9 shows screenshots.

Table 6 presents the results of applying the framework to evaluate the accessibility of the four video games. It includes positive factors, negative factors and areas for improvement, and the accessibility levels for visual, cognitive, motor,

Table 4. Information on the video games to be evaluated.

	Video game 1	Video game 2	Video game 3	Video game 4
Name	God of War (2018)	Tales of Arise	Red Dead Redemption 2	Jedi Fallen Order
Developer	Santa Monica Studios	Bandai Namco Entertainment	Rockstar Games	Respawn Entertainment
Publisher	Sony Interactive Entertainment	Bandai Namco Entertainment	Rockstar Games	Electronic Arts
Platforms	PlayStation 4 (2018), PC (2022)	PlayStation 4,5, Xbox One/Series S, PC	PlayStation 4, Xbox One, PC	PlayStation 4,5, Xbox One/Series X,S, PC
Genre	Action-adventure, Hack and Slash	Action-adventure, RPG	Action-adventure	Action-adventure
Game mode	Single-player third-person	Single-player third-person	Single-player (campaign) third-person	Single-player third-person
Awards and Nominations (IMDb, 2022)	262 awards and nominations, best game of the year (2018), best action-adventure game, best music, best game direction	Best RPG 2021, best art direction, game of excellence at Tokyo Game Show (2022)	20 awards and 26 nominations, best game of the year (2019), best narrative and soundtrack, best game design and art direction.	Best soundtrack and music, multiple nominations for best game of the year, best action-adventure game, best narrative, among others.
Score	Metacritic (93/100), Users (8.5/10)	Metacritic (87/100), Users (8.7/10)	Metacritic (97/100), Users (8.6/10)	Metacritic (81/100), Users (8.2/10)

auditory, and overall accessibility for each game. Figure 10 shows a graph with the level of accessibility due to disability of each game. All details, such as comments, screenshots, and complete accessibility evaluation templates for the four entertainment video games, can be found in [22].

4.3   Summary of Results

The evaluation process identified a range of strengths and weaknesses in the accessibility of the evaluated games. By evaluating compliance with the categorized Accessibility Guidelines, specific areas for improvement in terms of accessibility features were identified, highlighting both the positive aspects and shortcomings of each game. Some games excelled in aspects like audio descriptions for visually impaired players, while others lacked features to support players with motor impairments, such as customizable control schemes. Through the evaluation process, the accessibility levels of the selected games were compared for different types of disabilities, including auditory, visual, motor, and cognitive impairments. This comparative analysis allowed for a nuanced understanding of how games catered to diverse accessibility needs and where enhancements

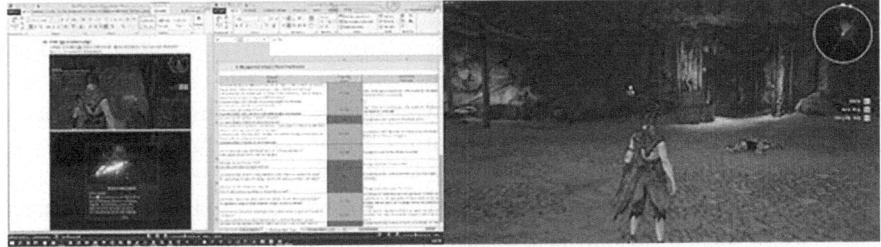

Fig. 7. Evaluator equipment layout

RESULTS		Values	% accessibility due to disability
1- Visual Impairment		8.5	56.7%
2- Cognitive Impairment		19.5	72.2%
3- Motor Impairment		13.5	67.5%
4- Hearing Impairment		11.5	60.5%
	SUM	53	
	% of questions answered	100%	
Number of questions NOT answered (all must be answered for the complete evaluation)		0	
Number of answered questions that count (without those NOT applicable)		81	
"Accessibility" percentage		65.4%	

(a)   (b)

Fig. 8. (a) Tales of Arise game accessibility percentage. (b) Tales of Arise game accessibility percentage graph.

Table 5. Example of a visual impairment guideline with its comment.

Guideline	Game Element	Question	Answer	Comments
Ensure no essential information is conveyed by a colour alone	Interface HUD	If the game colors were only black and white, can I identify the different elements from the game like teammates and enemies? You can use the Vi1 technique from the document.	Yes	The elements of the game are well defined by different symbols that are easy for the player to recognize.

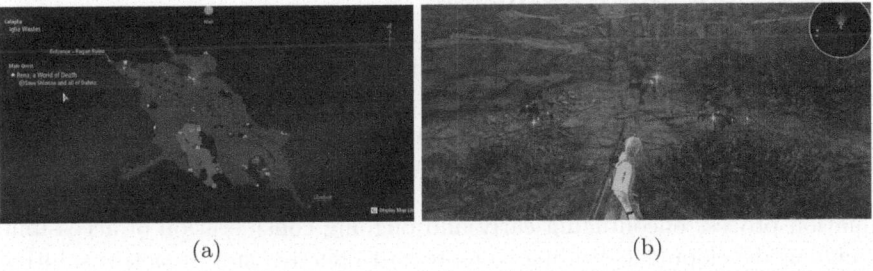

(a)   (b)

Fig. 9. (a) Interactive elements represented by symbols on the map. (b) Interactive game elements with a grayscale color filter.

could be made to better accommodate players with disabilities. The framework facilitated the validation of guideline compliance within each game, enabling developers to assess the extent to which their games met the established accessibility standards. By systematically evaluating the games against the categorized guidelines and using the validated Evaluation Tools and Techniques, developers could identify areas of non-compliance and prioritize improvements to enhance accessibility. The validation and application process provided valuable insights into the framework's strengths and limitations. The findings demonstrate its potential to empower developers to create more inclusive gaming experiences by guiding them in identifying and addressing accessibility issues within their games.

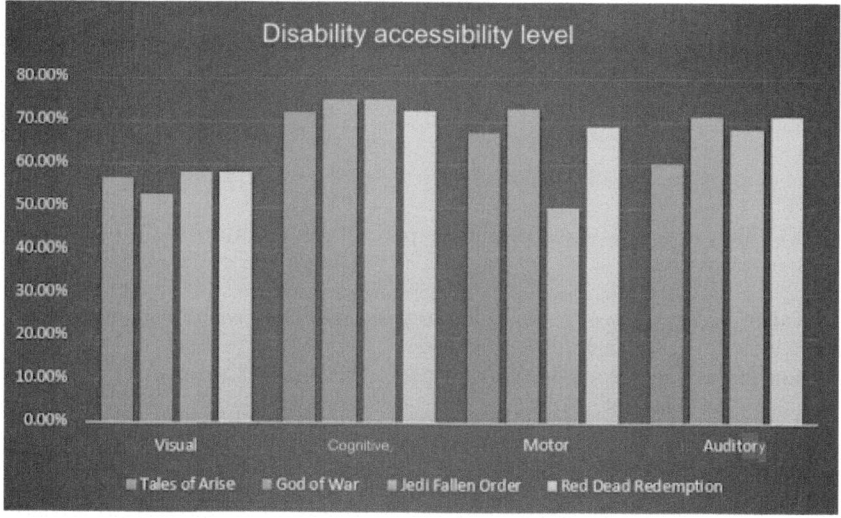

Fig. 10. Graph with the level of accessibility due to disability of each game.

5   Discussion and Conclusion

This work proposes a new framework specifically designed for video game developers to improve accessibility evaluation. The framework addresses limitations of existing methods by providing: 1) a clear and comprehensive list of accessibility guidelines for various disabilities and game elements, 2) validated tools and techniques to assess compliance with these guidelines, and 3) a structured evaluation process encouraging early and ongoing consideration of accessibility throughout development, leading to more cost-effective and proactive solutions.

This developer-oriented framework empowers video game creators to integrate accessibility features proactively. Its comprehensive guidelines and practical tools foster understanding of diverse player needs. By encouraging early and

Table 6. Accessibility level of the video games evaluated.

Video Game	Positive Factors	Negative Factors and Areas for Improvement	Visual (%)	Cogn. (%)	Motor (%)	Audit. (%)	Total (%)
Tales of Arise	The game has many accessibility features, including good default settings, visual cues for interactive elements, audio cues for actions, tutorials and hints, multiple save options, adjustable difficulty, controller support, and subtitles for all dialogue.	The game lacks options to customize text, colors, subtitles, and visuals. Subtitles don't indicate speakers, causing confusion when playing without sound. The game lacks alternatives for holding or repeatedly pressing buttons in combat. It doesn't allow a second player to control characters in combat, despite having four in battle and two in reserve. There is no training mode to practice combos and learn enemy attack patterns, and no story summaries to help players remember where they left off.	56.7	72.2	67.5	60.5	65.4
God of War	The game offers extensive accessibility options, including fully customizable keyboard and mouse controls, remappable buttons, vibration intensity settings, various assistance options, tutorials for new mechanics, multiple save options, adjustable difficulty, subtitles with speaker indicators and adjustable text contrast, directional audio cues, and no QTEs.	The game relies heavily on colors for information, has a fixed FOV, limited text customization, no controller remapping, confusing directional cues, and no time limits for battles. It also lacks a training mode for creating custom battles and practicing against specific enemies.	52.9	75.0	72.9	71.1	69.3
Jedi Fallen Order	The game provides audio cues for enemies and attacks, directional vibrations, adjustable difficulty with summaries, story recaps, controller and keyboard remapping, subtitles for all dialogue and background characters, and a glow for interactive items.	The game lacks colorblind options, uses colors for events that are unrecognizable in grayscale, has a complex map with no audio directions, and difficult combat with no way to focus on multiple enemies. It also lacks a training mode, doesn't allow visual customization, uses colors for unblockable attacks that are indistinguishable in grayscale, and requires manual saving at specific points, which can be frustrating if you die and haven't saved recently.s	58.3	75.0	50.0	68.4	63.8
Red Dead Redemption 2	The game offers colorblind modes, manual and automatic saving, detailed audio cues, tutorials, control remapping, assistance options, mission replay, optional challenges, adjustable difficulty, campaign story progression, vibration feedback, a clear map, and skippable sections.	The game lacks text size customization, has scattered tutorial prompts, a minimap without audio directions, and no custom mission creation. Controls can be complex with holding buttons and repetitive item collection. Interactive objects lack visual cues and there is no contrast option.	58.3	72.4	68.8	71.1	68.3

iterative evaluation throughout development, the framework allows developers to address accessibility concerns early, preventing costly fixes later. Additionally, the user-friendly design and structured process seamlessly integrate accessibility considerations into existing workflows, minimizing disruption and promoting a more holistic approach to game development.

The proposed framework has the potential to significantly improve inclusivity within the gaming landscape by raising developer awareness of accessibility through valuable resources and practical tools. This, in turn, empowers developers to create more accessible games, expanding the options and fostering a more inclusive gaming community for players with disabilities. Additionally, the framework can promote the adoption of consistent and effective best practices throughout the industry, ultimately leading to a higher overall standard of accessibility for video games.

It is important to acknowledge the proposed framework's limitations. The initial development focused on action-based third-person games, and further research is needed to explore its effectiveness in evaluating other game genres with unique accessibility challenges. Additionally, the framework's long-term impact and potential influence on industry-wide adoption require further investigation.

Recognizing the potential for further advancements, we propose future work in three key areas. First, expanding the framework's scope to encompass more game genres and platforms can broaden its reach and impact. Second, researching the framework's adoption within the industry can provide valuable insights into its real-world effectiveness. Finally, fostering collaboration between various stakeholders, such as HCI researchers, accessibility experts, and game developers, can further refine the framework and promote its widespread adoption, ultimately leading to a more inclusive gaming experience for all.

In conclusion, this work proposes a novel, developer-oriented framework for evaluating the accessibility of video games. This framework addresses the limitations of existing approaches by providing comprehensive, user-friendly, and efficient tools for developers to assess and improve the accessibility of their games. By empowering developers and promoting best practices, the framework has the potential to significantly contribute to a more inclusive and accessible gaming environment for all.

References

1. Aguado-Delgado, J., Gutiérrez-Martínez, J.-M., Hilera, J.R., de-Marcos, L., Otón, S.: Accessibility in video games: a systematic review. Univ. Access Inf. Soc. **19**(1), 169–193 (2018). https://doi.org/10.1007/s10209-018-0628-2
2. Araújo, M.C.C., Façanha, A.R., Darin, T.G.R., Sánchez, J., Andrade, R.M.C., Viana, W.: Mobile Audio Games Accessibility Evaluation for Users Who Are Blind, pp. 242–259. Springer International Publishing (2017). https://doi.org/10.1007/978-3-319-58703-5_18
3. Barlet, M.C., Spohn, S.D.: A practical guide to game accessibility. The AbleGamers Foundation Inc. https://accessible.games/wp-content/uploads/2018/11/AbleGamers_Includification.pdf. Accessed 25 Oct 2023

4. Cairns, P., Power, C., Barlet, M., Haynes, G., Kaufman, C., Beeston, J.: Enabled players: the value of accessible digital games. Games Cult. **16**(2), 262–282 (2019). https://doi.org/10.1177/1555412019893877
5. Cezarotto, M., Martinez, P., Chamberlin, B.: Developing inclusive games: design frameworks for accessibility and diversity. In: Sobota, B. (ed.) Game Theory, chap. 3. IntechOpen, Rijeka (2022)https://doi.org/10.5772/intechopen.108456
6. Entertainment Software Association: essential facts about the video game industry (2022). https://www.theesa.com/resource/2022-essential-facts-about-the-video-game-industry/. Accessed 25 Oct 2023
7. Gameaccessibilityguidelines.com: game accessibility guidelines — A straightforward reference for inclusive game design. https://gameaccessibilityguidelines.com/. Accessed 25 Oct 2023
8. Grammenos, D., Savidis, A., Stephanidis, C.: Designing universally accessible games. Comput. Entertain. **7**(1), 1–29 (2009). https://doi.org/10.1145/1486508.1486516
9. Granollers, T.: Usability evaluation with heuristics, beyond Nielsen's list. In: The Eleventh International Conference on Advances in Computer-Human Interactions (ACHI 2018) (2018). https://www.thinkmind.org/download_full.php?instance=ACHI+2018
10. Hassan, L.: Accessibility of games and game-based applications: a systematic literature review and mapping of future directions. New Media Soc. (2023). https://doi.org/10.1177/14614448231204020
11. Horowitz, A.: Accessibility by Numbers: a critical review of game accessibility guidelines, pp. 259–294. Springer International Publishing, Cham (2024). https://doi.org/10.1007/978-3-031-34374-2_10
12. IGDA: XRA's Developers Guide, Chapter Three: Accessibility & Inclusive Design in Immersive Experiences (2020). https://igda.org/resources-archive/xras-developers-guide-chapter-three-accessibility-inclusive-design-in-immersive-experiences-2020/. Accessed 25 Oct 2023
13. Jaramillo-Alcázar, A., Luján-Mora, S.: Mobile serious games: an accessibility assessment for people with visual impairments. In: Proceedings of the 5th International Conference on Technological Ecosystems for Enhancing Multiculturality. TEEM 2017, ACM (2017). https://doi.org/10.1145/3144826.3145416
14. Jaramillo-Alcázar, A., Salvador-Ullauri, L., Luján-Mora, S.: A mobile serious games assessment tool for people with motor impairments. In: Proceedings of the 2017 9th International Conference on Education Technology and Computers. ICETC 2017, ACM (2017). https://doi.org/10.1145/3175536.3175569
15. Leite, P.d.S., Almeida, L.D.A.: Extended Analysis Procedure for Inclusive Game Elements: Accessibility Features in the Last of Us Part 2, pp. 166–185. Springer International Publishing (2021). https://doi.org/10.1007/978-3-030-78092-0_11
16. McGonigal, J.: Reality is broken: why games make us better and how they can change the world. Penguin (2011)
17. Microsoft: Accessibility insights. https://accessibilityinsights.io/. Accessed 25 Oct 2023
18. Pilestone Inc.: color blind vision simulator. https://pilestone.com/pages/color-blindness-simulator-1. Accessed 25 Oct 2023
19. Porter, J.R., Kientz, J.A.: An empirical study of issues and barriers to mainstream video game accessibility. In: Proceedings of the 15th International ACM SIGACCESS Conference on Computers and Accessibility. ASSETS '13, Association for Computing Machinery, New York, NY, USA (2013). https://doi.org/10.1145/2513383.2513444

20. Powers, G., Nguyen, V., Frieden, L.: Video game accessibility: a legal approach. Disabil. Stud. Q. **35**(1) (2015). https://dsq-sds.org/index.php/dsq/article/view/4513/3833

21. Salvador-Ullauri, L., Acosta-Vargas, P., Luján-Mora, S.: Accessibility evaluation of video games for users with cognitive disabilities. In: Ahram, T., Karwowski, W., Vergnano, A., Leali, F., Taiar, R. (eds.) Intelligent Human Systems Integration 2020, pp. 853–859. Springer International Publishing, Cham (2020). https://doi.org/10.1007/978-3-030-39512-4_130

22. Shimabukuro, J.: Propuesta de un marco de trabajo para evaluar la accesibilidad de videojuegos de entretenimiento para los desarrolladores. Pontificia Universidad Católica del Perú, Lima, Perú (November, Tesis de pregrado (2023)

23. Sodhi, P., Girouard, A., Thue, D.: Accessible play: towards designing a framework for customizable accessibility in games. In: Companion Proceedings of the Annual Symposium on Computer-Human Interaction in Play, pp. 49–55. CHI PLAY Companion '23, Association for Computing Machinery, New York, NY, USA (2023). https://doi.org/10.1145/3573382.3616075

24. W3C Web Accessibility Initiative (WAI): WCAG 3 Introduction — w3.org. https://www.w3.org/WAI/standards-guidelines/wcag/wcag3-intro/. Accessed 25 Oct 2023

25. Westin, T., Ku, J.J., Dupire, J., Hamilton, I.: Game accessibility guidelines and WCAG 2.0 – a gap analysis. In: Miesenberger, K., Kouroupetroglou, G. (eds.) Computers Helping People with Special Needs, pp. 270–279. Springer International Publishing, Cham (2018). https://doi.org/10.1007/978-3-319-94277-3_43

26. Yuan, B., Folmer, E., Harris, F.C.: Game accessibility: a survey. Univ. Access Inf. Soc. **10**(1), 81–100 (2010). https://doi.org/10.1007/s10209-010-0189-5

Web Accessibility: An Overlooked Right

Carlos Simões[1,2]([envelope]) [ID], Letícia Seixas Pereira[1] [ID], and Carlos Duarte[1] [ID]

[1] LASIGE, Faculdade de Ciências, Universidade de Lisboa, Lisbon, Portugal
lspereira@ciencias.ulisboa.pt, caduarte@edu.ulisboa.pt
[2] Collaborative Laboratory for Labour, Employment and Social Protection
(CoLABOR), Lisbon, Portugal
csimoes@lasige.di.fc.ul.pt

Abstract. The digitalisation of the public sphere is an ongoing process accelerated by the ubiquitousness of the internet. For the over a billion people estimated to live with an impairment, this digitalisation comes with barriers that can represent an altogether exclusion from the digital realm, hindering their full participation in society. This context should compel stakeholders involved in the development of digital products to consider accessibility as an essential requirement. However, that may not always be the case. This work is the product of a scoping literature review guided by the overarching topic of accessibility in the context of the web. After arguing that disability as a phenomenon might be more prevalent than one would think, it frames web accessibility as a human right that benefits all individuals, while also having important dimensions that businesses would regret ignoring.

Keywords: Accessibility · Web Accessibility · Digital Accessibility · Impairments · Disability · Inequality

1 Introduction

Today the internet is ubiquitous. It is used as a gateway to essential services, healthcare, job opportunities, social activities and education. This digitalisation of the public sphere represents a major shift in paradigm that comes with many benefits. However, that digitalisation may also represent the mutation of physical barriers to digital ones [61].

For the over a billion people the World Health Organization (WHO) estimates live with an impairment around the world [67], those barriers can effectively represent an altogether exclusion from the digital realm, hindering their full participation in society. For that reason, web accessibility needs to be thought of as a necessity rather than just a quality attribute.

This work is the product of a scoping [33,53] literature review guided by the overarching topic of accessibility in the context of the web. It aims to provide an overview of the topic while substantiating arguments for its importance. It will first touch on the different types of impairments that interact with contextual

M. Antona et al. (Eds.): HCII 2024, LNCS 15379, pp. 103–122, 2025.
https://doi.org/10.1007/978-3-031-76818-7_8

factors to disable individuals, and then challenge the notion that phenomenon is reserved for a small segment of the population. Then, supported by the bibliography, it weaves considerations on the topic of web accessibility before presenting a general landscape of its implementation.

Throughout this work, the terms *impairment* and *disability* are used in an noninterchangeable way. Further reasoning for this is presented in Sect. 2 but, fundamentally, this decision was anchored in the dichotomy between those two terms set by the social model of disability. This model defines disability as a social creation stemming from the relationship between people with impairments and a disabling environment [48].

2   On Disability

One could be tempted to define disability solely in the context of health, however that would place the burden exclusively on the medical condition of an individual when there are other factors relevant to disabling someone that should be considered.

That understanding seems to be embodied in the United Nations' (UN) *Convention On The Rights Of Persons With Disabilities* (UNCRPD) and in the WHO's *International Classification of Functioning, Disability and Health* (ICF). Both adhere to the notion that disability arises from the interaction between a person with an impairment (e.g., a health condition) and that person's contextual factors (e.g., attitudinal and environmental barriers) [57,66].

The professionals involved in the development of websites and mobile applications are, most probably, not capable to alleviate the physiological condition impairing a user. Nevertheless, by knowing those conditions and deploying strategies to better accommodate people living with them, they might be able to dissolve some environmental barriers.

In an effort to better understand the notion of disability, this section will first present some of the underlying physiological conditions (impairments), and then try to bridge the gap between those that live with them and those that do not.

2.1   Different Types of Impairments

The ICF [66] categorizes different types of body functions that, when impaired, interact with contextual factors in disabling ways. We can leverage that taxonomy to better understand the types of impairments that the World Wide Web Consortium (W3C) recognises might hinder human-computer interaction (refer to Table 1). Those are: auditory, cognitive, learning, and neurological, physical, visual, and speech [70].

Auditory. Hearing loss can range from slight to profound, impact one or both ears and be able to be mitigated with auditory devices or not. These disparities might be explained by the existence of two types of hearing losses [28]:

Table 1. W3C's types of impairments and related ICF's body functions

ICF's body functions	W3C's types of impairments
Hearing functions	Auditory
Mental functions	Cognitive, learning, and neurological
Neuromusculoskeletal and movement-related functions	Physical
Seeing and related functions	Visual
Voice and speech functions	Speech

- **Conductive** hearing losses are caused by diseases or obstructions in the outer or middle ear. They affect all frequencies of hearing evenly and do not result in severe losses.
- **Sensorineural** hearing losses result from damage to the sensory hair cells of the inner ear or the nerves supplying them. They result in mild to profound losses and affect certain frequencies more than others.

Cognitive, Learning, and Neurological. Cognitive, learning, and neurological impairments are diverse in origin and impact [47]. They can either stem from neurological or mental health disorders and affect an individual's hearing, movement, vision and speech. However, they do not necessarily impact one's intelligence.

Examples include: attention deficit hyperactivity disorder (ADHD), autism spectrum disorder (ASD), memory impairments and dyslexia.

Physical. Physical, or motor, impairments could manifest as weakened and limited muscular control, limitations to sensation, joint disorders, pain that impedes movement, and missing limbs [70].

Dexterity impairments have the potential to greatly impact a user's interaction with the internet since they affect the hands and arms, body parts usually seen as indispensable to human-computer interaction. Impaired dexterity may come as a consequence of [54]:

- **Musculoskeletal impairments** arising in the muscle or skeletal system or in the interaction between them. They are usually caused by deformity, injury or disease. Examples include arthritis and carpal tunnel syndrome.
- **Movement disorders** result from damages to the nervous or neuromuscular system that can occur, for instance, after a stroke. Examples include ataxia and parkinsonism.

Visual. There are four critical visual functions [2]:

- **Visual acuity** is a measure of the ability of the eye to distinguish shapes and the details of objects at a given distance [29].

- **Contrast sensitivity** is the extent to which one can discern subtle differences in shades of gray.
- **Field of vision** is the visual area an eye sees at a given instant.
- **Color perception** refers to the eye's ability to interpret correctly the wavelengths of different colors.

When one or more of those four functions is affected, one's visual capabilities may be considered impaired. For example, difficulty to focus on far away or close objects (myopia and hyperopia respectively) and the distortion of what is being seen (astigmatism) will have negative impacts on an individual's visual acuity and contrast sensitivity. The presence of opacities (cataracts) in the eye lens will also prove detrimental to one's visual acuity while restricting the field of vision. Furthermore, the lack of the necessary cones in one's retina to interpret the color red (protanopia) will hinder color perception.

Speech. Speech impairments may be divided into either those that affect its production or its fluency [44]. The first, largely result from physical conditions affecting the face, mouth, tongue or vocal cords while the latter, may take the form of stuttering or apraxia of speech, a disorder impacting the brain pathways involved in sequencing the movements needed to speak.

2.2   Demystifying the Notion of "other"

The condition of the impaired is often seen as undesirable and the discourse about it relegated to a more seclusive realm of the public sphere [34]. However, one should acknowledge that the WHO estimates there are over a billion people living with some kind of impairment [67]. The immensity of this number lends itself nicely to the conclusion that, to live with an impairment does not place one in a unique and unheard of condition that is ought to be shunned and ignored by the public.

Instead, it would be of benefit to the population as a whole for the struggles of those living with an impairment to be discussed and, ideally, alleviated since it is likely an individual ends up living with an impairment at some point, as we will see in this section.

The passing of time is inevitable and with it comes ageing, something inexorable from the human condition. In recent decades, the Organisation for Economic Co-operation and Development (OECD) countries saw the share of population aged 65 and over double from 9% in 1960 to 18% in 2021 with projections indicating a rise to 27% by 2050. Declining fertility rates and a rising life expectancy – on average, in OECD countries, one can expect to live 19.5 more years at 65 – help explain this increase [38].

A number of impairments may arise from the degenerative effects of ageing [27]:

- Presbycusis is another word for age-related **hearing** loss. Its mere existence attests to the prevalence and normalcy of the issue. The deterioration evolves from the reduction in the ability to understand speech to the ability to detect, identify, and localise sounds [21].

- **Cognitive** impairments relating to memory or to maintaining focus and attention on an activity for a long time may become more common.
- **Psychical** impairments become more prevalent as movement range becomes limited and motor control declines.
- **Vision** is often affected since ageing individuals may have to deal with issues like the proneness for their eyes to get fatigued or dry, the thinning of the most sensitive cells of the eye (age-related macular degeneration) or the loss of the eyes' ability to focus on nearby objects (presbyopia).

Apart from the inevitability of ageing, during a lifetime one is also likely to suffer from a temporary impairment like a broken limb or the short-term effect of a medical intervention like an eye surgery.

Furthermore, it would be remiss to ignore situationally-induced impairments. The mobile computing paradigm brought upon an age where the user is no longer necessarily sitting in front of a desktop, but rather can be in an ample variety of situations, contexts and environments [65]. Navigating these situations while interacting with, for instance, a smartphone can be analogous to the experience of someone with a physiological impairment.

With Eurostat stating that 81.48% of the European Union's (EU) population was using smartphones to access the internet in 2021 [17], and the OECD announcing 127.9 as the number of mobile broadband subscriptions per 100 inhabitant in their member countries [37], we understand that universal usage of mobile devices as access points to the internet may be a reality sooner than later, and with it the rise of situationally-induced impairments.

Ultimately, if disability can come to be because of an inevitable physiological impairment, because of the contextual barriers formed by the way we interact with the internet today, or even because of a combination of both, then we need to understand it as a shared aspect of the human condition, and not as the condition of the "other". It is therefore, imperative to shift the focus from the condition of the impaired to the disabling aspects arising from contextual factors.

3   Web Accessibility

As discussed in Sect. 2, a disabling experience stems from the interaction between an individual's impairment and their contextual factors. If those contextual factors take on the form of online browsing, then, to ensure a non-excluding experience, web accessibility must be a concern.

During the development project of an online platform, there will, most likely, be a heterogeneous group of stakeholders involved. In a simple one, done in the context of a company, you might have [36]:

- A **client** working in a specific sector of the economy. They will probably want rapid development of a quality product.

– A **product owner** translating the client's needs into actionable tasks for the rest of the stakeholders and making sure the project is delivered.
– A **designer** working towards a visually appeasing and polished final product.
– A **development team** making decisions about the technological infrastructure and translating the design into code. Traditionally, this team will have **front-end** and **back-end** developers. The first specialize in the creation of the user interface, while the later will be involved in what happens server-side.

This rather heterogeneous group, or at least its last three members, seem to generally agree that web accessibility as a quality should be included in the design process [68]. However, that heterogeneity, in experiences, knowledge, and even in the used jargon, calls for an harmonization of all of web accessibility's complex socio-technical dimensions in an agreed upon definition for it.

In a study by Yesilada et al. [69], 300 participants with an interest in accessibility but different career and education paths, were tasked with choosing their preferred definition for web accessibility from a list of five. The majority opted for the W3C definition:

"Web accessibility means that people with disabilities can use the Web. More specifically, Web accessibility means that people with disabilities can perceive, understand, navigate and interact with the Web, and that they can contribute to the Web" [23].

In second came one from the US federal government:

"Technology is accessible if it can be used as effectively by people with disabilities as by those without" [46].

Nevertheless, some participants in the study criticized the distinction made between types of users - those with or without disabilities - by these definitions.

Trough the analysis of the responses given and sentiments shared, the authors concluded that, in order to find a definition with a high degree of consensus, it ought to be realistic and concise, should consider situational impairments and equal access, while not focusing on users with disabilities, and be proactive about accessibility as opposed to it being an afterthought.

Elsewhere, Petrie et al. [43] aimed to unify the definition of web accessibility by conducting an analysis of 50 definitions present in papers and guidelines. From them, they were able to extract six core concepts used by many:

1. Groups of users, characteristics, needs of users.
2. What users should be able to do.
3. Technologies used.
4. Characteristics of the website.
5. Design and development of the website.
6. Characteristics of the situations of use.

Incorporating them into a unique definition of web accessibility, they came up with:

"all people, particularly disabled and older people, can use websites in a range of contexts of use, including mainstream and assistive technologies; to achieve this, websites need to be designed and developed to support usability across these contexts" [43].

Although not particularly concise, this definition seems to be in agreement with Yesilada et al.'s assertion as to how a consensual definition of web accessibility should be produced. It is realistic, alludes to situational impairments when it speaks of a "range of contexts of use", mentions disabled people without placing the focus on that group and implies a proactive approach by suggesting web accessibility should be considered during the design and development phases.

3.1 It Benefits All

As alluded to in Sect. 2.2, during a lifetime, one is likely to have a disabling impairment that can hinder interaction with the web. This likelihood increases during the later phase, when the consequences of ageing are felt and can have a compounding effect resulting on the exclusion from digital participation. Pérez-Escolar and Canet [41] seem to confirm this by stating that the elderly are the most likely group to be excluded from the digital realm. The universality of the ageing phenomenon is a good argument towards understanding how an accessible web benefits all. However, more can be said on this.

Apart from accessibility, another concept commonly associated with the interaction between a user and the web is usability, which is defined by ISO 9241 as:

"the extent to which a system, product or service can be used by specified users to achieve specified goals with effectiveness, efficiency and satisfaction in a specified context of use" [40].

If we consider "specified users" to be those with impairments, and "specified context of use" the disabling environments or assistive technologies, that definition could easily be borrowed by accessibility. However, they are usually seen as distinct qualities of a web product, albeit, with some overlap. Usability is often correlated with the general user experience (UX) design and studies aspects that impact all users, often not sufficiently addressing the needs of people with impairments [49].

Nevertheless, better accessibility will often be directly correlated with better usability. Petrie and Kheir [42] shows that there is some communality between them, as more recently does Zhao et al. [71]. The latter, analysing accessibility issues from popular GitHub projects and their fixes, found that, among quality attributes, usability is the one interacting with accessibility more frequently, and that when accessibility issues were resolved, the usability issues were greatly improved. In sum, one can affirm that to alleviate the constraints of people with impairments will also result in a better user experience for all.

3.2   A Human Right

As the internet cements itself as the primary intermediary connecting individuals to essential services, healthcare, education, employment opportunities and social interactions, it becomes apparent that to hinder online participation equates to restricting involvement in society.

Article 1 of the UN's *Universal Declaration of Human Rights* (UDHR) states that:

"all human beings are born free and equal in dignity and rights" [56].

At its time of writing in 1948, it would be hard to envision the advent of the web. In 2006 however, it was already a reality. In that year the UN published the *Convention On The Rights Of Persons With Disabilities* (UNCRPD) where article 9 demands for accessible information and communications technologies [57]. On the same text, article 21 speaks on the right one with an impairment has to exercise freedom of speech, and to seek information on an equal basis with everyone else. Since public discourse is increasingly had online, and the internet became the *de facto* source of information, to not have an accessible web is to violate the UNCRPD.

While the UDHR sets a fundamental guiding norm of equality that is ought to be kept in mind as the web's ubiquitousness and importance expands, the UNCRPD situates web accessibility as a human right, qualifies it as necessary precondition for equality, and acknowledges its importance as a tool for social participation and inclusion [19].

A particular driver of social participation is also a human right. In article 23 of the UDHR, we can read that everyone has the right to work, and with it, the:

"right to just and favourable remuneration ensuring for himself and his family an existence worthy of human dignity" [56].

As technology advances, the way we exercise that right changes. In 2022, close to 30% of employed people in the EU reported using digital devices for the entirety or most of their working time [16]. Were those digital devices fully accessible, these jobs could probably be performed by people with impairments.

However, among people with impairments there still is a disproportionate rate of poverty and social exclusion compared with those without one. Eurostat data for 2022 shows us that, in the EU, 28.8% of the people in the first group were at risk of poverty or social exclusion, a number 10.5% higher that of the latter group [18].

A way to reduce that gap is to better assimilate people with impairments in the workforce, therefore allowing them to fully realize their human right. Nevertheless, several hypothetical factors might work against that assimilation. For one, in violation of the UNCRPD's article 9, those digital devices could be inaccessible. Another reason, could be an employers stigma towards those with impairments [20], which would violate article 1 of the UDHR. A third possibility might be the low education rate of those with impairments, which implies a violation of another human right, the one within article 26, the right to education. The strength of this last hypothesis increases when faced with UNICEF data showing us that, compared with children without impairments, children with impairments are 49% more likely to have never attended school [55].

The role of higher education, in particular as a device for the attainment of better living conditions, needs considering. According to Eurostat data [15], in 2022 in the EU, 86% of those that had completed a program of tertiary education were employed. That number drops to 74.2% when considering those that completed upper secondary or post secondary non-tertiary education and falls to 57.2% among those that, at best, attained lower secondary education.

Work towards the integral fulfillment of both the UDHR and UNCRPD still has to be done, and that seems to be in the UN's agenda with its 17 goals for sustainable development [58]. Among them, the most relevant to our discussion are:

- *"**Goal 1** - End poverty in all its forms everywhere"*.
- *"**Goal 4** - Ensure inclusive and equitable quality education and promote lifelong learning opportunities for all"*.
- *"**Goal 10** - Reduce inequality within and among countries"*.

Working towards generalized digital accessibility is a way to help attain goal 10, and also goal 4 if we consider how digital inaccessibility may be blocking people from obtaining an education in an increasingly digitalised world. As we have seen, full realization of goals 4 and 10 can potentially remove some of the people living with impairments from a self-perpetuating cycle of poverty and, therefore, not fully realize goal 1, but at least contribute towards it.

3.3   The Business Side

More than it being a fundamental human right, there are other angles to the accessibility question that businesses could regret ignoring.

Even with the higher risk for impoverishment that we have discussed in the previous section, the global disability market, considering people with impairments and their friends and family, commands over 13 trillion US dollars [10]. Given the demographic paradigm and the impacts of ageing we discussed in Sect. 2.2, we can postulate that with each passing year that figure will only increase.

In 2022, Eurostat estimated more than two thirds (68%) of the population between 16–74 in the EU had bought or ordered something over the internet in the 12 preceding months [13]. Other data points to 44.1% of large (250 or more persons employed) enterprises in the EU having e-commerce sales [14].

However, what is now a common practice for most of the population, may prove to be a tall task for people with impairments [51]. By building inaccessible e-commerce platforms, business are alienating a vast portion of their potential consumer base, therefore not fully realizing their earning potential and effectively losing money.

Apart from this opportunity to extend market reach, the W3C identifies three other added benefits from implementing accessibility [45]:

– It **drives innovation**: accessible design thinking may result in new and flexible ways to interact with websites. Furthermore, those solutions may end up improving the experience of all users (refer to Sect. 3.1).
  The W3C retells how Google's advances for accessible products and services, translated into innovative solutions for everyone. Among them are inventions already entrenched in our everyday lives like auto-complete and voice control. Additionally, those advances also play a part in propelling forward more contemporary innovations, such as artificial intelligence, that have only recently gained wider prominence.
  Concisely, and as Eve Anderson, senior director for Google, currently leading their accessibility effort, puts it:
    "The accessibility problems of today are the mainstream breakthroughs of tomorrow." [7]
  In the intersection between innovation and legal obligation, which we will touch on next, resides another example given by the W3C. In the early 2000s, students in the California State University (CSU) were unable to take advantage of an educational program built into Apple's iTunes because of it not being accessible to blind students. That resulted in teachers within the university being prohibited from using iTunes. In response, the tech company took note of the problem and worked towards making it more accessible. That software, and its educational programs were soon after being used in CSU, as the matter was solved trough innovation rather than litigation.
  Apart from an example as to how communication between societal stakeholders may bring forth accessibility, it also serves as a cautionary tale. If the adoption of accessibility is not a requirement, then the question becomes if market forces and technical change will or will not choose to enable access for those with impairments [6].
– It **minimizes legal risk**: the ratification of the UNCRPD by the EU in 2010 [59], led it to pass legislation like the *European Accessibility Act* (EAA) *(Directive 2019/882)* [12].
  The EAA identifies product and service features that must be made accessible. Among them are products like computers, operating systems, and smartphones, but also services like e-commerce, online banking and websites that provide information on transport services. From the 28th of June 2025, citizens will be able to file complaints with national courts if services or products do not respect the directive [11].
  Therefore, compliance with the eventual laws each country member will pass resulting from the transposition of the EAA, will mitigate the risk for an organization operating within the EU to be involved in legal action.
  In the United States of America, even though the country never ratified the UNCRPD [59], lawsuits have been filled under the Americans with Disabilities Act (ADA) because of inaccessible online platforms.
  Among them, a case filled in 2017 against a large sporting good corporation. The plaintiff argued the defendant failed to:

> *"design, construct, maintain, and operate its website to be fully accessible to and independently usable by the plaintiff and other blind or visually-impaired people"* [32].

– It **enhances the brand**: a commitment to accessibility can demonstrate a business' sense of Corporate Social Responsibility (CSR), which, in turn, may lead to enhanced brand image and reputation, increased sales and customer loyalty, improved workforce diversity among others [52].

Connected to CSR's are Environmental, Social, and Corporate Governance (ESG) factors. We can consider accessibility to be an ESG since it pertains to inclusion and human rights (refer to Sect. 3.2). Data pointing to the 35.3 trillion US dollars in investment driven by ESG's (an increase of 55% from 2016 to 2020) [22], allows us to postulate investors are increasingly interested in ESG's.

Organizations ought to take steps towards protecting and enhancing their brands in accordance to a CSR philosophy and with ESG's in mind. Publicly listed companies in particular need to take the latter in consideration, since studies [9,72] point to there being a correlation between ESG's and market value.

4   Web Accessibility in Practice

Up to this point, we have been discussing impairments that, conjugated with the environment, disable individuals. It is of particular interest to this work when that environment gains the form of a digital platform. To that point, we have been framing web accessibility as something beneficial to all, a human right and a potential advantage for businesses.

However, we are yet to address a critical element to this discussion. An analysis on its practical application is called for, in order to understand if web accessibility is already a reality, or if it is still an elusive necessity.

It would be difficult to have this discussion without a measure for accessibility. When the subject of study is the information on a web page or application, we usually refer to the W3C's *Web Content Accessibility Guidelines* (WCAG) [24]. In their most recent iteration – 2.2 published on the 5th October 2023 – there are 13 guidelines organized under four principles [62]:

– **Perceivable** – Users must be able to perceive the information being presented.
– **Operable** – User interface components and navigation must be operable. They cannot require an interaction the user cannot perform.
– **Understandable** – A user must be able to understand the information and the operation of the user interface.
– **Robust** – Users must be able to access the content as technology advances.

Every guideline has testable success criteria, each with its own level of conformance: A (lowest), AA, and AAA (highest).

Starting in 2019, the non-profit organization WebAIM publishes a yearly report on the accessibility of one million home pages. In 2023, they found that 96.3% of those pages had WCAG failures. Among them the most common were low contrast – present in 83.6% of pages – and missing alternative text – found in 58.2% [64].

The first constitutes a failure to meet success criterion *1.4.3 Contrast (Minimum)*, a level AA criterion for the guideline *1.4 Distinguishable*. The later represent failure in meeting the level A success criterion *1.1.1 Non-text Content* of the *1.1 Text Alternatives* guideline. Both are guidelines of the perceivable principle [63].

Elsewhere, Bi et al. [4] analyzed 1000 GitHub projects and found that, around 70% of them had reported accessibility issues. Similarly, Alshayban et al. [1] studied 1000 Android apps to find that most had accessibility issues. Likewise, Martins and Duarte [31] found that among close to three million pages, only less than 1% presented no accessibility issue.

4.1   Sentiments Towards It

We have previously established web accessibility's importance (refer to Sect. 3.2), yet we are now faced with a somewhat troubling picture of inaccessibility throughout the web. In this section, we will explore the sentiments towards it of some of the stakeholders mentioned in the beginning of Sect. 3 to understand if they explain a generalized disinterest.

In Inal et al. [25], 167 UX professionals from Nordic countries revealed, through an online questionnaire, how they view and practice accessibility. As to what pertains to their personal motivations in digital accessibility they rate being inclusive and designing better products as the two main propellers. They also mention motives like being ethical, complying with the law, and increasing revenue.

In Yesilada et al. [69], the 300 participants gave similar answers when asked as to their motivations for being involved with web accessibility. By decreasing number of respondents, some of the reasons were: being inclusive, design better products, be ethical and comply with the law.

Another study by Bi et al. [5], had 365 participants, the majority of which working either on web app or mobile app development, giving their opinions on statements about accessibility. Some noteworthy that gathered a relevant level of agreement (more than four in a six point Likert scale) are: accessibility needs to be incorporated into all software projects, it is not only for people who are unable to use standard software, and it is a marketing strategy.

Vollenwyder et al. [60], advances a study on the intention to consider web accessibility anchored on the *Theory of Planned Behavior* (TPB). A core concept associated to TPB is *intention*, the immediate antecedent to the performance of a behaviour. According to this theory, *intention* is formed by three factors:

1. **Attitude**, a personal opinion regarding the behaviour.

2. **Subjective norm**, the perceived social pressure to perform or not the behaviour.
3. **Perceived behavioral control** the perceived ease or difficulty of performing the behaviour.

These factors are influenced by *salient beliefs* emerging from the individual, social and informational backgrounds. The authors identified 12 of them associated with web accessibility and built around them a questionnaire that was answered by 342 participants, most of which, web practitioners like testers, managers, and developers.

The gathered answers allowed them to identify the main beneficial *salient beliefs* to web accessibility as:

– User advocacy, a subjective norm pertaining to the users demand for web accessibility.
– Self-perception as specialist, a subjective norm with perceived behavioural control implications, related to the individual's role as a web specialist.
– Product quality, an attitude correlating accessibility with better overall quality of the work.

Most of these motivations and perceptions have direct correspondence to topics we discussed previously. The notion that accessibility helps design better products for all was touched upon on Sect. 3.1. Web accessibility's potential to increase revenue, the legal risk of not complying with the law in what pertains to it, and its usage as a marketing strategy to enhance the brand was discussed on Sect. 3.3. Furthermore, the perception that, to design accessible platforms is to be ethical, may be rooted in the correlation between accessibility and human rights, established in Sect. 3.2.

Lastly, this section would be remiss to not address how the motivation to be inclusive, identified in Inal et al. [25] and Yesilada et al. [69], and the self-perception as specialist, the salient belief advanced by Vollenwyder et al. [60], can be a detriment to the narrative that there is no "other" (refer to Sect. 2.2) by problematically framing the question of accessibility as one where there are two non-intercepting groups, those that help by including, and those that are helped by being included.

Inclusivity may have as precursor empathy, which, according to Bennett and Rosner [3], may distance those that work on accessibility from the lives and experiences they hope to bring near. They present the idea that empathy may work as a mean of reinforcing on the web practitioner a feeling of superior training – or their self-perception as specialist, as Vollenwyder et al. [60] puts it – that makes them apt to resolve problems in domains they do not master.

They also point to how empathic modelling activities reproduce negative stereotypes, fail to highlight the challenges felt by those with impairments, and lead towards an inaccurate and incomplete notion of what makes an experience disabling. More disconcerting, these activities may even help practitioners distance themselves from those with impairments, therefore framing the latter's identity as one different from the former's, which consequently works against the notion that accessibility is not for the "other".

Although it can be framed somewhat problematically, empathy's ability to lead to the development of accessible solutions should not be disdained when it is genuine. However, that empathy should neither negate the fact accessibility is for all and not the "other", nor be used as false pretence aimed to cover another, legitimate, truer intention like the ones listed in Sect. 3.3.

In an hypothetical case of an e-commerce website, to claim accessibility was implemented purely because of empathy, without contemplating the increased revenue the interaction with the untapped market of people with impairments would generate, creates the false narrative that change happened, not because of the buyer's ability to advocate for it, but rather due to samaritanism on the seller's end. Ultimately, and paradoxically, this course of action guided by virtue signalling, could eventually even serve as a deterrent to the proliferation of accessibility were the paradigm to shift, and empathetic decisions started being met by the general public with indifference rather than praise.

Ultimately, respect among fellow humans should prevail as the guiding norm, and the fundamental rights for one's existence a constant not dependent on the good will, or empathy, of others.

4.2   Barriers

From the information gathered, it would not be a stretch to state that, in broad terms, stakeholders are in favour of implementing web accessibility. However, there must be some force pulling in the opposing direction. Otherwise, there would not be such a high prevalence of inaccessible platforms as the one reported in the beginning of this section.

A first clue as to why that is the case, may lead us to question if students are being adequately introduced to the problem. Cao and Loiacano [8], found that students of Computer Science or Information Technology programs, were not familiar with guidelines like the WCAG, even after having taken development and design courses.

This gap in knowledge tends to follow students to their professional careers. In fact, lack of training or of skills and knowledge is often cited as a challenge to the implementation of web accessibility [5,25], which among the stakeholders evidences a need for training in digital accessibility [39].

Other barriers to web accessibility pointed by participants of Inal et al.'s study [25] include time and cost constraints, placing the focus on other users, the work overload, and it not being a requirement neither for their organization nor for the client.

If we take a moment to analyze these barriers in light of what we have been discussing, we find that this line of though is fraught with potential issues, but also with a relevant insight serving as silver lining.

As alluded to in Sect. 2.2, the notion of "other" is one that needs to be applied cautiously. In this particular case one needs to understand that, if we say we are focusing on "other users", it creates the illusion that those with, and those without impairments are non intercepting and distinguishable groups, when in reality, most frequently, they are not. Furthermore, as seen on Sect. 3.1, to better prepare a platform to be used by someone with an impairment will often bring advantages to the whole user base.

Additionally, web accessibility not being a requirement is a paradigm being shifted by the legislative power. As discussed on Sect. 3.3, those organizations and clients referred to by the professionals in Inal et al. [25] have more to gain by being proactive on this matter and, therefore, avoid future legal actions that can result in costs that far outweigh the ones incurred on during the process of implementing web accessibility.

However, the notion that professionals do not have enough time for accessibility implementation because they are overloaded with work, is one requiring further investigation. The majority (55.7%) of the enquired estimated they spend under 10% of total working time on accessibility issues [25]. We can postulate this figure is connected to accessibility not being perceived as mandatory by their organizations, which therefore conditions them to divert their attention from the issue. It may also end up generalizing the idea accessibility is not as relevant as other software qualities, which can have a performative effect on the job market that ends up perpetuating the issue.

Martin et al. [30] studies 5920 job postings from 2062 different companies on LinkedIn to investigate if organizations seek software designers and developers versed in accessibility. They divided those posting into two categories: "general software roles" that represented close to 70% of the studied universe, and "accessibility specific roles". On the former group, less than 6% had the keyword "accessibility" on its description. Of the latter, it was required to have extensive technical accessibility knowledge, and to function as accessibility educators and advocates within the company.

This, in line with the sentiments gathered through the analysis of Inal et al., sets the tone for accessibility to be demoted in importance by workers of the first, bigger, group, while setting the second, smaller, group up for the inglorious and overloading task of being preaching advocates for the first's reluctant ears.

Moreover, Martin et al.'s data may also be correlated with another feeling shared by participants of Inal et al. that some workers are more responsible than others for the inclusion of accessibility in a project. This theory can work as a tactic of evasion of a responsibility that should be shared by all, and does a disservice to the idea that web accessibility should be a preoccupation throughout the entirety of the software development life-cycle [4, 6, 26, 68].

Apart from widespread understating that everyone will eventually have an impairment, for awareness of the accessibility issue to be more prevalent, these barriers dissipated, and their struggles alleviated, users with permanent impairments need to play an active role in promoting their needs among stakeholders [35]. However, that is hard to do from the frail position of the marginalized. To help exit that position, legislation and public opinion need to keep nudging stakeholders in the right direction until those with impairments can fully participate in our increasingly digital society and lobby for their interests. After all, structural changes trump punctual caritative actions as:

> "no individual is free and a full citizen if they are dependent on the will of others" [50].

5   Conclusion

Throughout this work, an overview of the web accessibility topic was provided, alongside arguments for the importance of its generalized implementation.

The framing of accessibility as a human right allows for a better understanding of the extent to which an inaccessible web can impose virtual barriers to the fulfillment of a complete and dignified existence for those living with impairments. Likewise, demystifying the notion of the "other" allows us to gain insight into the universality and prevalence of impairments, therefore further advancing the argument that web accessibility is a necessity.

However, fueled by the presented barriers, accessibility issues still abound online. Nevertheless, positive sentiments towards it from stakeholders, the benefits it brings to businesses, and an increasingly conscious legislative power, strengthen hope for a more accessible web in a near future.

Acknowledgements. This work was supported by FCT through the LASIGE Research Unit, ref. UIDB/00408/2020 (https://doi.org/10.54499/UIDB/00408/2020) and ref. UIDP/00408/2020 (https://doi.org/10.54499/UIDP/00408/2020), and by the COST Action LEAD-ME The Leading Platform for European Citizens, Industries, Academia, and Policymakers in Media Accessibility (CA19142).

References

1. Alshayban, A., Ahmed, I., Malek, S.: Accessibility issues in android apps: state of affairs, sentiments, and ways forward. In: Proceedings of the ACM/IEEE 42nd International Conference on Software Engineering, pp. 1323–1334. ICSE '20, Association for Computing Machinery, New York, NY, USA (2020). https://doi.org/10.1145/3377811.3380392
2. Barreto, A., Hollier, S.: Visual disabilities. In: Yesilada, Y., Harper, S. (eds.) Web Accessibility: A Foundation for Research, pp. 3–17. Springer, London (2019). https://doi.org/10.1007/978-1-4471-7440-0_1
3. Bennett, C.L., Rosner, D.K.: The promise of empathy: design, disability, and knowing the other. In: Proceedings of the 2019 CHI Conference on Human Factors in Computing Systems, pp. 1–13. CHI '19, Association for Computing Machinery, New York, NY, USA (2019). https://doi.org/10.1145/3290605.3300528
4. Bi, T., Xia, X., Lo, D., Aleti, A.: A first look at accessibility issues in popular GitHub projects. In: 2021 IEEE International Conference on Software Maintenance and Evolution (ICSME), pp. 390–401 (2021). https://doi.org/10.1109/ICSME52107.2021.00041
5. Bi, T., Xia, X., Lo, D., Grundy, J., Zimmermann, T., Ford, D.: Accessibility in software practice: a practitioner's perspective. ACM Trans. Softw. Eng. Methodol. **31**(4) (2022). https://doi.org/10.1145/3503508

6. Botelho, F.H.F.: Accessibility to digital technology: virtual barriers, real opportunities. Assistive Technol. **33**(sup1), 27–34 (2021). https://doi.org/10.1080/10400435. 2021.1945705, pMID: 34951832

7. Brownlee, J.: How designing for disabled people is giving google an edge (2016). https://www.fastcompany.com/3060090/how-designing-for-the-disabled-is-giving-google-an-edge. Visited on 15 Mar 2024

8. Cao, S., Loiacono, E.: Perceptions of web accessibility guidelines by student website and app developers. Behav. Inf. Technol. **41**(12), 2616–2634 (2022). https://doi.org/10.1080/0144929X.2021.1940278

9. Capelle-Blancard, G., Petit, A.: Every Little Helps? ESG news and stock market reaction. J. Bus. Ethics **157**(2), 543–565 (2017). https://doi.org/10.1007/s10551-017-3667-3

10. Donovan, R.: 2020 Annual Report: the global economics of disability (2020). https://www.rod-group.com/research-insights/annual-report-2020/

11. European Commission: European accessibility act: Q&A. https://ec.europa.eu/social/main.jsp?catId=1202&intPageId=5581. Visited on 25 Nov 2023

12. European Commission: Directive (EU) 2019/882 of the European Parliament and of the Council of 17 April 2019 on the accessibility requirements for products and services (Text with EEA relevance) (2019). http://data.europa.eu/eli/dir/2019/882/oj/eng

13. Eurostat: Digital society statistics at regional level (2023). https://ec.europa.eu/eurostat/statistics-explained/index.php?title=Digital_society_statistics_at_regional_level. Visited on 25 Nov 2023

14. Eurostat: E-commerce sales of enterprises by size class of enterprise (2023). https://doi.org/10.2908/ISOC_EC_ESELS. Visited on 25 Nov 2023

15. Eurostat: Employment by educational attainment level - annual data (2023). https://doi.org/10.2908/LFSI_EDUC_A. Visited on 3 Jan 2024

16. Eurostat: Eu employment: use of digital devices (2023). https://ec.europa.eu/eurostat/web/products-eurostat-news/w/ddn-20230627-1. Visited on 19 Nov 2023

17. Eurostat: Individuals - devices used to access the internet (2023). https://doi.org/10.2908/ISOC_CI_DEV_I, https://ec.europa.eu/eurostat/databrowser/view/isoc_ci_dev_i/. Visited on 12 Nov 2023

18. Eurostat: People at risk of poverty or social exclusion by level of activity limitation, sex and age (2023). https://doi.org/10.2908/HLTH_DPE010. Visited on 19 Nov 2023

19. Ferri, D., Favalli, S.: Web accessibility for people with disabilities in the European union: paving the road to social inclusion. Societies **8**(2) (2018). https://doi.org/10.3390/soc8020040

20. Friedman, C.: The relationship between disability prejudice and disability employment rates. Work **65**(3), 591–598 (2020). https://doi.org/10.3233/WOR-203113

21. Gates, G.A., Mills, J.H.: Presbycusis. Lancet **366**(9491), 1111–1120 (2005). https://doi.org/10.1016/S0140-6736(05)67423-5

22. Global Sustainable Investment Alliance: global sustainable investment review 2020 (2020). https://www.gsi-alliance.org/wp-content/uploads/2021/08/GSIR-20201.pdf

23. Henry, S.L.: Introduction to web accessibility (2022). https://www.w3.org/WAI/fundamentals/accessibility-intro/. Visited on 17 Nov 2023

24. Henry, S.L.: WCAG 2 overview (2023). https://www.w3.org/WAI/standards-guidelines/wcag/. Visited on 1 Dec 2023

25. Inal, Y., Guribye, F., Rajanen, D., Rajanen, M., Rost, M.: Perspectives and practices of digital accessibility: a survey of user experience professionals in Nordic countries. In: Proceedings of the 11th Nordic Conference on Human-Computer Interaction: Shaping Experiences, Shaping Society. NordiCHI '20, Association for Computing Machinery, New York, NY, USA (2020). https://doi.org/10.1145/3419249.3420119

26. Kulkarni, M.: Digital accessibility: challenges and opportunities. IIMB Manag. Rev. **31**(1), 91–98 (2019). https://doi.org/10.1016/j.iimb.2018.05.009

27. Kurniawan, S., Arch, A., Smith, S.R.: Ageing and older adults. In: Yesilada, Y., Harper, S. (eds.) Web Accessibility: A Foundation for Research, pp. 93–119. Springer London, London (2019). https://doi.org/10.1007/978-1-4471-7440-0_6

28. Kushalnagar, R.: Deafness and hearing loss. In: Yesilada, Y., Harper, S. (eds.) Web Accessibility: A Foundation for Research, pp. 35–47. Springer London, London (2019). https://doi.org/10.1007/978-1-4471-7440-0_3

29. Marsden, J., Stevens, S., Ebri, A.: How to measure distance visual acuity. Community Eye Health **27**(85), 16 (2014). https://www.ncbi.nlm.nih.gov/pmc/articles/PMC4069781/

30. Martin, L., Baker, C., Shinohara, K., Elglaly, Y.N.: The landscape of accessibility skill set in the software industry positions. In: Proceedings of the 24th International ACM SIGACCESS Conference on Computers and Accessibility. ASSETS '22, Association for Computing Machinery, New York, NY, USA (2022). https://doi.org/10.1145/3517428.3550389

31. Martins, B., Duarte, C.: A large-scale web accessibility analysis considering technology adoption. Univ. Access Inf. Soc. (2023). https://doi.org/10.1007/s10209-023-01010-0

32. Mendizabal, M.: Class action complaint and Jury Demand, Mendizabal V. Nike, INC., Case 1:17-cv-09498 (2017). https://www.classaction.org/media/mendizabal-v-nike-inc.pdf

33. Munn, Z., Peters, M.D.J., Stern, C., Tufanaru, C., McArthur, A., Aromataris, E.: Systematic review or scoping review? Guidance for authors when choosing between a systematic or scoping review approach. BMC Med. Res. Methodol. **18**(1), 143 (2018). https://doi.org/10.1186/s12874-018-0611-x

34. Munyi, C.W.: Past and present perceptions towards disability: a historical perspective. Disabil. Stud. Q. **32**(2) (2012). https://doi.org/10.18061/dsq.v32i2.3197

35. Mäkipää, J.P., Norrgård, J., Vartiainen, T.: Factors Affecting the Accessibility of IT Artifacts: a systematic review. Commun. Assoc. Inf. Syst. **51**(1) (2022). https://doi.org/10.17705/1CAIS.05129

36. Nicoara, R.: Working on a Team, pp. 187–197. Apress, Berkeley, CA (2023). https://doi.org/10.1007/978-1-4842-9663-9

37. OECD: mobile broadband subscriptions (2018). https://doi.org/10.1787/1277ddc6-en, https://www.oecd-ilibrary.org/content/data/1277ddc6-en. Visited on 12 Nov 2023

38. OECD: Health at a Glance 2023. OECD Publishing (2023). https://doi.org/10.1787/7a7afb35-en, https://www.oecd-ilibrary.org/content/publication/7a7afb35-en

39. Oncins, E.: Mapping the European digital accessibility field: the impact project. In: Proceedings of the 9th International Conference on Software Development and Technologies for Enhancing Accessibility and Fighting Info-Exclusion, pp. 33–37. DSAI '20, Association for Computing Machinery, New York, NY, USA (2021). https://doi.org/10.1145/3439231.3440608

40. Organization, I.S.: Standard 9241-11: ergonomics of human-system interaction - part 11: usability: definitions and concepts (2018). https://www.iso.org
41. Pérez-Escolar, M., Canet, F.: Research on vulnerable people and digital inclusion: toward a consolidated taxonomical framework. Univers. Access Inf. Soc. **22**(3), 1059–1072 (2023). https://doi.org/10.1007/s10209-022-00867-x
42. Petrie, H., Kheir, O.: The relationship between accessibility and usability of websites. In: Proceedings of the SIGCHI Conference on Human Factors in Computing Systems, pp. 397–406. CHI '07, Association for Computing Machinery, New York, NY, USA (2007). https://doi.org/10.1145/1240624.1240688
43. Petrie, H., Savva, A., Power, C.: Towards a unified definition of web accessibility. In: Proceedings of the 12th International Web for All Conference. W4A '15, Association for Computing Machinery, New York, NY, USA (2015). https://doi.org/10.1145/2745555.2746653
44. Roper, A., Wilson, S., Neate, T., Marshall, J.: Speech and language. In: Yesilada, Y., Harper, S. (eds.) Web Accessibility: A Foundation for Research, pp. 121–131. Springer, London (2019). https://doi.org/10.1007/978-1-4471-7440-0_7
45. Rush, S.: The business case for digital accessibility (2018). https://www.w3.org/WAI/business-case/. Visited on 25 Nov 2023
46. Section 508 standards: ICT accessibility frequently asked questions (2023). https://www.section508.gov/manage/accessibility-faq/
47. Seeman, L., Lewis, C.: Cognitive and learning disabilities. In: Yesilada, Y., Harper, S. (eds.) Web Accessibility: A Foundation for Research, pp. 49–58. Springer, London (2019). https://doi.org/10.1007/978-1-4471-7440-0_4
48. Shakespeare, T.: The social model of disability. In: Davis, L.J., ed. The Disability Studies Reader, vol. 2, pp. 197–204 (2006)
49. Henry, S.L., Abou-Zahra, S., White, K.: Accessibility, usability, and inclusion (2016). https://www.w3.org/WAI/fundamentals/accessibility-usability-inclusion/. Visited on 18 Nov 2023
50. Carvalho da Silva, M.: Cinismo no combate à pobreza. Jornal de Notícias (2023). https://www.jn.pt/1667884945/cinismo-no-combate-a-pobreza/. Visited on 3 Dec. 2023
51. Sohaib, O., Kang, K.: E-commerce web accessibility for people with disabilities. In: Goluchowski, J., Pankowska, M., Linger, H., Barry, C., Lang, M., Schneider, C. (eds.) Complexity in Information Systems Development, pp. 87–100. Springer International Publishing, Cham (2017)
52. Sprinkle, G.B., Maines, L.A.: The benefits and costs of corporate social responsibility. Bus. Horiz. **53**(5), 445–453 (2010). https://doi.org/10.1016/j.bushor.2010.05.006
53. Sutton, A., Clowes, M., Preston, L., Booth, A.: Meeting the review family: exploring review types and associated information retrieval requirements. Health Inf. Libr. J. **36**(3), 202–222 (2019). https://doi.org/10.1111/hir.12276
54. Trewin, S.: Physical disabilities. In: Yesilada, Y., Harper, S. (eds.) Web Accessibility: A Foundation for Research, pp. 19–33. Springer London, London (2019). https://doi.org/10.1007/978-1-4471-7440-0_2
55. UNICEF: Seen, counted, included: using data to shed light on the well-being of children with disabilities (2022). https://data.unicef.org/resources/children-with-disabilities-report-2021/. Visited on 19 Nov 2023
56. United Nations: Universal declaration of human rights (1948). https://www.un.org/sites/un2.un.org/files/2021/03/udhr.pdf
57. United Nations: convention on the rights of persons with disabilities (2006). https://www.un.org/disabilities/documents/convention/convoptprot-e.pdf

58. United Nations: transforming our world: the 2030 agenda for sustainable development (2015). https://sdgs.un.org/2030agenda

59. United Nations: United nations treaty collection - 15. convention on the rights of persons with disabilities (2023). https://treaties.un.org/Pages/ViewDetails.aspx?src=TREATY&mtdsg_no=iv-15&chapter=4&clang=_en. Visited on 25 Nov 2023

60. Vollenwyder, B., Iten, G.H., Brühlmann, F., Opwis, K., Mekler, E.D.: Salient beliefs influencing the intention to consider web accessibility. Comput. Hum. Behav. **92**, 352–360 (2019). https://doi.org/10.1016/j.chb.2018.11.016

61. Wadoux, J.: Digitalisation of services: ensuring equal access to all, including older people of today and tomorrow (2022). https://www.age-platform.eu/digitalisation-of-services-ensuring-equal-access-to-all-including-older-people-of-today-and-tomorrow/. Visited on 4 Jan 2024

62. WAI, W3C: Introduction to understanding WCAG (2023). https://www.w3.org/WAI/WCAG22/Understanding/intro. Visited on 1 Dec 2023

63. WAI, W3C: Web content accessibility guidelines (WCAG) 2.2 (2023). https://www.w3.org/TR/WCAG22/. Visited on 1 Dec 2023

64. WebAIM: the webaim million (2023). https://webaim.org/projects/million/. Visited on 1 Dec 2023

65. Wobbrock, J.O.: Situationally-induced impairments and disabilities. In: Yesilada, Y., Harper, S. (eds.) Web Accessibility: A Foundation for Research, pp. 59–92. Springer, London (2019). https://doi.org/10.1007/978-1-4471-7440-0_5

66. World Health Organization: The International Classification of Functioning, Disability and Health. World Health Organization, Geneva (2001). https://iris.who.int/bitstream/handle/10665/42407/9241545429.pdf?sequence=1

67. World Health Organization, World Bank: World report on disability 2011 (2011). https://iris.who.int/handle/10665/44575

68. Yeliz Yesilada, Giorgio Brajnik, M.V., Harper, S.: Exploring perceptions of web accessibility: a survey approach. Behav. Inf. Technol. **34**(2), 119–134 (2015). https://doi.org/10.1080/0144929X.2013.848238

69. Yesilada, Y., Brajnik, G., Vigo, M., Harper, S.: Understanding web accessibility and its drivers. In: Proceedings of the International Cross-Disciplinary Conference on Web Accessibility. W4A '12, Association for Computing Machinery, New York, NY, USA (2012). https://doi.org/10.1145/2207016.2207027

70. Zahra, S.A.: Diverse abilities and barriers (2017). https://www.w3.org/WAI/people-use-web/abilities-barriers/. Visited on 1 Dec 2023

71. Zhao, Y., Gong, L., Yang, W., Zhou, Y.: How accessibility affects other quality attributes of software? A case study of GitHub. Sci. Comput. Program. **231**, 103027 (2024). https://doi.org/10.1016/j.scico.2023.103027

72. Zhou, G., Liu, L., Luo, S.: Sustainable development, ESG performance and company market value: mediating effect of financial performance. Bus. Strateg. Environ. **31**(7), 3371–3387 (2022). https://doi.org/10.1002/bse.3089

Questionnaire and Interview to Understand Mathematics Teachers and Occupational Therapists' Usage of HandiMathkey

Nadine Vigouroux[1] , Jean-François Camps[2] , and Frédéric Vella[1(✉)]

[1] IRIT, UMR 5505, CNRS, UPS, 118 Route de Narbonne, 31062 Toulouse CEDEX 9, France
`Frederic.Vella@irit.fr`
[2] LNPL, EA 4156, UT2J, 5, Allée Antonio Machado, 31058 Toulouse CEDEX 9, France

Abstract. Typing mathematics is sometimes difficult with text editors for students with motor impairment and other associated impairments. The HandiMathKey is an application co-designed by mathematics teachers and occupational therapist. In this paper we report an mixed evaluation based on the UTAUT theoretical framework. We used questionnaire and interview to understand professional's usage of HandiMathkey. This study shows how the questionnaire and the interview complement each other, and how the two professionals can take a complementary approach to understanding the use and new needs of HandiMathkey as part of a user-centred design approach.

Keywords: Evaluation · assistive technologie · HandiMathKey · secondary students

1 Introduction

1.1 Problematic

Typing mathematics is sometimes difficult with text editor functions for students with motor impairment and other associated impairments (visual, cognitive). Studies [1, 2] and [3] reported design and evaluation of assistive technologies to input mathematical by disabled students. These studies show: 1) the usability of these solutions needs to be improved and 2) these evaluations have mainly involved students.

Digital technology can enable children with disabilities to enter mathematical formulae, for example using Word or free Office editors. These offer interfaces consisting of button bars associated with mathematical symbols. By clicking on these, the student can write a mathematical formula in the text editor. However, these symbols are difficult to visualise, and the small size of the buttons requires great precision on the part of the student, which can be tiring during maths lessons. To overcome these difficulties, there are three categories of software for entering mathematical formulas: interfaces integrated into Word or LibreOffice, online editors and applications [5]. However, these programs are not necessarily suitable for copying mathematical formulas in class because the symbols are not categorised, there are too many buttons, input is not done directly in the text editor sheet, there is a lack of symbols, it is impossible to modify the text in the text editor, and so on.

Poorly addressed input area in the accessibility field deals with the input of scientific elements including mathematical formulas. Indeed, learning in this subject requires inserting symbols not available on a conventional keyboard and writing in a non-linear way.

Firstly, ElSheikh and Najdi [4] studied the use of special math hardware keyboard. Their study reported that the math keyboard supports well the goal of mathematic communication for learning mathematics. However, at the elementary and middle school levels, it is difficult to be autonomous in mathematics for students who cannot write by hand [1] or who have grapho-motor disorders. Elliot and Bimes (2007) [2] reported that the speech modality has better benefits [3] for entering mathematical for people with motor impairments. The study of Anthony et al. (2005) demonstrated that the use of the multimodality combining handwriting and speech gives results in fewer errors and faster input of mathematical formulas than when using a keyboard and pointing device [3]. The MathTalk application is also a speech recognition software that allows the user to voice math for anybody. However, although such software with speech recognition is effective, it is also intrusive in school environments and therefore not suitable for classroom use.

Bertrand et al. [5] designed a virtual mathematical keyboard as an alternative to handwriting and speech, called HandiMathKey (HMK). It allows mathematical formulae to be entered using a pointing device or a touch tablet, using a text editor. The following section describes it.

1.2 HandiMathKey Context

Description. Bertrand et al., [5] deployed a user-centred design method involving the ecosystem (mathematics teachers and occupational therapists) of disabled students to design the HMK application. HMK's interface (see Fig. 1) consists of several areas: an area representing an azerty keyboard, an area containing common mathematical symbols and finally a 'contextual' area depending on the type of six mathematical formula topics (geometry, probability, arithmetic function). HMK works with both the Microsoft Office and Libre Office editors.

Evaluation with Students. 23 students (19 with hand motor impairment, 3 with visual impairment and 1 other with dyspraxia and dysgraphia disorders) in three classrooms of middle school during one school year have evaluated HMK. [9] partially reported the observations of 9 students with motor impairment who appropriated HMK due to the interface affordance. These observations also shown that the HMK learning phase is necessary for the students and that it can be more or less long depending on the associated impairment present (visuo-spatial disorders, memory, and attention).

On the other hand, few studies have looked at the point of view of the ecosystem/professional who work with young students to evaluate the acceptance and the use of HMK.

Now we plan to analyse professional feedbacks about the use of HMK.

To do this, in this paper we will set out the theoretical framework, then we will present the material and methods, then we will present the results, which will concern

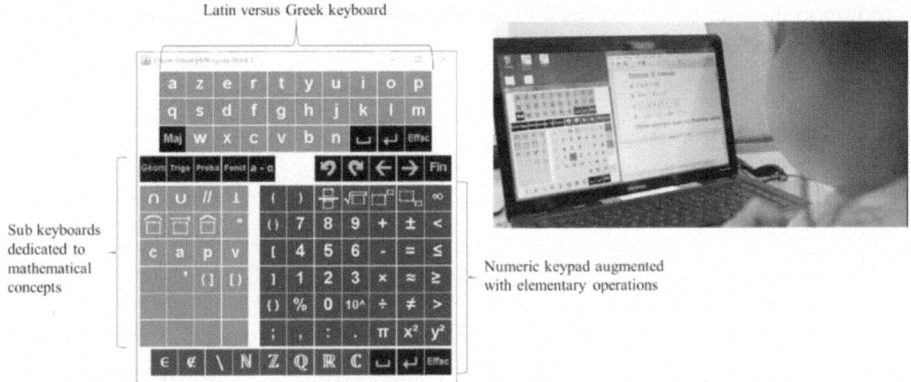

Fig. 1. HMK used at the Centre Jean Lagarde by a child with a disability.

the results of the questionnaire UTAUT and the interviews obtained from the teachers and occupational therapists, and finally we will conclude.

2 Theoretical Framework

Davis [10] proposed the TAM (Technology Acceptance Model). The objectives of this model were to study two variables, perceived usefulness and perceived ease of use, as determinants of the acceptance of a technology. The results of the work of Davis [10], are manifold, including:

- Confirmation of a significant correlation between perceived usefulness and intention to use a technology, and between perceived ease of use and intention to use a technology.
- Perceived ease of use also seems to have an influence on perceived usefulness. The perceived usefulness of a system will in fact be greater if the system is perceived as easy to use.

There have been a number of evolutions of the TAM model. Venkatesh et al. [11, 13] proposed the Unified Theory of Acceptance and Use of Technology (UTAUT) model. UTAUT is a model that integrates several models in the field of technology acceptance and use, including the TAM model, in order to identify the factors to be retained. When applying the UTAUT model to the context of using a digital application, several theoretical justifications support its appropriateness. Key determinants of technology acceptance are integrated in this model like: the perceived usefulness or performance expectancy which reflects the degree to which an individual will perform their task better. and the perceived ease of use the application. On another hand, the perceived ease of use or effort expectancy accounts for the measure of ease of use with the interface. A high level of perceived ease of use involves minimal effort for individual to interact.

The UTAUT model's emphasis on performance and effort expectancy is particularly relevant, as these digital applications need to demonstrate clear benefits and user-friendliness to gain acceptance. Perceived usefulness generally appears to be statistically more important than perceived ease of use and results are more mixed on the effect of social influences [12] (Fig. 2).

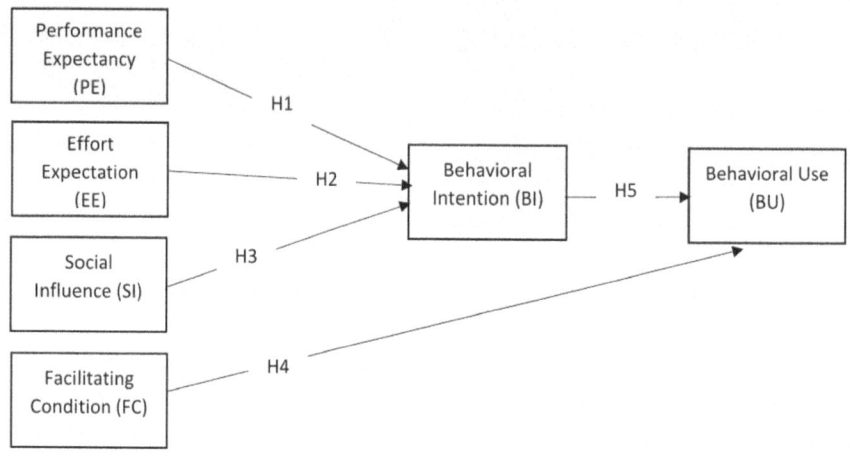

Fig. 2. Proposed theoretical model adapted from [11].

According to UTAUT model, "the behaviours of individuals can be inferred to a certain extent through behavioural intention which is a measurement of an individual's intent of doing something" (Min et al. [15]. We used the UTAUT model (Unified Theory of Acceptance and Use of Technology) as theoretical framework.

This model allows us to characterize dimensions on behavioural intentions and uses behaviour. The first three dimensions on behavioural intentions are: 1- Performance Expectancy (PE) which refers to professional's belief that HMK is a useful tool stating that they will intend to use it as a compensatory tool for students with learning disabilities. 2- Effort Expectancy (EE) which measures the ease of using HMK. 3-Social Influence (SI) as the HMK's perceived importance in the student's environment i.e., the impact of HMK use on the environment (family, friends, etc.). The two last focuses on use behaviour with 4- Facilitating Conditions (FC) evaluating the ease access to keyboard' functions and 5- Behavioural Intention (BI) which address conscious decision to use HMK.

Then, five hypotheses [15] were formulated and tested:

- H1: Performance expectancy will affect the behavioural intention.
- H2: Effort expectancy will affect the behavioural intention.
- H3: Social influence will affect the behavioural intention.
- H4: Facilitating condition will affect the use behaviour.
- H5: Behavioural intention will affect the use behaviour.

We used the hypotheses of Dwivedi et al. [15] to define the content of the web-online questionnaire (see 3.3). We use the hypotheses as indicators of the acceptability of using HMK.

3   Material and Methods

3.1   Description of the Multi-disciplinary Workshops

We carried out a mixed evaluation (questionnaire and interview) with five professionals (3 mathematics teachers and 2 occupational therapists) following a year of multidisciplinary workshops with secondary school pupils. These professionals led multidisciplinary workshops during the 2022–2023 school year. These workshops took place every two weeks. They consisted in having student's complete exercises involving the input of mathematical formulae, using the concepts taught by the teachers in their classes. 21 students from on 5th grade class and two 4th grade class took part in these workshops. Two classes used Microsoft Word and one class used Libre Office. Each mathematics teacher has his/her own class. The role of the occupational therapists was to assist the students by helping them to use HMK and reminding them of its functions. The teacher's role is to teach mathematical concepts using HMK to input mathematical formulas. At the end of the school year, we carried out a qualitative and quantitative evaluation.

3.2   Population

The occupational therapists (*ER4 & ER6*) have many years' experiences in supporting students at the Educational Medical Institute at the Centre Jean Lagarde and in proposing technical aids to facilitate access to digital tools. The three teachers (*EN2, EN3 & EN5*) also have experience of teaching classes with special needs students. They all volunteered and were behind the creation of the multidisciplinary workshops.

3.3   Mixed Evaluation

We used two methods: an online digital questionnaire and semi-structured interviews.

Questions for the UTAUT Model for HMK. We designed 16 questions to measure the actual use of HMK (see Table 1) in relation to its usefulness and perceived ease of use. A five-point Likert scale (strongly disagree, disagree, agree, strongly agree and no opinion) was used for the 16 questions. We invite the five professionals to complete an online digital questionnaire.

Semi-structured Interview. The semi-structured interviews involve guiding participants through a series of questions while allowing them the freedom to express their thoughts and feelings spontaneously. This method strikes a balance between structured and unstructured interviews, providing enough guidance to cover essential topics while being flexible enough to uncover unanticipated insights. This method allows delving deeply into the user's thought processes, capturing nuanced insights into how they interact with the software. The interview guides consisted of three sets of questions on the criteria of usefulness, usability and intention of use.

For the usefulness criterion, we wanted to know how HMK is useful. "What does HMK enable you to do that you couldn't do without it"?

Concerning the usability criterion, the semi-open questions aimed to obtain information such as "what did you want to do with HMK but were unable to do by questioning

Table 1. Questions to measure the use of HMK.

Questions	Hypotheses
1. HMK is an efficient tool (faster, fewer actions, etc.) for inputting mathematical formulae	H1
2. HMK is a useful tool for inputting mathematical formulae	H1
3. Using HMKhelps me to input my mathematical formulae better	H2
4. I can help children learn HMK quickly	H2
5. The HMK input procedure is clear and easy to understand	H2
6. I found it easy to learn how to enter mathematical formulas with HMK	H2
7. I am more like to use HMK if those around me (colleagues and occupational therapists) use it	H3
8. The people around me (colleagues and occupational therapists) think that I should use a tool like HMK to help my pupils understand mathematical formulae	H3
9. I can use all the symbols needed in HMK to enter all the mathematical formulae in my mathematics-teaching curriculum	H4
10. HMK enables me to use symbols to enter a particular mathematical formula	H4
11. I think that using HMK fits in well with the way I like to enter mathematical formulae	H5
12. I intend to use HMK in the future	H5
13. I would recommend HMK to friends and family.	H5
14. It is a good idea to use HMK to enter mathematical formulas	H5
15. I enjoy using HMK	H5
16. Using HMK makes entering mathematical formulas more motivating for me	H5

accessibility', "are there any uncorrectable input errors in HMK"? "What did you find difficult in using HMK"? "Did it take you a long time to learn how to use it"? etc.

For the intention of use, the questions were, "Why do you wish/do you not wish to continue to use the HMK application as part of your professional activities? What new features would you like to see implemented in HMK? Would you be willing to teach professionals how to use HMK?".

We conducted the interviews at the Centre Jean Lagarde by the authors from IRIT. Subsequently, we transcribed the interviews.

4 Results

4.1 Questions for the UTAUT Model for HMK

Despite the small number of respondents, the interest of this study lies in the disparity or complementarity of the point of view of mathematics teachers (EN) in one hand and the occupational therapists (ER) on the other. We computed the scale scores for each of the hypotheses (See Fig. 3). The values represent the number of occurrences of the Likert point for the questions in each hypothesis and for each class of professionals.

According to the UTAUT model H1, H2 and H3 have an impact on intention behaviour, while H4 and H5 influence use behaviour. If we look at the descriptive results for teachers (*EN*s), they agree/strongly agree that HMK is useful or very useful (H1). Teachers, on the other hand, were more weighted and mixed on the ease of use (scale between strongly agree, agree and disagree). For these two hypotheses H1 and H2, the results for occupational therapists (*ER*s) were either agree or strongly agree. This means that occupational therapists think that HMK is useful and easy to use. Concerning H3, *EN*s and *ER*s confirmed the importance of the human environment (parents, teachers, and friends) (agree, strongly agree scale and with no opinion. The same applies to H4, with *EN*s and *ER*s believing that easy access to HMK's functions encourages use behaviour (mainly agree and strong scale). For H5, the behavioural intention of *EN*s and *ER*s are very favourable (agree and strongly agree) for the intentions to use HMK.

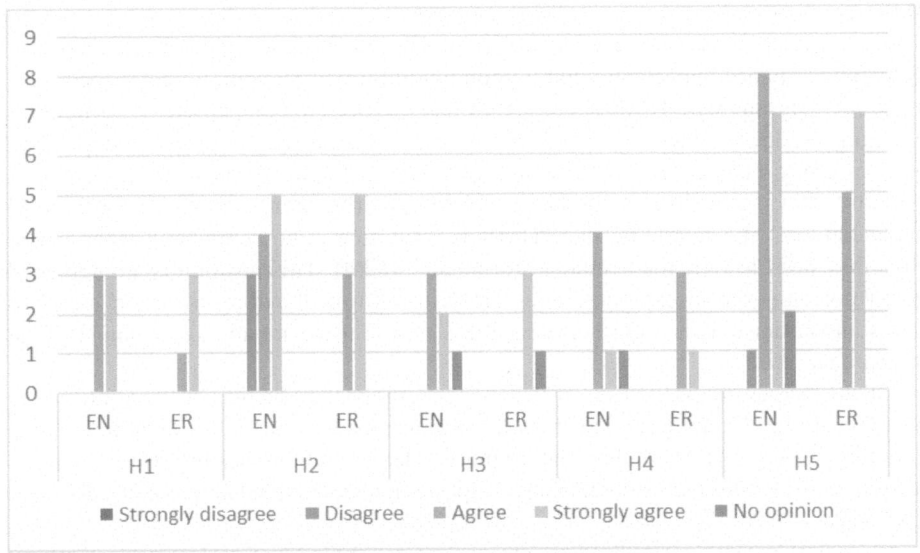

Fig. 3. Scores' hypotheses by teachers & occupational therapists.

4.2 Semi-structured Interview

In order to take these quantitative analyses by questionnaire further, we are going to analyze the verbatims of the respondents with regard to the 3 hypotheses H1, H2 and H3 which, according to the UTAUT model, contribute to usage intentions and usage behaviors

- H1: Performance expectancy or Perceived Usefulness will affect the intention of use.

This hypothesis could be reformulated in an operational way like this: "When HMK enables tasks such as mathematical writing to be carried out independently, it develops greater perceived usefulness". This dimension is part of the reason, which decide an individual to Accept & Use.

When looking for positive or negative arguments in teachers and therapists' statements, two dimensions are highlighted. On one hand, the proven ability to write mathematical formulae. For example, teachers generally confirm this ability: "HMK is useful for students (in Year 8), giving them better access to mathematical formulas". Moreover "they could write mathematical formulae without having to know the specific code of the word processor" (*EN2*). HMK eases cognitive workload whenever mathematics needs to be written. "This application opened up the use of virtual math keyboard to everyone, whatever the word processor". (*EN2*).

On the second hand, the topic addressed was the ability of HMK to rehabilitate student with writing disabilities. One teacher reported that "This system facilitates the written of mathematical formulae, particularly for students with visual impairment." confirming that this application has been developed for writing compensation (*EN3*). Teachers, together highlight the increase autonomy of the students provided by using HMK.

One occupational therapist (*ER4*) with a specific rehabilitation point of view, reported on the performance expectancy that " young people, step by step, … developed their autonomy in typing with HMK because they had this need to compensate for difficulties in writing, tiredness, slowness" …"when they were assessed, they were always dependent on a secretary, because in mathematics, they had difficulties accessing the different symbols… It was very difficult for them to find the position of the symbols in the classical maths editors." She concludes that "HMK is a solution to be completely autonomous when they need to type mathematical formulae". (*ER4*). This position is strengthened by her colleagues who explained that "HMK in term of handling is easier: easier to access and easier to use… Furthermore, I don't think there are any tools than HMK at the moment." (*ER6*).

On this perceived usefulness, one teacher concluded that she likes to "continue using the application with my pupils to show them that it's a tool that helps them to become more independent. And that also enables them to learn mathematics in a different, more fun way, with an interactive tool that also helps them to understand notation in a different way." (*EN5*).

Overall, the various stakeholders interviewed concluded that usefulness expectancy had been reached.

- H2: Effort expectancy (Perceived ease of use) will affect the intention of use.

The operational hypothesis could be written in these terms: a system like HMK that is easy to use and reuse develops greater Effort expectancy.

Like Performance expectancy, Effort expectancy is crucial for user acceptance, as evidenced one of the teachers who reported, "Over time, pupils started to use without me asking. They used it outside the classroom. It happened step by step without my help and so it enabled them to become autonomous." (EN2). The same teacher completed specifying "I found a correct level of usability in that the application HMK is based on the students' academic program in mathematics in Year 8. This ease of use has also been described by the two other teachers as "I find it fairly easy to access." (EN3) and "HMK is a very intuitive tool." (EN5) respectively. In fact, one teacher said that grouping the windows together had greatly improved HMK's user-friendliness. (EN3).

The occupational therapist approach is interesting as her point of view is focused on rehabilitation potentiality to compensate motor or visual impairments… An occupational therapist said that "HMK's features made it easy to learn the virtual keyboard, but that it was necessary to separate this learning from the physical keyboard' learning". (ER4). "Young used to use classical keyboard even when for word processor so they developed habits in using HMK whenever a symbol or formulae wasn't accessible directly on the classical keyboard. Young people used to type on their physical keyboards. And so, HMK comes in, they use HMK when the symbols aren't on the standard keyboard."(ER4).

"When HMK is used to…the symbols will…For example, for a fraction, they'll write the number first, use HMK to write the HMK code, then the number, then equal, and all this is done linearly. So this organization is very different and will suit some pupils better than others." (ER4). Despite these caveats, the second therapists indicated that: "I think you need a bit of guidance at first. But once you've got the hang of it, I think it's pretty easy to use… Today, it can be used quite intuitively, and learning is relatively easy." (ER6).

However occupational therapists focused on constraints which impact more or less on this Effort Expectancy. Therefore, HMK required the computer mouse device to operate. Even if the feedbacks seem to be fairly positive, there are factors that counterbalance these positive aspects: "Because there are all sorts of associated difficulties, visuospatial and motor impairment due to the fact that student leaves the physical keyboard to go and find the mouse. So, there's a movement in space, moving the mouse in space, already locating it on the screen and then clicking in the right place on HMK' virtual keyboard…". Spatial localization on virtual keyboard could be enhance by "coding new color blocks in the preexistent blue one." (ER4).

"Fatigability can also be visuospatial, visual. We all have young people typing and looking at their keyboards. Young people are not so independent that they can type without looking at the physical keyboard. They look at their keyboard and then they also control the screen. There's this constant switch between physical keyboard and screen. They're always, almost every time they type, checking. And then, when they need to call up HMK, there's "I'm grabbing my computer mouse" and then there's this visual control of the mouse pointer that they have to fetch from HMK…" (ER4).

Teachers perceived HMK as easy to use. The therapists place HMK in a context of use that requires a text processor, a physical keyboard and a computer mouse, and that the pupils could have some difficulties to coordinate the use of these different tools. But they conclude positively that HMK has given the pupils autonomy.

- H3: Social influence will affect the behavioural intention.

HMK Operational hypothesis: Promoting HMK to colleagues develops greater behavioral intention and then use intention.

When respondents are consulted about the possibility of promoting the tool, all consider the benefits to others of using HMK. Each in their own way, they communicate to others an interest in HMK like: "I would recommend this tool. Those who could not write, gave up using word processor and got help from their secretary. So, I think HMK enables them to be autonomous, and that's why I'd recommend it to my colleagues".

(*EN2*). More directly on the subject of the promotion, we can read "Yes, certainly. Yes, I would." (*EN3*). On this social influence, one of the teachers specified the social collaboration between teachers and occupational therapists. She described the situation as follows: "We worked as a team to organize the visual organization of the virtual keyboard for people with visual impairment. The motor impairment too, to organize the keys on the keyboard panel to minimize interactions as possible." Finally, she was arguing to others the autonomy's benefice gained with HMK (*EN5*).

Occupational therapists take a similar point of view. One therapist (*ER4*) indicated on promoting the tools with colleague's therapists or teachers "Yes, yes, yes, of course. As far as I am concerned, it is an interesting tool that really eases young people of the task of entering all the symbols and mathematics on the computer. It is free, there is still opportunity for improvement, but it really brings a lot of things together." (*ER4*). The other therapist (*ER6*) supports promotion: "Yes, I'd recommend it. That's more for the outside world. And then, internally, to continue to introduce it to our students here".

On the question of promotion to colleagues, all the respondents agreed on the merits of distributing this tool.

5   Discussion

The aim of this study was to measure, by means of an adapted questionnaire and additional interviews, the variables which, according to the UTAUT model, contribute to the development of behavioral intentions and ultimately to behavioral use.

Questioning the five hypotheses, all respondents are "agree to strongly agree" with an intention of use of HMK with special needs students (H5 hypothesis). Each of the four hypotheses described earlier (perceived and effort expectancies, social influence and facilitating condition) was validated. Interviews analyses clarified the way professionals are considering the way students used HMK in autonomy.

The results show that the classroom facilitates acceptability of HMK by student with disabilities. In general, young students adapt quickly to HMK, thanks to its intuitive layout. However, they necessarily need to be also accompanied in the learning of the mathematical editor.

The usability evaluation of the HMK tool is not only limited to feedback from users and their caregivers (teachers or occupational therapists). In fact, using the UTAUT model allows us to think about the design evolution cycle by structuring the designing phases to improve the various functionalities and user interface that could be obstacles to getting to grips with, accepting and using the HMK tool.

One important point of this study is to enable young to become autonomous. It is of fundamental importance for their studies, but more generally for their lives, that these students with special needs can become as independent as possible. Developing autonomy is both a learning objective and a way to engage students. As well as enabling students to work at their own pace and with a tool that better meets their needs, this autonomy can help teachers to manage their time better and improve students' learning abilities.

Fernandez-Batanero et al. [16] conducted a systematic review of studies regarding the impact of assistive technology for the inclusion of students with disabilities. Findings of this study include that the use of assistive technologies is successful in increasing the inclusion and accessibility of students with disabilities, although barriers such as teacher education, lack of information or accessibility are found. Autonomy enhances students' learning skill as mentioned by [17]. Autonomy learning is more efficient when using computers [17] and assistive technologies. To support the autonomy in learning mathematics for disabled students, HMK enables students to input mathematical formulae in autonomy as confirmed by professionals.

This work to develop ICT for pupils with special needs is part of a wider movement towards an inclusive policy, as set out in various French national education laws, decrees and circulars. Furthermore, Information Communication Technology has also an impact on motivation, engages low achievers, supports differentiation and improves behavior [18], or increases learner confidence [19]. Taking into account the impact of policies and ICT, the inclusive approach we advocate, beyond the development of a compensation tool, is to defend the rights of pupils to inclusion. According to Ebersold [20], these rights must include 4 dimensions: First of all, the "Taking part", so that each pupil can participate in the classroom in the same way as their peers. Secondly, the "being part of", which defines each individual as a full member of the class group. A third dimension characterizes social recognition, the feeling of existing with others, through others and finally this right must emancipate each individual by allowing them to "act on" their learning and other school or extra-curricular activities. These four dimensions must also be considered implicitly in every development of assistive technologies.

Working in the field of inclusion goes far beyond the development of ICT, but the ultimate aim is to enable pupils with special needs to be able to be pupils like everyone else [20].

6   Conclusion and Perspectives

In the course of this work, we evaluated HMK with professionals (3 maths teachers and 2 occupational therapists). To do this, we implemented an evaluation methodology based on the UTAUT model for the questionnaire, followed by an interview with each of the professionals.

The results of the questionnaire show that the professionals intend to use HMK because it is a need of the students. This shows the value of using the UTAUT model accompanied by an interview when the number of participants is low. This helps to support the responses to the questionnaires and to reinforce the intention to use HMK.

In the rest of our work, we will propose the UTAUT questionnaire to professionals (teachers and occupational therapists) who have downloaded and used it with HMK children. However, for the results of this questionnaire to be valid, we need to use it on a larger number of people and contextualise it in relation to the number of children, the situations in which they are used, the time they are used, etc.

In addition, the study clearly demonstrates the perceived usefulness and the perceived ease of use of HMK for disabled children from the point of view of the professionals. This confirms the usability of HMK by pupils [9]. It is also very interesting because it crosses the points of view of two classes of professionals (mathematics teachers and occupational therapists). This diversity of feedback is very interesting for the development and adaptation of HMK, both in terms of the accessibility of the HMK tool and the benefits of HMK for greater autonomy in the classroom to write mathematical formulae. This study also demonstrates the importance of the student ecosystem for the appropriation and acceptability of HMK.

However, these results should be considered relative to the low number of participants and should be confirmed on a larger population of professionals after annual use of HMK.

Acknowledgments. The authors would like to thank the respondents for participating in this study and for their involvement in setting up the interdisciplinary workshops. This work was carried out under the Hand'Innov agreement (IRIT and ASEI).

References

1. Benoit, H., Sagot, J.: L'apport des aides techniques à la scolarisation des élèves handicapés. La nouvelle revue de l'adaptation et de la scolarisation **43**, 19–26 (2008)
2. Elliott, C., Bilmes, J., Computer based mathematics using continuous speech recognition. Striking a C [h] ord: Vocal Interaction in Assistive Technologies, Games and More (2007)
3. Anthony, L., Yang, J., Koedinger, K.R., Evaluation of multimodal input for entering mathematical equations on the computer. In: CHI 2005 Extended Abstracts on Human Factors in Computing Systems, pp. 1184–1187 (2005)
4. ElSheikh, R.M., Najdi, S.D.: Math keyboard symbols and its effect in improving communication in math virtual classes. Int. J. Inform. Educ. Technol. **3**(6), 638–642 (2013)
5. Bertrand, E., Sauzin, D., Vella, F., Dubus, N., Vigouroux, N., HandiMathKey: mathematical keyboard for disabled person. In Computers Helping People with Special Needs: 15th International Conference, ICCHP 2016, Linz, Austria, 13–15 July 2016, Proceedings, Part II 15, pp. 487–494. Springer International Publishing (2016)
6. Pouplin, S., et al. : Effect of a dynamic keyboard and word prediction systems on text input speed in patients with functional tetraplegia. J. Rehab. Res. Dev. **51**(3), 467–480 (2014)
7. Windsteiger, W., Theorema 2.0: A graphical user interface for a mathematical assistant system. arXiv preprint arXiv:1307.1945 (2013)
8. Bertrand, E., Sauzin, D., Vella, F., Dubus, N., Vigouroux, N., HMK: mathematical keyboard for disabled person. In: International Conference on Computers Helping People with Special Needs, pp. 487–494. Springer, Cham (2016)
9. Vella, F., Dubus, N., Gallard, C., Malet, C., Ades, V., Vigouroux, N., Observation of Handi-MathKey appropriation phase by disabled students in a middle school. In: 15th International Conference of the Association for the Advancement of Assistive Technology (AAATE 2019), 31, 157–157 (2019)
10. Davis, F.D.: A technology acceptance model for empirically testing new end-user information systems: theory and results. Doctoral dissertation, Sloan School of Management, Massachusetts Institute of Technology (1986). https://dspace.mit.edu/handle/1721.1/15192
11. Venkatesh, V., Morris, M., Davis, G.B., Davis, F.D.: User acceptance of information technology: toward a unified view. MIS Q. **27**(3), 425–478 (2003)
12. Kefi, H., Mesures perceptuelles de l'usage des systèmes d'information : application de la théorie du comportement planifié, Humanisme et Entreprise **297**, (2010)
13. Venkatesh, V., Thong, J.Y., Xu, X.: Unified theory of acceptance and use of technology: a synthesis and the road ahead. J. Assoc. Inf. Syst. **17**(5), 328–376 (2016)
14. Min, Q., Ji, S., Qu, G.: Mobile commerce user acceptance study in China: a revised UTAUT model. Tsinghua Sci. Technol. **13**(3), 257–264 (2008). https://doi.org/10.1016/S1007-021 4(08)70042-7

15. Dwivedi, Y.K., Rana, N.P., Jeyaraj, A., Clement, M., Williams, M.D.: Re-examining the unified theory of acceptance and use of technology (UTAUT): towards a revised theoretical model. Inf. Syst. Front. **21**(3), 719–734 (2019)
16. Fernández-Batanero, J., M., Montenegro-Rueda M., Cerero, J. F., Inmaculada García-Martínez, I., G., Assistive technology for the inclusion of students with disabilities: a systematic review, Cultural and Regional Perspectives, accepted: 20 May 2022 / Published online: 10 June 2022; https://doi.org/10.1007/s11423-022-10127-7
17. https://snow.idrc.ocadu.ca/the-inclusive-classroom/3-1-0-creating-an-inclusive-classroom/3-1-2-developing-student-autonomy/
18. Balanskat, A., Blamire, R., Kefala, S.,: The ICT impact report: a review of studies of ICT impact on schools in Europe. Report, European Schoolnet, Brussels (2006)
19. Blamire, R.: ICT impact data at primary school level: the STEPS approach. In: Assessing the Effects of ICT in Education, Scheuermann, F., Pedro, F. (eds.) European Union/OECD, France (2009)
20. Ebersold, S.: Société inclusive, droits pédagogiques et fonctions de l'accessibilité. Revue française de pédagogie **220**, 47–60 (2023). https://www.cairn.info/revue--2023-3-page-47.htm

Design and Usability Testing of Home Rehabilitation Training Toys for Children with ADHD

Zhongqing Yao, Ziyun Lin[✉], Yefang Chen, Rong Luo, and Siu Shing Man

School of Design, South China University of Technology, Guangzhou 510006, China
carameloko616@gmail.com

Abstract. Attention Deficit Hyperactivity Disorder (ADHD) is a prevalent psychiatric disorder among children, with a significant impact on academic performance and social interactions. Conventional treatments, while helpful, cannot fully address the complex needs of children with ADHD. This study aimed to design a home rehabilitation training toy tailored to the characteristics of ADHD children to complement existing treatment modalities. By exploring current treatment modalities, including sensory integration comprehensive training, and conducting user research with parents of ADHD-diagnosed children, this research ensured the relevance and effectiveness of the designed toy. The product design concept was grounded in theories of sensory integration training, aiming to create A-Rounding relay, a toy that facilitates rehabilitation training through play within the home environment. The design implementation involved the creation of a toy featuring a ring-shaped track with LED strips and rotating blocks, promoting sensory stimulation and therapeutic exercises. Human-computer interaction considerations ensured optimal usability for children with ADHD. System Usability Scale (SUS) was used to assess the satisfaction level of children with ADHD regarding the toy and their understanding of its gameplay mechanism. Results indicated excellent usability of A-Rounding relay and satisfaction levels among participants. Future work will focus on developing a functional prototype and investigating the effectiveness of the product in training children with ADHD using assessment tools from the medical field.

Keywords: Tasks and Usability · Toy design · Interaction design · Design for children

1 Introduction

Attention Deficit Hyperactivity Disorder (ADHD), also known as Attention Deficit Disorder, is one of the common psychiatric disorders among children [1, 2]. According to a survey of American parents, the prevalence of ADHD among children aged 3–17 was about 9.8%, and approximately 23% of children with ADHD do not receive medication treatment [3]. Furthermore, there has been a growing trend in the number of children affected by ADHD in recent years. The adverse effects of ADHD, which may include a decline in academic performance, social difficulties, and strained family relationships, underscore the critical importance of early detection and intervention measures. Research indicated that conventional treatments such as medication and neurobehavioral therapy alone are insufficient to address the high prevalence of ADHD [4]. Simultaneously, within the field of human-computer interaction, there is a growing focus on designing for special needs children, with an increasing number of teams investigating rehabilitation methods that extend beyond conventional treatments. Therefore, this study aimed to investigate the characteristics of ADHD children and, based on this understanding, design a home rehabilitation training toy suitable for ADHD children to help improve their symptoms.

2 Research on Children with ADHD

2.1 Current Treatment Modalities for ADHD

With the advancement of medical technology and research, treatment approaches for ADHD have become increasingly refined, including pharmacotherapy [5], behavioral therapy [6], executive function training [7], and psychotherapy [8]. Among these, sensory integration comprehensive training stands as one of the primary modalities for the rehabilitation training of children with ADHD. This method involves stimulating multiple sensory systems in the human body to promote physical, intellectual, and emotional development in children [9]. Such multidimensional stimulation aids in improving attentional focus and enhancing self-control abilities in children with ADHD, while gradually fostering patience and confidence. Due to its evident efficacy, simplicity, and safety [10], sensory integration comprehensive training has gained widespread acceptance among children and parents. This makes it particularly suitable as a foundational principle for the design of rehabilitation toys for children with ADHD, especially considering the potential for enjoyable gamification in design.

2.2 User Research

In order to gain a comprehensive and authentic understanding of the actual use of sensory integration training toys by children with ADHD in their daily lives, as well as their social interactions, we conducted surveys with parents of children diagnosed with ADHD.

Some examples of questions are:

(a) What is the duration since your child was diagnosed with ADHD? (Fill-in-the-blank)
(b) Which of the following symptoms does your child exhibit? (Multiple-choice question)
(c) Has your child ever played with sensory integration training toys? (Single-choice question)
(d) Has your child's attention improved while playing with such training toys? (Single-choice question)
(e) Has your child had experiences playing with other typically developing children? (Single-choice question)
(f) How does he behave when playing with other children? (Multiple-choice question)

(g) Do you believe this type of game can motivate children? (Single-choice question)

Based on a survey of 45 questionnaires, it was found that the majority of children with ADHD exhibit characteristics such as difficulty sustaining attention, difficulty completing tasks in sequence, and a preference for stimulating activities. Most of them had undergone sensory integration training with some therapeutic effect. Additionally, ADHD children demonstrated a relatively positive attitude when playing with peers.

3   Product Design

3.1   Design Concept of A-Rounding Relay

Drawing inspiration from the identified pain points of children with ADHD, the product design concept of A-Rounding relay was based on theories such as sensory integration comprehensive training, a common treatment modality for ADHD. Brainstorming sessions and analysis of existing children's products were conducted to create a toy specifically tailored for children with ADHD. A-Rounding relay should facilitate rehabilitation training solely through play within the home environment. By integrating elements of sensory stimulation and therapeutic exercises, A-Rounding relay aimed to alleviate symptoms of ADHD while providing an enjoyable and stress-free experience for the children.

3.2   Design Implementation

Product Demonstration of Effects and Features. Based on the aforementioned design concept, after designing the gameplay mechanism and product details of the home rehabilitation training toy, we utilized the 3D modeling software Rhino to model the product's structure and appearance and employed Blender's Cycle renderer to create color schemes and textures. The final result is shown in Fig. 1. The following outlines the structure and gameplay mechanism of, as well as how the product was designed based on the principles of rehabilitation training needs for children with ADHD.

The main body of A-Rounding relay featured a ring-shaped track with a gap, allowing a small ball to roll along the track. In the center of the toy, there were LED strips and rotating blocks. The LED strips were used to guide children with ADHD to complete the track and allow the ball to pass smoothly, while the rotating blocks served as a reward mechanism at the end of each game.

A-Rounding relay was designed for two players. Before the game begins, each player receives their own track module and memorizes the corresponding color. Once the game starts, the small ball rolls along the track and the central LED strip randomly illuminates either yellow or green lights during the match. Children must add track modules according to the color of the lights as a reminder. If the color correspondence is incorrect, the game ends. Both players need to cooperate to ensure that the ball passes through as many gaps as possible and lasts for a longer duration. After the game ends, children can retrieve blocks from the rotating device in the center to create various interesting patterns. The longer they persist, the more blocks they receive. Successful attachment of track modules or game completion will be accompanied by sound feedback prompts.

Fig. 1. Rendering of A-Rounding relay

The ball consists of three different colors (blue, yellow, and green), which, in a constant state of motion, effectively attract children's attention visually. During gameplay, children need to engage multiple sensory systems, including visual, tactile, auditory, and proprioceptive senses, to achieve the goals of sensory integration comprehensive training. Children are required to act only when the corresponding color light is illuminated, which helps them develop cognitive sequencing skills and reduces disorganization in their daily activities. Following instructions to complete actions and gradually forming self-directed behavior patterns helps improve children's self-control abilities and has been shown to lead to progress through training [11]. Cooperative gameplay for two players stimulates children's interest in playing and satisfies their social needs. The rotating blocks visually record the duration of the game and provide rewards to children at the end of the game.

Human-Computer Interaction Considerations. Based on the data from "GBIT 26158–2010 Human dimensions of Chinese minors," the 50th percentile dimensions for boys aged 4–6 are as follows: height 1113 mm, hand length 123 mm, hand width 59 mm, and for girls aged 4–6, height 1109 mm, hand length 122 mm, hand width 57 mm, shown in Fig. 2, 3.

Taking into account the above body dimensions, the following product dimensions have been designed to provide the optimal experience for children: the maximum dimensions of the toy body are 40 cm in length, 8 cm in height, and the handheld slider for children measures 7 cm in length, 4 cm in width, and 4 cm in thickness shown in Fig. 4.

Research showed that environments with yellow and blue significantly enhance the attention and detail capture abilities of children with ADHD [12]. Therefore, considering this conclusion, the decision to set the main colors of the toy body as yellow and blue was aimed at assisting children with ADHD in effectively capturing instructions and executing the action of adding track modules during gameplay.

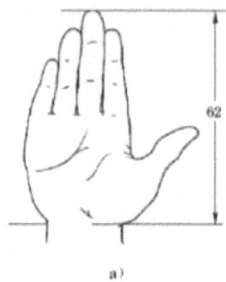 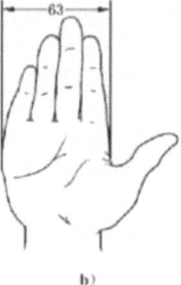

Fig. 2. Body Measurement Chart Including Hand length, hand width (GB/T 26158–2010)

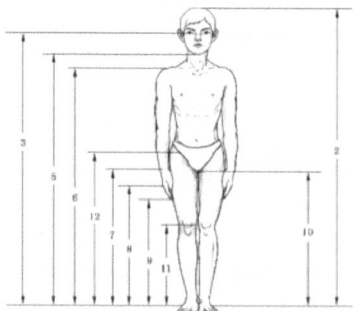

Fig. 3. Body Measurement Chart Including height, arm length, and other data (GB/T 26158–2010)

4   Usability Testing

4.1   Experimental Methodology

Serious games are designed and developed with a functional purpose, possessing dual attributes of entertainment and functionality. In the design and development process of serious games, it is crucial to assess and validate their effectiveness [13]. Rehabilitation training toys for children with ADHD in a home environment should provide effective therapeutic value, relieving symptoms after a period of use. Additionally, they should be enjoyable for children, providing a more relaxed and pleasant experience compared to other rehabilitation training tools. This project referenced usability testing methods from the serious games domain to design the experiment.

Common usability testing methods included think-aloud, interviews, and question-naires, among which think-aloud and interviews require higher language skills from children [14]. This experiment primarily utilized the System Usability Scale (SUS) for testing (Fig. 5), as initially developed by John Brooke in 1986. The SUS comprised 10 questions, covering three sub-scales: Satisfaction, Use Efficiency & Usability, and Effectiveness & Learnability. Odd-numbered items are positive statements, while even-numbered items are negative statements, rated on a 5-point scale (1 = strongly disagree to 5 = strongly agree). After scoring, the scores need to be converted: for odd-numbered

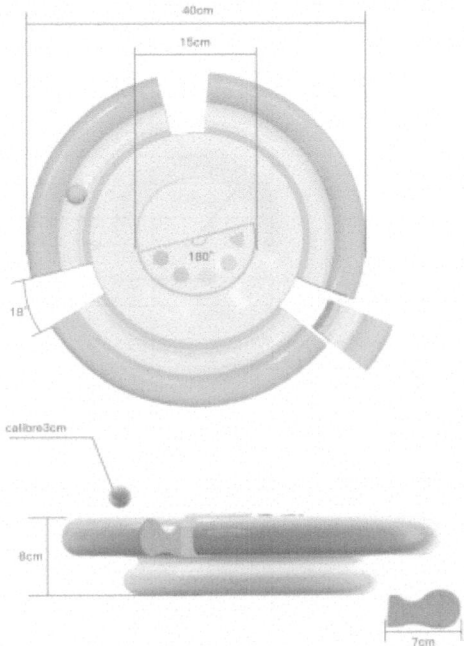

Fig. 4. Dimension drawing of A-rounding relay

questions, the converted score is the original score minus 1, and for even-numbered questions, the converted score is 5 minus the original score [15]. The converted scores of all questions are summed and multiplied by 2.5 to obtain the total SUS score. A score exceeding 70 is generally considered indicative of usability (Fig. 6).

Since a functional prototype had not yet been developed, we then used visual motion effects and product animations (Fig. 7) to test. Therefore, the main objective of this test was to assess the satisfaction levels of children with ADHD regarding the toy and their understanding of its gameplay. Furthermore, adjustments were made to the wording of the questionnaire based on children's comprehension abilities and cognitive levels, as shown in Fig. 8. Usability testing typically requires complementing with user interviews. Parents usually have some understanding of products for ADHD and are familiar with children's interests and the effects of using related products. Therefore, following the conclusion of the test, we conducted semi-structured interviews with parents to obtain specific recommendations for improving the product [15, 16].

4.2 Experimental Procedure and Results

In this experiment, a total of 5 children with ADHD and their parents were recruited. The children watched product demonstration animations with the assistance and guidance of experimenters while being accompanied by their parents. Subsequently, the

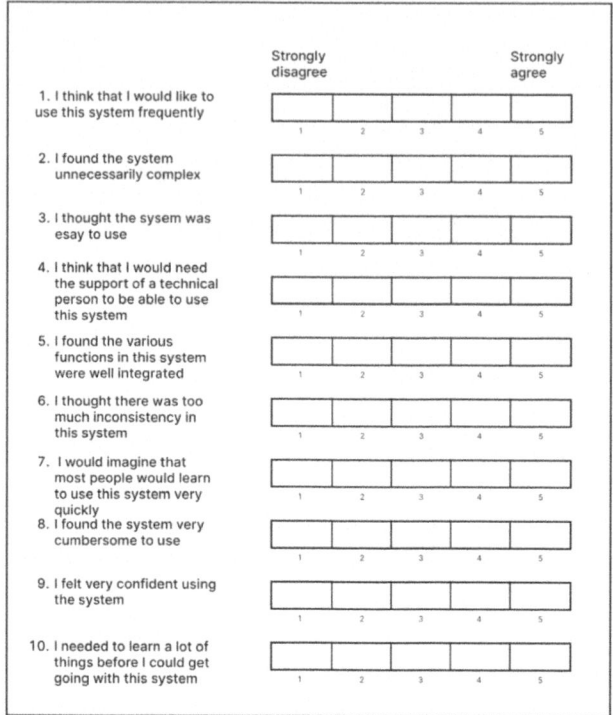

Fig. 5. SUS score

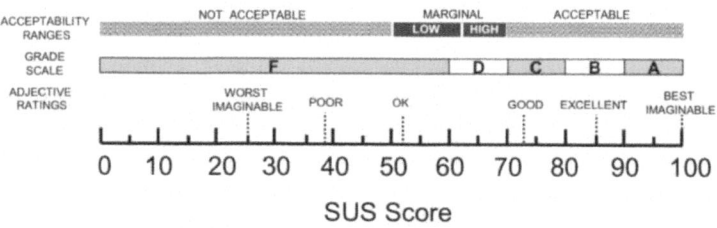

Fig. 6. A comparison of the adjective ratings, acceptability scores, and school grading scores in relation to the average SUS score

children were required to evaluate A-Rounding relay, and the experimenters' conducted interviews with the parents.

According to the aforementioned SUS calculation method, the usability assessment score table for this product is obtained (Fig. 9). The average score is 83.5, with a variance of 83.125. The SUS scores indicated excellent usability, supported by positive feedback from semi-structured interviews with parents. Most of them said that A-Rounding relay is helpful for children, especially those with sensory disorders. We also found that

Fig. 7. Product animation clips of A-Rounding relay

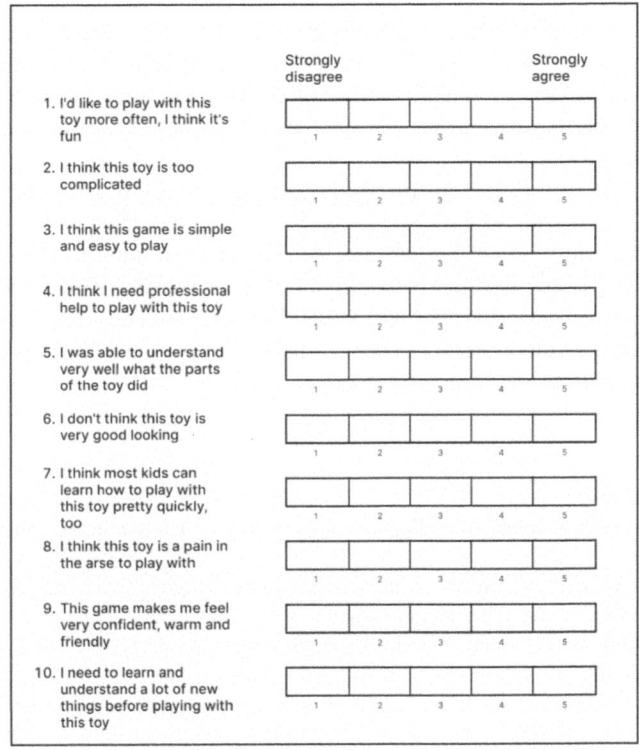

Fig. 8. SUS scale for describing improvements

children under the age of 6 are more likely to be interested in A-Rounding relay than older children. What's more, parental guidance in playing with the toys improves the effectiveness of training toys for children. The results of these interviews were highly informative for subsequent iterations of product features.

User	Q1	Q2	Q3	Q4	Q5	Q6	Q7	Q8	Q9	Q10	Final score
Child A	4	1	5	2	5	1	5	2	5	2	90
Child B	3	3	3	1	4	1	4	1	4	1	77.5
Child C	5	1	5	1	5	1	3	1	5	1	95
Child D	3	2	5	1	4	3	4	2	3	2	72.5
Child E	4	2	5	2	4	1	4	1	4	2	82.5

Fig. 9. Usability assessment score table

5   Conclusion and Future Work

This study made some progress in addressing the therapeutic needs of children with ADHD through the design and usability testing of home rehabilitation training toys. Integrating principles of sensory integration comprehensive training and human-computer interaction, A-Rounding relay offered an effective and enjoyable therapeutic tool for children with ADHD in home settings.

However, the usability test in this study focused solely on assessing the satisfaction level of children with ADHD regarding the product and their understanding of its gameplay mechanism. The effectiveness of the product in training was not investigated. In the future, we plan to develop a functional prototype using tools such as Arduino and three-dimensional printing. We will also utilize assessment tools from the ADHD medical field, such as the Schulte Grid, to continuously monitor changes in symptoms in children with ADHD after using the product.

References

1. Bitsko, R.H.: Mental health surveillance among children—United States, 2013–2019. **71**(2), 1–42 (2022)
2. Zentner, A.: Applied innovation: artificial intelligence in higher education (2022)
3. Danielson, M.L., et al.: State-level estimates of the prevalence of parent-reported ADHD diagnosis and treatment among US children and adolescents, 2016 to 2019. J. Atten. Disord. **26**(13), 1685–1697 (2022)
4. Muñoz, J.E., et al.: Design and creation of a BCI videogame to train sustained attention in children with ADHD. In: 2015 10th Computing Colombian Conference (10CCC). IEEE (2015)
5. Quinn, P.D., et al.: ADHD medication and substance-related problems. Am. J. Psychiatry **174**(9), 877–885 (2017)
6. Catalá-López, F., et al.: The pharmacological and non-pharmacological treatment of attention deficit hyperactivity disorder in children and adolescents: a systematic review with network meta-analyses of randomised trials. PLoS ONE **12**(7), e0180355 (2017)
7. Tamm, L., Nakonezny, P.A., Hughes, C.W.: An open trial of a metacognitive executive function training for young children with ADHD. J. Atten. Disord. **18**(6), 551–559 (2014)

8. Margraf, J., Schneider, S., Meinlschmidt, G.: Lehrbuch der verhaltenstherapie, vol. 3. Springer (2009). https://doi.org/10.1007/978-3-662-54911-7
9. Tzang, R.-F., et al.: Increased risk of developing psychiatric disorders in children with attention deficit and hyperactivity disorder (ADHD) receiving sensory integration therapy: a population-based cohort study. Eur. Child Adolescent Psychiatry **28**, 247–255 (2019)
10. Faramarzi, S., et al.: Effect of sensory integration training on executive functions of children with attention deficit hyperactivity disorder. **11**(1), 1–5 (2016)
11. Huang, W., Li, D.: Behavioral interventions for ADHD and their effectiveness. Adv. Soc. Sci. **1**(2), 37–48 (2012)
12. Duan, Y., Zhang, Y., Qiu, T.: The improvement of space textile color design on ADHD children's attention deficit behavior. Zhuangshi **6**, 124–126 (2022)
13. Zhang, J.: User experience design for cognitive screening of elderly based on serious game. Jiangnan University (2022)
14. Markopoulos, P., Bekker, M.: On the assessment of usability testing methods for children. Interact. Comput. **15**(2), 227–243 (2003)
15. Bangor, A., Kortum, P.T., Miller, J.T.: An empirical evaluation of the system usability scale. Int. J. Hum.-Comput. Interact. **24**(6), 574–594 (2008)
16. Wang, F.: Tangible Interaction Design of Children's Musical Toys based on Embodied Metaphor. Zhejiang Sci-tech University (2023)

Design for Older Adults

Navigating Ageing in Portuguese Transnational Families: The Role of Digital Technologies

Carlos Barros[✉] [iD] and Carla Ganito[iD]

Research Centre for Communication and Culture (CECC), Universidade Católica Portuguesa.
Palma de Cima, 1649-023 Lisboa, Portugal
{cbarros,carla.ganito}@ucp.pt

Abstract. Digital communication has an increasingly important role in relationships between members of transnational families since space tends to be resignified between the digital and the face-to-face as a way of maintaining relational dynamics. This paper presents qualitative research, conducted between the last quarter of 2022 and the first quarter of 2023, with Portuguese people who have adult children who have emigrated ($N = 20$). The results show us the importance of reflecting on the process of ageing in a transnational family, particularly considering the many challenges that digital technologies can enhance or create new ones, leading to an ambivalent situation.

Keyword: Transnational Families · Ageing · Digital Technologies

1 Introduction

Research into transnational families has recognised the impact of digital space on maintaining relational dynamics, since physical distance is a challenge to communication between the various members of these groups [3, 21]. In addition, research points to the importance of seeing care among the family group as multi-challenged, across sociocultural contexts and across borders, with members being both providers and recipients of support, where the digital context is part of the way distance is reinvented for presence [4, 10].

New forms of contact and presence are potentialized, as well as new challenges and risks that must be considered when understanding this relationship between family members, mediated by technologies – where tensions, ambivalence and new forms of interaction can naturally arise [6, 22]. The development of new interactions can challenge expectations and options throughout the life cycle, where family rituals can be reinvented and there is a greater accompaniment of adjustment dynamics in the face of stressful but expected phases (*e.g.* ageing; job transitions), but there can also be more ambivalent, whether in the use of digital tools or in the perception of what the frequency and intensity of interactions should be [6, 8].

Thomazini and Goulart [28] emphasize the need for careful reflection on the massive use of new information technologies in the family environment, namely by reducing direct (or physical) communication but promoting a communication channel between its members. However, it is necessary to think about the importance of these tools for families that are geographically distant. New information and communication technologies are particularly important in reducing physical distance since: "It is known that the changes brought about by the emergence of technology have been major and positive for society in the areas of communication, connection and social interaction." [25] (p. 78). In the same context, Bacigalupe and Parker [2] (p. 99) state that "although the use of ICT does not necessarily increase the migrants' desire to be present with their loved ones, it does activate the desire for a connection", being a form of dynamic 'activation' that can have various contours of cohesion, ambivalence or relational conflict.

A large part of intercultural communication turns to take place on the internet, and it is through this platform that forms of contact are created, since "the internet can be understood as a contact zone because it is a means of facilitating contact between different and geographically distant cultures, which would otherwise hardly be cultures in contact." [18] (p. 146). In fact, "the new means of mass communication give us an almost unlimited capacity to communicate, even geographical and cultural distances can now be reduced by technologies such as the internet (…)" [18] (p. 141).

In this context, the use of digital means plays an important role in maintaining family dynamics, especially for those in different countries. According to Bacigalupe and Parker [2] (p. 98), "information must flow through the family so that it can be significantly shared, evaluated, understood and utilized". McDevitt and Butler [23] underline the transformative role of these new technologies, which nurture the family system with new inputs that promote a re-signification of family dynamics over the course of a lifetime [7].

However, the fact is that transnational families benefit from new technologies to get closer to the *Other*, if only on a virtual level. It is in the attempt to be present, albeit virtually, that we can see a desire to connect with distant family members [3, 4].

In the Portuguese context, as a country with a long history of the social, economic, educational, political and psychological impact of migration, this aspect is particularly important, since Portugal is one of the European countries with the most emigrants [24] and with a very varied profile. In the last decade, with the *brain drain,* we have seen a confluence of different expectations, motivations and ways of connecting during migration processes. Emigrants now have more social capital (for example, from high levels of education and specialisation) and are trying to build their lives in such a way as to find their well-being in a new society where they are trying to integrate into work and social life [20].

These 'new' migrations suggest the importance of reflecting on cross-border dynamics, since these transnational family members can (with digital media) have continuous contact, reducing the generational gap and, at the same time, accompanying the adjustment challenges of those who have emigrated [6] as well as the ascending family figures who are left without support during ageing [8].

The challenge presented by the use of digital tools seems, firstly, to have an impact on the quality of relationships as a psychosocial construct; however, it is important to remember the individual impact that the use of these tools has, especially on ascending figures who have less digital literacy and skills. In an ageing society, where only the youngest age groups have been empowered by technology, it is important to create moments and ways of bridging intersectional vulnerabilities. The author Ganito [19] underlines the role of gender and elderly populations when it comes to (re)thinking the equal use of digital tools. In previous studies (*e.g.* Barros, Hanenberg & Santos [8]), we have seen that digital use in the family context becomes more difficult the older people get, but it is also more conducive to connection – whether with other family members who participate in the learning process, or with the social context where they seek training and social interactions.

This paper aims to focus on the meanings of ICT use in people over the age of + 45/50 years old, who live in Portugal and are the parental figures of young adult emigrants, considering the multidirectional impact of these transnational relationships. The main research questions are to:

a) How the impact of their digital environment increases the perception of belonging.
b) What are their uses of digital communication tools.

2 Methods

2.1 Participants, Instruments and Procedures

Using a qualitative approach, with snowball data collection, we interviewed Portuguese parents with adult children who had emigrated ($N = 20$). According to their self-identification, the majority were female ($n = 16$) and some were male ($n = 4$). Their ages ranged from 48 to 76 ($M = 60.83$; $SD = 9.15$).

The participants were invited to take part in the study through a website built for the purpose, which was publicised in various associations and organisations working on community issues in Portugal. The data was collected between the last quarter of 2022 and the first quarter of 2023.

For data collection, we used a script for individual semi-structured interviews, adapted from a previous study with adult children from similar transnational families [5, 6], to explore the perception of needs and adjustments to social realities in a post-constructivist strategy [16, 17].

Before the scripts were applied, they were discussed with experts on the topics to be developed ($n = 8$) and a focus group was held with people with identical profiles ($n = 7$) to ensure the rigor and appropriateness of the questions.

The interview script included seven main themes: *i)* characterization of the family; *ii)* motivations and cohesion in the transnational family; *iii)* maintaining the relationship with distance; iv) intergenerational support network; *v)* transmission of norms and values; *vi)* lifelong learning, namely how they manage ageing; and *vii)* how they perceive their psychological and social well-being.

All interviews were audio-recorded, transcribed and then the audios were destroyed, with the names of the participants and sensitive data changed to ensure confidentiality.

Before the interview, a brief socio-demographic questionnaire was administered.

2.2 Data Analysis

The data was codified in the *N-vivo* software (ed.14) and thematic analysis was carried out to explore the data and cross-check it with the previous literature by Charmaz [16, 17]. The sample size was based on the theoretical saturation of the N analysis.

To minimize bias, the collection and analysis of the data was analysed by the first author of the paper and discussed with the research team, to have a more reflexive and interdisciplinary approach to the phenomenon, from a post-constructivist perspective following Charmaz [15].

2.3 Ethical Issues

In accordance with the ethical principles of research, the project was approved by the Committee on Ethics in Technology, Social Sciences and Humanities (CETCH) of the Portuguese Catholic University, under reference CETCH2022–08. Also complies with the code of the American Psychological Association [1].

Informed consent was obtained from all subjects involved in the study.

3   Results and Discussion

To analyse and discuss in an integrated way, we opted for the presentation of results mediated by reflection and connection with the literature following Charmaz [16, 17] which allows us to co-construct applied social approaches.

3.1   Digital: New Perceptions of Belonging

The impact of digital means is recognised as high by all the participants, as they all report that it is a vital way of ensuring their connection with their emigrant children. As Lurdes (58-year-old woman) tells us:

"[...] distances are easily crossed with new technologies. With *WhatsApp*, especially, we're always in touch [...] of course it's never easy for all of us to be away, as parents we're always worried about her, but we take part in her life".

Curiously, the distance didn't minimise the strength of the relationships, instead, it gave new meaning to contact and presence, which corroborates the most recent literature on these topics (e.g. Baykara-Krumme & Fokkema, [9]; Barros, [6]; Mateia, [21]). Around half of the participants reported that they lived in ambivalence between what should be the appropriate time and content for their communication. However, they also indicated that they managed to mediate relationships by setting boundaries for themselves and their children, which improved their relationships. This is illustrated by an extract from the interview with Diana (53-year-old woman):

[…] I think our relationship has improved, in that respect it's improved, we're more… How can I put it… There's not so much mother and daughter, there are two more friends with a sense of family roles and she knows she can always count on me and I know that if I call her, I can also count on her […] we have a better sense of boundaries on both sides".

In the light of the most recent studies that indicate that space can not only be understood face-to-face, but also as a geography between the digital and the face-to-face with an impact on lives and the use of space (*e.g.* Shaw [26]), we found that the use of digital media not only has an impact on the family context, but also helps to connect with extra-family contexts with similar interests, promoting active ageing. As we illustrate with Fernanda's (61-year-old woman) narrative:

"The physical effects of getting older are more painful, as you start to feel a pain here and there, but my husband and I usually go hiking and we have a group of friends who get together and walk some of the trails there are here in the area. At least as long as our health allows, we intend to do that. [...] using social media has activated my connection with these people because that's where we organise walks, share tips and avoid the risks of our amateur sport".

Also, the beautiful narrative of Maria (71-year-old woman), referring to when she started volunteering to provide food support to vulnerable people, organised in *Facebook* groups:

"I don't want money; I don't want anyone to give me money. I want food, I want rice, I want pasta, I want sugar, I want milk. And why? Because I ask and here, I find the way to give my love to these people, since I can't give it any other way, I give a little bit of happiness and dignity. You don't know the joy I feel when I go to the house of a mum with five children to deliver a bag full of bread and cakes, where those children say to me, "Hey, do you have any Berlin balls?" [Portuguese popular sweet pastry]. You don't know the joy I feel, I feel like queen of the world because I've gone there to nurture a family who are waiting for me and who count on me as a friend".

This data makes us reflect on the psychosocial and systemic impact from the micro to the macrolevel, in which actions are interconnected and promote a learning environment that crosses the individual, their direct relationships (*i.e.* the family group), social and community relationships, to the specific cultural contexts where the subject is influenced, but also directly influenced by their behaviours [11–14].

3.2 Diverse Uses, Diverse Needs

The use of digital resources differs depending on whether it is for interpersonal communication or for participation in social networks. All the participants say that they contact their emigrant children on a daily or very frequent basis through messages and video calls on interpersonal communication apps (e.g., *Messenger* and *WhatsApp*).

Meanwhile, around three thirds of the participants indicated that they opened accounts on the social networks *Facebook* and *Instragram* to reduce the isolation and loneliness they felt when their children emigrated. These networks also serve today as a way of being involved in their children's lives through interaction on their *feeds*. Yet as a way of understanding some dynamics. Participant Inês (57-year-old woman) tells us:

"I have a shop selling handicrafts, when she [her daughter] sees handicrafts, she takes a photo and sends it to me on WhatsApp, which is why I say WhatsApp is marvellous. [...] Sometimes I'm on her Instagram and I see that she's sharing this and that and I think 'Well, ok, you're alive'. In this less private way, we can share with the world and also keep up with each other until we're only able to talk"

This dynamic subsequently seems to be extended to the various interactions and networks in which these people circulate, reflecting a relational behaviour similar to the perception of the group/individual similar to that with their children. An excerpt from Inês illustrates this behaviour:

"I think we're living in very complicated times in which selfishness, self-centredness, are undermining all that is social relationships and what is important, just look at social networks and the way people sometimes mistreat each other and don't see the other person's place. I'm in a group of travel lovers on Facebook, and I saw a lady just yesterday asking for help for twenty-five years of marriage and wanting a suggestion of a place where she could have an accessible meal celebration... You can't imagine how many people said to her "so it's twenty-five years and you're asking for an accessible restaurant?". Who knows how difficult it is for the lady? I've learnt from examples like this that it's better to send a private message than to reply in yet another comment."

The different uses – in one-to-one messaging/calling or participation in social networks, also alert us to the need to develop different learning and competencies in relation to digital tools. This is all more important when we refer to a social group that may, intersectionally, have less digital training.

According to researchers who explain the importance of understanding digital vulnerabilities, which are more pronounced in older people and take gender into account [19, 27], it is important to understand the use of digital technologies in different contexts throughout life, promoting appropriate learning for each context.

In this sense, we found that around a third of the participants, who are all retired and haven't had to use these tools in their jobs, find it more difficult to adapt digitally. However, several organisations are taking shape (*e.g.* senior universities, parish associations) that provide senior leisure and learning activities, which has greatly helped them to adapt. This is illustrated by the experience of Rita (62-year-old woman), a mum who tells us about the importance of learning and literacy networks in digital contexts, reflecting on her attendance at a senior university that offers ICT classes.

"I only joined now, I joined this year [...] I enrolled in English classes because I've always loved English, my father didn't let me continue studying when I was a kid. With my daughter moving to the United Kingdom, I was more quickly drawn to English and informatics, which is a new subject for me, and I really like it, I really enjoy being there, because I get to socialise with people my own age and others a bit older. [...] I learn and have fun with other people. Going to the senior university was fantastic!"

These findings point to the importance of reflecting on the impact of social actions that promote the development of competencies and, at the same time, enhance the perception of belonging and well-being. Ageing leads to a series of situations that have to be considered in the context of each person's resilience [19, 27] but it seems pertinent to consider transnational groups as examples of that connection and need for inclusion in diverse contexts [6, 9].

4   Conclusions

Although ageing is a global issue, along with globalisation and the phenomenon of transnational families, it seems increasingly important to highlight the role of digital communication technologies in both the family and social contexts.

In regards do our first research question of trying to understand how the impact of the digital environment of transnational families increases the perception of belonging for aging family members, we understood, that despite the fact that the less younger generations (starting with the over-50s) have less formal training in the use of digital tools, when part of transnational family contexts they end up having the support of other family members and/or community groups for digital training – which not only promotes their digital skills, but also ends up promoting attitudes of more interaction in less isolation.

As for our second research question about their uses of digital communication tools, it's important to note that different digital communication systems can have different uses and different contexts. That is: although flexible in its use, one-to-one interpersonal communication seems to take place on *Apps* that add chat functionality (e.g. *Whatsapp*), while non-direct communication, which can take place with extended family members or networks of friends, tends to take place on *Apps* with feeds (e.g. *Facebook*). In any case, we highlight the ability to socialise, moulded from the face-to-face reality, allowing navigation between a more or less private area of sharing.

In conclusion, digital environments seem to allow for a more accompanied perception of life cycle events, of which ageing is no exception, enabling connections to be made in various micro and macro-systemic networks.

5   Limitations and Suggestions for Future Studies

Although the study had a gender bias on data collection (which is usual in snowball sampling with theoretical saturation of themes), it did not allow us to analyse the impact of gender on the phenomenon under study. As such, we suggest the importance of continuing to collect data in order to triangulate information on the impact of vulnerabilities, in particular the gender and age of the participants.

Acknowledgments. To the participants in the study. To the collaborators at the research centers and faculties who provided logistical support at all times, namely CECC – Research Center for Communication and Culture. Finally, to the funding institutions that made it possible to explore the impact of science on the community. This article is an extract from the data collected during studies under a post-doctoral grant from the Portuguese Catholic University/PORTICUS, under reference GR-074770.

Disclosure of Interests. The authors have no competing interests to declare.

References

1. American Psychological Association. Ethics committee, rules and procedures (2018). https://www.apa.org/ethics/committee-rules-procedures-2018.pdf
2. Bacigalupe, G., Parker, K.: Conexões transnacionais através de tecnologias emergentes. Nova Perspectiva Sistêmica, **25**(56), 94–107 (2016). http://pepsic.bvsalud.org/pdf/nps/v25n56/n25a08.pdf
3. Baldassar, L.: Missing kin and longing to be together: emotions and the construction of co-presence in transnational relationships. J. Intercult. Stud. **29**(3), 247–266 (2008). https://doi.org/10.1080/07256860802169196
4. Baldassar, L., Merla, L.: Introduction: transnational family caregiving through the lens of circulation. In: Baldassar, L., Merla, L. (eds.) Transnational Families, Migration and the Circulation of Care: Understanding Mobility and Absence in Family Life, pp. 3–24. Routledge (2014)
5. Barros, C.: Famílias pelo Mundo: Solidariedade Intergeracional em Famílias Transnacionais [Families Around the World: Intergenerational Solidarity in Transnational Families.]. Doctoral Thesis. Faculdade de Psicologia da Universidade de Lisboa (2021). https://repositorio.ul.pt/handle/10451/50377
6. Barros, C.: Connection in transnational families. Presence between face-to-face and digital spaces in Portuguese Emigrants. Trends Psychol. (2023). https://doi.org/10.1007/s43076-023-00309-4
7. Barros, C., McGarrigle, J., Santos, A.S., Albert, I., Murdock, E.: Solidarity typologies in dynamics between portuguese emigrants and their parents. Human Arenas (2023). https://doi.org/10.1007/s42087-023-00368-0
8. Barros, C., Hanenberg, P., Santos, A.S.: Reframing Relational Space: Migration From The Perspective of Those 'Who Stay'. Hum. Arenas (2024). https://doi.org/10.1007/s42087-024-00403-8
9. Baykara-Krumme, H., Fokkema, T.: The impact of migration on intergenerational solidarity types. J. Ethn. Migr. Stud. **45**(10), 1707–1727 (2019). https://doi.org/10.1080/1369183X.2018.1485203
10. Bryceson, D.F.: Transnational families negotiating migration and care life cycles across nation-state borders. J. Ethn. Migr. Stud. **45**(16), 3042–3064 (2019). https://doi.org/10.1080/1369183X.2018.1547017
11. Bronfenbrenner, U.: Toward an experimental ecology of human development. Am. Psychol. **32**(7), 513–531 (1977). https://doi.org/10.1037/0003-066X.32.7.513
12. Bronfenbrenner, U.: The ecology of human development: experiments by nature and design. Harvard University Press (1979)
13. Bronfenbrenner, U.: Ecology of the family as a context for human development: research perspectives. Dev. Psychol. **22**(6), 723–742 (1986). https://doi.org/10.1037/0012-1649.22.6.723
14. Bronfenbrenner, U.: Making human beings human: biological perspectives on human development. Sage Publications (2005)
15. Charmaz, K.: Constructing grounded theory: a practical guide through qualitative analysis. Sage (2006)
16. Charmaz, K.: Constructionism and the grounded theory method. In: Holstein, J.A., Gubrium, J.F. (eds.) Handbook of Constructionist Research, pp. 397–412. The Guildford Press (2008)
17. Charmaz, K.: The construction of grounded theory: a practical guide to qualitative analysis. Artmed (2009)

18. Ferreira, C.: Identidades lusófonas em rede: importância da internet na relação dos emigrantes portugueses nos EUA com a cultura de origem. Anuário Internacional de Comunicação Lusófona 2009 (2009). https://core.ac.uk/download/pdf/229414638.pdf

19. Ganito, C.: Gendering old age: the role of mobile phones in the experience of aging for women. In: Human Aspects of IT for the Aged Population. Acceptance, Communication and Participation: 4th International Conference, ITAP 2018, Held as Part of HCI International 2018, Las Vegas, NV, USA, July 15–20, 2018, Proceedings, Part I 4 (pp. 40–51). Springer International Publishing (2018). https://doi.org/10.1007/978-3-319-92034-4_4

20. Gomes, R.M.: Fuga de cérebros: Retratos da emigração portuguesa qualificada. Bertrand Editora (2015)

21. Mateia, E.K.: O Impacto das novas tecnologias de informação e comunicação na família contemporânea: Um estudo sobre as «relações entre pais e filhos. [The impact of new information and communication technologies on the contemporary family: A study on the relationship between parents and children]. Master's dissertation, Universidade do Porto. Open Repository of the University of Porto (2018). https://repositorio-aberto.up.pt/handle/10216/117349

22. Matusitz, J., Musambira, G.: Power distance, uncertainty avoidance, and technology: analyzing Hofstede's dimensions and human development indicators. J. Technol. Hum. Serv. 31(1), 42–60 (2013). https://doi.org/10.1080/15228835.2012.738561

23. McDevitt, M., Butler, M.: Latino youth as information leaders: Implications for family interaction and civic engagement in immigrant communities. InterActions: UCLA J. Educ. Inf. Stud. 7(2) (2011). https://doi.org/10.5070/D472000698

24. Pires, R.P., Vidigal, I., Pereira, C., Azevedo, J., Veiga, C.M.: Emigração Portuguesa 2022: Relatório Estatístico [Portuguese Emigration 2022: Statistical Report]. Observatório da Emigração e Rede Migra, CIES-Iscte (2022). http://hdl.handle.net/10071/27896

25. Oliveira, C.: TIC'S na educação: A utilização das tecnologias da informação e comunicação na aprendizagem do aluno [ICT in education: the use of information and communication technologies in student learning]. Pedagogia em Ação, 7(1) (2015). https://periodicos.puc minas.br/index.php/pedagogiacao/article/view/11019/8864

26. Shaw, S.L.: Time geography in a hybrid physical–virtual world. J. Geogr. Syst. 25, 339–356 (2023). https://doi.org/10.1007/s10109-023-00407-y

27. Taipale, S., Wilska, T.A., Gilleard, C. (Eds.): Digital Technologies and Generational Identity: ICT Usage Across the Life Course. Routledge (2017)

28. Thomazini, M.G., Goulart, E.E.: Tecnologias móveis e relações interpessoais [Mobile technology and interpersonal relations]. Revista Educação Em Questão 56(49) (2018). https://doi.org/10.21680/1981-1802.2018v56n49ID14464

Learning Curve and Acceptability for Immersive VR Exergame Intervention Among Community-Dwelling Elderly Individuals in Shanghai: A Pilot Study

Jing Cao[1], Ling Yue[2], Siming Li[1], and Zhiqiang Wu[1(✉)]

[1] College of Design and Innovation, Tongji University, Shanghai, China
wus@tongji.edu.cn
[2] Shanghai Mental Health Center, Shanghai, China

Abstract.

Background: With the increasing prevalence of cognitive impairments among the elderly, such as mild cognitive impairment (MCI), finding effective interventions to enhance cognitive and physical function is crucial. Virtual reality (VR) exergames have emerged as a promising tool for this purpose, offering a combination of physical exercise and cognitive stimulation. However, little is known about the acceptance among community-dwelling elderly individuals, particularly those with cognitive impairments.

Method: This study recruited 8 cognitively normal (NC) and 23 individuals with mild cognitive impairment (MCI) elderly people, using MoCA assessment to ensure the representativeness of the sample. The study adopted the commercially available immersive VR game "The Lab," designed with exercise tasks including dog walking, mountain climbing, and drone protection. Participants were assessed on their willingness to engage in VR exergames and their performance was evaluated through multidimensional assessment and learning curve analysis.

Results: The study showed an average SUS score of 73.45, reflecting a good overall usability evaluation. Among the 29 valid samples, 72% of individuals expressed their willingness to continue using the system. Learning curve analysis revealed the elderly users' adaptation and learning efficiency towards VR technology. The study found significant differences($p < 0.01$) in the need for technical support between the NC and MCI groups, with the MCI group requiring more assistance. Furthermore, a notable difference ($p < 0.01$) was observed in game performance between the Low Willingness Group(N = 8) and High willingness groups(N = 21), with the latter demonstrating superior skills. Although NC group slightly surpassed MCI group in Game performance, this difference was not statistically significant. Remarkably, some MCI elderly individuals demonstrated learning enthusiasm and game performance comparable to those in the NC group.

Conclusion: This study is empirically investigating the acceptance of commercial VR exergames among community-dwelling elderly in Shanghai, with a focus on individuals with cognitive impairments. The findings reveal that VR exergames with adaptive difficulty adjustments, rich content provide good freedom and kinematic richness for the elderly, stimulating the complementary advantages of brain and physical intelligence. While some elderly individuals, particularly those with MCI, may require additional support, the study demonstrates the potential of VR exergames to provide inclusive services for elderly people with varying cognitive abilities. Importantly, the study highlights the need to enhance the health affordances of current exergame media to ensure that all elderly individuals can fully perceive and benefit from the health benefits of these games. This research provides preliminary data support for optimizing community digital health services and more effectively meeting the health needs of future elderly populations.

Keywords: Immersive VR · Exergame · Motor Learning Curve · Acceptability

1 Introduction

1.1 Research Background

Policy Support: Healthy Aging. The China aging development report (2024) forecasts that by 2030, seniors aged 65 and above will make up over 20% of the population, marking China's transition into a deeply aging society [1]. In response, the "14th Five-Year National Health Plan" [2] details strategies for citizen health monitoring and intervention, anticipating the health service industry's value to surpass 11.5 trillion yuan by 2035. The plan focuses on nationwide fitness and comprehensive elderly health assurance, aiming for over 65% of elderly individuals to have access to standardized health management services by 2025, through collaboration with medical institutions to boost preventive healthcare and health literacy.

User Characteristics: Shrinking Population and Service Shortage. Shanghai, a metropolitan city, was the first city in China to enter the aging society and is a large city with the highest degree of aging in China. According to the Shanghai's "2022 Elderly Population and Cause Monitoring Statistical Information" [3] reveals that 36.8% of its registered household population is aged 60 and above. This demographic shift underscores workforce shrinkage and aging population challenges. Alzheimer's disease and cognitive impairments are key health risks for the elderly [4, 5], highlighting the need for improved brain health and fall prevention strategies. Physical activity is recognized as essential for promoting healthy aging [6].

1.2 Bottlenecks in the Socialization of Virtual Reality Exergames for the Aged

Little Research on the Feasibility, Acceptability, and Potential Benefits. VR exergames are advancing as key tools for elderly entertainment and rehabilitation, combining physical and cognitive training to enhance the well-being of older adults [7, 8]. They have the potential to motivate seniors in daily care centers to adopt healthier, more active lifestyles [9]. However, the feasibility and acceptance of VR exergames in community or home settings for community-dwelling elderly remain understudied [10]. The effectiveness of VR in rehabilitation hinges on optimizing user experience to minimize dropouts, underscoring the necessity for high usability in these systems [11]. While some studies have focused on intervention methods [12, 19] and assessed effectiveness through pre- and post-intervention measures [6, 18], there is a gap in game performance evaluation and multidimensional data analysis, especially concerning the usability perceptions of cognitively impaired elderly who may have difficulty with self-reported questionnaires [13].

Limiting the Applicability of Research Findings for Design Practice. The integration of age-related declines in sensory, cognitive, and motor abilities into the design of virtual reality (VR) interactions presents a significant challenge. As individuals age, these declines can profoundly impact their capacity to adapt to and interact within VR environments, affecting their learning trajectory and overall proficiency with VR technologies. Despite the clear need, there is a notable scarcity of experimental studies that explore the influence of these perceptual abilities on user interaction behavior, which are critical for informing design considerations [14]. Furthermore, there is a significant gap in empirical data regarding the specific impact of age-related cognitive changes on performance in virtual tasks. Gaining an understanding of these data is essential for the development and refinement of design applications that are better equipped to serve the unique needs of the elderly population.

Anthropological Representation Concerns. Existing research exhibits biases in sample size [6, 10, 15–19], gender [6], and regional distribution [9, 10, 15], reducing its local applicability in China. The exclusion of elderly individuals with cognitive impairments in usability studies [6, 17, 18] may restrict the generalizability of findings, ignoring the unique challenges faced by this population in physical activity and motor learning.

Conclusion. The lack of research on the learning curve and acceptability of immersive VR interventions for the elderly brings uncertainty to the effectiveness of community promotion and the quality of sustainable services. Current research is insufficient for establishing a systematic design methodology for elderly-oriented exergames, particularly for those with mild cognitive decline.

1.3   Research Aim

Research Objective and Cooperation. This study aims to investigate the usability of VR games among elderly users, ensuring that the games are user-friendly and meet the elderly's needs. By incorporating learning curve, game performance evaluation and multidimensional data analysis, we seek to gain a more accurate understanding of the elderly users' experience and requirements. Investigation of the acceptability and explore the feasibility of providing cost-effective daily digital health services to elderly residents in Shanghai's communities through commercial virtual reality (VR) exercise games in collaboration with medical institutions and community centers.

Research Question

1. What differences exist in the acceptance and usability feedback of virtual reality technology as a potential low-cost intervention between elderly populations with mild cognitive impairment (MCI), and those with normal cognition (NC)?

2. Do significant differences exist in learning curves and performance outcomes in virtual reality games between elderly individuals with MCI and NC, as assessed by Montreal Cognitive Assessment (MoCA) scores?
3. Are there any differences in the preferences of elderly individuals for virtual game content, specifically regarding affinity for animal-related, nature-oriented, and competitive sports content?

2 Method

2.1 Participant Selection

From October to December 2023, in collaboration with the Shanghai Mental Health Center, this study recruited 31 community-dwelling elderly volunteers from the participants of Shanghai Brain Aging Study (www.shanghaibrainagingstudy.org), providing a targeted and representative sample. Participants underwent the Montreal Cognitive Assessment (MoCA), with 23 scoring 15 to 25 classified as mild cognitive impairment (MCI) and 8 scoring 26 to 30 considered cognitively normal (NC).

2.2 Game Selection Process

The research team curated games from Steam, adhering to criteria such as being free, offering immersive VR, exceeding 2000 user reviews, and having a "Very Positive" review summary. From the top-ranked games post-review rating, "The Lab" [20], App No.450390, was selected for its 0.94 recommend rate and "Very Positive" reviews from 6077 players since its 2016 release.

2.3 Statistical methods

The group differences of continuous variables were compared using t-test, and those of categorical variables with chi-square test/Fisher's exact test. RStudio R.4.2.1 and SPSS 16.0 statistical software was used to analyze the relevant data. Differences were considered statistically significant when $p < 0.05$.

2.4 Design of Physical and Mental Training Tasks Based on Commercial Games

Dog Walking and Play Segment. Participants are required to locate and pick up wooden sticks from the ground, engaging in play with a virtual dog by shaking or throwing the sticks. This involves squatting or lateral stretching, finger grasping, and rotational movements of the neck and elbow to swing and throw the arms.

Mountain Climbing and Sightseeing Segment. Participants use a controller interface to search for positioning points, plan climbing routes, and virtually climb mountains and enjoy the view from the summit, utilizing rotational movements of the neck, elbow, and whole body.

Fig. 1. In accordance with guidelines for physical exercising by organizations such as the WHO [5], we designed three physical and mental exercise segments based the content of The Lab.

Drone Protection and Shooting Game Segment. "Drone Protection," a 3D shooting competition game, requires participants to rotate the neck, elbow, and whole body while standing, shift weight, move in multiple directions, squat, and stretch laterally to enhance hand-eye coordination speed and accuracy during the defense and attack switch against multiple projectiles (Figs 1, 2, 3, 4 and 5).

2.5 Experimental Procedure Design

The study's protocol is meticulously organized into three phases: preliminary introduction, formal experimentation, and post-experimental interview.

1. Preliminary Introduction: 5 min

Participants receive a comprehensive briefing on the full-process audio and video recording. They sign an informed consent form and are screened for health risks, including heart disease, stroke, or fractures within the past six months. Prior virtual reality experience is also assessed. The experimental setup, including the computer, HTC VIVE controllers, and headset, is introduced to ensure participants understand their operation.

2. Formal Experimentation: 15–25 min

Environmental Introduction and Practice. After equipping participants with the gear, they are introduced to The Lab's environment. Basic controller actions like fist clenching and movement are demonstrated. Participants must complete two independent displacements to verify proficiency.

Task Instruction and Assessment. Participants progress through three detailed task scenarios. An initial comprehensive orientation checks for adverse reactions. Researchers then demonstrate task rules and standards, conducting a practice trial. In the formal assessment, verbal cues guide participants, with feedback provided after each attempt and a check on their willingness to proceed.

3. Post-Experimental Interview: 20 min

After the conclusion of the experiment, an in-depth interview session is conducted. Researchers initially request participants to recount and describe the scenarios, content, operation methods, and gameplay of the task segments. In cases of forgotten, researchers would assist participants to recall the memory. Subsequently, a semi-structured interview

1.Wearing devices   2.Practicing virtual handshakes   3.Practicing virtual displacement

Fig. 2. After equipping participants with the gear, they are introduced to The Lab's environment. Basic controller actions like fist clenching and movement are demonstrated. Participants must complete two independent displacements to verify proficiency.

format is employed to gain insights into participants' perceptions and opinions regarding their gaming experience.

2.6 Data Collection and Analysis

Interview and Questionnaires. This study uses an expanded SUS [14] with TAM [18] to assess game usability and acceptance, exploring dimensions like usefulness, ease of use, enjoyment, community use willingness, and self-efficacy in daily fitness. The SUS's limitation is its mix of affirmative and negative phrased items [21]. To address potential self-report challenges for elderly with cognitive impairments, an interview-based survey method is employed, enhancing data reliability by understanding participants' scoring logic. Questions Q5 to Q14 are rated on a 0 ("totally disagree") to 4 ("totally agree") scale, with a maximum sum of 40, then multiplied by 2.5 to scale the score from 0 to 100. A SUS score of 72.5 or above is good, and over 85.0 is excellent, indicating high user satisfaction [13, 22].

Data Collection, Analysis, and Quality Control. The experiment is fully recorded audio-visually for data traceability. A single researcher provides consistent instructional guidance. The team sets unified rules for data organization, cleansing, and coding, with pre-coding and discussions to refine procedures. Two researchers code the data independently, followed by statistical analysis and visualization of the synthesized results.

3   Result

3.1   Overview (See Table 1 for Details)

Two seniors withdrew after the first dog walking task due to sickness. The study included 29 participants (10 males, 34%; 19 females, 66%), divided into Normal Cognition (NC, n = 7) and Mild Cognitive Impairment (MCI, n = 22) groups. The average age was 69.74 years (M), SD 5.94; average education was 10.97 years (M), SD 2.82. SUS.

Table 1. Interview Data Overview

Interview Data Overview	Score Average ± Score Difference		
	All Subject (N = 29)	NC Group (N = 7)	MCI Group(N = 22)
Q0Gender	0.66 ± 0.48	0.57 ± 0.53	0.68 ± 0.48
Q1Age	69.74 ± 5.941	70.00 ± 7.16	69.23 ± 5.63
Q2Education	10.97 ± 2.82	12.29 ± 2.69	10.55 ± 2.79
Q3Moca Score	23.10 ± 3.33	27.29 ± 1.11	21.77 ± 2.60
Q4SUS Score	73.45 ± 14.31	81.07 ± 9.23	71.02 ± 14.93
Q5I think that I would like to use this exergame platform frequently in the community	2.79 ± 1.35	3.00 ± 1.00	2.73 ± 1.45
Q6I found the exergame platform unnecessarily complex	3.41 ± 0.98	3.57 ± 0.53	3.36 ± 1.09
Q7I thought the exergame platform was ease to use	3.24 ± 0.69	3.57 ± 0.53	3.14 ± 0.71
Q8I think that I would need the support of a technical person to be able to use this exergame platform	2.17 ± 1.28	3.14 ± 0.69	1.86 ± 1.28
Q9I found the various functions in this exergame platform ware well integrated	3.38 ± 0.62	3.14 ± 0.69	3.45 ± 0.60
Q10I thought there was too much inconsistency in this exergame platform	3.10 ± 0.56	3.14 ± 0.69	3.09 ± 0.53
Q11I would imagine that most elderly people would learn to use this exergame platform very quickly	1.83 ± 1.31	2.29 ± 0.95	1.68 ± 1.39
Q12I thought the exergame platform was cumbersome to use	3.52 ± 0.69	3.71 ± 0.49	3.45 ± 0.74
Q13I felt very confident using the exergame platform	3.38 ± 0.90	3.57 ± 0.53	3.32 ± 0.99

(continued)

Table 1. (*continued*)

Interview Data Overview	Score Average ± Score Difference		
	All Subject (N = 29)	NC Group (N = 7)	MCI Group(N = 22)
Q14I needed to learn a lot of things before I could get going with this exergame platform	2.55 ± 1.21	3.29 ± 1.11	2.32 ± 1.17
Q15 level of perceived pleasure of the dog walking exergame	2.48 ± 0.78	2.29 ± 0.49	2.55 ± 0.86
Q16level of perceived pleasure of the climbing exergame	2.34 ± 0.90	2.29 ± 0.49	2.36 ± 1.00
Q17 level of perceived pleasure of drone exergame	3.52 ± 0.57	3.86 ± 0.38	3.41 ± 0.59
Q18I feel a sense of accomplishment after completing this exergame training	2.62 ± 1.42	2.43 ± 1.51	2.68 ± 1.43
Q19I found the exergame training challenging	2.72 ± 0.80	2.86 ± 1.07	2.68 ± 0.72
Q20Daily exercise gives me a strong sense of health self-efficacy	3.31 ± 0.76	3.14 ± 0.90	3.36 ± 0.73

scores averaged 73.45 (M = 73.45, SD = 14.31) overall; NC scored 81.7 (M = 81.7, SD = 9.23), and MCI scored 71.02 (M = 71.02, SD = 14.93), showing positive usability. Questions Q6 to Q13 aligned with SUS, with both groups scoring over 3, indicating agreement. (see Table 1 for details).

Key issues affecting SUS scores included: Question 5 on future community technology use, with an overall score (2.79 ± 1.35); NC (3.00 ± 1.00) more proactive than MCI (2.73 ± 1.45). Question 8 on technical support needed a significant difference (p = 0.03), NC (3.14 ± 0.69) less than MCI (1.86 ± 1.28). Question 11 on quick learning received negative scores, NC (2.29 ± 0.95) and MCI (1.68 ± 1.30). Question 14 on pre-game learning showed cognitive load perception differences, NC (3.29 ± 1.11), MCI (2.32 ± 1.17). NC group has a higher acceptance of cognitive load.

Drone protection (Q17) scored high in enjoyment (3.52 ± 0.57), while mountain climbing (Q16) was lower (2.34 ± 0.90). Achievement (Q18) and challenge (Q19) scores were weakly positive, especially for NC's achievement (2.43 ± 1.51), with a large SD indicating disagreement. Health self-efficacy in daily life (Q20) was positively viewed by all, scoring (3.31 ± 0.76).

3.2 Willingness and SUS (See Table 2 for Details)

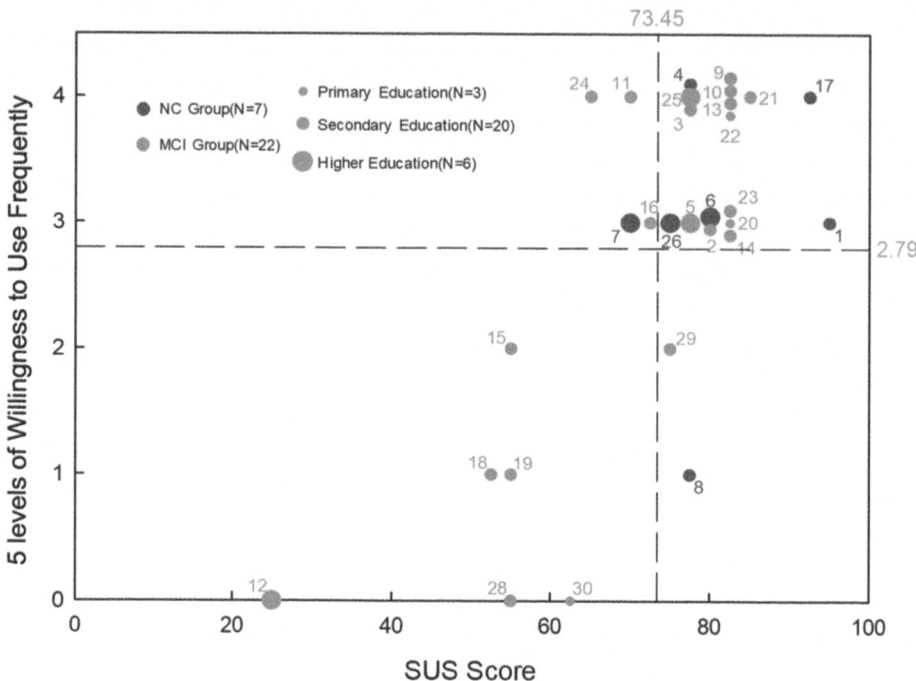

Fig. 3. Using a scatter plot with " Willingness Intention Total Score" and "SUS Total Score," the study categorized elderly users into three groups: High Willingness and High SUS Scoring Elderly (N = 17, Q4 "SUS score" = 82.06 ± 5.17, Q5 "Using Willingness in the community" = 3.53 ± 0.51), who showed strong technology use intentions and high SUS approval. High Willingness and Low SUS Scoring Elderly (N = 4, Q4 = 68.13 ± 5.5, Q5 = 3.50 ± 0.58) had above-average use intentions but below-average SUS scores, suggesting reservations in their approval of the technology. Low Willingness Elderly (N = 8, Q4 = 59.06 ± 16.7, Q5 = 0.88 ± 0.83) had the lowest scores in use intentions and relatively lower SUS, showing a general disinterest and lack of approval for the technology.

Low Willingness Group (Below Average = 2.79, N = 8). This Group provided lowest evaluation for Q8 Technical Support," = 1.25 ± 1.49, Q11 "Learnability for the Elderly" = 1.00 ± 1.31, Q14 "Cognitive Load" = 1.88 ± 1.25, highest evaluation for Q19"sense of challenge" = 3.00 ± 0.76, which show a pessimistic attitude towards the future use of the elderly.

Reasons. A) Functional decline (No.8,12,15,18,19): With reduced physical function, going to community centers to use technology becomes inconvenient. b) Psychological constraints (No.12,15,28): Facing a sense of mortality, elderly individuals tend to avoid crowds and prefer solitude. c) High substitutability (No.29,30): Preferring to exercise in real-life daily scenarios. d) Multiple residences (No.29): Inability to ensure long-term residence and consistent use. Use of the technology.

Table 2. Willingness /SUS Group data Overview

	Low Willingness (Below Average = 2.79, N = 8)									High Willingness with Low SUS Score(N = 4)					High Will High SUS (N = 17)
	N8	N12	N15	N18	N19	N28	N29	N30	SA ± SD	N7	N11	N16	N24	SA ± SD	SA ± SD
	F	M	F	F	F	F	F	F		F	F	M	F		
Q0	1	0	2	1	1	0	2	0	0.88 ± 0.35	3	4	3	4	0.75 ± 0.50	0.53 ± 0.51
Q1	73	82	76	68	69	65	72	73	72.25 ± 5.23	60	69	66	71	66.50 ± 4.80	68.76 ± 6.18
Q2	9	15	9	12	12	12	9	6	10.50 ± 2.78	13	12	9	12	11.50 ± 1.73	11.06 ± 3.13
Q3	26	21	24	25	17	20	25	18	22.00 ± 3.46	28	23	22	21	23.50 ± 3.11	23.53 ± 3.39
Q4	77.5	25	55	52.5	55	63	75	70	59.06 ± 16.74	70	70	72.5	60	68.13 ± 5.54	82.06 ± 5.17
Q5	1	0	2	1	1	0	2	0	0.88 ± 0.83	3	4	3	4	3.50 ± 0.58	3.53 ± 0.51
Q6	4	0	3	4	1	3	4	4	2.88 ± 1.55	3	4	4	2	3.25 ± 0.96	3.71 ± 0.47
Q7	3	3	3	2	3	2	4	3	2.88 ± 0.64	3	4	3	3	3.25 ± 0.50	3.41 ± 0.71
Q8	3	0	1	0	1	1	4	0	1.25 ± 1.49	4	0	1	2	1.75 ± 1.71	2.71 ± 0.77
Q9	2	2	3	3	4	4	4	4	3.25 ± 0.89	3	4	4	3	3.50 ± 0.58	3.41 ± 0.51
Q10	4	3	3	3	3	2	3	3	3.00 ± 0.53	3	2	3	3	2.75 ± 0.50	3.24 ± 0.56
Q11	3	0	0	1	3	0	0	1	1.00 ± 1.31	2	0	3	0	1.25 ± 1.50	2.35 ± 1.06
Q12	4	2	2	2	3	4	4	3	3.00 ± 0.93	3	4	4	3	3.50 ± 0.58	3.76 ± 0.44
Q13	4	0	2	4	2	3	4	4	2.88 ± 1.46	3	4	3	3	3.25 ± 0.50	3.65 ± 0.49
Q14	3	0	3	1	1	3	1	3	1.88 ± 1.25	1	2	1	3	1.75 ± 0.96	3.06 ± 1.03
Q15	2	1	2	3	3	3	2	4	2.50 ± 0.93	3	2	2	3	2.50 ± 0.58	2.47 ± 0.80
Q16	2	1	1	3	3	2	2	4	2.25 ± 1.04	3	3	2	3	2.75 ± 0.50	2.29 ± 0.92
Q17	4	2	3	3	3	3	3	4	3.13 ± 0.64	4	4	4	3	3.75 ± 0.50	3.65 ± 0.49
Q18	4	0	1	4	3	1	4	4	2.63 ± 1.69	4	4	3	2	3.25 ± 0.96	2.47 ± 1.42
Q19	4	2	3	3	2	3	3	4	3.00 ± 0.76	3	4	2	2	2.75 ± 0.96	2.59 ± 0.80
Q20	2	3	3	4	3	3	3	3	3.00 ± 0.53	2	4	4	4	3.50 ± 1.00	3.41 ± 0.80

High Willingness but Low SUS Group (N = 4). This group rated lower SUS Score (=68.13 ± 5.54), mainly reflecting negative evaluations for Q8(=1.75 ± 1.71), Q11(=1.25 ± 1.5), Q14(=1.75 ± 0.96), indicating they still face challenges in its usability.

Reasons. Aligning with the "Meaningful Experience"[23] framework proposed by Elisa et al. (2019): a) "Connectivity" with their daily life and cognitive background. b) Clarity in achieving health promotion "goals." c) "Coherence" in the integration of health intervention systems. d) Intuitive "resonance" that inspires competence, confidence, and pleasure. e) Recognition of the "meaning" and health value in frequent.

3.3   Drone Protection and Shooting Game Segment

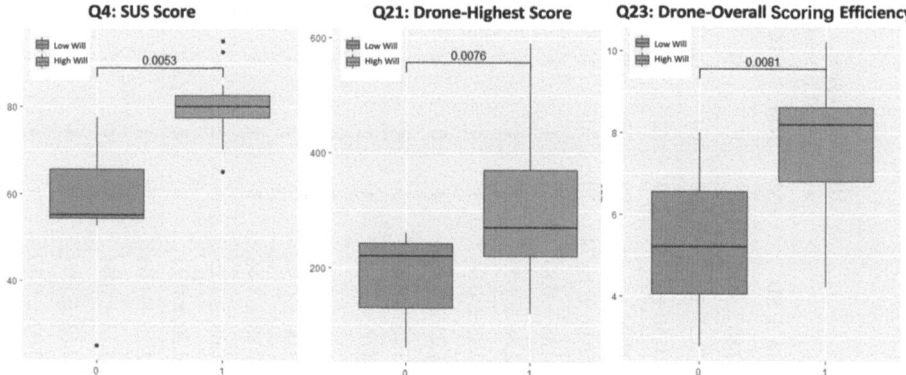

Fig. 4. Statistical analysis (see Table 3 for details) revealed significant differences between the Low Willingness Group(N = 8) and High willingness groups(N = 21) in three specific metrics: the SUS Total Score (p = 0.0053), Q21: Drone-Highest Score (p = 0.0076), and Q23: Drone-Overall Scoring Efficiency (p = 0.0081). Groups with low score for SUS and willingness perform worse in game scores of Drone Protection.

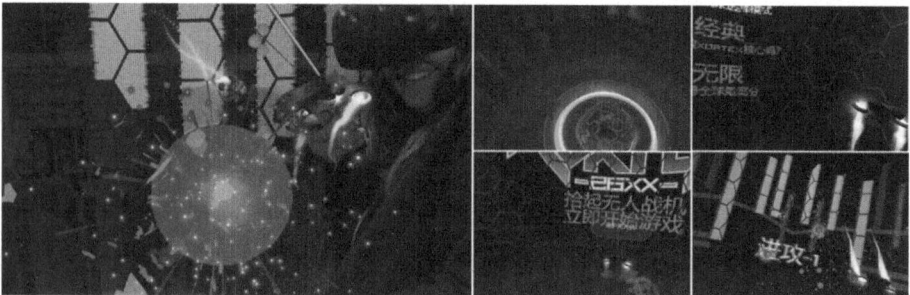

Fig. 5. Drone Protection Task Gameplay: Players must destroy enemy projectiles within a time limit while evading attacks, ending if their drone is hit. Points are scored by eliminating enemy fire, with efficiency boosted by strategic drone maneuvering for prolonged gameplay.

Visualization Analysis of Senior Participants' Performance
XXX

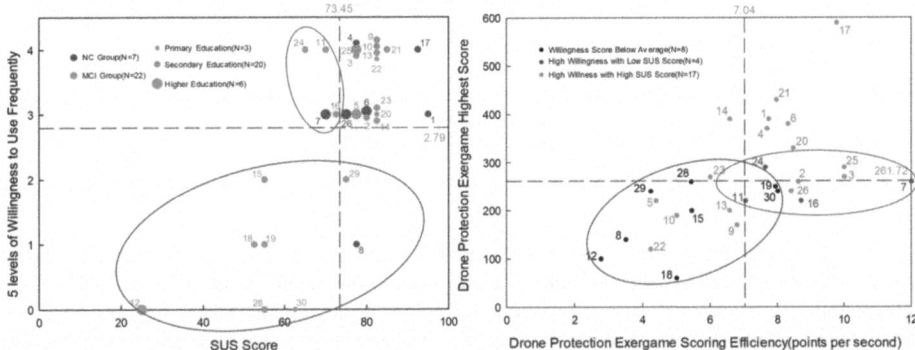

Fig. 6. A scatter plot analysis of highest scores and overall scoring efficiency in the drone task: show three main quadrant distributions. High Will and High SUS participants (green dots) excelled, taking down more projectiles and enduring longer, demonstrating superior gaming abilities. The Low Will group (N = 8, black dots) in the third quadrant had lower success rates, resulting in poor defense and rapid drone loss. Conversely, the High Will but Low SUS group (N = 4, blue dots), spread between the first and fourth quadrants, had average peak scores, indicating scoring efficiency despite facing quick defensive failures.

MCI and NC Learning Curve. In the drone protection task, elderly participants showed notable learning enthusiasm. After instruction, 13 seniors (45%) made three or more attempts; however, 5 seniors (17%, including 2 from the Low Will groups) only tried once. The Cognitively Normal (NC) group slightly surpassed the Mild Cognitive Impairment (MCI) group in score and efficiency, but not significantly. (See Table 3 for details).

The Low Willingness group struggled with gameplay understanding, underperforming. This included one-time quitters (e.g., No.8 NC, No.18 MCI) with extremely low scores; No progress types (e.g., No.12, No.19, No.30) showed no improvement after two attempts; and the striving but repeatedly learning types (e.g., No.15, No.29) had score fluctuations. Notable was participant No.28, an MCI individual with improved scores and doubled persistence time, showing balanced gameplay. (See Fig. 6 and Fig. 7 for detail).

Despite lower drone task performance, this group rated their enjoyment at 3.13 ± 0.64, finding the game relatively enjoyable. (See Table 2 for details).

4 Discussion

This study conducted an acceptability and feasibility survey of virtual reality (VR) games among elderly individuals with varying cognitive abilities residing in Shanghai communities. The findings reveal that both healthy and MCI elderly possess distinct experiences

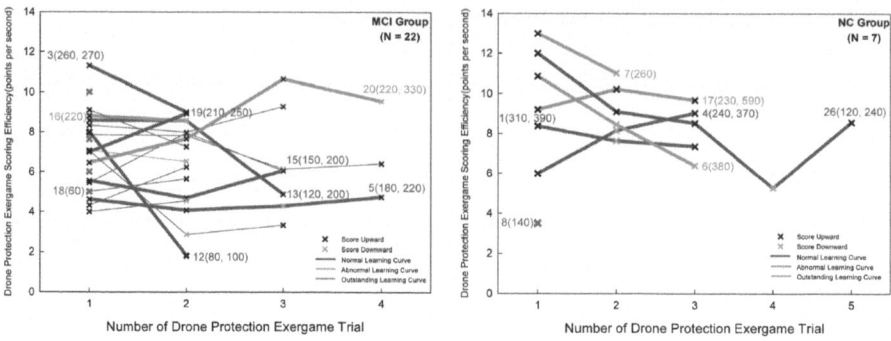

Fig. 7. Performance line charts for the MCI and NC groups, based on voluntary trials and round scoring efficiency, exposed learning curves. Color coding indicated round progress: yellow for declines both in score and efficiency, green for significant improvements. Cross markings showed current-round score, with black indicating an increase and gray a decrease from the previous round. Only 4 seniors regressed, while 20 improved with multiple attempts.

and perceptions of VR games, differing notably from those of younger individuals. Furthermore, most elderly participants demonstrated a pronounced willingness to engage with VR gaming experiences.

4.1 No Significant Difference Between MCI and NC?

In the drone protection task, significant differences in game performance were found between high and low willingness-to-use groups (p < 0.001), with better performance linking to positive usability ratings and future technology use intentions. Despite this, no significant difference in drone performance was observed between NC and MCI groups, as learning curves showed substantial variability within groups, masking inter-group differences.

Two participants (see Fig. 7 and Table 3 for detail), one from each group, are noteworthy. MCI's No.20 (female, 61, primary education, MoCA = 15) showed moderate cognitive impairment but demonstrated high learning enthusiasm and rapid body reactions intuitively. Her attack efficiency and score increased both by 50% over four attempts, reaching the highest score of 330 in her group by the fourth round.

NC's No.6 (male, 62, higher education, MoCA = 29) achieved the highest score in his group with an initial score of 380. He quickly mastered game rules and showed swift hand-eye coordination but did not improve in subsequent attempts. He expanded his defense strategy but struggled with sustained concentration and peripheral attention, leading to self-inflicted drone destruction.

The activity promoted physical engagement and cognitive function, offering a stimulating interactive experience. Some elderly individuals with cognitive impairments showed higher learning enthusiasm and even outperformed the cognitive normal group in some aspects. This underscores the advantage of exergames in enhancing embodied cognition [24] and complementing brain and physical intelligence. Exergames may be better suited for long-term community-dwelling senior use than cognitive games.

Table 3. Drone Protection Performance Data Overview (Notable cases listed)

No	Age	Edu	MoCA Score	Will	Total Trials	1st trial score	Highest score	1st trial scoring efficiency (point/sec)	Total Scoring Efficiency (point/sec)
N1	69	12	28	HWill	3	310	390	8.38	7.73
N3	61	12	22	HWill	2	260	270	11.30	10.00
N4	73	9	27	HWill	3	240	370	6.00	7.69
N5	81	15	23	HWill	4	180	220	4.62	4.39
N6	62	15	29	HWill	3	380	380	10.86	8.31
N7	60	13	28	HWill	2	260	260	13.00	10.21
N8	73	9	26	LWill	1	140	140	3.50	3.50
N12	82	15	21	LWill	2	80	100	8.00	2.77
N13	61	11	22	HWill	3	120	200	8.57	6.58
N15	76	9	24	LWill	3	200	200	5.56	6.11
N16	66	9	22	HWill	2	220	220	8.80	8.70
N17	72	12	27	HWill	3	230	590	9.20	9.77
N18	68	12	25	LWill	1	60	60	5.00	5.00
N19	69	12	17	LWill	2	210	250	7.00	7.93
N20	61	6	15	HWill	4	220	330	6.47	8.46
N26	81	16	26	HWill	5	120	240	12.00	8.40
N28	65	12	20	LWill	2	120	260	5.00	5.43
N29	72	9	25	LWill	3	240	240	7.06	4.24
N30	73	6	18	LWill	2	200	240	9.09	8.00

4.2 Can Game Scores Reflect the Physical Exercise Performance of the Elderly?

Of the 29 participants, around 59% rated the game usability above 82.06($\pm$5.17), and 72% were willing to continue using the games in their community. Exergames with adaptive difficulty are well-suited to the elderly's gradual learning process, offering interactive freedom and kinematic richness that enable diverse joint rotation combinations for task completion [25]. These aspects increase their appeal over activities limited to procedural movement.

The question of whether game scores can accurately reflect elderly physical exercise performance persists. In the Drone Protection Task, aggressive players with high scoring efficiency use small-amplitude movements and precise hand-eye coordination, requiring substantial cognitive processing like decision-making and reaction time, potentially enhancing cognitive abilities. However, their body movement amplitude is relatively small. Defensive players, with lower scoring efficiency, perform large-amplitude movements to dodge attacks, leading to more significant physical activity.

Determining how to measure the elderly's exercise performance scientifically using commercial games and providing data for long-term monitoring requires further research.

4.3 Health Knowledge or Health Beliefs?

The appropriateness of exergames for elderly individuals with physical decline needs further study. Nine participants reported health issues like knee problems, lumbar conditions, fractures, and lung diseases, with five showing less engagement willingness. However, four participants (No. 3, 5, 13, and 16) showed higher willingness; notably, No. 13 and 16 resumed 30-min to 1-h daily running routines after 9 months from post-fracture, demonstrating a strong commitment to exercise for health. Despite potential dangers, their health beliefs sustain a positive and proactive exercise attitude. (See Figs. 6, 7 and Table 3 for individual performance data).

Another noteworthy datum is that seven elderly individuals, accounting for 24%, did not derive a sufficient sense of achievement from completing the intervention exercises, indicating a potential lack of motivation for continued use. For instance, participant N1, (male, 69 years old, with moderate education, MoCA score = 28) recognized the task's value primarily for its recreational and leisure aspects rather than its potential health benefits. He noted, "I am well aware that this is a scenario game, like mountain climbing, but it relies on the power of the machine. This is the machine's accomplishment, not an achievement based on my physical capabilities. Moreover, the current difficulty and intensity of the exercise have not made me feel a sufficient health-promoting effect, neither cognitively nor physically." This suggests that while the training exercises were generally engaging and enjoyable, a segment of the elderly population may not fully appreciate their health benefits.

All these insights underscore the need to reframe the holistic value of these activities and community-based service, so as to enhance the health promotion features as affordances.

4.4 "Resonance" that Inspires Competence, Confidence, and Pleasure

In the experiment, 20% of elderly participants found the game content reminiscent of past pleasant experiences. For example, during the mountain climbing task, seniors remembered scenic views from their past. However, elderly individuals often favored shooting competitive games over those with rich biophilic elements, as the latter are more substitutable in daily life. Participant No.26 (male, 81, higher education, MoCA = 26) noted that the climbing task's paths diverged from his mountain viewing expectations: "The path I envision differs from what's allowed here; it's not real mountain climbing." Conversely, Drone Protection games heightened the elderly's perception of health promotion value, aligning with their health benefit expectations. Participant No.6 said, "This game is fun, like the shooting games I played on computers and phones ten years ago." The game content's resonance [23] enabled seniors to joyfully immerse themselves in the experience.

4.5   Need for Technical Support

Cognitively normal elderly individuals and those with cognitive impairments showed significant differences in their need for technical support (Question 8, p $=$ 0.03), with the NC group scoring 3.14 $\pm$ 0.69 and the MCI group scoring 1.86 $\pm$ 1.28. (See Tables 1 and 2 for detail) The NC group felt that technical assistance was unnecessary due to low system complexity, preferring video tutorials or posters for basic teaching and trial-and-error learning for advanced knowledge. Conversely, the MCI group, recognizing the importance of learning guidance and their limited memory capacity, often needed help operating everyday devices, reflecting individualized learning curves. The disparity in opinions suggests a future research opportunity to develop an inclusive elderly health intelligent service system, integrating resources at the societal organization level. This would require collaborative innovation among government departments, community center operators, medical institutions, and designers to address the inevitable bottleneck of service human resource scarcity.

5   Conclusion

In conclusion, for the first time, the present study has conducted a pioneering and comprehensive investigation into the acceptability of VR games among community-dwelling elderly in Shanghai. Amidst the escalating trends of aging and technological advancements, the demand for cognitive training among the elderly has grown substantially. This research thus bridges the gap between technology and the elderly care needs, contributing to the optimization of digital services and facilitating the future fulfillment of elderly health needs in a more effective manner.

Acknowledgments. This research was funded by the China Ministry of Science and Technology (STI2030-Major Projects-2022ZD0213100), three-year action plan for strengthening the construction of the public health system in Shanghai (GWVI-11.2-XD24), and Teaching Reform Project of Tongji University.

Ethics Approval. This study has been reviewed and received ethics approval from the Shanghai Mental Health Center (reference number 2021–54). Each individual provided their signature on a written consent document. To avert any possible bias regarding acceptance of the intervention, participants received no form of compensation.

References

1. A China Aging Development Report. Social Sciences Academic Press, Beijing (2024)
2. The webpage of 14th Five-Year National Health Plan. https://www.gov.cn/zhengce/content/2022-05/20/content_5691424.htm
3. The webpage of 2022 Shanghai Elderly Population and Cause Monitoring Statistical Information. https://wsjkw.sh.gov.cn/tjsj2/20230412/899c76cbff2e4c93997b03593ccb946e.html

4. Gallou-Guyot, M., Mandigout, S., Bherer, L., Perrochon, A.: "Effects of exergames and cognitive-motor dual-task training on cognitive, physical and dual-task functions in cognitively healthy older adults: an overview. Ageing Res. Rev. **63**, 101135 (2020)

5. World Health Organization: WHO Global Report on Falls Prevention in Older Age. World Health Organization: Geneva, Switzerland (2008); ISBN 978–92–4–156353–6

6. Campo-Prieto, P., Cancela-Carral, J.M., Alsina-Rey, B., Rodríguez-Fuentes, G.: Immersive virtual reality as a novel physical therapy approach for nonagenarians: usability and effects on balance outcomes of a game-based exercise program. J. Clin. Med. **11**(13), 3911 (2022)

7. Dong, J., Ota, K., Dong, M.: Why VR Games sickness? An empirical study of capturing and analyzing VR games head movement dataset. IEEE Multimedia **29**(2), 74–82 (2022)

8. Du, Z., Wang, T., Wang, F., Wang, S.: Augmented reality experience: an examination of viewer responses to sports videos. J. Consum. Behav. **23**(3), 1307–1328 (2024)

9. Goumopoulos, C., Drakakis, E., Gklavakis, D.: Feasibility and acceptance of augmented and virtual reality exergames to train motor and cognitive skills of elderly. Computers **12**(3), 52 (2023)

10. Mehrabi, S., et al.: Immersive virtual reality exergames to promote the well-being of community-dwelling older adults: protocol for a mixed methods pilot study. JMIR Res. Protoc. **11**(6), e32955 (2022)

11. Wang, L., Huang, M., Yang, R., Liang, H.-N., Han, J., Sun, Y.: Survey of movement reproduction in immersive virtual rehabilitation. IEEE Trans. Visual Comput. Graphics **29**(4), 2184–2202 (2023)

12. Sadeghi, H., et al.: Effects of 8 weeks of balance training, virtual reality training, and combined exercise on lower limb muscle strength, balance, and functional mobility among older men: a randomized controlled trial. Sports Health **13**(6), 606–612 (2021)

13. Costa, V., et al.: Evaluating the usability and safety of virtual reality application combined with the swalker for functional gait rehabilitation. Games Health J. **13**(5), 397–405 (2024)

14. Nielsen, J.: Usability Engineering. San Francisco, CA, USA: Morgan (1994)

15. Muñoz, J., et al.: Immersive virtual reality exergames for persons living with dementia: user-centered design study as a multistakeholder team during the COVID-19 pandemic. JMIR Serious Games **10**(1), e29987 (2022)

16. Ip, W.K., Soar, J., James, C., Wang, Z., Fong, K.N.K.: Innovative virtual reality (VR) application for preventing of falls among Chinese older adults: a usability and acceptance exploratory study. Hum. Behav. Emerg. Technol. **2024**(1), 5556767 (2024)

17. Campelo, A.M., Weisberg, A., Sheehan, D.P., Schneider, K., Cossich, V.R.A., Katz, L.: Physical and affective physical literacy domains improved after a six-week exergame exercise program in older adults: a randomized controlled clinical trial. Games Health J. **12**(5), 366–376 (2023)

18. Xu, W., Liang, H.-N., Yu, K., Wen, S., Baghaei, N., Tu, H.: Acceptance of virtual reality exergames among Chinese older adults. Int. J. Hum.-Comput. Interact. **39**(5), 1134–1148 (2023)

19. Dajime, P.F., Smith, H., Zhang, Y.: Bespoke exergames for balance improvement and fall risk reduction in community-dwelling older adults: a systematic review and meta-analysis of randomized controlled trials. IEEE Trans. Games **14**(4), 687–695 (2022)

20. The Lab game webpage. https://store.steampowered.com/app/450390/The_Lab/

21. Stanney, K.M., Kennedy, R.S., Drexler, J.M.: Cybersickness is not simulator sickness. In: Proceedings of the Human Factors and Ergonomics Society Annual Meeting, pp. 1138–1142. SAGE Publications, Los Angeles, CA (1997)

22. Oh, H., Son, W.: Cybersickness and its severity arising from virtual reality content: a comprehensive study. Sensors **22**(4), 1314 (2022)

23. Mekler, E.D., Hornbæk, K.: A framework for the experience of meaning in human-computer interaction. In: CHI '19: Proceedings of the 2019 CHI Conference on Human Factors in Computing Systems, pp. 1–15. Association for Computing Machinery, New York, NY, USA (2019)
24. Clark, A.: An embodied cognitive science? Trends Cogn. Sci. **3**(9), 345–351 (1999)
25. Levin, M.F., Demers, M.: Motor learning in neurological rehabilitation. Disabil. Rehabil. **43**(24), 3445–3453 (2020)

A Decision Support System for Matching Users and Fall Risk Detection Technology

Manila Caragiuli$^{(\boxtimes)}$ ⓘ, Agnese Brunzini ⓘ, Chiara Massera ⓘ, Mara Candelari ⓘ, and Michele Germani ⓘ

Department of Industrial Engineering and Mathematical Sciences, Università Politecnica delle Marche, Via Brecce Bianche 12, 60131 Ancona, Italy
m.caragiuli@univpm.it

Abstract. One of the most common issues among the older people is falling. Sensor technologies can control the risk of people to fall and make them aware of their health status. Numerous devices are available in the market and new brands are continuously deployed making challenging the choice of the ideal monitoring device. The present study aims at providing a methodology to identify older adults at risk of falls and guide the user in the choice of the best set of technology to control and prevent the fall risk.

Multidimensional health data of 121 older adults were collected, pre-processed and fed to five machine learning classifiers to automatically identify people at fall risk. A positive fall risk classification triggers a knowledge-based algorithm to identify the best matching device according to five categories (type, accessory parameters, accessory functions, technical requirements, and digital effort) and considering the user's clinical and social needs. This way, the algorithm is not constrained to a specific device but is able to handle several technologies and could be generalized to a larger pool of disease by properly training the ML classification models. Unlike common recommendation systems based on user preferences and user profiling, the proposed decision-support system does not require any a priori knowledge of the user preferences. Indeed, as a future development, it is planned to consider user's opinion obtained from usability and user experience tests to optimize the personalization of the assignment and improve the user's engagement.

Keywords: Personalized Healthcare · Older Adults · Fall Risk Assessment · Decision Support System · Sensors

1 Introduction and Research Background

Falls one are of the most common issues among older people. Indeed, according to the WHO, 684,000 deaths are annually associated with serious falls and further 37.3 million falls are severe enough to cause disability. Moreover, falls can have serious implications on the psychological and social side. Indeed, the anxiety and the fear of falling may lead to reduced physical activity and increased physical and social isolation undermining the life quality and increasing the frailty status of individuals. Older people are more likely to fall due to comorbidity, medications, reduced reflexes and reaction time, osteoporosis, reduced muscle tone, and visual problems. However, some risk factors are modifiable posing a chance to prevent the phenomenon. Indeed, environments should be well designed and managed to avoid darkness and barriers (carpets, stairs, furniture etc.). Sensor technologies can control the risk of people to fall and make them aware of their health status. Policymakers and healthcare providers can thus make appropriate plans for preventive interventions to reduce the rate of falls in older people and improve their independence.

There are many tools and ways to assess the fall risk among elderly people. Functional measures and physical performance tests are the most evident way to address it. The review article of [1] identified 26 fall-risk assessment tools, used in different settings. Timed-Up and Go test and Berg Balance Scale are some of the most widely adopted tools, also in community settings. However, their predictive performance varies substantially across studies [1, 2]. Sensor-based assessments (depth cameras, radio signal-based devices, inertial sensors) allow to conduct measurements in daily life, but the complexity is given by the location of the sensor and data processing. Questionnaires are easy to administer but have questionable predictive values that, however, could be improved by combining them with physical performance tests or including specific questions about fall history or medication use.

Lage et al. [3] developed a fall risk prediction model based on a multivariable logistic regression model and a test-retest approach. Age, zone, social community resources, physical exercise, self-perception of health, difficulty to keep standing, difficulty to sit and get up from a chair, strain to see, use of technical devices, hypertension, number of medications, and gender result to be relevant factors in the fall risk of community-dwelling adults aged over 65. The same approach was adopted by Smith et al. [4] investigating the influence of hip and knee osteoarthritis on falls and fracture risk. The findings report a 50% greater chance of experiencing a fall and over 80% greater chance of experiencing a fracture in the first year of diagnosis compared to the control group (without the disease and without fractures).

A logistic regression model was also developed by [5, 6] to evaluate the association of gait parameters with prospective falls, and to develop a fall risk index by investigating the causal relationship of multidisciplinary features, respectively.

Beside traditional approaches based on statistics, machine learning (ML), and deep learning (DL) models have become popular tools for fall prediction.

The study of Martinez et al. [7] proposed a model for fall risk classification of 510 individuals aged 20–60 years, based on deep neural networks and transfer learning. Data based on time-series inertial data (walk, jog, skip, upstairs, downstairs, and stay) measured by a smartphone placed on a gait belt near the hip, were fed to a fully convolutional neural network. The accuracy is 86%, the sensitivity 85% and the specificity 87%.

The article of Adeli et al. [8] developed a dynamic fall risk assessment tool for inpatients with dementia, based on Multi-Layer Perceptron with Adam optimization. This study also investigated the short-term risk by varying the extent of prediction and the last k days of measurements (the average values over the most recent 5 days, and the baseline 5 days). The best classifier included 3 longitudinal gait features (cadence, eMOS, UPDRS-III-gait) measured by ambient sensors, antipsychotic medications, and baseline STRATIFY scores. The highest AUROC was obtained for a fall prediction over the next 4 weeks and accounting for medications and gait assessments of the last 5 days.

The study of Buisseret et al. [9] found out that combining TUG test with Six-minutes walking test can improve the accuracy of the fall prediction by 12%, if compared to the individual TUG. Moreover, a convolutional neural network model based only on the kinematic data derived from the elderly walking six minutes, was developed. The findings revealed a comparable accuracy to that of the augmented TUG, making the model reliable for the fall classification task.

A framework for activity monitoring, fall detection and generating effective health recommendations, based on a fog-edge-IoMT architecture, was proposed by [10]. A combination of ML, federated learning, and deep learning enabled the system to outperform baseline ML models improving the accuracy by 10%-16%. Concerning the fall detection task, the proposed framework achieves a high accuracy in the range of 90%-94%.

The analyzed literature suggested that various Artificial Intelligence (AI) techniques have been used to predict the fall risk. Indeed, the progress in computing resources enabled processing large quantity of data collected through wearable devices while executing common activities of daily living, such as walking.

However, the largest evidence of predictive models for falls involves hospital settings or institutions, thus controlled environment, with people who already experienced previous falls or frailty status, whilst a more effective prevention could be provided in community-dwelling individuals. Moreover, the focus is on the identification of the risk, rather than its prevention.

This study is based on the assumption that some basic and useful training about fall risks should be provided to all older people as a preventive strategy. Moreover, it proposes a methodology to develop a decision-support system to support the general practitioner in the choice of the fall risk monitoring device that best matches the older adult's needs. Unlike a previous work published by the authors [11], the proposed methodology strengthens its generalizability taking advantage of machine learning techniques, and knowledge-based reasoning rules.

Despite the large availability of Internet of Things (IoT) devices for self-monitoring, their effectiveness could be undermined by the user compliance.

The work of [12] proposed a technique for automatic IoT device selection based on a policy based on user preferences. A user preference model based on Bayesian network associated with each device a degree of usage preference concerning several functions. Searching algorithms were used to find the device that maximize the user preference and fulfil the required functions. Among four optimization algorithms (hill climbing, simulated annealing, genetic algorithm (GA), and brut-force), GA provided the best balance between effectiveness and efficiency.

Sabatucci et al. [13] proposed a Device-Goal-Norm runtime model for the selection of equivalent devices to be used in an AAL application, by accounting for user preferences, and laws and regulations. The goal represents the conditions and the environment of application as well as its failure/success state. A validation procedure based on ad-hoc user profiles was carried out to assess the time to convergence and the ability to reach the goal of the algorithm. However, such implementation requires an a priori knowledge of the user's preferences.

Asthana et al. [14] proposed a system to suggest wearables and IoT devices for health monitoring through a ML and mathematical optimization approach. A decision tree classifier was trained on a public dataset to output the disease conditions a person is at risk of, and the corresponding measurements that need to be monitored. Then, an optimization model allowed to associate to the pathology the proper device based on the measurements to be monitored, and according to constraints including the budget, the cost of the device, and the resource capacities. Moreover, the system can update the choice of the device based on the monitored data. The classifier got a Root Mean Square error of 0.11. However, there is no validation about the proper assignment of the device, and the user's perspective is not considered.

A more recent work is proposed by [15]. Some ML models were fed with clinical health data of users to output the measurements to be monitored. Then, such output measurements, the features and functionalities of the devices, and the patient's feedback were used as input for the device recommendation system based on a Genetic Algorithm. However, the target of this study did not correspond to older adults and a validation procedure was not available since the source of the data came from a public dataset, preventing any patient involvement.

Despite, few studies attempted to provide the recommended device based on the user needs, the compliance of the user depends on the usability and acceptability of a monitoring device. An authors' previous study [16] applied usability and user experience protocols to investigate the experience of older adults when using self-monitoring and entertainment devices (pressure devices, smartphone, and tablet). Findings suggest that technology anxiety does not impact on the use of such technological devices. Indeed, the perceived usefulness of the device and the opinion of the relatives positively influence their use. Moreover, a continuous digital mediation and individual training sessions can encourage the device use. This is supported also by [17] and [18], finding out a general positive attitude toward technology among older adults (aged over 65). Features perceived as a barrier to the use of technology include the cost, the ignorance of the features, and issues about privacy and obtrusiveness.

This is why it is important to address a personalised strategy for the care of older adults. Concerning this aspect, literature is very scant in terms of recommendation systems for the choice of the optimal monitoring device.

The present study aims at providing a methodology to develop a tool able to classify older adults at risk of falls and guide the user in the choice of the best set of technology to control and prevent the fall risk. Some of the key benefits of the proposed approach include the multi-disciplinary approach and the personalization of the output based on the user's needs.

2 Materials and Methods

The purpose of this section is to describe the proposed methodology, illustrated in Fig. 1, to investigate the research problem.

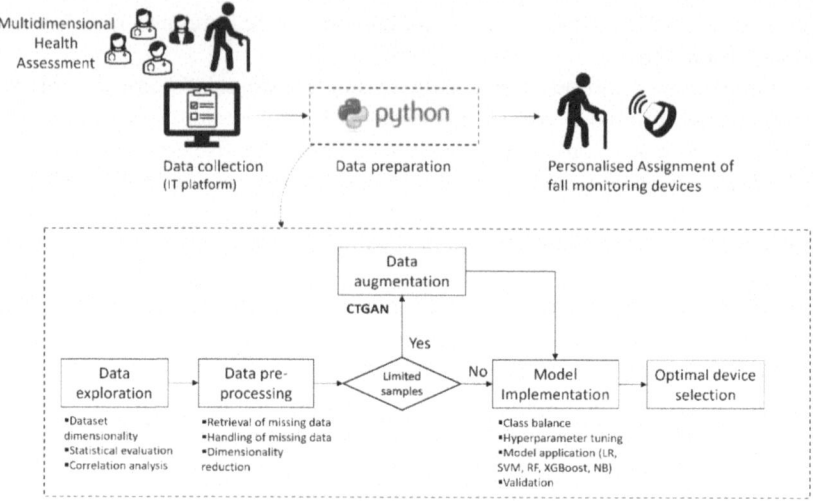

Fig. 1. Workflow of the proposed methodology

2.1 Data Collection

Data have been collected in the context of an Italian National Project (MOSAICO) funded by the ex-Ministry of Economic Development and Marche Region under the grant agreement for innovation. The target users were older adults greater than 75 years, living in small municipalities of Marche region (inner areas of Fermo and Macerata provinces affected by the earthquake of 2016). Respondents with severe cognitive impairment were excluded since most of the collected variables were assessed through anamnestic interviews. Eligible subjects signed a written informed consent to participate in this study.

A multi-disciplinary staff of doctors (cardiologist, nutritionist, physiatrist, psychologist, social operator) evaluated the social and health status of the users through face-to-face interviews, validated questionnaires available in the literature, physical performance tests, and clinical exams, as described in [11]. Data about socio-demographic information (age, education level, social relationship, living status, marital status, owning pets, environmental barriers etc.) as well as clinical aspects of users' life (mobility assessment, cardiovascular problems, nutritional status, cognitive and mood disorders, quality of life) have been collected in a software platform GDPR compliant. At the end of the screening, a final debriefing among the clinicians allowed to define the user need for a fall detection device.

2.2 Data Preparation

As stated by [19] and [2], data pre-processing has a strong influence on the accuracy of ML classification models, since errors or inconsistencies may worsen the performance of the models. Thus, a careful data preparation should be performed.

All the acquired data have been collected in a database according to the users' ID to preserve the user's privacy.

The dataset contains 121 samples and about fifty features of mixed data type (continuous and categorical) depending on the nature of the selected features. As output (target variables) different technologies for fall detection will be discussed in detail in the next sections.

All the categorical features have been encoded for further model development. The output variables have been encoded into binary Boolean values where 1 represents the presence of the fall risk, while 0 is the converse.

All the pre-processing steps have been done in Python (v3.10.11) through common libraries (Numpy, Pandas, Scikit Learn, Matplotlib). Missing data up to 25% were imputed through Multivariate Imputation by Chain Equation technique ('miceforest' library[1]). It allows to preserve the relationship between variables in the original data. In the other cases, missing data were deleted. Non-relevant features, identified through the support of the involved clinicians, were deleted to reduce the dimensionality of the database. Moreover, some feature engineering allowed to combine multiple features in a single one.

To increase the number of samples for reliable ML classifications a data augmentation process was applied to synthesize new data based on the real ones. To this purpose, a CTGANSynthesizer[2] from 'sdv' library was used.

Then, data were normalized through 'MinMaxScale[3]r' to scale data into the same range. Finally, class imbalance was handled by means of 'smotenc[4]', a technique suitable for mixed-type dataset that enables oversampling the minority class.

2.3 Model Implementation

The choice of the ML models to be used for the classification purpose came from a set of criteria mainly based on the dataset characteristics. Indeed, ML models able to handle mixed data type (continuous and categorical) and few records were selected. Table 1 reports the main characteristics of the considered ML models.

5 ML models (RF, LR, SVM, NB, and XGBoost) were implemented on the synthetic dataset. To improve the performance of the ML models, a Grid Search Cross Validation was applied to identify the combination of hyperparameters that gave the best performance on the synthetic data. This way a trade-off between bias and variance will prevent the model from overfitting or underfitting. However, the choice of hyperparameters to be tuned was limited to the computation power of the resources since the code was executed in Colab in a virtual machine with CPU.

To reduce the dependency on the training set a K-fold cross-validation was done by assuming K = 10. Thus, the dataset was divided into K equally sized parts each used as a test set for model validation at each training iteration.

As a further validation, the tuned ML models were applied to the real dataset used for the augmentation process.

---

[1] https://pypi.org/project/miceforest/.

[2] https://docs.sdv.dev/sdv/single-table-data/modeling/synthesizers/ctgansynthesizer.

[3] https://scikit-learn.org/stable/modules/generated/sklearn.preprocessing.MinMaxScaler.html.

[4] https://imbalanced-learn.org/stable/references/generated/imblearn.over_sampling.SMO
TENC.html.

Table 1. Main characteristics of the analyzed ML models.

ML model	Description	Strengths	Drawbacks
Random Forest (RF)	Ensemble learning method based on a collection of decision trees to improve predictive performance The classification result is determined by the majority voting of the classes returned by the individual trees	· Overfitting reduction; · Improved generalizability by aggregating predictions from multiple decision trees; · Suitable for high-dimensional data with complex decision boundaries; · Suitable for both categorical and continuous features; · Robustness to noisy data and missing values; · Insights into the most relevant features	· High computational power; · Time-consuming; · Less intuitive interpretation than decision tree
Logistic Regression (LR)	It is a binary classification technique that predicts the probability of an instance belonging to a particular class and outputs a value between 0 and 1	· Intuitive interpretation; · Probability estimate of an occurring event; · Suitable for binary target; · Often used in medical research for risk prediction	· Vulnerability to overfitting; · Failure in capturing complex and nonlinear relationships
eXtreme Gradient Boosting (XGBoost)	It is an ensemble method that combines multiple decision tress to make an accurate prediction	· Effective with large data sets; · Fast and efficient; · High accuracy; · It can capture complex nonlinear relationships; · Missing data handling capability; · Insights into feature importance	· Complex implementation; · Computationally intensive; · Sensitive to overfitting if not properly tuned
Support Vector Machine (SVM)	It finds the best possible decision boundary that separates the data points into different classes aiming at maximizing the margin between the boundary and the closest data points	· Suitable for high-dimensional data with few training examples; · Memory efficient; · Less prone to overfitting; · It can handle nonlinear data; · Suitable for classification and regression	· Limited interpretability for higher dimensionality; · Sensitivity to class unbalance; · Missing data handling problem; · Computationally expensive

(*continued*)

Table 1. (*continued*)

ML model	Description	Strengths	Drawbacks
Naive Bayes (NB)	It is a probabilistic classification algorithm derived from Bayes' probability theory. Indeed, the probability of a hypothesis A derives from the occurrence of the evidence	· Easy and fast; · Suitable for both binary and multi-class classifications; · It doesn't require larger amounts of training data; · It can handle both continuous and categorical data	· Features independence assumption; · Sensitivity to class unbalance

The algorithm performances were evaluated in terms of the area of the Receiver Operating Characteristic curve (AUROC), accuracy, precision, recall and f1-score. Accuracy enables to evaluate if the ML model correctly predicts the outcome. Positive predictive value or precision is computed as the ratio between the positives correctly identified (true positive) and all the predicted positives (true positive and false positive). Recall identifies the true positives among all the positive measures (true positive and false negative). F1-score represents the harmonic mean of precision and sensitivity.

2.4 Optimal Device Selection

- This is the final step of the methodological workflow proposed to identify the fall detection device that best matches the user's needs.
- Firstly, a proper set of fall detection monitoring devices was defined. Then a knowledge-based algorithm was developed considering the users' needs as well as the technological requirements.

Technology Selection. Wearable, environmental, or stand-alone portable sensors have been proposed for a comprehensive choice of the device that best matches the user's needs. Error! Reference source not found. Reports the assumed set of monitoring devices. The technology consists of commercial devices, available in the Italian market, compliant with the required monitoring parameter (fall event), and suitable for such a category of people. Indeed, one of the key aspects of the choice of the technology is related to user compliance and acceptability. Being the privacy and the obtrusiveness common issues among older adults [18], devices based on optical sensors were excluded. Moreover, it is worth mentioning that elderly people are prevented from using such kind of technology due to the perception of a vulnerable condition. Thus, "augmented devices" that provide additional functions compared to the baseline (fall detection) may improve the perceived usefulness of the technology in their daily life.

Device Selection Algorithm. Once the classification algorithm identifies a user as being at risk of falling, the device selection algorithm executes an automatic selection of the most suitable fall monitoring device for a certain user, from a pool of candidates based on

Table 2. Fall risk detection devices.

Device	Functionality description
WEAR2[5]	It is provided with a triaxial accelerometer with 9 levels of sensitivity able to automatically detect a fall event. A SOS button enables to manually send an alert request. In case of emergency an alert is automatically sent to caregivers via SMS and phone calls. It enables bidirectional communication by speakerphone, not only in case of emergency. The GPS allows to know the localization of the user. The geofence function alerts in case of departure from guard zones
Apple Watch[6]	Smart watch embedded with sensors for multiple vital sign monitoring (oxygen saturation, cardiac frequency, EKG, steps). It can automatically detect a fall event, and to manually send a SOS in case of emergency. The cellular version does not require a iPhone to make phone calls
Seremy[7]	It is a wristband designed to automatically detect a fall event and alert the caregivers via app notification providing info about the localization. A SOS button can be pushed in case of emergency to manually send alert requests. The device enables to detect the heart rate, and the number of steps. The geofence function alerts in case of departure from guard zones
Salvalavita Pocket[8]	Pocket device able to automatically detect a fall or manually send a SOS and alert caregivers via SMS and phone calls. The GPS function provides information about the localization of the device
SiDLY Care Pro[9]	It is a wristband able to automatically detect a fall and manually send a SOS in case of emergency, and alert caregivers via SMS or phone calls also providing a geographic localization. It enables to measure the heart rate, the blood oxygen saturation, and the number of steps. The geofence function alerts in case of departure from a predefined zone. It is possible to set up reminder for medications
FP2[10]	It is a presence sensor based on radar technology to detect the presence of multiple people and fall events. By connecting it to a hub it is possible to setup automations triggered by the detected presence (e.g., lighting)
Vayyar Care[11]	Environmental sensor based on radiofrequency for a continuous monitoring of fall event. It requires Internet connection to send alerts via SMS to caregivers

the user's needs. Indeed, despite being fall monitoring devices, the selected technology reported in Table 2 differs in specific features including the provided functions, the accessory parameters to be monitored, the degree of difficulty in using the device, and other intrinsic characteristics.

---

[5] https://www.microtecno.com/product/localizzatore-indossabile-gpsagps/.

[6] https://support.apple.com/kb/SP778?locale=it_IT.

[7] https://www.seremy.it/.

[8] https://www.beghelli.it/store/it/catalogo/salvalavita/dispositivi-salvalavita/salvalavita-pocket-gsm-131191.

[9] http://www.aditechsrl.it/healthcare/active-and-assisted-living/sidly-care.

[10] https://www.aqara.com/en/product/presence-sensor-fp2/.

[11] https://vayyar.com/care/b2b/overview/.

Unlike most recommender systems that are based on a single criterion such as the rating of an item, the proposed reasoning engine considers multiple criteria classified into five categories: type, accessory parameters, accessory functions, technical requirements, and technological effort. All the categories except the last one were filled with data available online from the suppliers' websites.

"Type" allows to discriminate devices between wearable and environmental.

"Accessory parameters" refers to a set of parameters other than fall event, that a device allows to measure. Indeed, multiparametric devices offer the possibility to monitor additional parameters being embedded with suitable sensors.

"Accessory functions" describes a set of additional services provided by the device such as geo-localization, communication, SOS function, reminder etc.

"Technical requirements" is strictly related to the required operating conditions as well as the use constraints provided by the device (i.e., device not suitable in the presence of certain pathologies, device not recommended for user monitoring in the presence of pets, smartphone required to use the device etc.).

"Technological effort" represents the difficulty in using a specific device considering the target of users (older adults aged > 75), and their digital divide. It is mainly based on the degree of familiarity with the technology. Indeed, users familiar with smartphones could be associated with any kind of smart device that requires some technical skills for its use (touchscreen, activation of Bluetooth, interaction with the device etc.). On the other hand, people who still have a fixed phone or a non-smartphone device should be associated with simple devices and minimal interaction with the technology. According to a prevention strategy, a priority is given to the parameters over the functions meaning that a multiparametric device is preferred over a device that can monitor one single parameter but provide several functions. Moreover, the categories "type", "technical requirements", and "digital effort" are assumed as constraints to filter the choice of the devices. The rationale behind the algorithm is to filter the dataset of fall monitoring devices by type, identify the devices able to measure as many parameters as required by the patient, apply the "technical requirements" constraints to discard uncompliant devices, then check by the function, and apply the "digital effort" constraint. Figure 2 shows a high-level workflow of the device selection algorithm. It is worth noting that the "technical requirements" constraint mainly depends on the parameters to be monitored, thus the choice to apply it after the parameters check.

A dataset of devices was thus defined consisting of attributes identified based on the aforementioned categories and as many records as the number of devices.

On the user side, a map of the user's needs concerning the aforementioned categories was defined with the aid of the clinicians' feedback to be used as reasoning rules in the user-device matching process (e.g., if a user has heart disease OR atrial fibrillation OR QT interval > 430 ms than the EKG parameter could be useful as an accessory monitoring; if a user is very active a wearable device is a proper choice). Thus, the dataset of devices is checked for correspondence with respect to the user's map, row by row, starting from the attribute of the type category. The check of each category allows to reduce the choice of potential fall monitoring devices. Moving to the parameters category, every time a positive correspondence is detected (revealing the user's need for a parameter that a device can measure), the name of that device is appended to an array, and by counting the occurrences of each device, it is possible to identify the devices that best match the user needs. If the devices with the highest occurrences are not compatible with the specified technical requirements, the algorithm discards those devices and applies again the technical requirement constraint among the remaining devices with the highest occurrences. This loop is iterated until a compatible device is obtained or until the set of devices filtered by "parameters" is empty. In that case, the algorithm can come back to the dataset filtered by type, drops the devices so far analysed, checks for the compatibility concerning the technical requirements, and then proceeds by analysis the functions. The set of devices filtered by function is then analysed in terms of digital effort. It is assumed as a weak constraint since the literature [16–18, 20, 21] states that older adults are prone to the use of technology if adequate training is provided thus the algorithm outputs a recommendation but does not preclude a device with slightly higher digital effort since it fulfils of the clinical and social needs of the user.

A simple application of the proposed algorithm will be presented in the next section as for illustrative purposes and as functional validation of the developed reasoning engine.

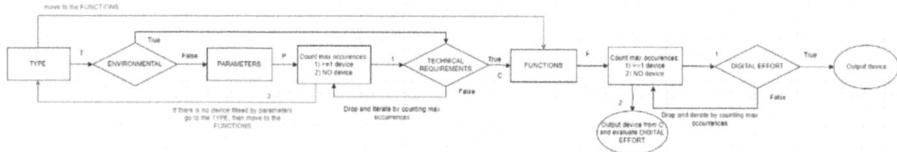

Fig. 2. High-level workflow of the device selection algorithm

3   Results

General descriptive statistics is reported in Table 3 to analyze the trends and patterns in some of the categorical and continuous data of the target population. Categorical features assume the presence of the descripted condition.

The ML models described in Table 1 were used for the fall risk classification purpose. Hyperparameters tuning was performed for each model to identify the best set of parameters able to improve the overall model performance. Table 4 reports the results of the fall risk classification algorithm.

Figure 3 reports the ROC of each model calculated on the real data. AUROC ranges 91%-94%. AUCROC values were estimated for SVM, LR, NB, RF, and XGBoost as 93%, 94%, 91%, 93% and 94%, respectively.

Concerning the algorithm validation, 5 users from the study sample were considered as a test set for a functional check. It is assumed that all the users require a fall detection monitoring device as output of the classification model. Table 5 reports the map of the devices features and user's needs according to some attributes pertaining the previously defined categories. Indeed, A represents the "type" category, B to E the "accessory parameters" (i.e., B: EKG, C: heart rate, D: blood oxygen saturation, E: steps), F-H concerns the "accessory functions" (i.e., F: reminder, G:communication, H: output call), I stands for the "digital effort", and J and K are part of the "technical requirements" (i.e., J: immunity to people/pets, and K: immunity to prosthesis).

Table 3. General characteristics of the sample study.

Characteristics	Mean ± sd (N = 121)	Characteristics	Counts (%) (N = 121)
Age (years)	82 ± 5	Gender (female)	64%
Weight (kg)	68.8 ± 13.4	Living alone	41%
BMI	28.5 ± 4.8	Physical Inactivity	31%
BBS	49 ± 8	Nocturia/Polyuria	46%
MNA_SF	13 ± 2	Heart disease	53%
Skeletal Muscle Mass (kg)	22.9 ± 6.5	Hypertension	93%
Cardiac frequency (bpm)	66 ± 12	Diabetes	17%
PCS12	43.73 ± 9.05	Orthostatic Hypotension	27%
MCS12	46.47 ± 9.29	Low MMSE level	35%
Max handgrip strength (kg)	19.6 ± 8.5	Owning a Smartphone	27%

Table 4. Performance metrics of the ML models

ML Model	Best parameters	Dataset	A	P	R	F1
RF	(Criterion = gini, max_depth = 10, max_features = log2, min_samples_split = 8, n_estimators = 100)	TEST	86%	82%	84%	83%
		REAL	87%	89%	78%	83%
XGBoost	(Gamma = 0.5, lambda = 1, learning_rate = 0.1, max_depth = 3, min_child_weight = 0, n_estimators = 100, multi_strategy = one_output_per_tree)	TEST	88%	84%	87%	85%
		REAL	88%	91%	78%	84%
LR	(C = 100, Max_iter = 1000, Solver = liblinear)	TEST	86%	81%	85%	83%
		REAL	89%	90%	84%	87%
SVM	(C = 100, gamma = 0.01, kernel = rbf)	TEST	84%	79%	84%	82%
		REAL	89%	90%	84%	87%
NB	(alpha = 0.5, var_smoothing = 1e-09)	TEST	84%	84%	76%	79%
		REAL	85%	88%	75%	81%

A: Accuracy, P: precision, R: recall

The algorithm checks the correspondences between the users' values and the dataset of devices row by row starting from the TYPE evaluation. User 1 requires an environmental device, the monitoring of heart rate, functions including reminder and output call, no particular problems concerning the digital effort, a device compatible with people/pets and prostheses. All the rows associated with wearable devices are dropped from the device dataset. Moving forward to the analysis of technical requirements a match occurs

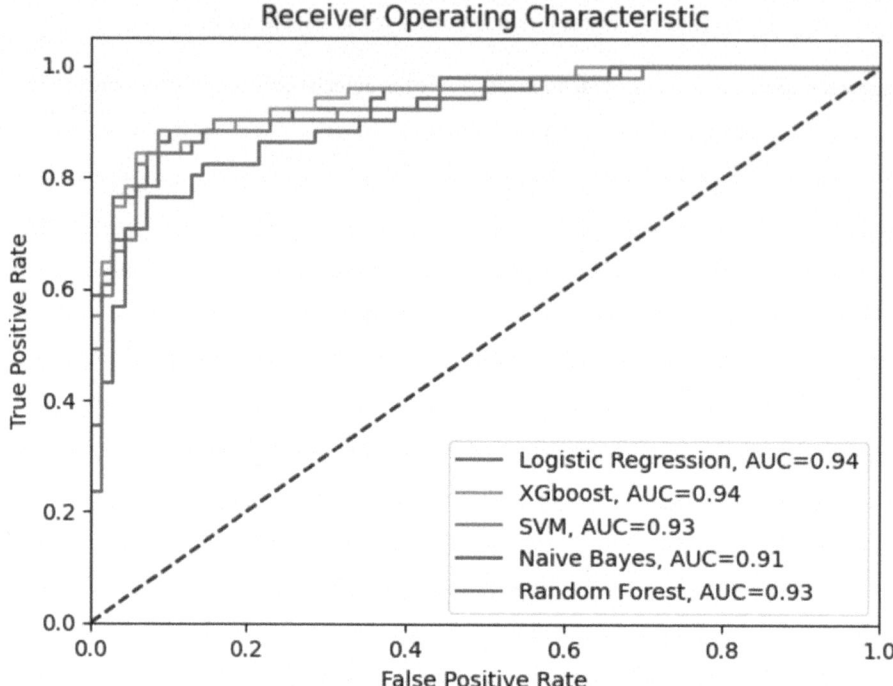

Fig. 3. ROC curves of the ML models

Table 5. Map of the devices' features and user's needs according to type, accessory parameters, accessory functions, technical requirements, and digital effort categories.

DeviceName	A	B	C	D	E	F	G	H	I	J	K
WEAR2	W	0	0	0	0	0	1	1	0	N/A	1
Seremy	W	0	1	0	1	0	0	0	0	N/A	1
SiDLY Care Pro	W	0	1	1	1	1	1	0	0	N/A	1
Applewatch	W	1	1	1	1	1	1	1	1	N/A	0
Salvalavita Pocket	W	0	0	0	0	0	1	0	0	N/A	1
Vayyar Care	E	0	0	0	0	0	0	0	0	0	N/A
FP2	E	0	0	0	0	0	0	0	0	1	N/A
User 1	E	0	1	0	0	1	0	1	1	1	1
User 2	E	0	1	0	0	1	0	1	1	0	1
User 3	W	1	1	1	1	0	0	0	0	N/A	1
User 4	W	0	1	0	1	0	0	0	0	N/A	0
User 5	W	0	0	0	0	0	1	1	0	N/A	0

in FP2 meaning that it fulfils these requirements. This way the algorithm recommends it as the best choice.

Concerning User 2, an environmental device is required with no particular restrictions, thus the algorithm suggests both the environmental devices Vayyar Care and FP2. Conversely, User 3 requires a wearable device, thus all environmental solutions are discarded. The analysis of the parameters suggests that Seremy can measure 2 parameters, SiDLY 3 and Applewatch all the required parameters. Thus, Applewatch is the preferred choice, however, being not compatible with prostheses (that users have) it is discarded and the algorithm must search among the remaining devices, filtered by parameters, the ones that can monitor as many parameters as possible. SiDLY Care Pro is the closest device with the second maximum occurrence thus, after the technical requirement check it is subjected to the digital effort check. Since there are no particular constraints, it is output as a best matching device.

User 4, instead, requires only two parameters to be monitored thus three possible devices result (Seremy, SiDLY Care Pro and Applewatch). Given that there are neither particular constraints to be applied nor functions to be fulfilled, the last evaluation is based on the digital effort. The user is not familiar with the technology, thus Applewatch is discarded and the user is free to choose between Seremy and SiDLY CarePro.

Lastly, User 5 is not required to monitor any parameters but two functions that are provided by only two devices (WEAR2 and Applewatch). This time the algorithm checks directly for the digital effort since no parameter is involved and recommends WEAR2 as fall detection monitoring device.

4   Discussion

The technological revolution in IoT and AI fostered the development of monitoring devices for potential continuous monitoring of vital signs parameters, and user activity.

Numerous devices are available in the market and new brands are continuously deployed making challenging the choice of the ideal monitoring device.

This work proposed a methodology aimed at developing a decision-support system in the selection of a fall monitoring device suitable for older adult needs. A data synthetization approach is proposed when dealing with limited samples. Despite this can lead to overfitting [2], preventing the model from generalizing the learning to unknown new datasets, some authors [22, 23] reported a higher accuracy in the detection of falls. Moreover, to improve the reliability of the trained ML models, a real dataset was used as further validation. Five ML models (RF, LR, SVM, NB, and XGBoost) were implemented to classify the individuals at fall risk. A general improvement in the quality metrics was observed in the test data, except for recall. By observing prediction results obtained on real data, it is possible to note that all the models result in an optimal AUROC (91–94%) and high accuracy (85%-89%). LR achieved the highest AUROC (94%), as supported by [24]. The precision ranges from 88% to 93%, whilst the recall exhibits slightly lower values in the range of 75%-84%. As in all ML models, the performance of the model strictly depends on the computational resources. In this study the code was executed in Colab in a virtual machine with CPU, thus a tradeoff between the hyperparameters tuning and the computational time and requirements was mandatory. However, results are encouraging, indeed, LR and SVM obtained the best overall results with 89% accuracy and 84% recall. XGBoost reported the highest precision (91%), followed by LR and SVM (90%), whilst NB performed worst (85%, 75%, and 88%, respectively).

A positive output (fall risk detection) triggers a knowledge-based algorithm to identify the best matching device according to five categories (type, accessory parameters, accessory functions, technical requirements, and digital effort). This way, the algorithm is not constrained to a specific device but can handle several technologies based on the identified categories. As assumed by [12], the device identification and selection process is mainly based on the parameters and functions devices can fulfil, rather than the brand, the aesthetics or the cost. Indeed, cost is perceived by older adults as a barrier in the use of technology monitoring devices [17, 18, 25].

Unlike common recommendation systems based on user preferences and user profiling, the proposed decision-support system does not require any a priori knowledge of the user preferences. Indeed, as a future development, it is planned to consider the user's opinion obtained from usability and user experience tests, to optimize the personalization of the assignment and improve the user's engagement [26].

This work assumed that some basic and useful training about fall risks should be provided to all older people. However, the proposed decision-support system may allow for planning specific strategies in at-risk of fall people to minimize the risk over time. Indeed, physical activity and exercise programs have been found to be protector of falling [3].

5 Conclusion

Falls and their related injuries are a serious threat to quality of life of older people as well as society.

In this study, a methodology aimed at developing a decision-support system in the selection of a fall monitoring device suitable for older adult needs is proposed. Given the limited size of the sample study, synthetic data were generated through a CTGAN based on a real dataset and used to train five common ML models. Beside cross-validation, the performance of the classifiers was validated on a real dataset of 121 older adults for fall risk detection. LR and SVM obtained the best overall results with 89% accuracy and 84% recall. XGBoost reported the highest precision (91%), followed by LR and SVM (90%).

Depending on the output of the ML model prediction, an algorithm for fall detection device selection is triggered. Given the large variety of monitoring devices available in the market, such a reasoning engine aims at supporting the general practitioner in the choice of the fall detection device that best fits the user's needs. Multiple selection criteria were clustered into five categories (type, accessory parameters, accessory functions, technical requirements, and technological effort) and prioritized to drive the reasoning process. Currently, a preliminary investigation of the user preference is not required but as a future development, the personalization of the device selection could be investigated also in terms of usability and acceptability of the technology to increase the engagement of the users in self-monitoring.

Moreover, an automatic integration and categorization of the devices can improve the scalability of the system as well as its generalizability to handle numerous devices and monitoring devices pertaining to different diseases. Indeed, the positive outcomes of the classifiers suggest that the model is valid and translation, allowing its application in a real-world scenario. This way, a longitudinal study involving real users may enable evaluating the long-term effectiveness of the fall risk model providing useful insights into its clinical application. To improve the prevention efficacy of the system, data acquired from wearable sensors should be investigated and used to build a dynamic fall detection model.

Acknowledgments. The authors would like to acknowledge Manuel Cretone and Eleonora Vincenzetti for their valuable contribution to the research activity.

Disclosure of Interests. This research was funded by the Ministry of Enterprises and Made in Italy (ex Ministry of Economic Development) and Marche Region under the tender for Innovation Agreements. Project title: MOSAICO—Models, products and services to make the life of frailty people socially active and inclusive in communities spread across the territory. CUP: I36J20000910001.

References

1. Park, S.-H.: Tools for assessing fall risk in the elderly: a systematic review and meta-analysis. Aging Clin. Exp. Res. **30**, 1–16 (2018). https://doi.org/10.1007/s40520-017-0749-0
2. Millet, A., Madrid, A., Alonso-Weber, J.M., et al.: Machine learning techniques applied to the development of a fall risk index for older adults. IEEE Access **11**, 84795–84809 (2023). https://doi.org/10.1109/ACCESS.2023.3299489
3. Lage, I., Braga, F., Almendra, M., et al.: Older people living alone: a predictive model of fall risk. Int. J. Environ. Res. Public Health **20**, 6284 (2023). https://doi.org/10.3390/ijerph201 36284
4. Smith, T.O., Higson, E., Pearson, M., Mansfield, M.: Is there an increased risk of falls and fractures in people with early diagnosed hip and knee osteoarthritis? Data from the Osteoarthritis Initiative. Int. J. Rheum. Dis. **21**, 1193–1201 (2018). https://doi.org/10.1111/1756-185X. 12871
5. Al Abiad, N., van Schooten, K.S., Renaudin, V., et al.: Association of prospective falls in older people with ubiquitous step-based fall risk parameters calculated from ambulatory inertial signals: secondary data analysis. JMIR Aging **6**, e49587–e49587 (2023). https://doi.org/10. 2196/49587
6. Caragiuli, M., Brunzini, A., Germani, M., et al.: A prediction algorithm for fall risk assessment among community-dwelling elderly people (2023). https://doi.org/10.11159/icbes23.149
7. Martinez, M., De Leon, P.L.: Falls risk classification of older adults using deep neural networks and transfer learning. IEEE J. Biomed. Health Inform. **24**, 144–150 (2020). https://doi.org/ 10.1109/JBHI.2019.2906499
8. Adeli, V., Korhani, N., Sabo, A., et al.: Ambient monitoring of gait and machine learning models for dynamic and short-term falls risk assessment in people with dementia. IEEE J. Biomed. Health Inform. **27**, 3599–3609 (2023). https://doi.org/10.1109/JBHI.2023.3267039
9. Buisseret, F., Catinus, L., Grenard, R., et al.: Timed up and go and six-minute walking tests with wearable inertial sensor: one step further for the prediction of the risk of fall in elderly nursing home people. Sensors **20**, 3207 (2020). https://doi.org/10.3390/s20113207

10. Ghosh, S., Ghosh, S.K.: FEEL: FEderated LEarning framework for ELderly healthcare using edge-IoMT. IEEE Trans. Comput. Soc. Syst. **10**, 1800–1809 (2023). https://doi.org/10.1109/TCSS.2022.3233300

11. Brunzini, A., Caragiuli, M., Massera, C., Mandolini, M.: Healthy ageing: a decision-support algorithm for the patient-specific assignment of ICT devices and services. Sensors **23**, 1836 (2023). https://doi.org/10.3390/s23041836

12. Al-Shaboti, M., Chen, A., Welch, I.: Automatic device selection and access policy generation based on user preference for IoT activity workflow. In: 2019 18th IEEE International Conference On Trust, Security And Privacy In Computing And Communications/13th IEEE International Conference On Big Data Science And Engineering (TrustCom/BigDataSE), pp 769–774. IEEE (2019)

13. Sabatucci, L., Cossentino, M., Di Napoli, C., Susi, A.: A model for automatic selection of IoT services in ambient assisted living for the elderly. Pervasive Mob. Comput. **95**, 101845 (2023). https://doi.org/10.1016/j.pmcj.2023.101845

14. Asthana, S., Megahed, A., Strong, R.: A recommendation system for proactive health monitoring using IoT and wearable technologies. In: 2017 IEEE International Conference on AI & Mobile Services (AIMS), pp 14–21. IEEE (2017)

15. Bokharaei Nia, M., Afshar Kazemi, M., Valmohammadi, C., Abbaspour, G.: Wearable IoT intelligent recommender framework for a smarter healthcare approach. Library Hi Tech **41**, 1238–1261 (2023). https://doi.org/10.1108/LHT-04-2021-0151

16. Brunzini, A., Caragiuli, M., Atzori, F., et al.: Digital technology for elders better living: a usability and user-experience assessment. In: Proceedings of the 16th International Conference on PErvasive Technologies Related to Assistive Environments. ACM, New York, NY, USA, pp. 123–130 (2023). https://doi.org/10.1145/3594806.3594846

17. Harris, M.T., Blocker, K.A., Rogers, W.A.: Older adults and smart technology: facilitators and barriers to use. Front. Comput. Sci. **4** (2022). https://doi.org/10.3389/fcomp.2022.835927

18. Vassli, L.T., Farshchian, B.A.: Acceptance of health-related ICT among elderly people living in the community: a systematic review of qualitative evidence. Int. J. Hum. Comput. Interact. **34**, 99–116 (2018). https://doi.org/10.1080/10447318.2017.1328024

19. Rehman, R.Z.U., Zhou, Y., Del Din, S., et al.: Gait analysis with wearables can accurately classify fallers from non-fallers: a step toward better management of neurological disorders. Sensors **20**, 6992 (2020). https://doi.org/10.3390/s20236992

20. Ding, E.Y., CastañedaAvila, M., Tran, K.-V., et al.: Usability of a smartwatch for atrial fibrillation detection in older adults after stroke. Cardiovasc Digit Health J **3**, 126–135 (2022). https://doi.org/10.1016/j.cvdhj.2022.03.003

21. Xia, Y., Yu, M., Huang, Y.: Digital technology for business management innovations in community ageing. Acad. J. Manage. Soc. Sci. **6**, 104–109 (2024). https://doi.org/10.54097/a6540d21

22. Yokota, S., Ohe, K.: Construction and evaluation of FiND, a fall risk prediction model of inpatients from nursing data. Jpn. J. Nurs. Sci. **13**, 247–255 (2016). https://doi.org/10.1111/jjns.12103

23. Santos, G., Endo, P., Monteiro, K., et al.: Accelerometer-based human fall detection using convolutional neural networks. Sensors **19**, 1644 (2019). https://doi.org/10.3390/s19071644

24. Agrawal, D.K., Usaha, W., Pojprapai, S., Wattanapan, P.: Fall risk prediction using wireless sensor insoles with machine learning. IEEE Access **11**, 23119–23126 (2023). https://doi.org/10.1109/ACCESS.2023.3252886

25. Chan, D.Y.L., Lee, S.W.H., Teh, P.-L.: Factors influencing technology use among low-income older adults: a systematic review. Heliyon **9**, e20111 (2023). https://doi.org/10.1016/j.heliyon.2023.e20111
26. Baig, M.M., Afifi, S., GholamHosseini, H., Mirza, F.: A systematic review of wearable sensors and IoT-based monitoring applications for older adults – a focus on ageing population and independent living. J. Med. Syst. **43**, 233 (2019). https://doi.org/10.1007/s10916-019-1365-7

When a Digital Social Network Helps Seniors Live with Cancer: The French Case of Chronic Lymphocytic Leukemia (CLL) on Facebook

Juliette Charbonneaux[✉] and Karine Berthelot-Guiet

GRIPIC CELSA Sorbonne University, Neuilly-sur-Seine, France
`juliette.charbonneaux@sorbonne-universite.fr`

Abstract. This paper aims to investigate the search for online information and support for older patients, in France, focusing on a particular type of cancer, Chronic Lymphocytic Leukemia (CLL), and a specific social media: Facebook. It raises the following question: How can a digital tool like Facebook, whose accompanying discourses a priori exclude its use by so-called "elderly" population groups, constitute a means of exchange around CLL, a cancer that primarily affects the elderly? This question is addressed using a semio-discursive and communicative analysis of three contemporary (2022–2023) French Facebook groups, the publications they offer, and the comments and exchanges they provoke. Through this analysis, the paper shows how Facebook is today a place to discuss, also, serious illness, painful symptoms, and difficult treatments, all in a tone that easily supports seriousness and even pathos.

Keywords: Cancer · Facebook · Leukemia · seniors · social media

1 Introduction

The approach we propose in this article is developed within an integrated cancer research site or "Siric" CURAMUS (Cancer United Research Associating Medicine, University & Society) linked to the Groupe Hospitalier Pitié Salpêtrière - Sorbonne Université site (Paris, France). CURAMUS has three integrated research programs (neuro-oncology, rare immuno-hematological cancers, and microsatellite instability cancers). Each program includes dedicated human sciences research, with shared features such as the question of equality/inequality in access to treatment, transforming patient representation from patient to person in the context of personalized medicine, and improving care and dialogue between doctors, patients, and caregivers (family, friends, professional caregivers, etc.).

The program "Rare and Aggressive Hematologic Cancers in the Ecosystem" focuses on several pathologies, including chronic lymphocytic leukemia (CLL), in the case of rare chromosomal abnormalities. Aside from the cases analyzed in the CURAMUS program, chronic lymphocytic leukemia is the most common type of leukemia in adults (19,000 new cases and approximately 4,500 deaths in the U.S. in 2023) [1] From a

M. Antona et al. (Eds.): HCII 2024, LNCS 15379, pp. 194–213, 2025.
https://doi.org/10.1007/978-3-031-76818-7_14

medical and biological point of view, the program is based on cohorts that are unique in the world. Chronic lymphocytic leukemia, or CLL, is an immunohematological cancer and is defined on the website of the French National Cancer Institute (INCA) as a "hematological malignancy. It is characterized by an excessive accumulation in the bone marrow, blood, lymph nodes, and spleen of a type of white blood cell called B lymphocytes that have become abnormal. This cancer is also known as a blood or bone marrow disorder. From a medical and biological point of view, LLC's CURAMUS program is based on cohorts that are unique in the world.

Within this framework, human and social science research focuses on the needs and experiences of patients, including asymptomatic, untreated CLL patients. These patients live under a "Sword of Damocles". Moreover, for those diagnosed at a younger age, often at the time of a routine check-up, CLL is a "discreet intruder" [2] whose diagnosis falls on asymptomatic patients, invisible and often "forgotten" by medical institutions for lack of care to receive. The waiting is difficult: "sick without really being sick, newly diagnosed asymptomatic patients (…) find themselves in an unclear and anxiety-provoking situation", all the more so since "the active surveillance phase" can last from a few months to several decades.

As a result, patients often age without symptoms and are joined by those whose symptoms lead them to consult a medical team. According to INCA, "the median age at diagnosis is 71 for men and 73 for women. Given that "the 5-year survival rate is over 80%," the challenge for those affected is not only to find the treatment they need but also perhaps just as importantly, to learn to live with it.

Our discussion is taking place within a framework that has been promoted in France for several years, that of "health democracy". As stated on the website of the Ile-de-France Regional Health Agency (ARS), the aim is to involve as many stakeholders as possible in the implementation and development of health policy, in a spirit of dialogue and consultation. This is achieved by recognizing the rights of users of the health system and encouraging their active participation. Institutionalized by the 2002 Law on "Patients' Rights and the Quality of the Health System", health democracy defines the participation of users in the operation of the health system and highlights the notions of "accreditation of associations and training of users' representatives". The Law of 2016 on the "Modernization of our Health System" confirms health democracy by strengthening the place of health system users in regional and national bodies; it also specifies their rights (information on costs, health data, etc.).

In this context, the concepts of "expert patient" and, more recently, "patient partner" have emerged. They are recognized and promoted by the institutions, which define them as "patients who, over time, have acquired a sound knowledge of their illness, thanks in particular to therapeutic education. He or she does not replace the caregiver, but encourages dialogue between the health care team and the patient, facilitates the expression of other patients and contributes to a better understanding of the discourse of the health care team" (Haute Autorité de Santé - HAS). However, the notion of "expert patient" remains complex and problematic due to the vagueness of its definition and "the lack of a reference framework regarding the expertise of the expert patient". Nevertheless, "this gap could be one of the obstacles to a form of recognition for patient experts" [3].

Earlier work on the specific case of glioblastoma (a rare and severe form of brain cancer) showed how specific digital environments, in particular online forums or discussion forums, could play a unifying role and facilitate the emergence of this recognition among patients, their families, and caregivers. We focused, in particular, on the means of expression of the patient's families and not of the patients themselves, as online forums could provide. We developed the idea of family and relative expertise.

The present paper is an extension of that consideration, moving the focus from glioblastoma to CLL, but also from forums to other digital devices and, in particular, from Instagram to the social network Facebook, not because discussion forums are not present in the digital environment that unfolds around CLL. There are many of them, as a simple query on the Google search engine shows: reference sites appear in the field of health information (Doctissimo, Journal des Femmes santé), but also in the field of associations related to this cancer (Laurette Fugain association, Ligue contre le cancer) or even in specialized fields such as insurance (Ameli insured forum). Moreover, these forums will still be active and mobilized in 2023, unlike the case of glioblastoma, for which we have seen a mothballing of similar spaces for several years to the benefit of Facebook.

From this observation, we focus on this particular social network, which also has the advantage of allowing consistent expression: without offering the possibility of writing lines without counting, as in forums, Facebook's architext does not constrain writing as much as X's with its famous 240 characters, to name one. What is more, this social network seems particularly interesting to study in this case because it raises the following tension: How can a digital tool like Facebook, whose accompanying discourses a priori exclude its use by so-called "elderly" population groups, constitute a means of exchange around CLL, a cancer that primarily affects the elderly?

This question is addressed using a semio-discursive and communicative analysis of three contemporary French Facebook groups, the publications they offer, and the comments and exchanges they provoke. This analysis is based on the variety of signs that can be written on the screen (texts, images, hypertext links, and other "small forms"). To analyze and deconstruct the main features of these Facebook accounts.

This research, like our research into glioblastoma and the potential uses of A.I. connected objects for non-verbal people [4], has the peculiarity of being theoretical research whose results will enable translational research in the short term, i.e., as usual in medical research, from the laboratory to the patient's bedside. In our case, the goal is to create, in the coming years, a "Digital Observatory for Patients and Caregivers" to provide the right information in the right form to those who need it most and/or those who wait.

This first research on the digital presence of CLL patient and caregiver associations will proceed as follows: First, we will look at the digital environment that the social network Facebook offers and has offered on the one hand to older people, given that the vast majority of CLL patients are over 70, and on the other hand to patient and caregiver associations in general. The result will be a study of the digital representations and stereotypes of older people and their Internet use. Then, we will take a closer look at the three French Facebook groups most active in the field of CLL and their respective statements about their aims: portraits and ages of CLL patients will emerge. On the other hand, we will focus our analysis on the first type of exchange content that can be observed when Facebook is used both as a source and as a means of sharing information. This aspect is all the more important given the need for information in the face of an "invisible disease," [2] waiting for the symptoms for diagnosed asymptomatic patients or of elements that allow one to understand the disease for patients who have just been diagnosed with symptoms. Age is an essential factor in this regard.

In addition, Facebook seems to be a platform for action, especially for the leaders of the associations, who are often the administrators of the accounts, to ensure that the needs related to CLL are understood and recognized and that these needs become all the more specific as the patients grow old. Finally, adopting the scale of the individual, the patient, or his or her entourage, we will focus on another part of the content exchanged on these Facebook accounts. Facebook then appears as a possible place, maybe a forum for expressing "digital affects", as revealed by the preponderance of individual/personal testimonies. From the collective of associations, via the individual level, we tend towards a new form of collective: the "emotional community".

2   LLC on Facebook: The Overall Environment and the Muted Age Issue

First, we will look at the digital environment that the social network Facebook offers and has offered to older people, given that most CLL patients are over 70 and to patient and caregiver associations in general. The result will be a study of the digital representations and stereotypes of patients and caregivers, exploring whether age is an issue. Then, we will take a closer look at the three French Facebook groups most active in the field of CLL and their respective statements about their aims: portraits and ages of CLL patients will emerge.

2.1   Portraits of a Corpus

A query on the French Google search engine for CLL shows that CLL is the third possibility automatically suggested by the system, after "leukemia" alone and "fulminant leukemia". Given that Google is by far the leading search engine, used by about 90% of the French population [2], this type of result is interesting and all the more relevant to comment on. We can build a reliable corpus through the natural referencing of the topic, the site, or the account on a social network. This point is confirmed by using Google Trends France to compare queries over the last 15 years for 'leukemia,' 'LLC,' and 'over sixty-five.' The resulting maps show a very strong correlation with the average age of the French population: the older the population, the more llc is searched. This is the case in Nord, Alsace, Lyon, Burgundy, Brittany and Paris. These results are confirmed by comparing the results of Google Trends France, crossing only "leukemia" and "LLC," and the maps of the distribution of the over 65s in the country, produced by the Observatoire des Territoires, proposed by the French government.

There is enough Google search for LLC and, among other things, age, especially in the sense of "being old". To select a relevant corpus of social network accounts, let us look at the general environment the Web creates around LLC.

Predictably, searching for "LLC" on Google France gives access to the first page of results starting with a page in French from the Canadian Cancer Society, then, as the Google system always suggests, to the "most frequently asked questions" concerning "how does CLL develop / how to treat CLL / what are the symptoms of CLL / what is the least serious form of leukemia ". Then, two suggestions for research papers, and finally, a list of websites, starting with the Institut du Cancer, alternating with sites issued by university hospital groups, pharmaceutical groups, publishing houses dedicated to pharmacology and medical education, and, in a distant place, rare enough to be worth mentioning, Wikipedia.

The page continues in its current configuration with "related searches" such as: "life expectancy," "is it fatal," "treatment," "symptoms," "complications," "age," "diagnosis," and "diet". The list continues with a strong presence of associations, some French, Canadian, Belgian, and Swiss media, and, far away, "Doctissimo". We point out the position of Doctissimo because, in France, it is usually a reference for the search for information, in the first place, by the general public. For example, in our early work on forums for glioblastoma patients and their families, Doctissimo appeared very high on the Google search results page via Forum-doctissimo. Doctissimo is the leading French site in terms of audience. It is dedicated to health and well-being. The main players seem more specialized for a more common pathology (than glioblastoma) like CLL.

These results contain almost exclusively websites. For this reason, the search "LLC social networks" was then carried out on Google France. The results first present the Vidal site (dictionary of French medicines), which undoubtedly owes its position to a promotional purchase. Then, "How to live well with CLL" and "Is CLL tiring?." The emphasis is placed on lived experience, on feeling. Thus, we enter the enunciative territory of social networks, which mobilize representations of "participating" and "friendship," of "sharing" [6], and open the door to a double mention of the association *Vivre avec une LLC*, which successively presents two testimonies. Then comes *ELLye*, an association dedicated to several types of hematological cancers and the major generalist associations in the fight against cancer.

We completed the constitution of the corpus of Facebook pages LLC by searching the social network itself and entering "Chronic Lymphocytic Leukemia LLC". The cohabitation of full name and acronym avoids references to accounts on all types of leukemia. The main results were: "Vivre avec une leucémie Lymphoïde Chronique - LLC", then "Leucémie Lymphoïde Chronique - LLC selon RV", and "Leucémie Lymphoïde Chronique - LLC-leucémie Aïgue Lymphoïde - LAL". We have also added the ELLye Facebook group, a partner association of the CURAMUS research program to which we belong. Finally, only 3 Facebook pages remain as our request to join the "Leukemia Lymphoïde Chronique - LLC-leucémie Aïgue Lymphoïde - LAL" has not yet been accepted after several months.

Our precise fieldwork is a corpus consisting of 3 Facebook accounts: the first one is linked to a hematological multipathology association (ELLye), the second is a page proposed by an individual "Leucémie Lymphoïde Chronique - LLC selon R.V". And the third is a page "Vivre avec une leucémie Lymphoïde Chronique - LLC," proposed by the pharmaceutical company Astra Zeneca, explicitly identified in the "About" section (architext), under the tab "Details on Living with an LLC," third and last tab after "General Information and Contact Details," then "Page Transparency". The account's non-promotional, non-commercial purpose is strongly asserted: "The Living with Chronic Lymphocytic Leukemia - LLC Facebook page is in no way: - an area for promoting products marketed by AstraZeneca; - a sales area; - a customer service area". More specifically, we have gathered for analysis all the posts and comments (written and emoticon) present on these three accounts.

2.2 Implicit Portraits of Senior Citizens

The decision to focus the corpus on Facebook is based on several factors:

First, it is generally considered one of the oldest (founded in 2004) and one of the most famous "social networks". Second, because of its numerical weight, in 2017, 2.13 billion monthly users, or more than a third of the world's population, and in 2023, 2.989 billion monthly active users, placing it first in the ranking of the world's most "active" social media platforms. It has become an integral part of everyday life. Third, Facebook is becoming a social network for older people in France: The long initial lockdown due to the Covid 19 epidemic has "converted" many seniors to Facebook in France. Compared to 12% in 2018, they represented 43% of users in 2022.

On the whole, the network is going through a real process of seniorization, which is leading to a disaffection on the part of younger users, especially grandchildren. When the network remains shared, it generates different practices: "While Facebook registration is now transgenerational, the age divide within Facebook is still very present, depending on user activity configurations. It is likely simplistic to say that Facebook use has become normalized due to an aging population. Not only do older people not use Facebook in the same way as younger people, but older people are most concerned about their profile and e-reputation [8].

Older people post links, statuses and photos on their wall and sometimes comment on them, unlike younger people who post more text. Senior citizens prefer mediatization and join groups that share their interests (sports, creative hobbies, their town's page, etc.) and enjoy sharing their political opinions. (francebleue.fr).

Finally, their relationship to "informational public space" is specific, as seniors "link their use of Facebook to topics covered in the media" [7].

As a result, social network accounts dedicated to a disease whose specificity is to be diagnosed at over 70 years of age are bound to find their audience on Facebook France and must be there to find their "followers. "At least CLL on Facebook is obvious, if not pleonastic. Thus, social network accounts dedicated to a disease whose specificity is to be diagnosed at over 70 years of age are bound to find their audience on Facebook France and must be there to find their "followers. "It is hardly surprising, then, that the subject of age and old age is rarely a topic of discussion in account administrators' posts. In logic, this is a kind of presupposition: "semantic information which, though not thematically posited by the proposition, is nevertheless part of its literal meaning" [8]. There is no need for words; it is a matter of course.

The topic of aging comes up more often with the users of the three accounts than with their administrators. We will come back to this later. However, one exception partially confirms the obvious rule of age: the welcome banner of the "Vivre…" account shows a photo of a "typical" French elderly couple, short, white-haired (a certain visual fusion), surrounded by two children. They look fit and radiant, even from behind, and the white hair suggests that the children are their grandchildren. Representing them from behind allows all participants to identify with them, even though this type of choice can have negative connotations. This identifies the elderly as the main people affected by the pathology and the target of the proposed Facebook page. Lastly, the first names of the people participating in the exchanges are clearly dated. "Maryvonne, Monique, Christiane, Lucette, Alain, and Jean-Paul" are the first names of people aged between 70 and 80 (INSEE).

We can see how the strength of the media and promotional representations is remarkable: this single representation of seniors obeys in every respect the media stereotypes developed over the last ten years: the careful selection of good-looking, not-so-old people, very dynamic, beautifully tanned, hair beautifully gray or white, doing physically and intellectually demanding activities [9].

Now it is time to look at what the 3 Facebook accounts in the corpus offer to these implicit seniors.

3   What is Being Shared: Facebook Finding, Sharing, and Acting on Information

We will now focus our analysis on the first type of exchange content that can be observed when Facebook is used as a source and a means of sharing information. This aspect is all the more important given the need for information in the face of an "invisible disease," waiting for the symptoms for diagnosed asymptomatic patients or for elements that allow one to understand the disease for patients who have just been diagnosed with symptoms. Age is an important factor in this regard.

In addition, Facebook seems to be a platform for action, and the accounts administrators use it to ensure that the needs related to CLL are understood and recognized and that these needs become all the more specific as the patients grow old.

Although all are dedicated to LLC, the aim and type of enunciation are very different between the 3 Facebook groups in our corpus. The notion of information is present in widely differing senses: "Vivre," for example, offers a broad range of information, advice, and guides, while the "LLC selon…" account focuses on highly specialized information. Finally, the ELLye account provides information on its various offline services to inform patients and their families.

Although the 3 Facebook groups in our corpus are all dedicated to LLCs, the goal and the type of enunciation are very different. The idea of information is used in very different ways: "Vivre," for example, offers a wide range of information, advice, and guides, whereas the "LLC selon…" account focuses on highly specialized information. Finally, the ELLye account provides information on its various offline services to inform patients and their families.

3.1 Information and Ethos

More precisely, we will see how these enunciative regimes work, what discursive ethos the enunciators produce, and which model readers they address to propose what relationship.

In Aristotelian rhetoric, ethos refers to the work done by the speaker to construct, through his speech, "an image of himself that is capable of convincing the audience by winning its confidence" [10]. It is entirely linked to the act of enunciation: the image of the self, the organization, or the association constructed both linguistically and visually. Through analysis, we gain access to this ethos, which is distinct both from the so-called target ethos, that is to say, the image that the speaker intended to transmit, and from the prediscursive ethos, which is the image that the receivers may already have of the sender's ethos because they already know it and "even if the recipient does not know anything about the speaker's ethos, the mere fact that a text belongs to a genre of discourse or a certain ideological positioning creates expectations about the ethos".

Displaying an ethos coexists with constructing a model receiver, again through the message. [11] The ideal receiver, inspired by Eco's notion of the model reader [12], can think, construct, and find his or her way in the given message, here on a Facebook page. Eco assumes that the text only provides some of the elements of meaning and that it requires the interpretive cooperation of the reader. By favoring certain references, turns of phrase, types of vocabulary, genres, and images, etc., the authors of the message try to impose certain frames of expression, presuppositions, limits of interpretation; they act on the message so that a model recipient exists, because "a text is a product whose interpretative destiny must be part of its generative mechanism".

Generally speaking, what is shown and said refers to competence on the receiver's part, i.e., the ability to understand certain aspects of the message. The type of vocabulary, the syntactic elaboration, and the style of sentences constitute a specific linguistic competence. Encyclopedic competence is a predictive calculation of the amount of knowledge about the world an interlocutor is likely to have, which implies that the whole is difficult to limit and constantly evolving.

On these aspects, considering all that is visible and readable is included in the exchanges in question, we will return to the messages produced by the 3 Facebook accounts of the LLC: Facebook's system, its architext proposing, imposing, or preventing certain things, administrators' posts (writings, videos, images, links, etc.). Users' comments will be the subject of analysis in part 3.

The choice of the digital platform Facebook is in itself a first framework because "the sites of the so-called 'social' Web want to be perceived as places where people 'talk' and 'discuss,' not as devices that perform a skillful montage of writings" [6]. Hence, the proximity of the "Like" and "Comment" buttons: "While the 'Like' stands out for its economic, minimalist character, the composition of a 'Comment' involves the author in the production of a new small text to be read".

3.2 How to Live with an LLC User's Guide

"Vivre Avec une Leucémie Lymphoïde Chronique - LLC" (linked to Astra-Zeneca, see the corresponding website) is an account that has a rather large number of participants, with a total of 1.7 K likes and 2.1 K followers on a specific pathology. The "Page" section links it to the topic of medicine and health. It describes itself, as the Facebook system invites it to do, as a "testimonial and self-help site" designed to collect and disseminate "information and slice of life ". It establishes the link with the account of the association ELLye by publishing the fact that it follows it.

The first publication dates back to July 28, 2022, with a "Welcome to your "Living with Chronic Lymphocytic Leukemia - CLL" page. This page belongs to you. Patients and caregivers, this community has been created so that you can support and connect. Here and on our website, https://vivreavecunellc.fr/, you'll find information and news about the disease, as well as testimonials from patients and their families affected by chronic lymphocytic leukemia. We'll talk about managing the side effects of treatment, nutrition, exercise, sexuality, art, sleep, travel… We'll talk about living with the disease together!

In September, Blood Cancer Awareness Month and World Chronic Lymphocytic Leukemia (CLL) Awareness Day, we welcome you to our Living with CLL page.

See you soon for a new feature! See you in September for the launch of this new community! Until then, take care. From the outset, the speaker, represented here by the administrator and those who write the posts, presents himself as external to the "community" he addresses and for whom the account is intended. A whole game of "we," "us," "our," and "you," "for you" is set up. The main future topics are announced, and the claim to provide information and news (the difference needs to be specified, which assumes that readers know it and are familiar with the different online and offline media forms of information). The community is explicitly offered as a gift; its usefulness is taken for granted and not justified. Only its composition is described in detail. The target audience and the model reader are clarified.

The rhythm of publications is very regular (every 2–3 days), and they are based on a fairly stable discursive pattern: an informative post by the administrator, exchanges in comments between patients, and many digital reactions to posts (likes, shares, emoji reactions…). The types of information published correspond to the variety announced in the initial post: practical life, diet, hobbies, possible reactions to treatments, disease progression (stress 01/11/22 with an explanatory diagram), living with the disease (17/11/22, driving 18/10/22, credit 29/09/22), sports (yoga 11/10/22), nutrition (06/10/22, 15/09/22), after the announcement (12/01/23), prevention, explanations on certain dimensions of the disease (mention of "décryptage", form "le savez-vous? "for example 11/05/23, 13/10/22, 11/10/22). In addition, information is provided on associations and the world of cancer, with a focus on life outside cancer and outside the Internet (Christmas, World Cancer Day, Rugby World Cup, July 14, CML Day on 09/22, CLL Awareness Day on 09/01 with explanatory video, etc.), incentives for digital reading, patient testimonials (e.g., 03/18/23, 12/06/22, 09/19/22), videos by medical specialists (11/24/2022, 10/27/22, 09/14/22).

It is worth noting that this account's visual and written aspects are extremely polished, linking its production to an entity that has the means to implement this professional level on Facebook.

From an enunciative point of view, "administrator" posts are highly ritualized around seasonal or weekly headings, such as "Samedi qui bouge" and "Jeudi Nutri". Most of the posts have a structure of the type: a question (rhetorical?), followed by a quick answer or immediate proposal of a list of tips, or even injunctions (systematic use of the imperative), in the form of a "to-do list," and a final call to share ("your tips" for the question of pain). These posts are generally written in a "positive" tone, and there is a strong desire for buy-in. The way the information is presented is similar to how some self-help books are written.

If the term "chemobrain" is technical, the term "chronic" shows a possible misunderstanding of the meaning of the term, especially when applied to cancer, which to the general public is a disease that has a beginning, a course, and an end, whatever that may be.

One message does not fit either of these two cases: it is about sexuality, a subject the administrator feels the need to justify as "a subject you have urged us to address". The users were at the origin of the request. The contributions take the following form: a list of facts (effects of the disease and treatments on libido), a list of statistics with an "i" for info in pictogram form, as if it were necessary to support the appearance of this subject, then a list of advice on who to contact: partners, care teams, associations. We can assume that the subject of sexuality suffers doubly from the discursive taboo that it is subject to when it comes to the sick and, even more so, to the elderly.

In theoretical texts (Google Scholar), sexuality in cancer is discussed for breast, female genital, and prostate cancer. In other cases, it appears in the context of life after cancer. As for the association "sexuality and the elderly," it generates responses that explicitly describe the subject as "hidden" and "taboo".

The administrator's main ethos, and the account in general, is that of an advisor. Giving advice is kind, but it is also an intrusive form of verbal exchange, with the expertise of a confident tone and recurring turns of phrase, a mentor, coach, or guide position. Hence, the word "vivre" in the name is important since it is a guide to life that's being suggested or even attempted to be imposed through imperative pronunciation. It is about being the "good" patient who feels things and complements them with what the site suggests, looking for solutions to the different stages and feelings associated with CLL. Imagine checking off every item on every to-do list you make.

Personal management of items other than treatment is highly valued and even encouraged. It is about letting yourself be carried along by the list of lists constituted by the Facebook architecture. In this way, patients and their relatives are, in a way, brought into a common form, where individualities enter to emerge transformed on the scale of the collective, communicating in the list of tasks to be done to be "well" when ill.

3.3   A Strong Ethos of Association Commitment

ELLyE - Ensemble Leukemia Lymphomes Espoir weighs more on Facebook with 8.4 K Likes - and 8.5 K Followers. It is given as an association for patients and relatives affected by lymphoma, CLL, and Waldenström's disease, and the "page" is categorized as a "non-profit organization". The home banner announces the 9th ELLYE national meeting on February 3, 2024. Its first post, January 29, 2018, announced to be a list, a research tool with a large place given to research and trials: "The ORELy platform, freely accessible online, lists, in French and updated, all the clinical trials open in France in the field of lymphoma. ORELy is a platform for all those involved in clinical research, patients, and health professionals. ORELy is a research tool for lymphoma studies, in the spirit of democracy in healthcare, and contributes to the development of clinical research by encouraging patient participation in clinical trials/, www.orely.org". They engage people to take part in a study initiated in the CURAMUS program and now going on with.

Their publications are very regular, several times a week. They are mainly about calls for donations, "days of" receipt of donations, reactions to current events (e.g., abolition of the AME in the immigration law), news from the association and its volunteers (information meetings, races, etc.), patient testimonies, etc. Participants react mostly with emoticons, re-shares, and few comments (support, requests for more information, reactions to general news).

Ellye has a strong French associative ethos and shows it by displaying its links with other associations: "#jesuissolidaire mask action link with Renaloo and AIDES - distribution of masks on January 6, Place de la République, Paris". They show their activity in the field of the defense of associations: "Our associations, members of the collective Action Patients, speak out against the cuts in the Aide Médicale d'Etat (AME), a blatant attack on the part of the population living in France. It is no secret, and it has been all over the media since France's migration policy came under scrutiny by the authorities. The AME is contested on the grounds of the number of beneficiaries (411,364 by 2022), the cost to the state (968 million euros by 2022), and the alleged attraction it exerts on unselected immigration (denied by the Evin-Stefanini report). For our associations, it is not only normal that people living in France, no matter how foreign, have access to the AME; it is a necessity". This kind of outspokenness is typical of the French associative scene. It is often seen as militant than a simple meeting of interests. In this respect, ELLye has a classic ethos. It has an ideological perspective and is concerned with preserving acquired advantages in the health care and French social security systems. It took a stand on national authorities' slowness and participated in the "No to glyphosate" public debate.

ELLye's Facebook account makes numerous references, materialized by links to the association's website. Content follows the festive calendar. For 2024, there is a classic message of good wishes, unrelated to illnesses and citing the Olympic Games: "We send you our best wishes for 2024 and wish you peace, serenity, and well-being for the New Year. See you soon for this Olympic year and our national and regional events.

On your marks…". The classic associative work of appealing to and highlighting the receipt of donations (Breast Cancer Association) is strong.

When it comes to providing information on pathologies, Facebook is not the place where ELLye chooses to share information. Instead, it sends participants there in "real life" and organizes meetings, discussions, etc., in the form of "e-cafés," e-meetings, hospital meetings, and webinars: "LLC according to …" has a very different, technical tone on treatments and trials, among oneself strong technical info and almost incomprehensible, no keys to enter the meaning; technolect, excluding jargon but in a form that is significant: that of advice. Moreover, advice, even when well-intentioned, is an intrusive form of verbal exchange.

3.4   Hypertechnicity and the Limits of Its Informative Value

The third and last account is confidential. Although declared "open to all," it has only 50 members. Created on July 11, 2022, it offers about four monthly publications, and its administrator is named and identified. The tone and vocabulary used are highly specialized, if not hyper-specialized, especially regarding the names of treatments, despite a description in the "About" section stating that it is intended to provide "information and help on CLL from a non-professional". The effect is striking. It excludes from the outset those - no doubt many - who are unfamiliar with it: "Clinical trials of fixed-duration treatment in first-line IBRUTINIB + VENETOCLAX for CLL. FIXED-DURATION (F.D.) IBRUTINIB + VENETOCLAX IN FIRST-LINE CHRONIC LYMPHOCYTIC LEUKEMIA. PFS progression-free survival. O.S. overall survival = survival (alive). uIGVH = unmutated IGVH See more". This is not unrelated to the fact that the administrator's posts attract very few comments and/or anonymous questions, which are often answered in a hasty and unemphatic way and do not lead to any substantive exchange.

The information provided is second-hand. It refers to the original media, national, regional, or foreign daily press, or studies published in national or international journals. Images are rare and are, in fact, graphic representations of the results of research, all of which are "second-hand".

Overall, this Facebook account does not have a visual identity, not even that of the profile banner. As for the posts, we have already mentioned the general technicality of the content, which is all the more surprising since the administrator declares himself "non-professional". However, most posts have a typical structure: "IF you have…" or, more directly: "second-line treatment recommendation clinical trials molecules and results table". The participants' contributions are as direct: "Hello everyone…diagnosed with CLL - what can I expect?

Age is mentioned in a neutral, technical way: "If you're over 80 and taking ibrutinib as a first-line treatment, it is important not to stop taking it for more than seven days if possible. You will improve the time to relapse. Fortunately, all the negative criteria for CLL do not influence your life expectancy (del 17p might not mutate, etc.). Source Enrica Antonia Martino."

Therefore, the discursive ethos observed is technical and specialized, with a strong knowledge of the names of molecules, their combinations, and ongoing trials with a sharp follow-up of research and treatments carried out in the USA. The remaining receptors, the others having been sorted out and dismissed by "jargon" or "pharmaceutical technolect," don't seem to mind. They respond. It is a highly technical, expert relationship.

3.5   Of Sites and Social Networks: Discursive Economy of Information About LLC on the Web

We will now compare the previous elements with the results of an analysis carried out on the websites of associations and profit-making organizations for caregivers (family and friends) and patients [5].

They all offer a wealth of administrative information (assistance, files, taxes, etc.), financial advice and contingency plans, participation spaces, and calendars of events.

One category of sites stands out: it is more specialized, focusing on the disease, medical research, and more technical information, rather than "target" (mixed professional patients and caregivers) as is the case with "LLC Selon…".

The sites of the associations have more visible content, as they are more focused on the caregivers' expectations than those of the profit-making organizations. On this point, the issue is rather neutralized on Facebook between "ELLye" and "Vivre avec…" and the latter account, linked to Astra Zeneca, is more informative than the association's account. Indeed, many private actors "provide public health information via the Internet" [13]. On the other hand, what these accounts have in common - although this is much more obvious in the ELLye account - is that they "consider social networks as relays for websites that provide information to Internet users ". Facebook accounts are interesting in their own right, however, because of the interpersonal exchanges they involve: "Overall, social networks appear to have created opportunities for interpersonal engagement, interactivity, and dialogue that are qualitatively different from those offered by traditional websites" [14].

In 2023, the split between the website and social network was stable for the multiple actors surrounding a disease like CLL and providing information. Each has a different raison d'être, as "social media constitute (…) a communication tool perfectly suited to the communication objectives of these organizations, in particular associations (…) which have few resources and few professional (volunteer) skills for their communication.

4   What is Being Shared 2/2: Facebook, a Space for Expressing "Digital Affects"

The discourses and publications analyzed are also made up of "digital affects", understood as "a capacity to feel or bring to life emotions" [15]. These affects are themselves enabled by the fact that the digital device studied promotes the elaboration of "techniques of the self", which enable "individuals to perform, alone or with the help of others, a certain number of operations on their body and soul, their thoughts, their conduct, their mode of being", according to Michel Foucault's notion taken up by Alexandre Coutant [16].

4.1   The Importance of Individual Testimony

Among the digital "techniques of self" is a very particular narrative: the testimonial. The group "Vivre avec une LLC" (Living with CLL) has made this one of its defining characteristics, with the words "Vivre Avec une Leucémie Lymphoïde Chronique - LLC" (Living with Chronic Lymphocytic Leukemia - CLL) is a testimonial and self-help site. Ellye, for its part, offers a "we are patients" sub-heading that makes it easier to locate testimonials. Analysis of glioblastoma forums had already identified this mode of narration, encouraged or even demanded by the communicative organization of these systems, as a privileged form of authority based on expertise linked to the experience of and in the disease [17]. At the level of F.B. groups, we find it in two forms that vary according to the enunciator.

The associations, for their part, opt for the publication of fairly short videos (around 3 min) devoted to the narration by a patient seated facing the camera of his or her life with CLL since diagnosis. The auto-biographical mini-narratives follow a relatively stabilized and conventional pattern: presentation of the patient, date and stage of diagnosis, the introduction of treatment, and daily life with treatment. A positive tone prevails, built around "hope" and "confidence". Alain, for example, concludes by urging us to "trust the nursing staff" on the "Living with CLL" group (06/12/2022). These individual biographies come close to exemplum through the micro-narrations, the obligatory "narrative detours" that engage the discourse and produce a singularized and singularizing narrative [18] that articulates a collective value through the creation of a kind of common repertoire for group members who are understandably encouraged to pursue community engagement by joining, offline, the associations in question. On the Ellye group page, for example, we find the testimony of Christophe (13/11/2023), who, after recounting the ups and downs of his illness, from announcement to relapse, calls for people to join the association. In support of this invitation, his words, "It is very good therapy to look after others; it does me a lot of good," have been extracted and added to the list.

This emphasis on testimonial accounts has a dual effect: it contributes to the associations' communication by promoting them while at the same time establishing personal experience as a form of knowledge to be shared. This is a dimension to which members adhere, as evidenced by the number of shares, reactions, and comments following the videos mentioned. It is precisely in the spaces reserved for comments that the second form of testimonial at work takes shape: patients and, sometimes, their loved ones seize the opportunity to recount, in a necessarily fragmented form, snippets of their lives with cancer from the pivotal moment of announcement/diagnosis.

The announcement of the diagnosis occupies a very special place in the stories. This act marks a temporal break in individual history, and thus takes on the status of an event, a "sharp edge" that tears the fabric of our habits, our daily routines, our projects, and our memories" [19]. As one patient recounts on the "Living with CLL" group (08/06/2023): "The first day I saw people, I had the impression they had no faces. I was alone and far from my family and couldn't see them for four days. You wake up at night and think you're having a nightmare, but then you're not. Then, the treatments make you feel like you're living your life on the side, at least for me. At the moment, I'm in remission, but I'm having just as much trouble living the same nightmare but in the opposite direction".

As we can see, we are no longer dealing with a linear narrative, following a well-orchestrated chronological coherence, but with as many micro-narratives as there are themes proposed, whether on the initiative of the administrators or because the dialogic logic at work in the comments area constantly restarts the narrative machine, as new small texts are added to the screen. As the words of this patient suggest, however, the emotions expressed are decidedly less positive than in the videos, starting with fear. "Once I stayed for more than ten minutes, they stopped bombarding, but I was still well irradiated under the machine, and it lasted for months," says one patient. "I'm claustrophobic; I'm always afraid of this machine," replies another member of the "Living with CLL" group (23/03/2023). "I have low-grade lymphoma, fortunately without treatment for the moment, but I'm panic-stricken about chemo," confesses yet another patient on the same site (14/09/2023).

As Françoise Le Corre explains: "What happens when pain or illness occurs? It seems that the person is subject to a kind of "law of gravitation" that can be expressed as follows: whenever the body imposes itself, becomes heavier, takes up space, the subject tends to fade away or fail. He loses sight of himself. He undergoes a kind of involution in the body. He becomes wrapped up in it. The space occupied by the body makes the subject difficult to see. Opaque. For the patient himself and those around him" [20].

This "suffering body" is the other subject of patients' affective narratives. In the fragments written by them, the description of symptoms is given pride of place, no doubt because it makes visible and explicable cancer whose "invisible" nature is experienced as an additional burden, as stated, for example, by a participant in the "Living with CLL" group (01/09/2023): "The invisible disease! You can't see it on the outside! So we put on a smile and act "as if"!"With the distance afforded by the mediation of screen writings [21], the forced smile can thus fade away and give way to a detailed and often painful description of what the sick body is undergoing". Hello, following my chronic lymphocytic leukemia, I have had very low immune defenses since March 2023. Every week, I have a 2-h infusion, and I have fewer worries about infection, whereas before, I had bronchitis after bronchitis. I even fractured two ribs while coughing", recounts, for example, a member of "Vivre avec une LLC" (Living with CLL) (23/11/2023). "I can't live a normal life, but I also have fibromyalgia and a thyroid storm, and it's getting very heavy and complicated with all 3″, replies another member.

These "emphases on the body and everyday life" (16) are the result of the multiple self-writing favored by the Facebook device in which, as Hélène Bourdeloie writes, "the relationship to the body is hybridized," "between the digital self (its online data) and the physical/biological/material self" [22]. This hybridization enables small-scale regaining of control on the scale of the senior individual, who can thus regain control over his or her subjectivity via his or her biographical narrative, but also, as we shall see, on the scale of a community united in the sharing of emotions.

4.2   From the Individual to the Collective: Towards an "Emotional Community"?

LLC-related Facebook groups, for instance, involve seniors in the "expressivism" that, for Laurence Allard, defines online modes of expression, emphasizing "identity production and social recognition through self-exposure" [22]. "Through their posts and participation in devices, the living asserts their digital selves and give themselves in representation," she argued (22). Indeed, from the very first publication, the individual weaves himself to others and, in so doing, to a shifting collective, perceptible through the phenomenon of conscription (writing together or gathering of writings and images) as defined by Gomez-Mejia [23]: "[it] refers to seeing one's name written with other names. The devices of the contemporary Web, he continues in this sense, multiply the conscriptions of Internet users' names and effigies within automatically generated lists and mosaics and promote the possibility of seeing one's name written with a third-party actor". Within these lists and mosaics, which form a "collective individual" out of "collectives of individuals" [24], various semiotic and discursive features are deployed to promote commonality.

First and foremost, the relationship with time. While the forums lead to a narrative identity centered on the different times of the disease [25], on Facebook, the common calendar is split into two: the words spoken show a link between this very particular temporality and the broader one of ritual events that can be celebrated on the same device, outside the strict support group. In 2022, as in 2023, the "Vivre Avec la LLC" association wished its members a Merry Christmas and a Happy New Year. "The festive season is often synonymous with joy. However, when you're suffering from cancer, it can be difficult (...). How do you manage your holiday season?" the page read on December 29, 2022. Group members then react, multiplying the signs (745 reactions and 48 shares for this post) and wishes. "Courage and Happy New Year to all. Thank you for life's little pleasures", writes one participant.

Conjunctural and structural events are all occasions to manifest other digital affects that can be grouped under the paradigm of mutual support. The list of successive comments, both joined and disjoined, is striking for its warm expressions of support for another person, who may be an individual or a single speaker. For example, a patient writing on "Living with CLL": "I have low-grade lymphoma, fortunately, untreated for the moment, but I'm panic-stricken about chemo," receives the following brief message in reply: "Don't worry too much, the support is top-notch these days. Courage" (14/09/23). This "other" also turns out to be generalized, extended to the whole of a community that never ceases to expand as comments are added around the same post on the one hand and as posts accumulate on the other, with the effect of scrolling suggesting that you can potentially unroll ad infinitum the list of messages but also the names of your fellow sufferers: Facebook's architext encourages a virtuous cumulative principle in which words of support addressed to one become addressed to all. For example: "I have a blood disease that may evolve like you…COURAGE, you need support….and I sympathize even if it doesn't relieve you…!!!" (09/12/23). "Thank you so much for your sublime comments," writes yet another member on June 21, 2023, around a post about the fête de la musique in France, addressing all the speakers/scribers in the group.

Hyperbole, assertive lyricism, and capital letters accumulate to form a common, emphatic statement. As Anne Beyaert-Geslin reminds us, quoting an axiom of Barthes: "Emphasis is a force for cohesion" [26]. Cohesion between senior participants is made all the easier by the fact that, on these pages, there is a profound "decontextualization of the disease and the patient" [27], in the sense that material living conditions and "socio-economic" aspects are completely absent from the messages, as we have already seen in the case of glioblastoma [25]. Here again, a very strict boundary is established - and desired. - between an "inside," that of life in the face of disease, and an "outside" that ultimately encompasses everything else. This divide produces a desingularization of individual situations, reinforcing the feeling of belonging to a single collective.

"The same way of signifying an emotion can suggest the existence of an 'emotional community,'" Virginie Julliard and Fanny Georges [15] argued about online mourning. The words of support and encouragement, very similar in their expression, already make it possible to grasp the contours of such a community in the specific context of LLC. Added to this, perhaps more surprisingly for a population of senior citizens, is the sharing of the same "semiotic predilection," that "phenomenon of active differentiation within the semiotic form" which amounts to "creating different texts from the same space given to see" [6]. In the present case, this predilection relates to the extremely recurrent use of emojis and animated GIFs, those classic "small forms" of the contemporary Web, which "smooth and standardize the composition of contemporary Web screens (…)" [6].

Members of Facebook groups make widespread and recurrent use of emojis to end their comments with a complementary or additional affective connotation. Among these emojis are the little heads that cry, smile, or send heart-shaped kisses. For example, a participant writes at the end of his comment (17/08/2023) on the "Living with CLL" group: "I hope that everyone who is ill keeps hope and, above all, courage, because life is always an eternal struggle". We also frequently find the sign of joined hands, palm against palm, mobilized to give thanks or to ward off fear, as if in a secular prayer. "I've had this since 2010, and as I get older, it gets harder, and the fear gets worse and worse," says another sufferer in the same post dedicated to the fatigue she feels.

We can see how "insofar as emoji tend to redouble the content of the information transmitted semantically; it is the interest of the semiotic form of these additions that predominates, precisely because of the extra playful and emotional connotations they bring"[28]. The same applies to the other recurring type of "small form," animated gifs. They, too, come with their own set of affective connotations, with the emphasis on comfort. Here is an example, from a post published on September 28, 2023: After the following text "it takes courage to fight against such diseases, you must persevere and think of better days, which I wish for all of you. I supported my husband in this battle, and now he's at his best". The participant publishes a gif of these two panda bears, wishing "get well soon".

In the case studied here, the use of these "small forms" by senior citizens goes even further than the "surplus" since it sometimes suffices on its own without any accompanying text. In such cases, only the emotional connotation, and perhaps also the mastery of digital writing that the use of these forms signifies, takes precedence. Thus, the February 4, 2023 post published by "Living with an LLC" and dedicated to World Cancer Day elicits 27 separate comments. Half of them are animated gifs with no accompanying words. These include a circle of colorful hands holding each other, a heart bursting into fireworks with the words "Thank you," a series of three hands clasped in prayer, and an image of six people performing Usain Bolt's victory gesture. In contrast, the word "respect" is displayed, again the heart bursting into fireworks. Then, three comments later, two fairies and a "courage" gif.

"Observing small forms allows us to observe a phenomenon of stereotyping the 'image of text' on contemporary screens," emphasize the authors of "Le Numérique comme écriture" [6]. In this case, observing small forms shows that this stereotyping disregard potential boundaries between generations, which are nonetheless very much present in the escorting and social discourses accompanying this or that medium, digital or otherwise. It also ignores borders between national cultural spaces since the forms mobilized are accessible to all users of the objects and practices of the industries of contemporary digital capitalism, and the language of these industries, English, is mixed with that of the enunciators, in this case, French. In this configuration, the question arises as to whether the assertion that "the uses of signs charged with emotional value participate in the construction of enunciative positions (subjectivization)" [15] still holds or whether it needs to be qualified by envisaging an extreme homogenization of positions that would once again blur the contours of digital subjectivation.

5 Conclusion

The original analysis presented in this article further develops previous work based on studying another type of cancer and other digital spaces. It shows just how much Facebook is now being used by senior citizens in their search for specific information and day-to-day support in the context of a cancer like CLL. In this sense, it also extends other research devoted to the theme of identities and "digital eternities". In one of them, Sophie Pène wrote [29]: "Digital death and the digital discourse on human death, which are common topics of discussion on the Web, bear witness to the fact that digital identity is now applied to anthropologically essential situations - life, death, changes of state". Today, the digital identity of senior citizens is therefore also concerned with the major change of state that is the announcement of a cancer diagnosis. This marks a significant change from what the same researcher observed about Facebook in the early 2010s: "the illnesses we talk about are colds, flu, gastroenteritis, as unpleasant but light-hearted and comical obstacles".

Our analysis has clearly shown how this social network is today a place to discuss, on the contrary, serious illness, painful symptoms, and difficult treatments, all in a tone that easily supports seriousness and even pathos, this "discursive construction of the emotion the speaker intends to provoke in his audience" [30]. What is more, it is a space in which, through the medium of testimonies, patients can return to themselves and their bodies, thus escaping, for the duration of writing/reading, "the neutrality in which they are locked in exchange for healing" [31]. On the other hand, this is not a space cannibalized by individualism, as many contemporary social discourses tend to suggest: we do discover a "new way of taking care of one another (that) takes shape, at a distance, through the written word and the image, as a collective" [29].

However, this analysis also highlights the extent to which the dynamics of digital "care" are strongly conditioned by two types of capital-intensive industries. The first is the health and pharmaceutical industries, as demonstrated by the discreet but decisive presence of the Astra Zeneca laboratory in our corpus and results. This industry is invest-ing in Facebook to extend its influence, adopting a genuine consultancy posture applied to a list of care-related fields that seems capable of growing indefinitely. This dynamic also extends the contours of what Foucault defined as "bio-power," in which not only companies in the healthcare sector are participating but also those in the digital sector, the GAFAMs, who "after a stranglehold on the form of text, which materialized in the stable structure of architexts, the big digital companies have moved on to a stranglehold on textual content" [32]. This is the other major type of influence: Facebook, whose architext conditions the ways in which people write on-screen, is leading senior citizens to participate, in their turn, in a homogenization of modes of expression that disrupts the boundaries between linguistic spaces, between individual and collective, between private and public...

Sophie Pène concluded from her work on mourning on Facebook that "an industry of digital death is in place," which she also called for to be considered from the angle of "social network ethics". [29] Our article, on the other hand, highlights certain aspects of an "industry of digital sickness and disease" in which senior citizens find themselves more or less unwillingly embroiled and which needs to be monitored vigilantly, with the same ethical concerns in mind.

The research presented in this article is, as we said, both an extension to other forms of cancer of our work on the online presence of patients and caregivers in the specific case of glioblastoma neurological cancer. We are thus exploring the recurrent and possibly specific forms of these dialogues via forums and social networks. We therefore have several projects to carry out, on the other cancers in the CURAMUS program (hepatology-gastro, neuro and hemato) and on other social networks that could be involved. We will then be able to present and question the expertise of patients and caregivers, and culminate in the production of a dynamic digital observatory for patients and caregivers of selected cancers, to finally produce and make available information and relays that are currently lacking or insufficiently developed and known. This could be done in conjunction with patient associations, and as part of a broader framework for health democracy.

References

1. Emadi, A., York Law, J.: Leucémie lymphoïde chronique (LLC), Le Manuel MSD (2023)
2. Tinland, J.: La leucémie lymphoïde chronique un intrus; souvent discret est un objet de réflexion philosophique. Med. Sci. (Paris), 718–721 (2022)
3. Gross, O., Gagnayre, R.: Hypothèse d'un modèle théorique du patient-expert et de l'expertise du patient: processus d'élaboration. Hors Série « les Actes » Revue Recherches Qualitatives **15**, 147–165 (2013)
4. Charbonneaux, J., Berthelot-Guiet, K.: Of Seals and Humans. Media and scientific discourses about a caregiving medical device. In: Kalra, J., Lightner, N., (eds.) Healthcare and Medical Devices. AHFE (2023) International Conference. AHFE Open Access, vol. 79, pp. 170–180 (2023)
5. Rouquette, S., Chauzal-Larguier, C.: Analyses des stratégies de communication numérique à destination des proches aidants. In: Pinède, N., Massou, L., Mpndo-Dicka, P., Présence numérique des organisations, ISTE Editions (2023)
6. Souchier, E., Candel, E., Jeanne-Perrier, V., Gomez-Mejia, G.: Le numérique comme écriture. Théories et méthodes d'analyse, Armand Colin (2019)
7. Bastard, I., Cardon, D., Charbey, R., Cointet, J.P., Prieur, C.: Le numérique pour quoi faire ? Configurations d'activités et structures relationnelles. Sociologie **1**, 54–82 (2017)
8. Angenot, M.: Interventions critiques. Volume 1 Questions d'analyse du discours, de rhétorique et de théorie du discours social. Chaire James McGill (2002)
9. Berthelot-Guiet, K.: New media, new commodification, new consumption for older people. Human Aspects of IT for the Aged Population, ITAP 2018, Held as Part of HCI International 2018 Las Vegas, USA, July 15–20, Proceedings, pp. 33–52. Springer (2018). https://doi.org/10.1007/978-3-319-92034-4_33
10. Maingueneau, D.: "Problèmes d'ethos", Pratiques no. 113–114 (2002)
11. Berthelot-Guiet, K.: Analyser les discours publicitaires. Armand Colin (2015)
12. Eco, U.: Lector in Fabula, Le livre de poche (1989)
13. Romeyer, J.: TIC et santé : entre information médicale et information de santé, TIC et société n°1 (2008)
14. Lovejoy, K., Saxton, G.-D.: Information, community, and action: how nonprofit organizations use social media. J. Comput.-Mediated Commun. **17**(3), 1, pp. 337–353 (2012). https://doi.org/10.1111/j.1083-6101.2012.01576.x
15. Julliard, V., Georges, F.: Produire le mort: Pratiques d'écriture et travail émotionnel des deuilleurs et des deuilleuses sur Facebook. Réseaux **210**, 89–116 (2018)

16. Coutant, A.: Des techniques de soi ambivalentes. Hermès, La Revue **59**, 53–58 (2011)
17. Berthelot-Guiet K., Charbonneaux, J.: Entre déjà-dit et jamais-dit. Cancers rares et quêtes d'autorité numérique. Argumentation et Analyse du Discours [En ligne], 26 (2021), mis en ligne le 14 avril 2021, consulté le 02 janvier 2024. http://journals.openedition.org/aad/5161, https://doi.org/10.4000/aad.5161
18. Abiven, K.: L'exemplum : un modèle opératoire dans la lettre familière? Exercices de rhétorique, n° 6, [En ligne] (2016)
19. Arquembourg, J.: Le Temps des événements médiatiques. De Boeck Supérieur, Paris (2003)
20. Le Corre, F.: Le corps souffrant: que devient la personne? Laennec **52**, 30–42 (2004)
21. Jeanneret, Y., Souchier, E.: Pour une poétique de l'écrit d'écran. Xoana **6**, 97–107 (1996)
22. Bourdeloie, H.: Usages des dispositifs socionumériques et communication avec les morts: D'une reconfiguration des rites funéraires. Questions de Commun. **28**, 101–125 (2015)
23. Gomez-Mejia, G.: Les fabriques de soi ? Identités et industrie sur le web. MKF, Paris (2016)
24. Wrona, A.: Face au portrait De Sainte-Beuve à Facebook. Hermann, Paris (2012)
25. Berthelot-Guiet K., Charbonneaux, J.: Vers une entraide numérique intergénérationnelle ? Le cas du Glioblastome sur les forums de discussion en ligne Revue française des sciences de l'information et de la communication, 19, [En ligne] (2020)
26. Beyaert-Geslin, A.: L'image ressassée. Photo de presse et photo d'art. Commun. Lang. **147**, 119–135 (2006)
27. Azeddine, L.: Le cancer et ses récits: quelles places des malades et des maladies? Les Enjeux de l'information et de la communication, pp. 1–7 (2007)
28. Mercier, A.: Les modalités de la colère citoyenne sur Twitter. Quaderni n° **104**, 63–88 (2021)
29. Pène, S.: Facebook mort ou vif : Deuils intimes et causes communes. Questions de Commun. **19**, 91–112 (2011)
30. Plantin, C., Doury, M., et Traverso, V.: Les émotions dans les interactions. Arci/Presses universitaires de Lyon, Lyon (2000)
31. Baudrillard, J.: L'Échange symbolique et la mort. Gallimard, Paris (1976)
32. Saemmer, A.: De l'architexte au computexte. Poétiques du texte numérique, face à l'évolution des dispositifs. Commun. Lang. **203**, 99–114 (2021)

Timing of Micro-error Occurrence in Tablet-Based VR-IADL: Differences in Characteristics Between MCI and Healthy Elderly

Shoichiro Imanishi[1], Tania Giovannetti[2], Hayato Ohwada[1], and Takehiko Yamaguchi[3(✉)]

[1] Tokyo University of Science, Noda-City 2641, Yamazaki, Japan
7424503@ed.tus.ac.jp, ohwada@rs.tus.ac.jp
[2] Temple University, 1801 N Broad St, Philadelphia, PA 19122, USA
tgio@temple.edu
[3] Suwa University of Science, Chino-Shi 5000-1, Toyohira, Japan
tk-ymgch@rs.sus.ac.jp

Abstract. The increase in the number of dementia patients has become a social problem, with 50 million people suffering from dementia as of 2018, and this number is expected to increase to 152 million by 2050. MCI is a preliminary stage of dementia, and it has been reported that some patients can recover to a normal cognitive state with appropriate treatment. Thus, early detection and treatment of MCI are important. This project developed the Virtual Kitchen Challenge (VKC) system to measure cognitive function. Micro-errors (ME), which are subtle action difficulties, were observed during VKC tasks, and previous studies have demonstrated that MEs tend to occur at action transitions, which is related to the closeness of the action. This study hypothesized that there may be a difference in the number and timing of MEs in MCI patients compared to healthy elderly (HE) individuals due to their cognitive decline. In this study, 13 HE and 12 MCI participants were asked to perform a VKC task to determine whether there was a difference in the number of MEs and the ME timing. The experimental results revealed that the MCI patients exhibited more MEs than the HE participants, especially between subtasks.

Keywords: cognitive science · dementia · micro-error

1 Introduction

1.1 Dementia

Recently, the number of people with dementia has increased worldwide. According to a report by the International Alzheimer's Association, there were 50 million people with dementia in 2018, and this number is expected to increase to 152 million by 2050 [1]. In Japan, there were approximately 4.62 million people with dementia in 2012, and this

M. Antona et al. (Eds.): HCII 2024, LNCS 15379, pp. 214–228, 2025.
https://doi.org/10.1007/978-3-031-76818-7_15

number is expected to increase to approximately 7 million by 2025 [2]. Alzheimer's disease accounts for 60%–70% of all dementia cases [3]; however, there is no fundamental treatment for this disease, and the main focus of treatment is slowing the progression of the disease.

1.2   Mild Cognitive Impairment

Mild cognitive impairment (MCI) is a preliminary stage of dementia, and it is estimated that approximately 50% of MCI patients will progress to dementia within five years. However, 14%–44% of MCI patients can recover to normal cognitive status with appropriate treatment [4]. Thus, early detection and treatment of MCI is important [5].

Currently, brain imaging are using functional magnetic resonance imaging and cognitive function tests, e.g., the Mini Mental State Examination (MMSE), the Revised Hasegawa Scale of Dementia, the Montreal Cognitive Assessment, the Clinical Dementia Rating, and other cognitive function tests [6, 7]. These tests ask the subjects to answer questions about their immediate memory, calculation, and disorientation abilities, and the scores are used to assess cognitive function. However, even though the MMSE has high accuracy in identifying severely impaired stages, it exhibits low accuracy in terms of identifying the MCI stage. In addition, the test is time consuming; thus, a new screening method is required (Fig. 1).

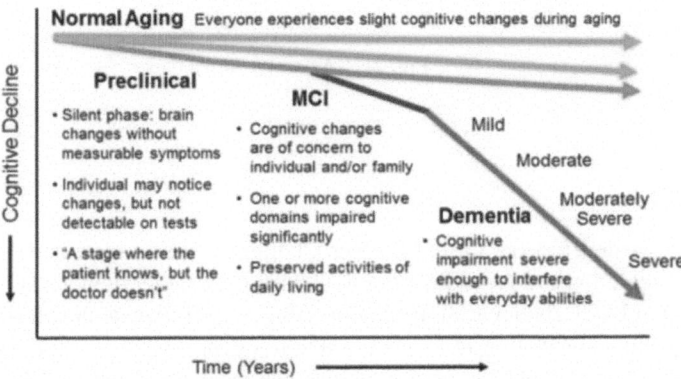

Fig. 1. Changes in cognitive function in normal aging and dementia [8]

1.3   Instrumental Activities of Daily Living

The instrumental activities of daily living (IADL) are complex activities that are performed with an action plan, e.g., cooking, laundry, shopping, money management, and answering the telephone.

MCI has been shown to have impaired behavioral functioning in IADL tasks [9, 10].

1.4 Naturalistic Action Test

The Naturalistic Action Test (NAT) task was developed to evaluate IADL performance [11]. This test discriminates between healthy subjects and MCI patients based on differences in the frequency of human errors due to behavioral dysfunction. However, the NAT task has several disadvantages, e.g., a large amount of equipment must be prepared, a large space is required to perform the test, waste is generated because coffee and sandwiches are prepared, and an experienced observer is required to observe the test subject (Fig. 2).

Fig. 2. NAT task

1.5 VR-IADL

In our project, we developed a Virtual Kitchen Challenge (VKC) system that uses virtual reality (VR) technology to reproduce the NAT task on a tablet device [12]. Similar to the conventional IADL, behavioral dysfunction due to cognitive decline has been found in the VKC, with a correlation in its occurrence frequency. Reproducing the NAT task on a tablet device eliminates the identified disadvantages and enables data analysis by acquiring data about the subject's touch, drag, and other movements.

The VKC has three modes, i.e., basic training, a breakfast task, and a lunch task, each of which has its own instructions and tests. Several main tasks are defined for the breakfast and lunch tasks, and each main task involves several subtasks. Note that the task order is not specified because the participants are asked to think and act according to their own plans. The following shows each task and the objects that appear in the breakfast and Lunch tasks.

Breakfast Task (Three Main Tasks)

- Toast task (seven subtasks)

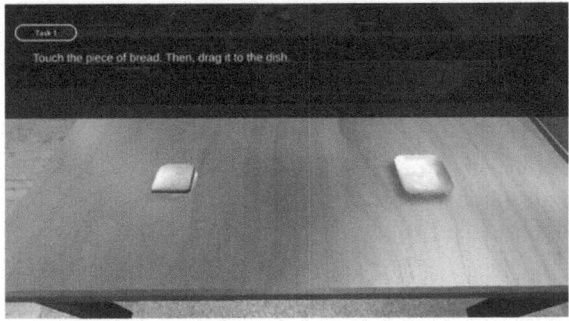

Fig. 3. Training task

Fig. 4. Breakfast task

Fig. 5. Lunch task

1. Put the bread in the toaster.
2. Lower the toaster lever.
3. Wait until the toast is done.
4. Move the toast to the plate.
5. Open the lid of the grape jam.
6. Take grape jam with a knife and spread it on the bread.
7. Take butter with a knife and spread it on the bread.

- Coffee task (six subtasks)

  1. Open the lid of the instant coffee.
  2. Take instant coffee powder with a spoon and put it into a mug.
  3. Stir the contents of the mug with a spoon.
  4. Open the lid of the sugar pot.
  5. Take sugar with spoon and place in a mug.
  6. Pour the cream into the coffee.

- Quit button task (one subtask)

  1. Press the QUIT button.

Lunch Task (Five Main Tasks)

- Sandwich Task (nine subtasks)

  1. Move a bread to a plate.
  2. Open the lid of the grape jam.
  3. Take grape jam with a knife and spread it on the bread.
  4. Open the peanut butter lid.
  5. Take peanut butter with a knife and spread it on the bread.
  6. Heap bread on top of bread.
  7. Take out aluminum foil.
  8. Wrap the sandwich in aluminum foil.
  9. Put the sandwich in the box.

- Juice task (five subtasks)

  1. Open the lid of a juice container.
  2. Pour juice into the bottle.
  3. Close the lid of the bottle.
  4. Close the cup of bottle.
  5. Put the bottle in the box.

- Snack task (three subtasks)

  1. Take out aluminum foil.
  2. Wrap cookies in aluminum foil.
  3. Put the cookies in the lunch box.

- Box task (one subtask)

  1. Close the lunch box.

- Quit button task (one subtask)

  1. Press the QUIT button.

Table 1. Objects in the breakfast task

#	Object Type	Object
1	Target	AluminiumFoil
2	Target	Bread
3	Target	Cap
4	Target	Cookie
5	Target	CookieDish
6	Target	Foil
7	Target	GrapeJelly
8	Target	GrapeJellyCap
9	Target	Juice
10	Target	KitchenPaper
11	Target	Knife
12	Target	Lunchbox
13	Target	PeanutButter
14	Target	PeanutButterCap
15	Target	SaladBowl
16	Target	Thermos
17	Target	ThermosCap
18	Target	ThermosCup
19	Target	UpperPivot
20	Target	Whitedish
21	Target	WrappedCookie
22	Target	WrappedSandwich
23	Target	WrappedSnack
24	Distractor	Fork
25	Distractor	Glass
26	Distractor	Razor
27	Distractor	SprayBottle

1.6 Micro-error

In the VKC task, subtle action difficulties, which are referred to as micro-errors (ME), can occur. Figure 3 shows an example of an ME. In Fig. 3, normal behavior would move the beverage straight to the bottle; however, when an ME occurs, the finger is attracted to an object that is unrelated to the task (i.e., the cup), which is referred to as the distractor, and the movement is modified (Figs. 4 and 5).

Table 3 shows the five types of MEs addressed in this study. Note that the ME shown in Fig. 3 corresponds to the reach-with-object ME (Fig. 6).

In a previous study, significant differences were observed in the number of ME occurrences in NAT tasks between older adults and young adults [13]. It has been shown

Table 2. Objects in the lunch task

#	Object Type	Object
1	Target	BreadDish
2	Target	Butter Dish
3	Target	Creamer
4	Target	GrapeJelly
5	Target	GrapeJellyCap
6	Target	InstantCoffee
7	Target	InstantCoffee
8	Target	InstantCoffeeCap
9	Target	InstantCoffeeCap
10	Target	Knife
11	Target	Mug
12	Target	Spoon
13	Target	SugarPot
14	Target	SugarPotCap
15	Target	Toast
16	Target	ToastDish
17	Target	Toaster
18	Target	ToasterLever
19	Target	Whitedish
20	Distractor	Ashtray
21	Distractor	IceCreamScoop
22	Distractor	PaintBrush
23	Distractor	SaltShaker

that the number of MEs in MCI is sensitive to task difficulty, and task difficulty is defined by the cognitive load, e.g., the number of task steps and the number of interfering stimuli [14]. The number of task steps and the number of interfering stimuli shown in Tables 1 and 2 indicate that the lunch task is more difficult than the breakfast task.

1.7 Previous Study 1: ME Occurrence Rate when the Viewing Angle and Position of the Distractors Vary

This study investigated the number of MEs that occurred when the viewing angle and the position of the interfering stimulus were varied in a specific environment [15]. Here, the viewing angles were 5°, 10°, 20°, and 30°, the interfering stimuli were placed vertically

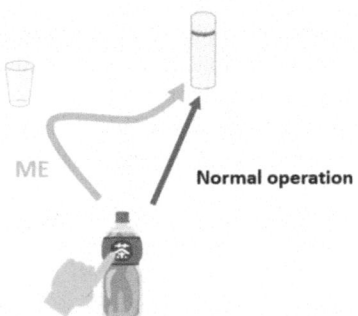

Fig. 6. Micro-error

Table 3. Type of MEs

Reach-Touch	Reach out and touch unwanted objects.
Reach-No-Touch	Reaches for unwanted object but corrects behavior before touching it.
Reach-With-Object	Move your finger to a non-target location while gripping the object.
Extra-Action	Grasping and moving objects without purpose.
Wandering	Wandering finger movement.

and horizontally, and the number of MEs was measured. The experimental results showed a positive correlation between the viewing angle and the number of MEs, indicating that MEs were more likely to occur as the viewing angle increased. This suggests that changes in spatial cognitive load caused by changes in the viewing angle may have affected the number of MEs.

1.8 Previous Study 2: ME Occurrence Rate when Taking Food and Drink Freely

This study investigated the occurrence of MEs in a task involving freely taking snacks and beverages laid out on a desk [16]. The experimental results revealed that the number of MEs was 1.7 times higher in elderly people than in normal university students, that the number of MEs increased with the presence of a distractor, and that the number of MEs decreased when the subjects were allowed to determine the placement of the objects. In addition, the results revealed that MEs occurred more frequently between tasks than within tasks. This suggests that the degree of action closeness (the degree to which the next action is facilitated by the previous action) is related to this phenomenon.

1.9 Objective

Previous studies have demonstrated that MEs are more likely to occur in action selection situations, which is due to the differences in cognitive load depending on the closeness of the action. In the VKC, at the start of a subtask, the next action is facilitated by the previous task. In contrast, at the start of the main task, it is necessary to plan the action for the task; thus, the cognitive load is higher at the beginning of the main task. This study hypothesized that MEs are more likely to occur under higher cognitive loads, but MEs may occur under lower cognitive load in patients with MCI because they exhibit cognitive decline compared to healthy older people.

Thus, this study attempted to determine whether there is a difference in the number of ME occurrences between the subtasks of the main task in healthy elderly subjects and patients with mild dementia.

2 Methodology

2.1 Measurement Environment

This experiment was conducted in cooperation with Professor Tania Giovannetti of Temple University.

Here, the subjects performed a total of six VKC tasks (basic training instruction, basic training test, breakfast instruction, breakfast test, lunch instruction, and lunch test) twice at intervals of 4–6 weeks. The order of the breakfast and lunch tasks was performed in consideration of counterbalancing. The subjects performed the VKC tasks using a tablet device or laptop computer with a touch screen, and their movements were filmed. The following is a description of the subject's condition at the time of measurement (Fig. 7).

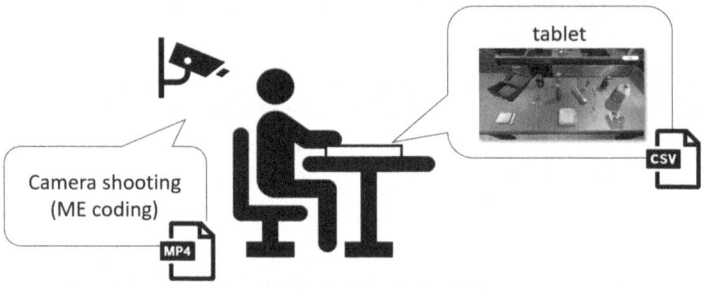

Fig. 7. Measurement environment

2.2 Participants

A total of 25 subjects (13 healthy elderly (HE) and 12 MCI patients; M = 74.04, SD = 8.33537) participated in this experiment.

2.3 ME Coding and Data Preprocessing

Based on the acquired video recordings, an experienced observer identified the location where the ME occurred, and the output was linked to the time of the video. The results were stored in CSV files.

Based on the obtained csv files, the subject's behavior was divided into subtasks and reflecting the ME coding data.

From the data, it was possible to identify when MEs were occurring (between main tasks, between subtasks). The ME data were output to a csv file for each subject.

2.4 Statistical Analysis

Among the six VKC tasks, only the basic training instruction, basic training test, breakfast instruction, and lunch instruction tasks were used to analyze the data acquired for the breakfast and lunch tests because these were training tasks to confirm the actions required to perform the tasks. Similarly, the ME coding and data preprocessing steps were only performed on the breakfast test and lunch test data.

In this study, Mann–Whitney's U-test was used for testing, and Cliff's delta was used for effect sizes. The indicators analyzed in this study are shown in Table 4.

Table 4. Types of indicators

BreakfastMECount	The ME count in the Breakfast test
LunchMECount	The ME count in the Lunch test
TotalMECount	ME count for both tests
TotalMEBtwMain	ME count between main tasks in both tests
TotalMEBtwSub	ME count between sub tasks in both tests
TotalMERatio	Ratio of ME count between subtasks in total ME count in both test

3   Results and Discussion

3.1 Results of Statistical Analyses

The results of the statistical analyses are shown in Table 5 and Figs. 8, 9, 10, 11, 12, and 13. In these figures, the label is 0 for HE and 1 for MCI.

Table 5. Results of the statistical analyses

	p_value	p(<.05* <.01** <.001***)	Z_value	Cliff's delta
BreakfastMECount	6.888.E-08	<.001***	5.39	0.88301
LunchMECount	5.179.E-05	<.001***	4.05	0.65545
TotalMECount	1.090.E-07	<.001***	5.31	0.8734
TotalMEBtwMain	8.357.E-03	0.008**	2.64	0.42949
TotalMEBtwSub	4.122.E-07	<.001***	5.06	0.82853
TotalMERatio	5.079.E-03	0.005**	2.8	0.46314

3.2 Interpretation and Discussion of Results

The results demonstrated that there was a significant difference in the number of MEs in the breakfast task, the lunch task, and the sum of both tasks. These results indicate

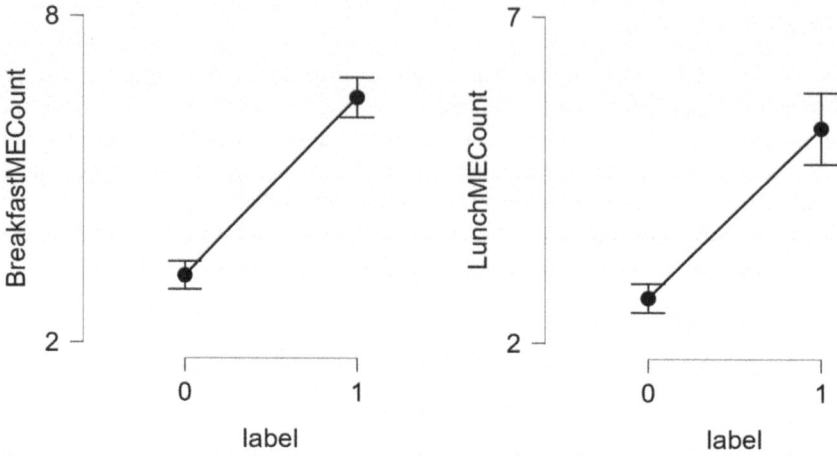

Fig. 8. The mean and standard error plot of BreakfastMECount

Fig. 9. The mean and standard error plot of LunchMECount

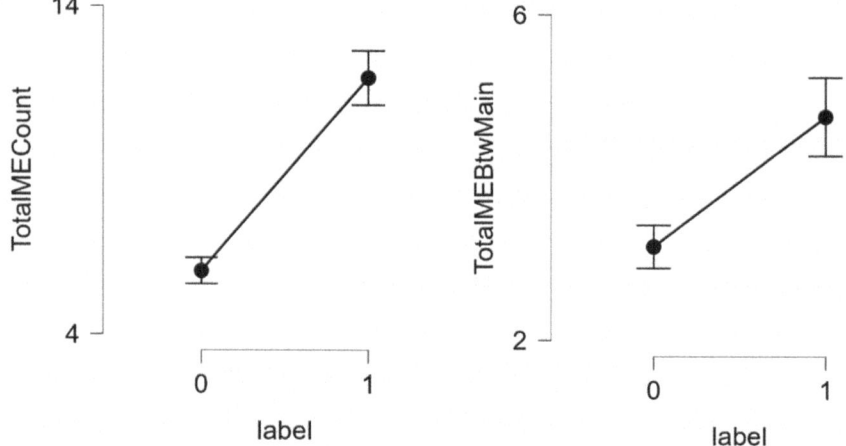

Fig. 10. The mean and standard error plot of TotalMECount

Fig. 11. The mean and standard error plot of TotalMEBtwMain

that there was a significant difference in the number of MEs between the MCI and HE participants.

In addition, when comparing the effect size, the lunch task exhibited a smaller effect size than the other two indices, which indicates that the rate of increase in the number of MEs was lower. For discussion, we compared the ME counts of the breakfast and lunch tasks using data from both subjects. The results are shown in Table 6 and Fig. 14.

The results demonstrate that the number of MEs decreased in the lunch task compared to the breakfast task, which is not in line with previous studies that showed the number of MEs increases in response to task difficulty. Task difficulty is defined by the number

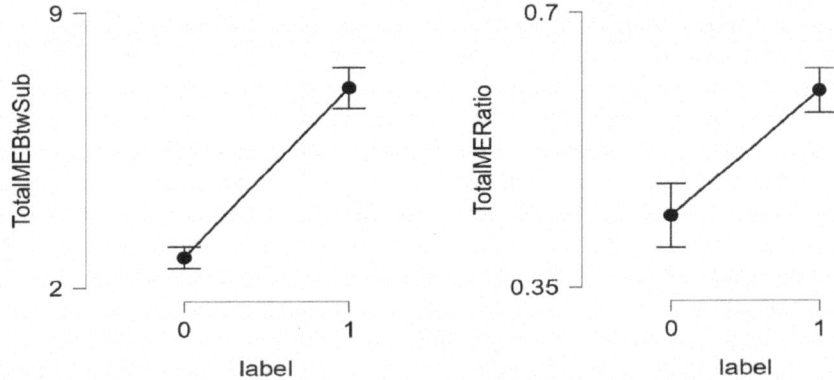

Fig. 12. The mean and standard error plot of TotalMEBtwSub

Fig. 13. The mean and standard error plot of TotalMERatio

Table 6. Results of paired t-test

Measure1	Measure2	p(<.05* <.01** <.001***)	Cohen's d
BreakfastMECount	LunchMECount	<.001***	0.488

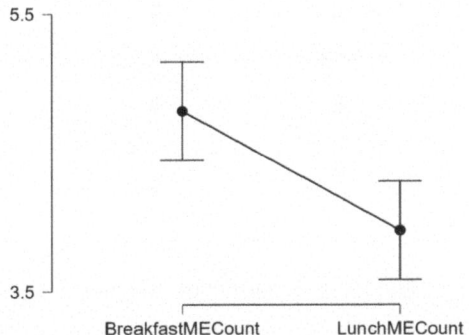

Fig. 14. Difference in the number of MEs between tests

of distractors and the number of task steps. In this study, the number of distractors in the breakfast and lunch tasks was equal; thus, the number of task steps was directly related to task difficulty. Here, the breakfast and lunch tasks included three and five main tasks, indicating that the lunch task was the more difficult task.

The following three points are discussed to examine why the above results were obtained.

The first is the possibility that the number of task steps has a small effect on task difficulty. As mentioned previously, task difficulty is determined by the number of task steps and the number of distractors; however, it is unclear to what extent either of these factors contributes to task difficulty. In addition, from a cognitive load perspective, the number of distractors may contribute more to task difficulty, and the number of task steps may not affect task difficulty to the same extent.

The second possibility is that other factors may be involved in the difficulty of the task. Although the number of main tasks in the two tasks differs, the number of subtask steps and the degree of closeness of each subtask in the main task also differ, which suggests that these factors may influence the difficulty of the tasks. For example, in the lunch task, the box task involved only one subtask. In contrast, the sandwich task involves nine subtasks, which is significant difference in the number of required actions. In addition, in the breakfast coffee task, the closeness of the actions of the sugar and cream pouring subtasks is relatively small. In contrast, in the lunch juice task, the closeness of the actions of the juice lid opening subtask and the juice pouring subtask is large.

The third possibility is that the real number of task steps in the breakfast task differs from the defined task steps. Many subjects performing the breakfast task make coffee while they are baking bread, as shown in Fig. 15, and they may switch between these tasks frequently. Thus, the actual number of main task steps differs from the originally defined number of main task steps, which may have led to the above results.

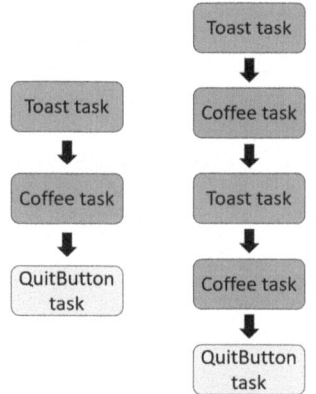

Fig. 15. Example of task switching

Significant differences were observed for both main task MEs and subtask MEs in the total number of MEs, and more significant differences were confirmed for the subtask MEs. Significant differences were also observed in terms of the main task and subtask ratio of MEs. These results indicate that there were differences in the timing of ME occurrence among the participants, and that the MCI patients exhibit an increased number of MEs between subtasks compared to the HE participants. This is considered to be due to the difference in cognitive load. The lower the cognitive load, the easier it is to make action plans; however, the MCI patients may not be able to form action plans due to cognitive decline; thus, MEs are more likely to occur. In addition, MEs occur between subtasks because the determined action plan may have been forgotten or failed during execution of the task. As a result, it is necessary to rethink the action plan, which may increase the cognitive load more than the original load; thus, MEs are likely to occur.

4 Conclusion and Outlook

4.1 Conclusion

The results of this study indicate that individuals with MCI exhibit more MEs than HE individuals, especially in terms of MEs between subtasks, thereby proving the hypothesis in this study.

4.2 Outlook

Future work will include the development of a machine learning classification model for MCI patients using the indices suggested in this study. In addition, due to the time constraints of the ME coding, some data were not available for analysis; thus, conducting the same test with a larger sample size is expected to provide more reliable results.

This study focused on the timing of MEs; however, in observing the VKC behavior of the participants, there may be differences in task switching. And it may be beneficial to investigate whether significant differences are observed in these indices among the participants.

In addition, this study compared HE and MCI participants; however, a comparison with dementia patients (e.g., Alzheimer's disease) is also required in the future.

References

1. Alzheimer's Disease International. World Alzheimer Report. (2019). https://www.alzint.org/u/WorldAlzheimerReport2019.pdf
2. Comprehensive Promotion of Dementia Policies - Bureau of Health and Welfare. Ministry of Health, Labour and Welfare, Bureau of Health and Welfare for the Elderly (2019). https://www.mhlw.go.jp/content/12300000/000519620.pdf
3. Queensland Brain Institute. Type of dementia (2023). https://qbi.uq.edu.au/brain/dementia/types-dementia
4. Yamamoto, H.: Current topics on mild cognitive impairment (MCI). J. Neuropsychiatry **113**, 584–592 (2011)
5. Malek-Ahmadi, M.: Reversion from mild cognitive impairment to normal cognition: a meta-analysis. Alzheimer Dis. Assoc. Disord. **30**, 324330 (2016)
6. Kato, S., Suzuki, Y., Kobayashi, A., Kojima, T., Ito, H., Honma, A.: Correlation analysis with HDS-R score using prosodic features of elderly people. Trans. Japan. Soc. Artif. Intell. **26**, 347–352 (2011)
7. Fujiwara, Y., et al.: Brief screening tool for mild cognitive impairment in older Japanese: validation of the Japanese version of the Montreal Cognitive Assessment. Geriatr. Gerontol. Int. **10**, 225–232 (2010)
8. Temple University Mild Cognitive Impairment. (2023). https://medicine.temple.edu/departments-centers/research-centers/alzheimers-center-temple/stay-informed/mild-cognitive
9. Wadley, V.G., Okonkwo, O., Crowe, M., Ross-Meadows, L.A.: Mild cognitive impairment and everyday function: evidence of reduced speed in performing instrumental. Am. J. Geriatr. Psychiatry **16**, 416–424 (2008)
10. Schmitter-Edgecombe, M., McAlister, C., Weakley, A.: Naturalistic assessment of everyday functioning in individuals with mild cognitive impairment: the day-out task. Neuropsychology **26**, 631–641 (2012)

11. Schwartz, M.F., Segal, M.E., Veramonti, T., Ferraro, M.K., Buxbaum, L.J.: The naturalistic action test: a standardised assessment for everyday action impairment. Neuropsychological **12**, 311–339 (2002)
12. Yamaguchi, T., Foloppe, D.A., Richard, P., Richard, E., Allain, P.: A dual-modal virtual reality kitchen for (re)learning of everyday cooking activities in Alzheimer's disease. Presence Tele Oper. Virtual Environ. **21**, 43–57 (2012)
13. Giovannetti, T., et al.: The virtual kitchen challenge: preliminary data from a novel virtual reality test of mild difficulties in everyday functioning, Neuropsychological **26**, 823–341 (2019)
14. Seligman Sarah, C., Tania, G., John, S., Libon David, J.: A new approach to the characterization of subtle errors in everyday action. Clin. Neuropsychol. **28**, 97–115 (2014)
15. Taisei, A., Yamaguchi, T., Tania, G., Maiko, S.: Basic study on incidence of micro-error in visual attention- controlled environment. In: HCI International 2020 - Late Breaking Papers: Cognition, Learning and Games, pp. 3–12 (2020)
16. Suzuki, K., Sasaki, M.: Task constraints acting on potential unit selection of actions: an analysis of micro-slips observed in everyday tasks. Cognit. Sci. **8**, 121–138 (2001)

Augmented Reality in Senior Communities: A Comparative Study of Urban and Rural Settings

Jie Ling[1] ⓘ, Nahua Huang[1] ⓘ, Qiyang Lei[1] ⓘ, Dan Li[1] ⓘ, and Li Ou Yang[2](✉) ⓘ

[1] Zhongkai University of Agriculture and Engineering, Guangdong 510220, China
[2] The Guangzhou Academy of Fine Arts, Guangdong 510261, China
oylee@163.com

Abstract. As the trend of societal aging intensifies, the design of senior-friendly communities becomes crucial. In recent years, augmented reality (AR) has emerged as a promising technological approach, garnering widespread attention from researchers. AR enhances and optimizes real-world scenes digitally, offering a range of functionalities and services. It serves as a tool to improve the quality of life and overall experience for the elderly; provides effective assistance in senior-friendly communities; and offers navigational features and real-time prompts, aiding seniors in seamlessly navigating their surroundings and accessing pertinent information. This study targets residents aged 50 and above from urban and rural settings. Through a review of literature and drawing from both domestic and international theories and practical experiences, the study employs AR to conduct comparative testing on life quality enhancement and supportive services. Observational records and structured interviews are used to compile feedback. The results indicate that urban residents have a higher acceptance and satisfaction rate with AR technology, particularly among newcomers. The findings elucidate the potential of using AR in designing cross-cultural environments within senior communities, offering new solutions for barrier-free and accessible experiences. This is vitally important for supporting sustainable development in an aging society and paves the way for future innovations in design and technology applications.

Keywords: Augmented Reality · Senior-Friendly Communities · Accessibility · Universal Design

1 Introduction

As global demographic structures continue to evolve, the aging of populations has become an increasingly prominent issue. According to United Nations data, by 2050, the global population aged 65 and above is expected to reach 1.6 billion, nearly 16% of the total population [1]. With the rising proportion of elderly individuals, older workers may need to extend their working years to support their retirement, potentially impacting the career development and employment opportunities for younger generations. The housing market and urban planning may need to adjust to cater to the specific needs

M. Antona et al. (Eds.): HCII 2024, LNCS 15379, pp. 229–247, 2025.
https://doi.org/10.1007/978-3-031-76818-7_16

of the elderly. Policymakers might have to reform the existing social welfare systems. Overall, the trend of societal aging presents numerous social and economic challenges while also demanding higher quality of life for the elderly. Against this backdrop, the design and implementation of senior-friendly communities become particularly vital. The World Health Organization (WHO) introduced the concept of 'age-friendly communities' in its 2002 "Active Ageing: A Policy Framework" [1], which refers to living environments that meet the physiological, psychological, and social needs of the elderly, a design philosophy proven by many studies to significantly enhance the quality of life for seniors.

From a macro perspective, meeting the needs of the elderly has profound implications for the overall development of society, not just economically but also culturally and politically. On one hand, the elderly, with their wealth of experience and wisdom, can continue to contribute to economic development as volunteers, knowledge sharers, or consumers. Their involvement can foster knowledge dissemination, encourage innovation, and increase societal productivity, thereby generating economic benefits. Furthermore, by focusing on the physical and mental health of the elderly, society can reduce the demand for medical resources and effectively lower healthcare costs. On the other hand, as custodians of culture and tradition, fulfilling their needs facilitates the preservation and transmission of cultural heritage. Their stories, experiences, and wisdom act as bridges connecting the past with the future, crucial for maintaining the cultural continuity of society. Therefore, building age-friendly communities to encourage the active social integration of the elderly helps enhance community cohesion and improves society's capacity to adapt to various challenges, providing stability and continuity that aid in maintaining balance during social transitions. On a micro level, creating communities that cater to the needs of the elderly not only alleviates the burden on families caring for their older members but also significantly reduces feelings of loneliness among the elderly, thereby preventing psychological health issues like anxiety. Thus, carefully designing age-friendly communities that meet the needs of the elderly not only highlights societal concern for the welfare of the elderly but also directly reflects the overall quality of life and level of civilization in society. However, despite considerable research focus on the physical and service design of elderly communities, how to further enhance these communities' functionalities and accessibility through modern technology remains an area ripe for exploration.

Augmented Reality (AR) technology, promising in enhancing the quality of life for the elderly, overlays virtual information onto the real world, offering rich, interactive user experiences. Specifically, it enriches the sensory experiences of the elderly through visual, auditory, and even tactile feedback, providing intuitive experiences and interaction. Operationally, AR guides users step-by-step, gradually increasing task complexity to enhance their mastery of technology. Moreover, gamification elements within AR, such as rewards and achievements, effectively motivate the elderly to learn and use new technologies, preventing cognitive decline. Importantly, AR also fosters interactions among elderly community members, reducing feelings of loneliness and strengthening community cohesion and social networks through shared AR activities and games.

There is a need for continuous exploration of how to effectively integrate AR technology into elderly communities to meet their growing and evolving needs, thereby enhancing their quality of life. Additionally, research should delve into how modern technology can further improve the functionality and accessibility of these communities. In recent years, AR technology has been applied in various domains due to its unique advantages. In the context of age-friendly communities, AR can provide navigation assistance, health monitoring, and interactive entertainment, helping the elderly better adapt to and enjoy their daily lives, thus offering multiple potential enhancements to their quality of life.

Despite the recognized potential of AR technology, its practical application still faces several challenges. These include acceptance of the technology, user experience, proficiency, and social engagement. Furthermore, systematic comparative analysis of the effectiveness and acceptance of AR in elderly communities across different regions, particularly between urban and rural areas, is relatively scarce. This paper aims to identify inequalities in access to health resources and technical support between urban and rural elderly communities. Providing insights into the characteristics of urban and rural markets helps businesses develop products and services suitable for different regions. Additionally, this research can guide governments and policymakers in adjusting and optimizing AR application services, crafting fairer and more effective policies to better meet the specific needs of the elderly, ensuring the balanced development of AR technology across regions.

This study seeks to fill this research gap by comparing the application effects and acceptance of augmented reality technology among elderly communities in urban residents of Shenzhen and rural residents of Linzhou. This paper aims not only to elucidate the practical utility of AR technology in advancing the development of elderly communities but also to offer strategic recommendations on how to promote this technology in an aging society.

2   Literature Review

With technological advancements, augmented reality (AR) has emerged as a significant field of study, particularly in enhancing and improving the quality of life for the elderly. This section reviews the literature related to the application of AR technology in the elderly domain over the past five years, with a specific focus on its use in the design of age-friendly communities.

2.1   Overview of Augmented Reality Technology

An analysis of publication trends from the CNKI database over the past five years, from 2019 to 2024, shows that 291 papers were published, averaging about 58 papers per year. This indicates a steady growth in research on AR in the design field. Most of these studies are related to children's picture book design or interactive design, with a few focusing on the preservation of digital cultural heritage. The peak in publications in 2023 suggests that AR technology might have moved from rapid initial growth to a more mature and in-depth research phase. Fourteen papers particularly highlighted the effectiveness of AR technology in enhancing user experience, focusing on how augmented reality can enhance interactive experiences and behavioral responses (Fig. 1).

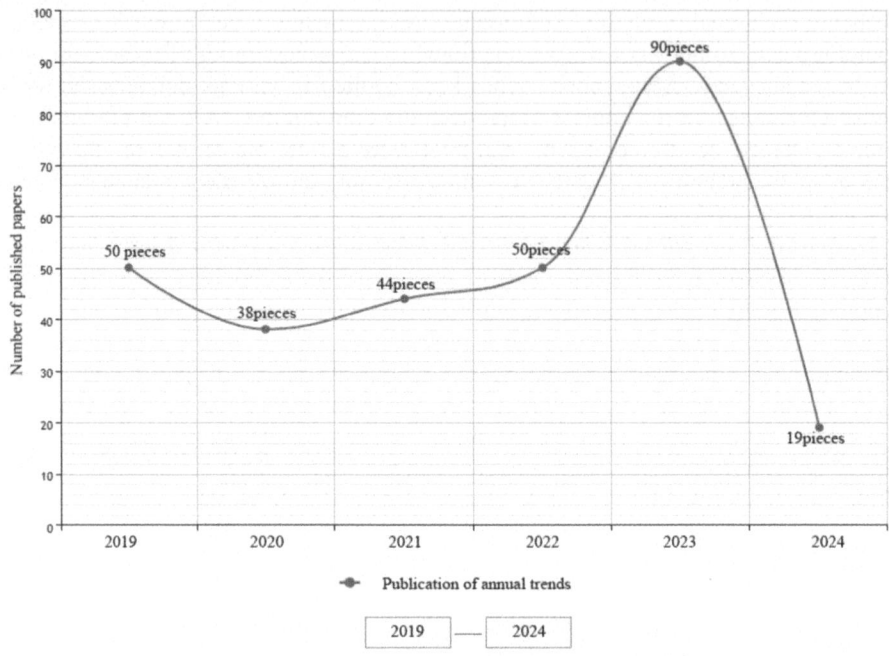

Fig. 1. Research Development Trends Graph. (Made by the Author)

Firstly, addressing the challenge of enhancing user experience, especially for the elderly, literature [2] suggests that a key to improving the overall experience of elderly users with AR navigation systems lies in reducing cognitive load. This indicates that AR designs intended for the elderly should simplify operation processes and provide more intuitive interface designs. Secondly, research documented in literature [3] also aids in enhancing the AR experience for tourists, studying different interaction methods in AR's application in tourism and cultural experiences. Although this provides insights applicable to our study, the age range of participants in these studies, between 18 to 32 years, may not directly translate to the elderly population. Therefore, the design of AR in age-friendly communities must also consider differences in physical capabilities, cultural and social needs, and economic sustainability. Nonetheless, these studies provide a crucial theoretical foundation for our research.

2.2 Development and Applications of Augmented Reality Technology

Development of AR Technology. The origins and evolution of augmented reality (AR) technology have been significantly explored [2]. In the early 1990s, Tom Caudell and his colleagues at Boeing coined the term "augmented reality" and developed a system to assist mechanics by overlaying digital information via a see-through head-mounted display (S-HMD). This period saw the emergence of various AR systems primarily aimed at sectors such as medical, entertainment, and military.

Following these developments, scholars like Ronald Azuma in 1997, defined AR in a widely accepted report that outlined its three main features: the combination of real and virtual, real-time interaction, and accurate 3D registration. In 2000, Bruce Thomas introduced the first outdoor AR game, AR Quake, which brought AR into real-world settings. As mobile devices such as smartphones continually evolved, an increasing number of AR applications began to surface. The debut of Google Glass in 2012 marked a significant resurgence in interest in AR, leading to increased research and development by corporations and academic institutions. Today, AR technology has found extensive applications across gaming, military, education, healthcare, and retail sectors.

Reflecting on policy documents and action plans over the past eight years, the inclusion of virtual reality technologies in China's "Thirteenth Five-Year Plan" in 2016 marked a turning point for national policy attention towards AR as a component of virtual reality technologies. In 2020, the Ministry of Industry and Information Technology highlighted the promotion of applications combining 5G with VR/AR, indicating policy support for the dissemination of AR technology. The "Fourteenth Five-Year Plan" in 2021 emphasized virtual and augmented reality technologies as key sectors in building a digital China, underlining further national commitment to advancing AR technology. The "Virtual Reality and Industry Application Integration Development Action Plan (2022–2026)" released by the State Council in 2022 set specific development targets and action plans for virtual reality technologies, including augmented and mixed reality, further underscoring the importance placed on AR technology.

Applications of AR Technology for the Elderly. Given the scarcity of domestic research on the application of augmented reality (AR) technology in the realm of gerontology, this study has shifted its focus to international literature. An analysis of significant research from the past five years (referenced in Table 1) reveals several factors influencing the adoption of AR among the elderly, including improvements in quality of life, assisted interactions, rehabilitation training, cognitive enhancements, and mental health benefits. These factors guide efforts to increase the elderly's acceptance and usage of AR technology.

It is essential to conduct in-depth analyses of AR technology applications across different environmental contexts and to summarize insights for future research directions. This approach not only helps understand the immediate benefits of AR for elderly users but also explores how these technologies can be tailored to meet their specific needs in various settings, thereby enhancing their overall well-being and engagement with their surroundings.

It is noteworthy that although the studies by Anne R. Smink [7] and others were not solely focused on the elderly, they discussed the reasons why people use media technologies, referencing the Uses and Gratifications (U&G) theory. This theory is often employed as a framework to map user needs and gratifications obtained. The gratification derived from media, sometimes referred to in the literature as media experience, is defined as "the emotional, intuitive, or perceptual experiences encountered by individuals at specific moments when interacting with specific media." The sum of these gratifications constitutes overall engagement with media technology, a critical component of media technology and a key indicator of whether individuals will continue using a technology.

To understand why people, use AR applications, researchers have collected extensive lists of gratifications associated with traditional and social media, given that these gratifications have been well-studied in relation to both types of media. They then expanded

Table 1. AR technology in the international perspective of the research field and implications

Researcher	Main Viewpoint	Key Area	Implications for Research
Po-Jung Chen [4] (2020)	Application of AR in Tai Chi training for the elderly	Human-computer interaction and Gerontology	AR design should include systematic guidance, simplifying and personalizing Tai Chi training based on user capability
Yen-Fu Chen [5] (2020)	The potential of games and AR technology in promoting cognitive health and social participation among the elderly	Cognitive psychology	AR games should enhance cognitive health and social interaction, considering users' needs, preferences, and cultural backgrounds
Reem Sulaiman Baragash [6] (2022)	Comprehensive review of AR and VR technologies in enhancing physical health, cognitive abilities, psychological health, and social welfare of the elderly	Holistic health	Provides guidance for future technological development and practices to improve the quality of life for the elderly
Anne R. Smink [7] (2022)	Comprehensive understanding of consumer behavior regarding AR application usage, revealing key factors affecting user experience and preferences	Market research, User behavior analysis	Offers insights for application developers on how to effectively use AR technology to enhance user experience and satisfaction

these lists to include gratifications related to AR applications, as using AR might bring about novel gratifications (e.g., enhanced reality sensation). They identified eleven types of gratifications: hedonic (enjoyment, stimulation, diversion, identification), utilitarian (practical use, timeliness, efficiency), social (social interaction, empowerment), and those related to technology (innovation, enhanced reality).

Research shows that both new and traditional media largely fulfill the same human needs—cognitive, social integration, tension release, affective, and personal integrative needs—with digital media focusing more on social and technology-related gratifications. These gratifications are closely related to the dimensions measured in this study and are indicators for assessing user experience and technology acceptance.

Furthermore, it's important to note that within the domestic mobile internet domain, a 2016 study titled "Design of an Augmented Reality Navigation System for the Elderly" [2] discussed how AR technology can enhance spatial navigation capabilities for the elderly. This study demonstrated through the practical application of a designed navigation system that it is user-friendly, can reduce cognitive load for elderly users, and improve their navigation experiences. AR navigation systems effectively help the elderly understand and adapt to their living environments, which is closely related to the navigation assistance function tests in this study.

As technology matures and application scenarios expand, AR technology is expected to see broader application and faster development in the coming years. With improvements in hardware devices, such as smart glasses and other sensors, and advances in software algorithms, AR technology will provide users with a more immersive and natural interactive experience.

2.3 Design Principles and Practices for Age-Friendly Communities

In the design of age-friendly communities, augmented reality (AR) technology plays a central and significant role. From 2012 to 2024, only 13 articles in domestic literature discussed the application of AR technology in relation to elderly design, and just seven of these directly related to assisting the elderly or enhancing their overall experience. This indicates that while AR technology is considered a powerful tool to support elderly living, specific application studies in the design of elderly communities are still relatively scarce.

An analysis and summary of the literature (Table 2) from the past five years in the domestic academic field concerning the design of age-friendly communities reveals that researchers have primarily focused on social participation and community integration of the elderly, intergenerational communication, and building diverse stakeholder relationships.

International Concepts. Xiaojing Hu [8] and others have explored the practices in building age-friendly communities internationally. Firstly, in countries like the USA, Canada, the UK, and Japan, the cooperation between governments and non-profit organizations plays a crucial role in constructing age-friendly communities. This partnership model provides necessary financial support and policy guidance. Secondly, the comprehensive content of community construction includes aspects such as health environments, health services, community activities, urban planning, land use, transportation, housing, community nursing, and social participation. Thirdly, projects like the "Lifetime Neighbourhoods" in the UK particularly emphasize empowering residents, encouraging them to actively express their needs and participate in community changes. Lastly, the rapid development of healthy communities, such as the "Healthy Toronto Initiative," which promotes the development of age-friendly communities through environmental renovations, park projects, and health service systems, is highlighted.

Domestic Concepts. Domestic scholars focus on constructing age-friendly communities based on basic needs, social needs, and the community environment. Their research methods include surveys, observations, and interviews with friends or community members. These mixed methods of objective and subjective assessments lead to more accurate evaluations and specific implementation suggestions. Researchers explore various elements of constructing age-friendly communities from different perspectives, providing valuable samples and insights for further studies.

Table 2. A summary of the research on the design of elderly friendly community in domestic academia

Researcher	Main Viewpoint	Implications for Research
Li Xiaoyun (2019) [9]	Analysis of the content framework and theoretical basis of age-friendly communities from an international perspective	Research shifts from a single perspective to a multidimensional one, aiming to construct communities that foster positive intergenerational interactions as a future development goal
Zhou Yanmin (2020) [10]	Impact of outdoor environment design in age-friendly communities on social interactions among the elderly	Design should focus on the psychological aspects of elderly communities, addressing social needs with accessible and diverse spatial planning to facilitate intergenerational interaction
Zhang Jia'an (2021) [11]	Advocates for multi-stakeholder cooperation and emphasizes the local characteristics in the construction of age-friendly communities	Suggests improving the physical and social environments of communities to enhance intergenerational communication and social participation, aiming for harmonious community integration
Hu Xiaojing (2021) [8]	Summarizes international experiences in constructing age-friendly communities	Highlights the importance of developing a comprehensive content system for health communities, building balanced multi-stakeholder relationships, and establishing a tiered collaborative construction mechanism

While the design of age-friendly communities has achieved significant progress, with continuous enrichment of research content and improvement of theoretical frameworks, and increasingly diverse methodologies, there remain some deficiencies:

The Depth of Research Needs Strengthening. While there is considerable focus on urban age-friendly communities, studies on rural or remote age-friendly communities are less frequent. More effective assessment methods and comprehensive impact analyses are also needed.

Although the Academic Backgrounds of Researchers Are Becoming More Diverse. The construction of age-friendly communities involves multiple disciplines such as architecture, urban planning, sociology, and gerontology. Research from a single perspective often does not adequately address the issues at hand, hence interdisciplinary studies are necessary to enrich research content and facilitate the integration of disciplinary knowledge.

How to improve the construction system of age-friendly communities in China based on existing theoretical foundations and more effectively explore the acceptance of augmented reality (AR) design among the elderly requires deeper investigation and experience summarization, integrating knowledge across various disciplines. Enhancing the development of age-friendly communities in China is a direction that necessitates collective effort.

2.4 Technology Acceptance Model (TAM)

The Technology Acceptance Model (TAM) is a widely used model in the field of information systems, devised to predict and explain user behavior towards technology acceptance. Originally proposed by Fred Davis [12], the model focuses on two key beliefs: Perceived Usefulness and Perceived Ease of Use. TAM has been extensively applied in studies of various technologies and systems, such as e-learning, online shopping, and enterprise resource planning (ERP) systems, to understand the motivations and barriers to new technology adoption by users.

2.5 Research Questions

This study aims to address the following key questions:

Experience. What are the differences in experience when elderly individuals use AR tools in urban versus rural areas?

Acceptance. How does the acceptance of different AR tools vary among elderly individuals in urban and rural areas?

2.6 Theoretical Framework

The theory of age-friendly communities emphasizes that communities should provide a supportive living environment for the elderly to promote their independence, social participation, and quality of life. The application of AR technology can enhance these aspects within this framework by offering interactive entertainment, education, and health promotion activities, thereby boosting elderly individuals' social engagement and life satisfaction. Drawing on the Technology Acceptance Model (TAM), this framework incorporates specific variables to extend the modified model of AR technology in age-friendly communities (Fig. 2).

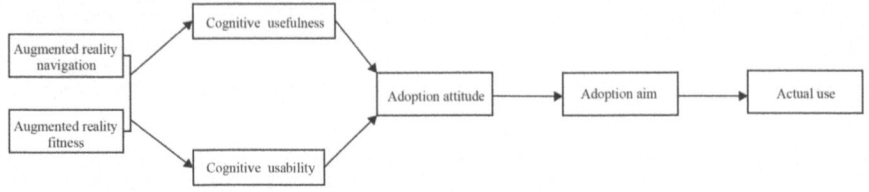

Fig. 2. Extended Technology Acceptance Model

3   Methodology

3.1   Research Design

This study employs a comparative research methodology to explore and compare the effects of Augmented Reality (AR) technology in different elderly communities, both urban and rural. The study involves two typical cases: urban residents of Shenzhen and rural residents of Linzhou. These locations represent typical environments for urban and rural elderly communities, respectively. Participants selected for the study are residents aged 50 and above, with 10 subjects from each location to ensure comparability of data. Experiments were designed around enhancing quality of life, assistance methods, and providing navigation and real-time prompts.

Experimental scenarios involving AR technology were selected:

Experiment One: Quality of Life Enhancement

Urban residents used AR-enhanced large screens for Tai Chi and dancing.

Rural residents used an everyday jump rope app.

Observation metrics include participation level, emotional response, physical vitality, perceived ease of use, usefulness, attitude towards use, intention to use, and actual usage (Fig. 3).

Fig. 3. Urban Residents Interacting with AR Screen. (Photography by the Author)

Experiment Two: Assistance Method. Utilized AR's measuring functionality to assess everyday items (3–5 items).

Functionality: Measuring the distance with a ruler.

Observation metrics include task completion rate, perceived ease of use, usefulness, attitude towards use, intention to use, and actual usage.

Experiment details: The setup included AR measuring tools capable of precisely measuring the radius of circular objects and accurately capturing and measuring the dimensions of rectangular objects. This was used to assess the practical effects of AR technology and its acceptance among the elderly (Fig. 4).

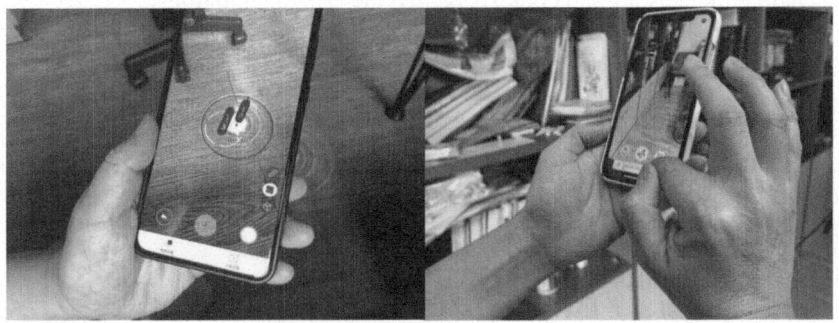

Fig. 4. People Using AR Software for Measurement. (Photography by the Author)

3.2 Data Collection Methods

Observational Records: We will monitor the elderly's behavior as they use devices for everyday activities such as navigation and information retrieval. Notes will include user proficiency, technology acceptance, and difficulties encountered.

Semi-structured Interviews: To gauge the initial perceptions and potential barriers to the use of AR technology in age-friendly communities, participants will use AR devices for a period after an introductory demonstration. This will be followed by semi-structured interviews focusing on the usefulness, ease of use, attitudes towards, and willingness to use AR technology. The interviews will aim to deeply understand the individual's feelings towards AR technology, gathering their views, concerns, and suggestions that may encourage acceptance and usage.

Questionnaire Design: The questionnaires will include basic demographic information, assessments of perceived ease of use, and usefulness of AR technology, intentions to use, and actual usage records.

3.3 Experimental Procedure

Training and Guidance: Participants will be introduced to the operation of AR and given preliminary guidance on its use.

Free Operation and Observation: Elderly participants will freely use AR tools during various sessions, with observations and records taken.

Interviews and Feedback: Post-use, participants will undergo semi-structured interviews to provide in-depth personal feedback and insights.

3.4 Data Analysis Methods

Quantitative Analysis: Data will be coded and analyzed using statistical software (IBM SPSS Statistics 26), employing descriptive statistics and correlation analysis to evaluate the relationships between perceived ease of use, usefulness, intention to use, and actual usage.

Qualitative Analysis: Content analysis of the interview data will be conducted to extract detailed descriptions of perceived ease of use and usefulness, aiding in understanding the reasons and contexts behind the statistical findings.

3.5 Ethical Considerations

Participants will give informed consent, ensuring they understand the study's purpose, methods, and potential risks. All collected data will be anonymized to protect participants' privacy rights.

4   Research Results and Discussion

4.1 Participant Characteristics

This study involved 20 participants, equally divided between genders with 10 males (50%) and 10 females (50%). The age range of participants was from 50 to 80 years. Ten participants were from Shenzhen, a coastal first-tier city in China with well-equipped urban facilities, higher levels of education, and above-average per capita income. The other ten were from Linzhou, an inland city located in a mountainous region characterized by a prevalence of elderly residents due to younger people working outside the area. Linzhou has average sports facilities, lower educational levels, and below-average income levels.

4.2 Analysis of Experimental Results

Enhancement of Quality of Life. Urban participants generally believed that augmented reality (AR) technology significantly enhanced their daily quality of life, particularly in entertainment and fitness. Observations from the first experiment showed that AR smart screens provided a platform for intergenerational communication, enriching interactions between grandchildren and grandparents. Furthermore, traditional square dancing, usually requiring multiple pieces of equipment and dependent on a lead dancer, was innovatively transformed by AR technology. Participants could now initiate dance activities anytime and anywhere with AR devices, enhancing social connections within the community and offering relaxation for both body and mind. Overall, AR technology demonstrated unique value and potential in enhancing community cohesion and improving residents' quality of life.

Semi-structured Interview Analysis. Random interviews were conducted on-site with ten elderly individuals aged between 60 and 80, to understand their attitudes and preferences towards AR Tai Chi and other fitness facilities in the park. Firstly, despite AR Tai

Chi being a novel form of exercise, most elderly showed little interest, preferring traditional fitness equipment available in parks or engaging in simple activities like walking. Secondly, many found the smart screens too complicated to operate, even with instructions, favoring direct interaction with traditional equipment. Additionally, some elderly chose specific equipment tailored to their physical discomforts. When asked about trying AR Tai Chi, they expressed willingness but noted limited time to engage beyond their usual routines. It was noted that for those over eighty, the purpose of exercise was less about health benefits and more about the activity itself. Lastly, while other games on the AR device attracted children, some elderlies were reluctant to compete for usage, opting instead for other types of equipment.

In rural elderly communities, ten individuals aged 60–80 were invited for testing. Although open to new technologies, the lack of infrastructure and limited experience with personal electronic devices posed challenges. With no AR smart screens available in the mountainous areas, similar functions had to be tested using apps. The use of AR fitness apps on phones required maintaining a certain distance, which was problematic for the elderly, citing issues such as small screen sizes and pace. Testing with iPads yielded better feedback from those aged 50–60, but those over 60 were still reluctant to interact with screens.

Elderly individuals demonstrate diverse and personalized needs in their fitness activities. They prefer straightforward, direct, and easy-to-operate methods of exercise. While emerging AR technology holds potential, its practical application must consider the habitual and real needs of the elderly more thoroughly.

Assistive Methods. The AR ruler tool, a mobile app, was used to test the elderly in both urban and rural settings, allowing for a comparative evaluation using the same testing tool. Following a brief training on the AR ruler, the usage among the elderly was assessed using observations and paper-based surveys. The survey included multiple-choice questions for perceived usefulness and a three-point Likert scale for other questions.

Perceived Ease of Use. Ease of Learning Evaluation: In both urban and rural areas, 40% of the elderly found the AR ruler tool easy to learn. However, the negative feedback in urban areas was as high as 60%, which might indicate higher expectations or dissatisfaction due to inconvenience among urban elderly. In rural areas, negative feedback was lower (40%) with 20% neutral, suggesting possibly better adaptability to technology or lower expectations compared to urban elderly.

Perceived Usefulness. Perception of Technological Advantages: Urban elderly primarily valued convenience (70%), while rural elderly appreciated cost savings (60%). This could reflect different challenges and needs in their daily lives. Perception of Future Applications: Urban elderly were more inclined to see AR technology applied in interior decoration (80% positive), whereas rural elderly found it more useful for measuring land and furniture (60% positive). This indicates significant differences in application contexts between environments.

Attitude Towards Use. Accuracy Satisfaction: Positive feedback on accuracy was higher among rural elderly (40%) compared to urban elderly (20%). This might mean that rural elderly have lower expectations for accuracy, or their use cases do not require high precision. Overall Experience Satisfaction: Negative feedback was slightly higher among urban elderly (50%) compared to rural (40%), with more neutral feedback in rural areas, suggesting a higher acceptance of the experience among rural elderly.

Intent to Use. Continued Usage Intent: 70% of urban elderly expressed a willingness to continue using the AR ruler, compared to only 20% in rural areas. This could be due to urban elderly more quickly recognizing the convenience and benefits of AR technology after use.

Task Completion Rate. Actual Use: Positive feedback was higher in urban areas compared to rural during actual use, but rural areas had more neutral feedback and very low negative feedback (0%). This may indicate that although rural elderly/s experience was not as positive as that of urban elderly, their acceptance was good (Table 3).

4.3 Discussion

In this study, we observed and analyzed the actual effects of augmented reality (AR) technology among elderly residents in urban Shenzhen and rural Linzhou. The results indicate that elderly individuals in urban environments exhibit higher acceptance and satisfaction levels with AR technology. Specifically, urban elderly demonstrated greater proficiency and less frustration in using AR for everyday navigation and information retrieval. Urban elderly community participants universally reported that AR technology significantly facilitated their daily lives, especially in navigating complex routes and accessing health information.

Differences in Technology Acceptance Between Urban and Rural Areas. Significant differences in technology acceptance between urban and rural elderly communities may be related to disparities in infrastructure, previous technology exposure, and age. Observations of emotional experiences with AR technology across different age groups revealed some disparities. Middle-aged individuals around 50 years old generally showed a pleasant and positive attitude towards experiencing AR technology. In contrast, individuals aged 60 to 70 appeared somewhat impatient during the experience. Upon inquiry, it was found that they found the AR interfaces complex and challenging due to limited exposure to new technologies in their youth and a lack of experience with modern devices during their younger years. Despite this, the middle-aged group around 50 was more willing to adopt new technologies but generally felt that AR needed improvement in terms of convenience and appeal.

Potential Barriers to Augmented Reality Technology. Following the experience with AR devices, a deeper discussion was initiated with the elderly based on questions designed for the survey. When asked whether they would recommend AR technology to family and friends, most elderly respondents said they would not. Upon further inquiry, it was discovered that their main concern was the practical utility of AR technology in everyday life. Although the younger segment of the elderly population was not unfamiliar with AR technology, after actual use, they commonly felt that the technology needed further enhancement in terms of convenience and practicality. For example, when using the AR ruler function, they felt it was not as quick and convenient as traditional rulers,

Table 3. Overall insights about AR assistive tools

Survey Dimension	Positive Feedback (%)	Neutral/General Feedback (%)	Negative Feedback (%)
Perceived Ease of Use: Ease of Learning Assessment			
City	40.00	0.00	60.00
Rural	40.00	20.00	40.00
Perceived Usefulness: Perception of Technological Advantages			
City	70.00 (Convenience)	40.00 (Cost Saving)	30.00 (More Accurate)
Rural	60.00 (Cost Saving)	40.00 (More Accurate)	30.00 (Convenience)
Perceived Usefulness: Perceived Applicability			
City	80.00 (Interior Decoration)	50.00 (Everyday Object Measurement)	40.00 (Land Measurement, Furniture Measurement)
Rural	60.00 (Land Measurement, Furniture Measurement)	50.00 (Interior Decoration)	30.00 (Everyday Object Measurement)
Usage Attitude: Satisfaction with Accuracy			
City	20.00	60.00	20.00
Rural	40.00	40.00	20.00
Usage Attitude: Overall Experience Satisfaction			
City	30.00	20.00	50.00
Rural	20.00	40.00	40.00
Usage Intent: Continued Usage Intention			
City	70.00	20.00	10.00
Rural	20.00	40.00	40.00
Task Completion Rate: Actual Use			
City	70.00	20.00	10.00
Rural	60.00	40.00	0.00

and the experience was mediocre. Therefore, they would only use AR technology if no other tools were available. However, when discussing the future prospects of AR technology, this group was optimistic about its potential and believed that the technology needed further improvements. While AR technology currently lacks commercial application scenarios and people are cautious about investing in new technologies, the elderly indicated that if AR technology were made more user-friendly, they would definitely be willing to undergo extensive training to enhance their ability to use it. This suggests that there is considerable potential for the application of AR technology in elderly communities.

Recommendations for Policy and Practice. The acceptance levels among elderly individuals are significantly influenced by their perceptions of ease of use and usefulness. Through a comparative study of urban and rural residents aged 50 and above, the researcher analyzed data and interview content to identify six key factors that affect elderly users' adoption of AR technology (Table 4).

Table 4. Influencing Factors for the Implementation of AR Technology

Factor	Specific Description
Educational Resources	Urban residents usually have better educational resources, making them more likely to accept and learn new technologies
Cultural Differences	There are cultural differences between urban and rural areas, with urban residents possibly being more open and willing to embrace new things
Technical Support	Urban areas may have more technical support and service points to assist elderly people with issues encountered while using new technologies
Lifestyle Needs	Urban elderly might prefer using new technologies that enhance life efficiency due to faster life pace and higher demands for convenience
Policy Support	Urban governments may be more inclined to promote technological innovation and application, enhancing residents' acceptance of new technologies through supportive policies and promotions
Infrastructure	Urban areas generally have more developed networks and infrastructure, which are crucial for the promotion and use of new technologies

Based on the research findings, it is recommended that policymakers and community planners consider the following aspects:

Customized Training Programs. Develop multi-level training courses tailored to the varying needs and technical familiarity of elderly users. These courses should range from basic device operations to advanced feature utilization, ensuring that each user can learn within their comfort zone.

Simplified User Interfaces. Design more intuitive and simplified user interfaces that reduce operational steps, use large fonts, and high-contrast colors to accommodate the visual needs of older adults. Consider introducing voice control features to allow those who are unaccustomed to or unable to use manual controls frequently to easily use AR technology.

Enhanced Community Support Networks. Establish AR technology support centers in both urban and rural areas, providing onsite assistance and regular technical check-ups. These centers could serve as community hubs where older adults can learn about and discuss new technologies, increasing their confidence and interest in using such technologies.

Strengthened Policy Incentives. Governments could offer tax incentives, subsidies, and other motivational measures to encourage more technology companies to develop AR applications suitable for the elderly. Moreover, governments should enhance efforts to promote the use of new technologies among older adults, aiming to shift traditional perceptions of technology.

Conduct Targeted Needs Assessments. Regularly conduct surveys to gauge older adults' needs and feedback on new technologies to ensure that the developed products and services genuinely address their real-life issues. These surveys could be conducted through community events, online surveys, or in collaboration with partner organizations.

Establish Senior Tech Ambassador Programs. Select technologically skilled and helpful older adults to serve as "Tech Ambassadors" within their communities. They could provide one-on-one assistance and training, making the dissemination of technology more personalized and approachable.

5 Conclusion

This study explored the effectiveness of augmented reality (AR) technology in urban and rural elderly communities and compared the acceptance and satisfaction levels of the elderly in these environments. The results highlight the great potential of AR technology to improve the quality of life for the elderly, while also revealing some key implementation challenges.

5.1 Main Findings

According to the study and observations, there are clear differences in the experience and acceptance levels of urban and rural elderly individuals when using AR tools. These differences are mainly influenced by education levels, infrastructure, previous technology exposure, and community support.

Differences in Experience. Urban elderly: Generally, have a more positive experience and adapt quickly to new technology. However, complex interface designs can sometimes lead to negative experiences.

Rural elderly: Limited by a lower frequency of technology exposure and poor infrastructure, although they are open to technology that can improve their quality of life, operational difficulties impact the overall experience.

Differences in Acceptance. Urban elderly: More likely to continue using AR tools, benefiting from good infrastructure and peer recommendations.

Rural elderly: Show curiosity and interest at initial contact but have lower continuous usage intentions and acceptance, mainly due to a lack of ongoing technical support and resources.

5.2 Future Outlook

While this study provides preliminary insights, it has the following limitations: it is confined to specific urban and rural communities and does not cover a broader area, lacks detailed analysis of AR operation and long-term impacts, and needs to integrate more disciplinary perspectives, such as psychology and design, to fully assess the application of AR technology. The research focuses on short-term experiences; future studies should conduct long-term tracking to evaluate the continued impact of AR on the lives and health of the elderly.

Future research should develop customized AR applications tailored to the characteristics of the elderly, optimize user interfaces and interaction designs. Conduct cross-regional studies to explore usage patterns and acceptance in different cultural contexts. Investigate the application of AR in elderly health management, especially in cognitive and psychological health. Research effective policy support and technology promotion strategies to ensure the widespread adoption and sustained use of AR technology. Pay attention to the ethical and privacy issues involved in the use of AR technology to ensure the safety of technology applications and respect the privacy rights of the elderly.

Acknowledgments. This study was supported by several esteemed institutions and projects: the 2024 Top Courses "Design Composition" (KA24YY044) and "Design Fundamentals (Three-Dimensional Space)" (6040324137); the 2023 School-Level New Agricultural Science Teaching Research and Reform Practice Project, which focuses on the deep integration of information technology with "Design Composition" education under the philosophy of "Tolerating Mistakes and Seeking Beauty, Integrating Skills to Have Beauty, and Honoring Schools to Promote Beauty"; the interim results of the ideological and political demonstration course "Fundamentals of Design (Three-Dimensional Space)" at Guangzhou Academy of Fine Arts in 2021 (Project Number: 6040321061); and the Guangzhou Academy of Fine Arts Graduate Program "Cultural Elements and Creative Design Education" (Project Number: 6040122027SFJD). Their generous support has been instrumental in facilitating this research.

References

1. Ageing and Health. https://www.who.int/news-room/fact-sheets/detail/ageing-and-health. Accessed 21 May 2024
2. Yang, Q., Wan: Design of navigation application system for the elderly based on augmented reality technology. Video Eng. **40**, 39–42 (2016). https://doi.org/10.16280/j.videoe.2016.11.008
3. Wang, J., Chen, Y., Hang, L.: Research on the impact of interaction methods and gender differences on tourism augmented reality user experience. Library Inf. Serv. **65**, 117–130 (2021). https://doi.org/10.13266/j.issn.0252-3116.2021.17.012
4. Chen, P.-J., Penn, I.-W., Wei, S.-H., Chuang, L.-R., Sung, W.-H.: Augmented reality-assisted training with selected Tai-Chi movements improves balance control and increases lower limb muscle strength in older adults: a prospective randomized trial. J. Exerc. Sci. Fit. **18**, 142–147 (2020). https://doi.org/10.1016/j.jesf.2020.05.003
5. Chen, Y.-F., Janicki, S.: A cognitive-based board game with augmented reality for older adults: development and usability study. JMIR Ser. Games **8**, e22007 (2020). https://doi.org/10.2196/22007
6. Baragash, R.S., Aldowah, H., Ghazal, S.: Virtual and augmented reality applications to improve older adults' quality of life: a systematic mapping review and future directions. Digital Health **8**, 205520762211320 (2022). https://doi.org/10.1177/20552076221132099
7. Smink, A.R., van Reijmersdal, E.A., van Noort, G.: Consumers' use of augmented reality apps: prevalence, user characteristics, and gratifications. J. Advert. **51**, 85–94 (2022). https://doi.org/10.1080/00913367.2021.1973622
8. Hu, X., Huang, J.: Creating age-friendly and healthy communities: international experience and inspiration. Shanghai Urban Plan. Rev. 1–7 (2021)
9. Li, X.: A review of the research progress of foreign age-friendly communities. Urban Develop. Stud. **26**, 14–19 (2019)
10. Zhou, Y., Wang, C.: Research on the outdoor environment design of elderly-friendly communities that creates a good social atmosphere—taking a continuous follow-up survey of a community in Beijing as an example. Shanghai Urban Plan. Rev. 15–21 (2020)
11. Z'hang, J.: Paths to build age-friendly communities from the perspective of community capacity building. J. Northwest Normal Univ. (Soc. Sci.). **58**, 107–119 (2021). https://doi.org/10.16783/j.cnki.nwnus.2021.06.012
12. Davis, F.D.: A technology acceptance model for empirically testing new end-user information systems: theory and results (1985)

Estimating Subjective *Ikigai* of Older Adults Based on the Analysis of Voice Communication in Social Activities: A Case Study of Frailty Check Activity Scenes

Takahiro Miura[1]([⊠]), Ken-ichiro Yabu[2], Emiko Uchiyama[3],
Kenta Kamikokuryo[4], Vincent Hernandez[4], Bo-kyung Son[5],
and Katsuya Iijima[5]

[1] National Institute of Advanced Industrial Science and Technology (AIST),
6-2-3 Kashiwanoha, Kashiwa, Chiba 277-0882, Japan
miura-t@aist.go.jp
[2] Research Center for Advanced Science and Technology, The University of Tokyo,
4-6-1, Komaba, Meguro-ku, Tokyo 153-8904, Japan
[3] Graduate School of Engineering, The University of Tokyo,
7-3-1, Hongo, Bunkyo-ku, Tokyo 113-8656, Japan
[4] Tokyo University of Agriculture and Technology,
3-8-1, Harumicho, Fuchu, Tokyo 183-8538, Japan
[5] Institute of Gerontology (IOG), The University of Tokyo,
7-3-1, Hongo, Bunkyo-ku, Tokyo 113-8656, Japan

Abstract. As birthrates decline and the population ages globally, the healthy age of older adults is increasing, and the need for sustainable participation in society is growing. Older adults can experience subjective well-being, namely, a sense of Ikigai (motivation to live), when they readily engage in meaningful activities. However, to support this, there is a need for a system that recommends such activities, and a method to measure the subjective experience of Ikigai in specific activities is yet to be developed. This study investigates the estimation of social engagement in enhancing the *Ikigai* of older adults based on communication during the volunteer activity. Focusing on voice communication during frailty checkup activities, we aim to develop a method to measure the subjective perception of *Ikigai* using objective indicators. We analyzed speech data from 16 older volunteers using advanced audio processing techniques and sentiment analysis. Based on our findings, it seems that individual speech features and group interactions can provide some indication of an individual's *Ikigai*.

Keywords: Older adults · frailty checkup · *ikigai* · voice communication · supervised learning

---

T. Miura and K. Yabu—Contributed equally to this work.

1   Introduction

One of the most pressing contemporary issues globally, including regions like North America, the EU, and East Asia, is the development of countermeasures against declining birth rates and population aging. In Japan, for instance, the percentage of individuals aged 65 and over was 29.1% in 2023, and it is projected to increase to 40.5% by 2055 [1, 2, 21]. Thus, it is crucial to present and implement a sustainable social model that can ensure the continued development of society, even in a society with a decreasing birth rate and an increasing aging population.

In a hyper-aged society with a low birthrate, people in other age groups must participate in various fields of society because the productive-age population is small [26]. Most older adults in Japan are not regarded as needing nursing care or support [24]. They can live independently and engage in various social activities such as employment, hobbies, and volunteer activities [4, 10, 16, 25, 27, 33, 35]. The frailty check (FC) program, a crucial initiative, screens the frailty conditions of older adults in community-dwelling active older adults, providing essential support [14, 18, 20, 32, 36].

Meanwhile, these social activities are seen as having preferences that depend on the characteristics of individual older adults [3, 8, 17]. When older adults are able to continue such activities easily, they can experience a sense of *Ikigai* (motivation to live) [15, 23, 28, 34]. However, it would be beneficial for individuals to engage in activities that give them a sense of *Ikigai*. An established system currently needs to be established to offer recommendations. Measurement of the subjective *Ikigai* condition in a specific activity is necessary for providing recommendation support, but the method for this purpose has yet to be developed.

Therefore, this study aims to develop a method to measure the subjective perception of *Ikigai* by older adults during social activities based on objective indicators. In particular, this paper focuses on voice communication among older adults during frailty checkup activities and extracts the characteristics of the communication situation. In addition, we attempted to estimate the Ikigai and other related indices that these older adults felt during their activities based on the features mentioned above.

2   Method

2.1   Participants

The study involved 20 older adults (9 males and 11 females) who participated as volunteer supporters in a frailty check activity. The participants conducted a pre-activity meeting, the actual frail check activity for older adults with frailty, and a post-activity roundtable discussion during the frail check activity. We used the SONY ICD-TX660 voice recorder to record voices, which was attached to the chest position of each person. Of these participants, 16 provided speech data for a total of approximately 48 h (3 h per participant). Before and after the frailty check activity, they answered the *ikigai*-related questionnaires, including the

Japanese version of PANAS (J-PANAS) [31], PEAQ [38], and State Eudaimonic Scale [39].

They were volunteers for frailty checkup activities 2–3 times a month and were asked to help with measurements about 2–3 times during the year. After this measurement period, we also asked the participants to answer the questionnaires mentioned above.

2.2 Feature Extraction from the Voice During Frailty Checkup Activities

First, the Whisper model [29,30] was used to extract relevant audio segments to preprocess the collected audio data. This process involved isolating specific sections of speech that were crucial for further analysis. Then, as feature extraction, the openSMILE toolkit was employed to perform feature extraction using the ComParE 2016 feature set of 6,373 features [11,22,40].

In order to refine the feature extracted from the dataset, sentiment analysis was conducted to identify and select segments with high sentiment likelihood. For this purpose, a Random Forest classifier trained on the Toronto Emotional Speech Set (TESS) dataset [13], which includes seven types of emotional speech, was employed. This classifier demonstrated an accuracy, precision, recall, and F1 score of over 98%. We only selected segments with a sentiment likelihood greater than 75% for further analysis.

The preprocessing steps resulted in a feature set comprising 18,237 utterances and 6,375 dimensions. On average, each participant contributed 1,140 utterances. The extracted features include a variety of acoustic parameters critical for subsequent analyses, providing a robust dataset for exploring the characteristics of speech in the context of frailty.

2.3 Acquisition of Voice Interaction Among the Participants

In addition to the personal voice recorder to capture their conversations, ambient microphones (Zoom H3-VR) were placed to monitor and record group communication among participants. We used audio data collected from the IC recorders and ambient microphones to analyze the voice interactions during individual activities. When participants engage in conversation nearby, their voices are picked up by the IC recorders of all nearby individuals. This phenomenon can be used to detect conversations and identify participants involved. Using the audio data, we estimated the presence of conversation between some participants based on the occurrence of overlapping voices.

Particularly during the roundtable discussion following the checkup, the amount of speech was measured to evaluate each participant's contribution. The ambient microphones captured the overall acoustic environment, allowing for an assessment of individual speech contributions within the group setting. This enabled the distribution of speech among participants to be captured.

2.4   Analysis

We first calculated a connection between the questionnaire results and the extracted features described in the feature extraction section. From the results of the J-PANAS, factor scores for negative and positive were obtained, and these were designated as hedonic factors. We also derived eudaemonic factor scores by using the PEAQ and the State Eudaimonic Scale and combined the two sets of scores due to their strong correlation in this study. We used supervised learning (elastic net method) to create regressors for these hedonic and eudaemonic factor scores using *glmnet* package on R [12,37,41]. Based on the regression results, each participant was ranked by their estimated value. RMSE (Root Mean Squared Error), R^2, and MAE (Mean Absolute Error) were obtained for the results estimated by the elastic net. The rank correlation coefficients ρ between the ranked values of the subjective/estimated quantities were also calculated and evaluated.

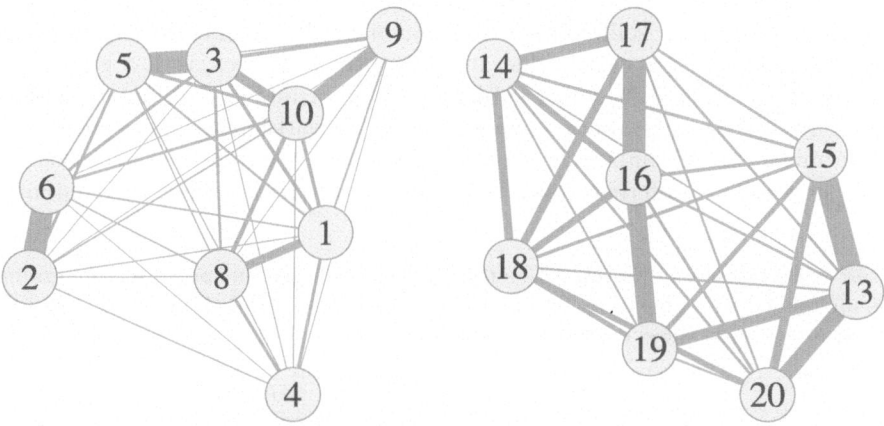

Fig. 1. Examples of a network diagram of conversation frequency. The number on the edge means the participant number. Note that the network also includes persons other than those who responded to the questionnaire (No. 17 and above).

For the interaction in speech, we created a network diagram based on the exchange matrix of the number of conversation detections and extracted five parameters related to centrality using *centiserve* package on R [19]. Figure 1 shows examples of a network diagram of conversation frequency. Specifically, the five parameters are order centrality, eigenvector centrality, PageRank, Bonacich's power centrality, and information centrality [5–7]. A regressor was constructed using the multiple regression analysis to determine the relationship between these and the aforementioned hedonic and eudaemonic elements, and each person was evaluated in the same way as in the previous paragraph.

3   Results and Discussion

Table 1 shows the performance of estimating subjective scores based on speech feature groups. In one-time frailty checkup, the hedonic positive and eudaemonic scores were estimated quite accurately, with a rank order correlation exceeding 0.5, indicating a high level of correlation based on Cohen's criteria [9]. The hedonic and eudaimonic scores were generally better estimated over the entire period than the one-time frailty check activity scores. However, the coefficient of determination did not show a high performance.

Table 2 displays the estimated performance of subjective scores based on speech interaction. The estimations of hedonic negative scores were relatively well done. The rank correlation for hedonic negative scores was above 0.3, indicating a moderate level of correlation.

When comparing the results in Tables 1 and 2, it is evident that the estimation of subjective scores after extracting features based on each person's speech generally performed better. This result could be because the subjective scores were obtained even for soliloquies, which may have allowed individuals to express their true feelings more clearly than in social situations such as dialogues. However, there were cases in which subjective scores could be estimated to some extent, even when only interactions were used. In particular, higher coefficients of determination and rank correlation coefficients were obtained for hedonic (negative) scores. This difference may be attributed to the fact that the content of

Table 1. Performance of estimating subjective scores based on speech feature groups. The underlined items mean the lowest for each category in RMSE and MAE, and the highest for R^2, and those exceeding 0.5 in ρ.

	RMSE	R^2	MAE	ρ
Hedonic (Negative)	<u>0.71</u>	0.13	<u>0.50</u>	0.45
Hedonic (Positive)	0.80	0.18	0.58	<u>0.59</u>
Eudaemonic	1.32	0.20	0.97	<u>0.59</u>
Hedonic (All period)	0.54	<u>0.23</u>	0.44	<u>0.59</u>
Eudaemonic (All period)	<u>0.27</u>	0.18	<u>0.22</u>	<u>0.86</u>

Table 2. Performance of estimating subjective scores based on speech interaction. The underlined items mean the lowest for each category in RMSE and MAE, and the highest for R^2, and those exceeding 0.5 in ρ.

	RMSE	R^2	MAE	ρ
Hedonic (Negative)	0.89	<u>0.30</u>	0.76	0.46
Hedonic (Positive)	<u>0.88</u>	0.17	<u>0.69</u>	0.19
Eudaemonic	1.20	0.13	0.93	0.15
Hedonic (All period)	0.59	0.33	0.47	<u>0.53</u>
Eudaemonic (All period)	<u>0.30</u>	<u>0.60</u>	<u>0.22</u>	<u>0.68</u>

the interactions with others differed from chatting for interaction, as these interactions were volunteer activities conducted with a sense of contribution. In the future, we plan to explore the factors that caused these differences and establish a method for estimating ikigai-related indices from objective indices by constructing a regressor based on both voice and interaction-related features.

4   Summary and Future Work

This study investigated how social activities affect older adults' subjective well-being, or *Ikigai*, in the context of Japan's aging society. Specifically, we focused on voice communication during frailty checkup activities and developed a method to measure subjective perceptions of *Ikigai* based on objective indicators. By analyzing voice data from 20 older volunteers using advanced audio processing techniques and sentiment analysis, we found that subjective well-being can be estimated from both individual speech features and group interactions. This research lays the foundation for recommending social activities that foster a sense of purpose and motivation among older adults, contributing to forming more inclusive and vibrant communities.

Future work aims to establish a method for estimating *Ikigai*-related indices from objective measures by constructing regression models that combine features related to both voice and social interactions. Further, we intend to develop a systematic activity recommendation system that supports older adults in finding and engaging in activities that give them a sense of purpose and fulfillment.

Acknowledgment. This work was supported by JST-Mirai Program (Grant number: JPMJMI21J1) and JSPS KAKENHI (Grant number: JP21H04580).

References

1. Annual Report on the Aging Society. (2017) (in Japanese). http://www8.cao.go.jp/kourei/whitepaper/w-2017/zenbun/29pdf_index.html. Accessed 31 Mar 2024
2. World Population Prospects. (2022). https://www.un.org/development/desa/pd/sites/www.un.org.development.desa.pd/files/wpp2022_summary_of_results.pdf. Accessed 31 Mar 2024
3. Amagasa, S., et al.: Types of social participation and psychological distress in Japanese older adults: a five-year cohort study. PLoS ONE **12**(4), e0175392 (2017)
4. Austin, E.N., Johnston, Y.A., Morgan, L.L.: Community gardening in a senior center: a therapeutic intervention to improve the health of older adults. Ther. Recreation J. **40**(1), 48 (2006)
5. Bonacich, P.: Some unique properties of eigenvector centrality. Soc. Netw. **29**(4), 555–564 (2007)
6. Borgatti, S.P.: Centrality and network flow. Soc. Netw. **27**(1), 55–71 (2005)
7. Brin, S., Page, L.: The anatomy of a large-scale hypertextual web search engine. Comput. Netw. ISDN Syst. **30**(1–7), 107–117 (1998)
8. Chang, P.J., Wray, L., Lin, Y.: Social relationships, leisure activity, and health in older adults. Health Psychol. **33**(6), 516 (2014)

9. Cohen, J.: A power primer. Psychol. Bull. **112**(1), 155 (1992)

10. Desai, R.A., Maciejewski, P.K., Dausey, D.J., Caldarone, B.J., Potenza, M.N.: Health correlates of recreational gambling in older adults. Am. J. Psychiatry **161**(9), 1672–1679 (2004)

11. Eyben, F., Wöllmer, M., Schuller, B.: Opensmile: the Munich versatile and fast open-source audio feature extractor. In: Proceedings of the 18th ACM international conference on Multimedia, pp. 1459–1462 (2010)

12. Friedman, J., Hastie, T., Tibshirani, R.: Regularization paths for generalized linear models via coordinate descent. J. Stat. Softw. **33**(1), 1 (2010)

13. Friesen, E., MacDougall-Shackleton, P., Chmiel, A., Dhar, S.C., Wilbiks, J.F., Fox, E.: Toronto Emotional Speech Set (TESS) (2020). https://doi.org/10.5683/SP2/E8H2MF. Accessed 31 Mar 2024

14. Fujisaki-Sueda-Sakai, M., Takahashi, K., Yoshizawa, Y., Iijima, K.: Frailty checkup supporters' intentions to participate in human-resource development and training activities. J. Frailty Aging **9**, 238–243 (2020)

15. García, H., Miralles, F.: Ikigai: The Japanese Secret to a Long and Happy Life. Penguin (2017)

16. Gottlieb, B.H., Gillespie, A.A.: Volunteerism, health, and civic engagement among older adults. Canadian J. Aging/La Revue canadienne du vieillissement **27**(4), 399–406 (2008)

17. Huxhold, O., Miche, M., Schüz, B.: Benefits of having friends in older ages: differential effects of informal social activities on well-being in middle-aged and older adults. J. Gerontol. B Psychol. Sci. Soc. Sci. **69**(3), 366–375 (2014)

18. Ishii, S., et al.: Development of a simple screening test for sarcopenia in older adults. Geriatr. Gerontol. Int. **14**, 93–101 (2014)

19. Jalili, M., et al.: CentiServer: a comprehensive resource, web-based application and R package for centrality analysis. PLoS ONE **10**(11), e0143111 (2015)

20. Johnson, H.H., Glascoff, M.A., Lovelace, K., Bibeau, D.L., Tyler, E.T.: Assessment of public health educator practice: health educator responsibilities. Health Promot. Pract. **6**(1), 89–96 (2005)

21. Kaneko, R., et al.: Population projections for Japan: 2006–2055 outline of results, methods, and assumptions. Jpn. J. Popul. **6**(1), 76–114 (2008)

22. Kaya, H., Karpov, A.A.: Fusing acoustic feature representations for computational paralinguistics tasks. In: interspeech, vol. 2016, pp. 2046–2050 (2016)

23. Matsuda, Y., Baba, A., Sugawara, I., Son, B.K., Iijima, K.: Multifaceted well-being experienced by community dwelling older adults engaged in volunteering activities of frailty prevention in Japan. Geriatr. Gerontol. Int. **24**, 273–278 (2024)

24. Miura, T., Nakayama, M., Hiyama, A., Yatomi, N., Hirose, M.: Time-mosaic formation of senior workforces for complex irregular work in cooperative farms. In: Universal Access in Human-Computer Interaction. User and Context Diversity: 7th International Conference, UAHCI 2013, Held as Part of HCI International 2013, Las Vegas, 21–26 July 2013, Proceedings, Part II, 7, pp. 162–170. Springer (2013)

25. Morrow-Howell, N., Hinterlong, J., Rozario, P.A., Tang, F.: Effects of volunteering on the well-being of older adults. J. Gerontol. B Psychol. Sci. Soc. Sci. **58**(3), S137–S145 (2003)

26. Muramatsu, N., Akiyama, H.: Japan: super-aging society preparing for the future. Gerontologist **51**(4), 425–432 (2011)

27. Nelson, M.E., et al.: Physical activity and public health in older adults: recommendation from the American College of Sports Medicine and the American Heart Association. Circulation **116**(9), 1094 (2007)

28. Okuzono, S.S., et al.: Ikigai and subsequent health and wellbeing among Japanese older adults: longitudinal outcome-wide analysis. In: The Lancet Regional Health–Western Pacific, vol. 21 (2022)

29. OpenAI. Whisper (2024). https://openai.com/index/whisper/. Accessed 31 Mar 2024

30. Radford, A., Kim, J.W., Xu, T., Brockman, G., McLeavey, C., Sutskever, I.: Robust speech recognition via large-scale weak supervision. In: International Conference on Machine Learning, pp. 28492–28518. PMLR (2023)

31. Sato, A., Yasuda, A.: Development of the Japanese version of Positive and Negative Affect Schedule (PANAS) scales. Jpn. J. Pers. **9**(2), 138–139 (2001)

32. Son, B.K., et al.: The co-design/co-development and evaluation of an online frailty check application for older adults: participatory action research with older adults. Int. J. Environ. Res. Publ. Health **20**(12), 6101 (2023)

33. Son, J.S., Nimrod, G., West, S.T., Janke, M.C., Liechty, T., Naar, J.J.: Promoting older adults' physical activity and social well-being during COVID-19. Leis. Sci. **43**(1–2), 287–294 (2021)

34. Sone, T., et al.: Sense of life worth living (ikigai) and mortality in Japan: Ohsaki Study. Psychosom. Med. **70**(6), 709–715 (2008)

35. Speake, D.L., Cowart, M.E., Pellet, K.: Health perceptions and lifestyles of the elderly. Res. Nurs. Health **12**(2), 93–100 (1989)

36. Taniguchi, Y., et al.: Associations of aging trajectories for an index of frailty score with mortality and medical and long-term care costs among older Japanese undergoing health checkups. Geriatr. Gerontol. Int. **20**(11), 1072–1078 (2020)

37. Tay, J.K., Narasimhan, B., Hastie, T.: Elastic net regularization paths for all generalized linear models. J. Statist. Softw. **106** (2023)

38. Waterman, A.S., Schwartz, S.J., Conti, R.: The implications of two conceptions of happiness (hedonic enjoyment and eudaimonia) for the understanding of intrinsic motivation. J. Happiness Stud. **9**, 41–79 (2008)

39. Waterman, A.S., et al.: The questionnaire for eudaimonic well-being: psychometric properties, demographic comparisons, and evidence of validity. J. Posit. Psychol. **5**(1), 41–61 (2010)

40. Weninger, F., Eyben, F., Schuller, B.W., Mortillaro, M., Scherer, K.R.: On the acoustics of emotion in audio: what speech, music, and sound have in common. Front. Psychol. **4**, 292 (2013)

41. Zou, H., Hastie, T.: Regularization and variable selection via the elastic net. J. R. Stat. Soc. Ser. B Stat Methodol. **67**(2), 301–320 (2005)

ProbinShasthoBondhu: A User-Centered mHealth App for Enhancing Elderly Health Management in Bangladesh

Sumyia Afnan Mukta[1,2], Mahfuja Khanam[1,2], Kalpika Paul[1,2], Azrin Ahmed[1,2], Ashraful Islam[1,2(✉)], and Asif Mahmood[2]

[1] Center for Computational and Data Sciences, Independent University, Bangladesh, Dhaka, Bangladesh
{2321672,2021967,1921641,1921996,ashraful}@iub.edu.bd
[2] Department of Computer Science and Engineering, Independent University, Bangladesh, Dhaka, Bangladesh
asif.mahmood@iub.edu.bd

Abstract. Current global demographic changes require the expansion of healthcare technologies, as seniors are more vulnerable to chronic diseases and mental illness, impacting their strength, mobility, and physical and mental well-being. As a result, seniors using smartphones require specific apps for physical and mental health, as well as emergency medical care. This work presents a methodical approach to designing a specific healthcare and fitness app dedicated to seniors while focusing on a user-centered design (UCD) strategy as well as studying their characteristics through surveys. The development of 'ProbinShasthoBondhu', a Bangla mobile health (mHealth) app aimed at Bangladeshi seniors, is presented here. It includes a variety of personalized features, such as various exercises like cardio and yoga, meditation techniques, medication management tools, and an emergency SOS button to quickly seek medical assistance. To test the usability and user experience of Probin-ShasthoBondhu, several usability scales were used, including the System Usability Scale (SUS) and User Experience Questionnaire Short version (UEQ-S). The results show a favorable overall SUS score of 60.3, indicating good usability. This study adds to the expanding literature on healthcare technologies for seniors by demonstrating the ability of UCDs to meet their specific requirements and ensure that mHealth apps will be more effective in promoting their health and well-being.

Keywords: Senior · Exercise · Usability · User Interface Design · Recipes

1 Introduction

Smartphone-based mobile health (mHealth) apps have become widely popular due to their apparent benefit to personal health and well-being. The usual features include an exercise plan, nutrition guide, and medication reminders, etc.

S. A. Mukta, M. Khanam, K. Paul and A. Ahmed—Contributed equally.

This is particularly necessary for seniors who often suffer from chronic diseases. A smart mHealth app can assist them in maintaining an active and healthy lifestyle to improve their vulnerability to various health conditions [6,12,14]. However, seniors are generally less adept at using cutting-edge technologies, especially smartphones, thus unable to utilize the full benefits of mHealth solutions [8,13]. Therefore, a better understanding of the needs and challenges of seniors is essential to provide effective mHealth solutions tailored to the health and well-being of the aging population.

Several senior-focused mHealth apps have emerged in recent years. The 'Elderly Care: Health+ Protect App' [2] uses reminders to promote regular care for mental and physical health. The 'Senior Fitness-Workout for 50+' app [3] offers health-promoting exercises for seniors, such as sit-ups, knee pain relief, hip strengthening, neck exercises, and chair yoga. The 'Sensalus' app [4] is a holistic solution for seniors, including things such as exercise, nutrition, stress management, and sleep. 'All Well Senior Care' [5] provides day-to-day health and wellness information, while 'Health Pal' [1] is also an integrated solution, with features such as health tracking, exercise, health-specific statistics, and reminders. These apps cater to seniors and improve their lives by providing health, safety, and fitness solutions. However, these apps' interfaces are primarily in English, and consequently, non-English-speaking people may find it difficult to understand and use their features properly. This is particularly problematic in developing countries like Bangladesh [10] where a mHealth app for seniors with a Bangla user interface would be more suitable.

This work presents the design, development, and evaluation of a mHealth app for the elderly people of Bangladesh. The design process is guided by user-centered design (UCD) methodology and the app is named 'ProbinShasthoBondhu' (can be translated as 'Elderly Health Companion') and its user interface is designed from scratch in Bangla language. The design process incorporates a preliminary survey to identify the habits and preferences of the senior populace, which guided the design and implementation of features tailored to the specific needs of the target user base [7,9]. Specifically, the app included several features such as an emergency SOS button, a medicine reminder, an exercise guide, information about healthy food and nutrition, tips about sound sleep, etc. Notably, the app features built-in profile management to allow multiple users sharing a single device, which is commonly found in developing countries like Bangladesh.

A prototype app was developed and distributed among senior citizens of Bangladesh. Afterwards, a usability and user experience survey was conducted among the users and their responses were analyzed to evaluate the application's effectiveness. ProbinShasthoBondhu obtained a good System Usability Scale (SUS) score of 60.3 and an above-average score of 1.306 in the User Experience Questionnaire-Short version (UEQ-S) confirming its comfortable user experience. Moreover, the majority of the participants were found to be willing to continue using the app and recommend it to other elderly people, corroborating its effectiveness.

The following section of the chapter describes in detail the design process of the ProbinShasthoBondhu app as well as its core features. The evaluation of the app's usability and user experience is presented afterward with a critical discussion of the app's performance results.

2   Interactive Prototype Development

This section articulates the ProbinShasthoBondhu interactive app prototype design and development process. The process starts with a survey to better understand the needs and habits of the target user base. Their responses were then analyzed and a set of core feature requirements were identified. These features were implemented in an interactive app prototype focusing on empathy and ease of use.

2.1   Design Requirement Analysis

A survey was conducted among the seniors (above 50 years of age) for the purpose of initial requirement analysis. The questionnaire includes several questions about features they would like to see in the app and their habits and thoughts about healthy lifestyles.

2.1.1   Survey Design: The survey questionnaire was composed of several sections. It began with a description of the study to help participants understand about its purpose. Firstly, the participants were asked to provide some demographic information such as age and gender. The following sections contained questions about features like exercise, nutrition, sleep, and mindfulness. Some sections also included questions about participants' exercise habits, dietary preferences, sleep patterns, and overall attitude toward health and well-being. The survey was designed to be brief, requiring minimal time commitment from the participants. Additionally, participants' personal information such as email addresses, phone numbers, or names was not collected.

2.1.2   Participants: The survey was circulated across various social media platforms, including Facebook, Messenger groups, and WhatsApp groups. Participation was restricted to individuals aged 50 and above, aligning with the target demographic of the app prototype. The participants were also required to have basic smartphone proficiency.

A total of 73 participants responded to the survey (40 male and 33 female) with an average age of 58.42 years (*standard deviation* (SD) 7.49). Majority of the participants were in the age group of 50-60 years, with a few in the older age groups (n=10, 60-70 years; n=3, 70-80 years; n=3, Above 80 years).

2.1.3   Measures and Data Analysis: We utilized Google Forms to conduct the survey, as it is a well-known and accessible platform. The survey responses encompassed Likert scales and yes/no questions. The responses were analyzed in Google Sheets to calculate various statistics such as mean, SD, and distribution of individual question responses. This helped us better understand the habits, attitudes, and needs of the target user base of the ProbinShasthoBondhu app.

2.1.4   Findings: The analysis of the survey responses revealed the following insights:

- **Communication:** Participants highly desired the inclusion of an Emergency SOS button in the app, with 78.1% responding affirmatively. Pressing this button would initiate a direct call to a predefined contact belonging to a family member or a caregiver in case of emergencies.
- **Health Information Sharing:** Many mHealth apps ask users to share various health information such as chronic diseases, co-morbidity information, and medication schedules for the purpose of providing personalized suggestions. To measure whether the users feel comfortable sharing such data, a Likert scale ranging from 1 to 5 was employed, where 1 denoted 'Not very comfortable' and 5 signified 'Very comfortable'. The results showed a predominant comfort rating of 4 out of 5. Notably, a significant majority of participants (70.2%) preferred a medicine reminder feature to help them maintain their medication schedule.
- **Attitudes Towards Health:** The survey revealed that a substantial portion of participants (78.2%) recognize the importance of lifestyle factors such as regular exercise and nutrition in maintaining overall health and well-being. A majority of participants (72.6%) mentioned health benefits as their primary motivation for engaging in regular exercise. However, many participants faced barriers to maintaining a regular exercise routine, with lack of time and interest being the main reasons cited by the majority (74%). They preferred having an exercise reminder feature with various degrees of recurrence, e.g. daily (35.5%), weekly (23.3%), monthly (6.8%), and customized (27.3%).
- **Exercise for Seniors:** Most participants preferred walking as their primary form of exercise, with a preference rate of 86.3%. Other exercise options include yoga (26%), jogging (24.7%), and swimming (15.1%). The widespread popularity of walking emphasizes its convenience and accessibility as a viable exercise option, particularly for seniors without mobility issues.
- **Nutrition:** When questioned about nutrition and dietary requirements, 49.3% of participants assessed their current lifestyle as moderate (3 out of 5 on a Likert scale). When queried about the importance of nutrition advice, an overwhelming 74% affirmed its significance. Moreover, participants concurred that maintaining a healthy diet necessitates access to proper recipes. 56.3% of the participants reported utilizing a healthy recipe app to aid in meal planning.
- **Mindfulness, Meditation, and Better Sleep:** When asked if they had tried meditation, 38.4% of participants responded negatively, meaning, they never attempted meditation for mindfulness. Among those who had tried meditation, varied experiences were reported, including better sleep (46.9%), peace of mind (50%), improved focus (23.4%), and enhanced cognitive abilities (12.2%). Many participants (46.6%) preferred a feature providing tips to improve sleep quality and manage sleep disorders.

2.2   Prototype Design and Development

The analysis of survey responses provided valuable insights regarding the habits and preferences of the seniors, which guided the development of the Probin-ShasthoBondhu app prototype. The prototype was designed with a central focus on user-friendliness, ensuring that user interfaces were simplified to enhance accessibility for elders.

The prototype was designed using Figma[1]. The Figma prototype can be easily distributed for testing purposes via a hyperlink, allowing it to be accessed on any online platform connected to the internet, including smartphones. Bangla was chosen as the interface language to cater to the needs of Bangladeshi seniors. The app followed a UCD approach, aiming to provide a seamless and intuitive experience for seniors. Through careful consideration of user needs and preferences, it addressed the specific health requirements of seniors, ultimately fostering a better quality of life for its users.

3   Prototype and Its Features

The ProbinShasthoBondhu app follows a UCD strategy that caters to the unique needs of seniors. The app features emergency assistance, medication management, personalized exercises and yoga, healthy food and nutrition planning, sleep enhancement, and mindfulness activities which aim to enable seniors to manage their health and well-being.

3.1   Login Page

The app begins with a simple 'Login' page, as seen in Fig. 1. Users are required to log in primarily to allow multiple persons to use their separate profiles on the same smartphone. This is useful when multiple persons share a single smartphone, which is particularly common in low- and middle-income countries like Bangladesh. The login process also helps maintaining privacy by ensuring that only authorized users can access sensitive health information. We maintained a minimalist design for senior citizens to facilitate easy navigation and interaction with the login page while providing clear instructions for inputting valid information. After successfully logging in, users are taken to a Dashboard where they can access various app features such as exercise, food and nutrition, sleep, and mindfulness.

3.2   Emergency SOS

The 'Emergency SOS' button is located at the top-right corner of the Dashboard, which can call a predefined number swiftly with a single tap. This feature can be useful in case of an emergency to contact family members or caregivers. Figure 2 illustrates this feature.

---

[1] https://www.figma.com/.

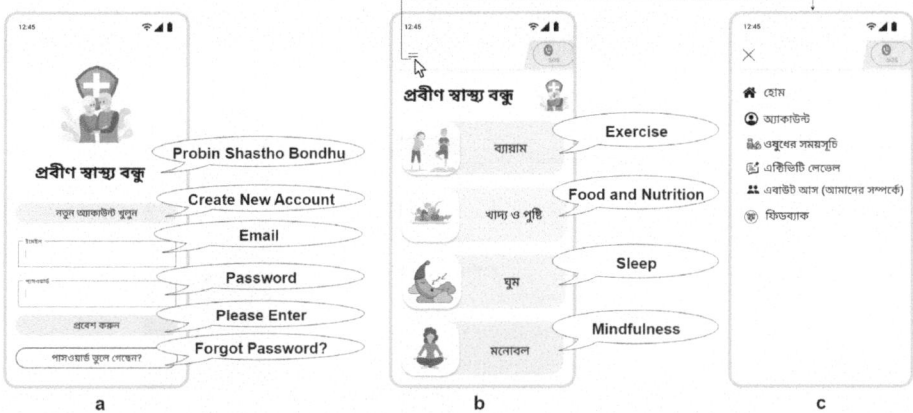

Fig. 1. The user interface of ProbinShashthoBondhu app prototype: (a) The Login screen containing app's logo as well as fields to enter email and password. (b) Dashboard containing several buttons for accessing specific features such as exercise, food and nutrition, sleep, and mindfulness. (c) A menu presenting various options such as home, account, medicine timings, activity level, about us, and feedback.

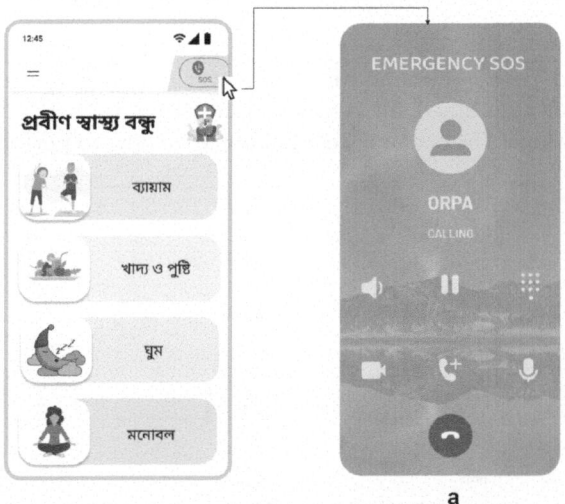

Fig. 2. The 'Emergency SOS' feature for seniors allows them to call for help in case of an emergency. (a) ORPA is set as an emergency contact for immediate assistance.

3.3   Medicine Reminder

The 'Medicine Reminder' section seen in Fig. 3 facilitates organized medication management with customizable reminders, ensuring seniors take their medications in a timely and systematic manner. This feature can be helpful to maintain a regular medication schedule with appropriate dosage, especially for those who need to administer several medicines regularly.

Fig. 3. The 'Medicine Reminder' feature. (a) Entering medicine information. (b) duration of medicine intake in days and a date range selector (c) medication reminder via notifications to take the prescribed medicine at the specified time.

3.4   Exercise

The 'Exercise and Yoga' section in Fig. 4 offers various types of exercises and yoga routines specifically designed for seniors, complete with video demonstrations, and clear instructions. Users can access guidance on how to perform the exercises or yoga poses.

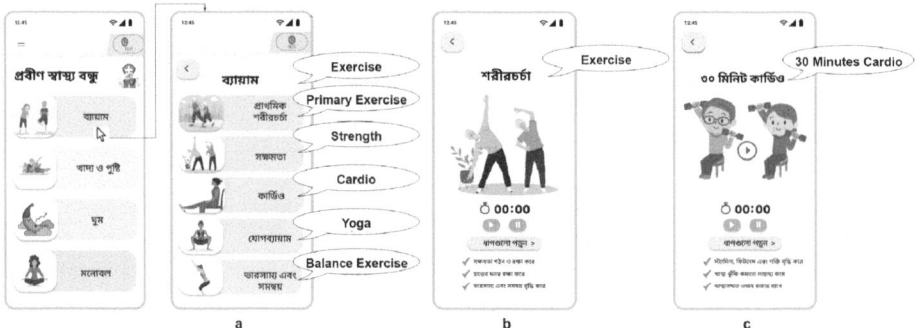

Fig. 4. The 'Exercise' feature, focused on promoting physical activity and healthy living: (a) Different exercise or activity categories such as cardio, and yoga (b) Setting a timer for exercise to keep activities on track. The button below the timer shows the exercise steps and the benefits related to the exercise routine, which would keep them motivated. (c) a video demonstration of the cardio exercise to follow along. The benefits related to the cardio routine being shown below the video as well.

3.5   Food and Nutrition

In the 'Food and Nutrition' section (seen in Fig. 5), users can access nutrition tips, healthy recipes, and information on essential food elements, enhancing their understanding of vital nutrients. This section is particularly beneficial for seniors who may have various health conditions such as heart disease, diabetes, hypertension, etc. A balanced diet can play a crucial role in helping them maintain their health and nutrition.

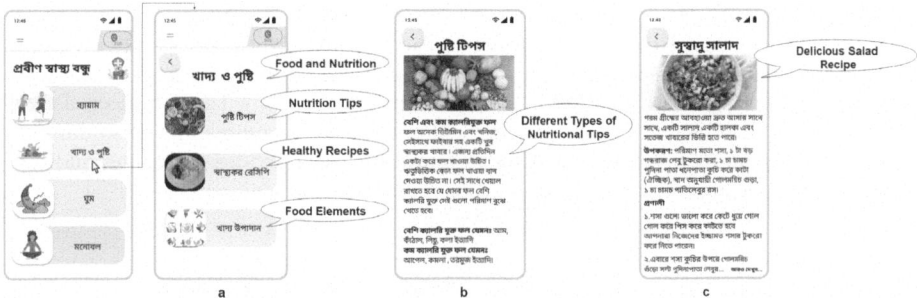

Fig. 5. The 'Food and Nutrition' feature focused on providing nutritional information and healthy diet tips as well as recommendations. (a) Secondary dashboard featuring 'Nutrition Tips', 'Healthy Recipe' and 'Food Elements' in Bangla (b) The 'Nutrition Tips' feature provides a detailed description and guidance on maintaining a balanced diet. (c) 'Delicious Salad' presents a healthy and colorful mixed vegetable salad dish recipe for seniors.

3.6   Sleep and Relaxation

The 'Sleep and Relaxation' section in Fig. 6 offers a holistic approach to promoting sound sleep and relaxation. Users can access sleeping tips, relaxing music, natural sounds, and bedtime stories to enhance their sleep quality and relaxation experience.

3.7   Mindfulness

The 'Mindfulness' feature seen in Fig. 7 incorporates guided meditation, soothing music, and positive affirmations, aimed at enhancing thinking abilities and reducing stress.

4   Usability and User Experience Evaluation

The ProbinShasthoBondhu app was methodically designed with the primary purpose of effortlessly integrating technology into seniors' lives to improve their

Fig. 6. The 'Sleep and Relaxation' feature of the ProbinShashthoBondhu application. (a) A menu with various options such as 'Sleep Tips,' 'Relaxing Music,' 'Nature's Sound,' and 'Bedtime Stories.' These options help the seniors with their sleep as well as wellness. (b) The 'Sleep Tips' feature provides advice or recommendations related to improving sleep quality. (c) The 'Nature's Sound' section provides a calming auditory experience via natural sounds to aid sleep or relaxation for seniors.

Fig. 7. The 'Mindfulness' feature: (a) Various menu options such as 'Meditation', 'Soothing Tunes', 'Motivational Quotes' and 'Story and Poetry'. (b) This 'Meditation' option provides information for relaxing the mind. Categories include 'Gardening', 'Religious Activities', and 'Leisure Activities'. (c) The 'Motivational Quotes' option include a list of podcasts to listen to, which would motivate the seniors, and promote a positive and fulfilling approach to aging.

health management. The design principles are based on empathy and simplicity, and they promote accessibility and user-friendliness, taking into account the special demands and potential obstacles that elders may have while adopting new technologies. The app prototype was distributed among Bangladeshi seniors and another survey was conducted among the app users to measure and evaluate its usability and user experience.

4.1 Post Survey Design

A survey-based evaluation was employed to gather quantitative feedback from participants. It took participants 10 to 15 min to complete the survey which began with an overview of the study and a consent form. Basic demographic information such as age and gender were collected. Following this, participants rated the app's usability using the SUS and UEQ-S.

4.2 Participants

To reach out to a diverse range of participants, the survey was distributed across various social media platforms, including different mailing lists. Participation criteria included being at least 50 years old and having basic proficiency of operating a smartphone. They did not require any English language proficiency since the prototype was developed in Bangla.

A total of 20 participants completed the survey, comprising 11 females and 9 males. Participants ranged in age from 50 to over 80, with a significant concentration in the 50-60 age bracket. The mean age of participants was 59.5 years (SD 8.26) (n=14, 50-60 years; n=4, 60-70 years; n=1, 70-80 years; n=1, 81 or above).

4.3 Measures and Data Analysis

The survey was conducted using Google Forms and their responses were collected and analyzed using Google Sheets. The analysis reveals various user experience aspects of the ProbinShasthoBondhu app such as user impressions, ease of use, and intention to continue using the app. Various statistics such as mean, standard deviations, and frequency distributions were also computed to gain insights about the quality of the data. This approach facilitated a comprehensive assessment of the app's performance and acceptability among the target users.

4.4 Findings

4.4.1 SUS: SUS is a widely-used tool for assessing perceived usability which is employed in approximately 43% of usability studies [11]. The SUS comprises a concise and universal 10-item questionnaire, alternating between positive and negative statements to mitigate response biases. Respondents rate these statements on a five-point Likert scale, ranging from 1 (strongly disagree) to 5 (strongly agree). A final usability score, ranging from 0 to 100, is calculated based on all 10 items, with adjustments if needed.

The analysis (Table 1) of the system's usability reveals a mean SUS score of 60.3 (median=53.8, SD=17.58, min=22.5, max=90.0). The mean and median of the SUS score are relatively close together, showing that the distribution is not heavily skewed. The range of the data (22.5 to 90.0) is quite wide, spanning nearly the entire possible range of SUS scores (0 to 100). This shows that the distribution is not heavily concentrated around a single value. The SUS scores follow a roughly normal (Gaussian) distribution, with a slight skew towards the left.

The median score of 53.8 suggests that half of the users rated the system's usability above this value, indicating an overall positive reception. With a standard deviation of 17.58, there is moderate variability in user perceptions. While many users found the system highly usable, some rated it lower, highlighting areas for improvement. The mean score of 60.3 is rated as 'Good', indicating the system's effectiveness in usability. This acceptability rating also suggests that the system is well-received by most users.

Figure 8 illustrates the participants' votes ratio on 5-point Likert scales for individual SUS items. There appears to be a significant divide in opinion among participants, with responses polarized towards the extreme ends of the scale for many questions. This polarization suggests that users had quite contrasting experiences or perceptions regarding the system's usability. Table 1 presents the mean SUS scores for the individual questions.

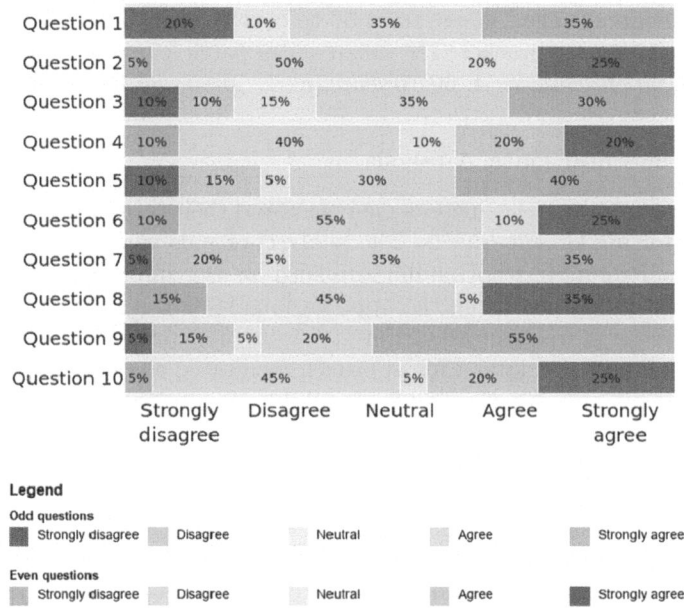

Fig. 8. Participants' votes for individual SUS items

Looking at the odd-numbered questions (phrased positively), a sizable portion of respondents selected 'Strongly agree' for several questions (e.g., Question 1, Question 7), indicating that a notable group found the system highly usable and easy to use. However, there is also a considerable percentage who responded with 'Strongly disagree' with these positive statements, pointing to usability issues experienced by another segment of users. The even-numbered questions (phrased negatively) reinforce this divide, with a substantial number of participants responding 'Strongly agree' to the fact that the system was cumbersome or difficult to use (e.g., Question 2, Question 10). A few questions, like Question 5 and Question 6, had a more balanced distribution of responses, suggesting some aspects of the system were perceived as moderately usable by many participants.

Table 1. Average SUS Score for Each Question

SL	SUS Question	Mean Score (SD)
1	I would like to use this system frequently.	3.65 (1.5)
2	The system was unnecessarily complex.	2.9 (1.33)
3	The system was easy to use.	3.65 (1.31)
4	I would need the support of a technical person to use this system.	3 (1.38)
5	The various functions in this system were well-integrated.	3.75 (1.41)
6	There was too much inconsistency in this system.	2.75 (1.41)
7	Most people would learn to use this system very quickly.	3.75 (1.29)
8	The system was very cumbersome to use.	2.95 (1.61)
9	I felt very confident using the system.	4.05 (1.32)
10	I needed to learn a lot before I could get going with this system.	3.15 (1.39)
	Overall Mean and SD	**3.36 (1.4)**

Figure 9 provides a graphical representation of the SUS study score and ratings. The distribution shows that the majority of individual scores are clustered around the middle range, which falls within the 'OK' category. This suggests that the overall usability of the system is generally acceptable but not outstanding. However, there are also several scores that fall into the 'Marginal' range (orange), indicating that some users or aspects of the system are experiencing usability issues that are less than optimal. Additionally, there are a few outlier scores that fall into the 'Poor' or 'Not Acceptable' range (red), suggesting that a small number of users or specific tasks may have significant usability problems with the system. On the positive side, there are also a handful of scores that fall into the 'Excellent' or 'Best Imaginable' range (dark green), indicating that some users or aspects of the system have exceptionally good usability.

4.4.2 UEQ: The UEQ assesses various aspects of user experience, including efficiency, effectiveness, and satisfaction. Unlike SUS, it puts two opposite-meaning terms such as 'complicated' and 'easy' at the ends of a seven-point scale ranging from -3 (most negative) to +3 (most positive).

Table 2 presents the result of the survey using UEQ, with the mean and variances for each item as well as their respective scales. The table's scales allow us to identify mean scores ranging from 1.1 to 1.6 among items 1 to 4 for Pragmatic Quality, and a mean of 1.2 to 1.6 with variances ranging from 2.1 to 3.3 among items 5 to 8 for Hedonic Quality.

Figure 10 shows an analysis of Pragmatic Quality, Hedonic Quality, and overall scores, comparing them with reference values obtained from the official UEQ website (www.ueq-online.org). The mean scores obtained from the survey for Pragmatic Quality, Hedonic Quality, and overall were 1.275, 1.338, and 1.31 respectively. When compared to the reference values, the Hedonic Quality score

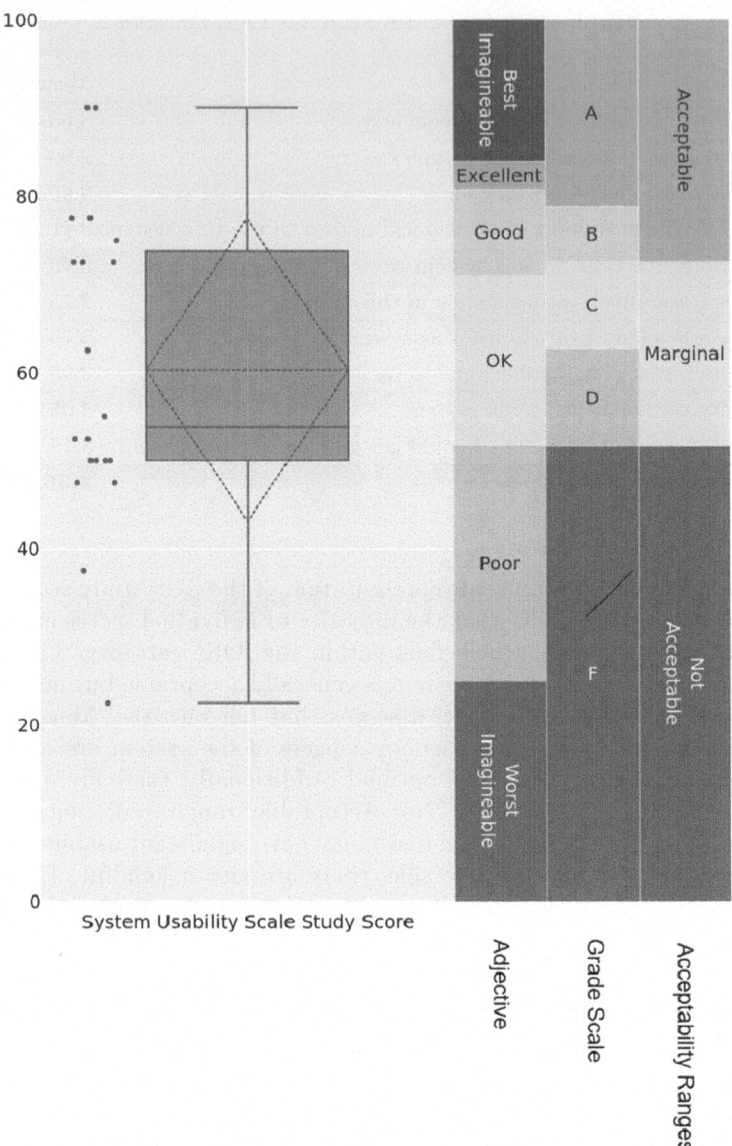

Fig. 9. SUS study score results

of 1.338 was classified as 'Good' while both Pragmatic Quality and overall scores fell in the 'Above Average' category.

4.4.3 Feature Popularity: The analysis of survey responses also reveals the popularity of individual features of the ProbinShasthoBondhu app among the participants. 'Exercise' and 'Food and Nutrition' features were found to be the

Table 2. UEQ Results from survey

UEQ Question (Negative/Positive)	Scale	Mean	Variance
1. obstructive/supportive	Pragmatic Quality	1.6	3.0
2. complicated/easy		1.4	3.1
3. inefficient/efficient		1.1	4.1
4. confusing/clear		1.1	4.2
5. boring/exciting	Hedonic Quality	1.2	3.3
6. not interesting/interesting		1.6	2.1
7. conventional/inventive		1.3	2.4
8. usual/leading edge		1.4	2.7
Overall		1.306	2.386

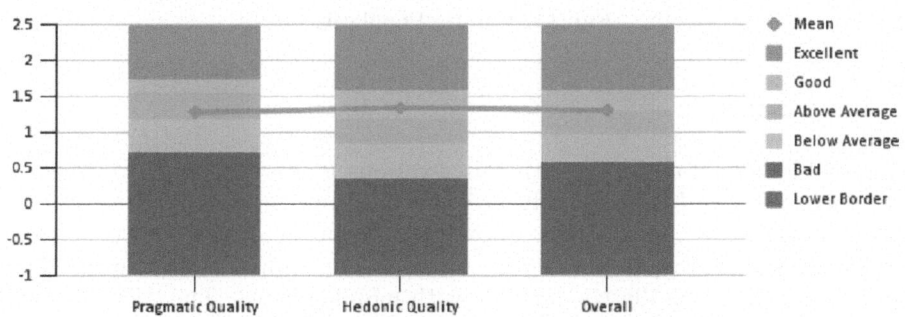

Fig. 10. Benchmark comparison of UEQ scores

most popular, each receiving 65% of the votes from participants (seen in Fig. 11). Following closely behind was the 'Sleep and Relaxation' feature, which obtained 60% of the votes. The 'Mindfulness' feature category received 25% of the votes, which was the least popular.

When participants were specifically questioned about features aimed at enhancing sleep quality, 60% of them expressed that they found 'Sleep Tips for Seniors' to be the most valuable. This suggests that most participants believed that receiving guidance on improving their sleep habits was important. Additionally, 50% of participants favored 'Sleep Time Stories' as a valuable feature. This indicates that a significant portion of participants found the idea of listening to bedtime stories beneficial for promoting better sleep.

4.4.4 Willingness to Use and Recommend: 55% of the survey participants indicated that they were interested in using the app themselves. Additionally, the same percentage of the participants, 55%, were willing to recommend the app to others. This indicates that a majority of participants not only saw value in using the app personally but also believed it could be beneficial for others in their age group.

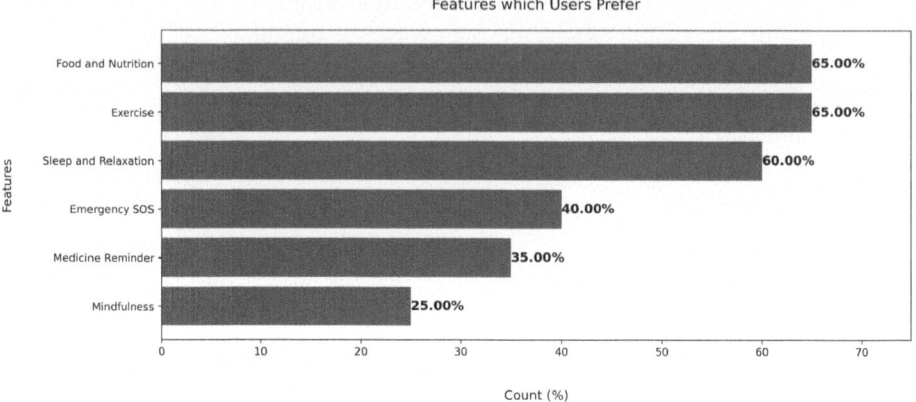

Fig. 11. Feature Popularity

5   Discussion

Using mobile apps for elder health raises various issues that require attention. The rapid rate of technological advancement needs an ongoing effort to stay up-to-date on the latest devices and accessories. Given the diversity in technology literacy among seniors, it is essential to assess the simplicity of use for those who may not be naturally comfortable with mobile phones. The 'Usability and User Experience Evaluation' section provided insights into the usability and user experience of the ProbinShashthoBondhu app. The SUS evaluation revealed a mean SUS score of 60.3, which is rated as 'Good', indicating the system's effectiveness in usability and overall positive reception by most users. The UEQ-S results showed a mean score of 1.275 for Pragmatic Quality, 1.338 for Hedonic Quality, and an Overall mean score of 1.306. These scores were above the reference values, indicating good performance in terms of practicality, enjoyment, and overall user satisfaction. Among the app's features, 'Exercise' and 'Food and Nutrition' were the most popular, receiving 65% of the votes from participants, followed closely by 'Sleep and Relaxation' with 60% of the votes. Additionally, 55% of participants expressed their willingness to use the app themselves and recommend it to other seniors for improving sleep.

6   Conclusion

This study has centered on the purpose, perspectives, and development of a mHealth app ProbinShasthoBondhu for Bangladeshi seniors. A preliminary survey was conducted to gain a reliable understanding of the habits, attitudes, and preferences of the target user base. The app was designed afterward guided by these insights, and essential functionalities were incorporated into the app. A prototype with a Bangla user interface was developed using Figma to enhance accessibility for the nation's populace. This design process was adopted to ensure user-friendliness of the app so that it would be beneficial to the aged population with a diverse range of technology proficiency.

The app prototype was then distributed and a usability and user experience survey was conducted among the users. The app obtained an overall 60.3% score in SUS, indicating good usability and acceptability. The UEQ score of 1.306 was classified as 'Above Average' compared to reference benchmark scores. A deep inspection of survey responses revealed some polarization among the participants on some aspects of the application. Therefore there is room for further improvements in the design to mitigate this issue. However, majority of the participants found several features substantially effective and expressed their interest to continue using the app, as well as recommending it to their peers. In conclusion, the ProbinShasthoBondhu app is poised to significantly improve the lives of senior citizens, catering to their specific health requirements and fostering a better quality of life.

References

1. Health pal - fitness, weight loss coach, pedometer - apps on google play (01 2014). https://play.google.com/store/apps/details?id=com.androidapps.healthmanager
2. Elderly care: health + protect - apps on google play (07 2016). https://play.google.com/store/apps/details?id=com.levstone.mobility.trustedelderlycare
3. Senior fitness-workout for 50+ - apps on google play (01 2019). https://play.google.com/store/apps/details?id=fitness.com.senior
4. Sensalus. senior fitness - apps on google play (12 2022). https://play.google.com/store/apps/details?id=com.sensalus.android
5. All well senior care - apps on google play (10 2023). https://play.google.com/store/apps/details?id=com.atman.allwell
6. Ehn, M., Eriksson, L.C., Åkerberg, N., Johansson, A.C.: Activity monitors as support for older persons' physical activity in daily life: Qualitative study of the users' experiences. JMIR mHealth and uHealth **6**, e34 (02 2018). https://doi.org/10.2196/mhealth.8345
7. Handojo, A., Adrian, J., Purbowo, A.N.: Elderly healthcare assistance application using mobile phone. In: International Conference on Soft Computing, Intelligent System and Information Technology (ICSIIT) (09 2017). https://doi.org/10.1109/icsiit.2017.69
8. Helbostad, J., et al.: Mobile health applications to promote active and healthy ageing. Sensors **17**, 622 (03 2017). https://doi.org/10.3390/s17030622, https://www.ncbi.nlm.nih.gov/pmc/articles/PMC5375908/
9. Kalimullah, K., Sushmitha, D.: Influence of design elements in mobile applications on user experience of elderly people. Proc. Comput. Sci. **113**, 352–359 (2017). https://doi.org/10.1016/j.procs.2017.08.344
10. Khatun, F., Heywood, A.E., Ray, P.K., Hanifi, S., Bhuiya, A., Liaw, S.T.: Determinants of readiness to adopt mhealth in a rural community of bangladesh. Int. J. Med. Inform. **84**, 847–856 (10 2015). https://doi.org/10.1016/j.ijmedinf.2015.06.008
11. Lewis, J.R., Utesch, B.S., Maher, D.E.: Measuring perceived usability: the sus, umux-lite, and altusability. Int. J. Human-Comput. Interact. **31**, 496–505 (06 2015). https://doi.org/10.1080/10447318.2015.1064654

12. Maresova, P., et al.: Consequences of chronic diseases and other limitations associated with old age – a scoping review. BMC Public Health **19** (11 2019). https://doi.org/10.1186/s12889-019-7762-5, https://bmcpublichealth.biomedcentral.com/articles/10.1186/s12889-019-7762-5
13. Ramdowar, H., Khedo, K.K., Chooramun, N.: A comprehensive review of mobile user interfaces in mhealth applications for elderly and the related ageing barriers. Universal Access in the Information Society (07 2023). https://doi.org/10.1007/s10209-023-01011-z
14. Yerrakalva, D., Yerrakalva, D., Hajna, S., Griffin, S.: Effects of mobile app interventions on sedentary time, physical activity and fitness in older adults: systematic review and meta-analysis (preprint). Journal of Medical Internet Research **21** (04 2019). https://doi.org/10.2196/14343

Research on Augmented Reality Design of Diet for Elderly Patients with Chronic Kidney Disease

Wang-Chin Tsai[1], Chien-Hua Kuo[2,3](✉), and Chuan-Fang Lee[4](✉)

[1] Department of Creative Design, National Yunlin University of Science and Technology, Yunlin, Taiwan
wangwang@yuntech.edu.tw
[2] Graduate School of Design, National Yunlin University of Science and Technology, Yunlin, Taiwan
D11230015@yuntech.edu.tw, tp0017@mail.tut.edu.tw
[3] Department of Fashion Design, Tainan University of Technology, Tainan, Taiwan
[4] Department of Industrial Design, National Yunlin University of Science and Technology, Yunlin, Taiwan
leecf@yuntech.edu.tw

Abstract. In the social environment of an aging population, the demand for medical care is increasing, and the impact of mobile medicine on medical staff, patients, and the quality of care is becoming increasingly important. However, in the context of limited medical resources, how to effectively assist patients to control dietary intake and improve the deterioration of renal function so as to avoid the progression to end-stage renal disease has become an important issue. This study combined scientific and technological services with dietary education to build an augmented reality application platform of dietary guidance and dietary knowledge, which was integrated into the patients' daily life. Patients could inquire relevant dietary knowledge through smartphones, and master and improve dietary knowledge in a short time. Through the operation mode of augmented reality and the use of virtual models or action presentation, patients could more intuitively understand the nutritional composition of food, such as protein, portion size, and carbohydrates to help them establish correct nutritional knowledge concepts. The platform of this study conformed to the principles of convenience, usability, and correctness, which accelerated the cultivation of patients' food identification and the ability to choose food. Through the intelligent platform, patients could be provided with relevant dietary recommendations, who were assisted in formulating diet management plans. The daily life quality of patients with chronic kidney disease was improved from the dietary level, delaying the deterioration of renal function, thus reducing medical costs and the burden of medical staff, and creating new service modes to improve medical quality. This study developed a system of Web Augmented Reality combined with chatbot through system process construction, response presentation, emotional connection and interaction, and functional requirements, which was applied to the interactive process of patients with chronic kidney disease. Through the intervention of health education knowledge and nutrition education, it was practically applied to daily life to achieve the service process

M. Antona et al. (Eds.): HCII 2024, LNCS 15379, pp. 273–289, 2025.
https://doi.org/10.1007/978-3-031-76818-7_19

and experience of self-health management of diet, so as to help patients maintain healthy body functions and promote healthy aging.

Keywords: Augment reality design · Chronic kidney disease · Elderly

1 Reason and Purpose of the Plan

According to the statistics of Taiwan's National Health Insurance Administration, the payment of chronic kidney disease reached NTD 51.3 billion in 2018, accounting for nearly 7% of the total health insurance [1]. The number of medical treatments reached 364,000 people, the number of peritoneal dialysis and hemodialysis reached 90,000, and chronic kidney disease ranked first in Taiwan continuously. However, patients have no obvious symptoms in the early stage of chronic kidney disease, making it difficult to detect the disease. Coupled with the low self-recognition rate of patients, it results in missing the opportunity for treatment. The gradual decline of renal function progressing to end-stage renal disease requires lifelong renal washing to maintain physiological function. After being diagnosed by doctors, patients with chronic kidney disease are given different care goals and different health care contents according to the stage of chronic kidney disease and are referred to dietitians for regular nutritional assessment and follow-up. Modifying patients' self-care behavior, the deterioration of renal function may be improved through effective control of dietary intake [2]. Studies have confirmed that through the intervention of nutrition health education, patients can improve their care knowledge and diet skills, which can help delay the decline of renal function. Moreover, the earlier the start of diet control can have more obvious effect [3]. After the intervention of nutrition health education, guiding the correct diet concepts and knowledge, and taking food correctly can effectively reduce the deterioration of kidney, and improve the discomfort of complications, thus promoting the improvement of quality of life [4]. In addition, maintaining a good nutritional state, patients should abide by the dietary principles and pay attention to five categories of food: protein, potassium, phosphorus, sodium, and water.

In the context of the approaching aging society, people's demand for care is increasing, and the impact of mobile medicine on caregivers, patients, and care quality is becoming increasingly important. Mobile medicine is defined as the use of existing developed mobile applications for planned health care services [5]. After receiving the complete care plan from the hospital, patients can manage their health at home by themselves. Taking the seamless service of continuous medical treatment and care without interruption as the principle, through the intervention of mobile devices, convenience can be improved. It can also simplify the operation process of nursing staff, thereby improving the quality of medical care and implementing patient care. In addition, health information can be obtained, shared, and effectively controlled at any time. It has positive effects on information transmission and improving communication among caregivers and promoting the positive development of daily healthy life.

In this study, patients with chronic kidney disease diagnosed by doctors having a glomerular filtration rate of less than 60 mL/min/1.73 m^2, with a disease course of more than 3 months and experience in using smartphones were selected as the investigation subjects, and chronic kidney disease patients in National Taiwan University Hospital Yunlin Branch were selected for investigation. As shown in Fig. 1, the hospital and patients with chronic kidney disease were taken as the main subjects. Through the combination of scientific and technological services and dietary education, with the application of Web Augmented Reality to dietary guidelines and dietary knowledge development, patients with kidney disease could learn and improve the effectiveness of dietary knowledge in a short time. Through the operation of smartphones combined with Web Augmented Reality (Web-AR), it could meet the convenience, usability, and correctness, accelerating the cultivation of the ability to identify and select food, understanding the nutritional composition, portion size, and calories of food, and improving the knowledge and concept of correct diet. They could establish a suitable nutrition plan to improve the daily life quality of patients with chronic kidney disease from the dietary level, delay the occurrence of dialysis stage, and develop innovative service processes. Therefore, medical staff could know the dietary status and body values of patients, give dietary advice through messages, and assist patients' dietary habits in daily life. It would achieve convenient and immediate results, thus increasing the willingness to use, and then reducing the expenditure of medical costs and the burden of medical staff and creating a new service mode to improve the effectiveness of medical quality.

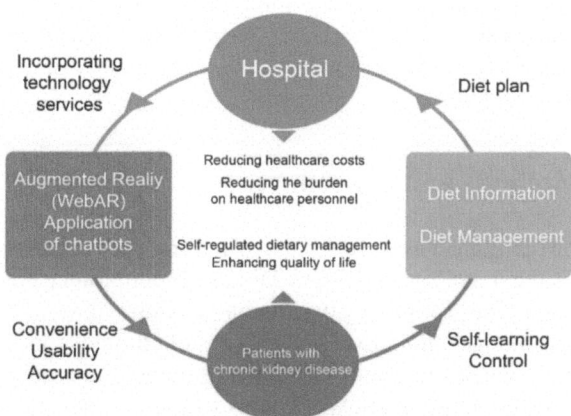

Fig. 1. Research Structure.

Dietitians mainly use food models as teaching equipment when teaching patients dietary knowledge, through which patients are taught correct diet related knowledge. According to the patient's illness and physical condition assessment, tailor-made diet plan and guidance are given. In the process, patients understand the nutritional composition of the food, such as consumption (protein intake, potassium ion, and phosphorus ion), portion size, and calories, etc., and establish the correct nutritional knowledge and concepts. Patients understand the needs of the body, who can choose food more confidently, and improve good eating habits from daily life, and further helping them delay or even improve their conditions, to make the body healthier (Wu, 2016). In the process of teaching, dietitians need to rely on food models as teaching materials. The teaching materials mainly focus on the six food categories recommended by the Health Promotion Administration (2018), which are whole grains, vegetables, beans, fish, eggs and meat, dairy products, fruits, oils and nuts and seeds. Dietitians can only provide partial food models to teach patients due to the large number of food categories, the diversity of food on the market, and the high costs of teaching materials. Under the circumstances of environmental restrictions, the ingredients and calories of each food are different, making it difficult to fully teach patients dietary knowledge. Patients can only learn from a small sample of ingredients, and teaching effectiveness is confined. For patients, after consulting with dietitians and learning preliminary nutrition knowledge, they should be able to identify and select food, as well as have correct dietary knowledge and concepts [6]. However, due to the limitation of teaching materials, patients can only understand part of dietary knowledge, resulting in limited learning effectiveness. In addition, there are many kinds of food, it is difficult to apply the food models to the food encountered in daily life. It needs continuous self-learning and exploration for the future life, taking more time to establish correct eating habits [7]. Moreover, after patients with chronic kidney disease who are diagnosed with Stage III kidney disease, they need to strictly restrict their daily meals to prevent and delay their entry into the final dialysis period. However, diet education and management are important links in self-care. Therefore, this study was intended to promote the improvement of dietary knowledge and concepts for patients with chronic kidney disease to improve their quality of life. The intervention was conducted through the application of Web-AR in mobile medicine to evaluate the effectiveness of dietary knowledge improvement and quality of life in patients with kidney disease [8].

2   Research Methods and Procedures

In the first stage, the literature data were discussed and analyzed in the early stage, and the diet sector in the Manual of Chronic Kidney Disease Health Management was taken as the reference indicator. The preliminary discussions and interviews with relevant doctors and dietitians were conducted to introduce the issues of chronic kidney disease patients from the perspectives of self-diet control and management. The primary purpose of this study was to explore the needs and expectations of mobile medical service planning based on the impact of patients with chronic kidney disease on daily life and changes in dietary habits.

In the second stage, the main initial research data were summarized and analyzed, and the clinical experience of medical staff interviews was sorted out, and the needs were determined to establish a database. From the perspective of self-diet management, the concept of Web-AR was introduced in mobile medicine, the design of patient-related services was proposed with the establishment of prototype, and the function of image recognition technology and 3D model were developed for querying the food system and teaching patients the knowledge of diet health education. Then the establishment of the system was confirmed through expert interviews.

In the third stage, pre-test of dietary knowledge and Web-AR operation instructions were conducted according to patients with chronic kidney disease recommended by doctors. The feedback was obtained from users' feelings after operation test, obtaining relevant suggestions on diet management effectiveness, preference, operation experience of Web-AR experience and functions of LINE chatbot. An overall improvement and proposal were made as a reference for assisting chronic kidney patients and improving the effectiveness of diet learning in the future, so as to meet the needs of patients.

2.1 Analysis of Interview Data

At this stage, the primary data were collected after interviews with experts through structured questionnaires and individual case interviews. The problems that patients with chronic kidney disease often encountered in self-management of diet were understood. The needs were learned through interviews with patients with kidney disease at various stages, experts, and dietitians. It mainly includes the followings: (1) diet conditions and problems of patients with chronic kidney disease in the early and late stages; (2) the diet plans assessed, treated, and formulated by medical staff; (3) needs and expectations of Web-AR in mobile medicine. This stage was used to plan the system, build a diet database, and develop Web-AR application to meet user needs.

Interview of Medical Staff

1. B Individual case interview method (medical staff).
2. Interviewees: Attending physician, Nephrology Department, National Taiwan University Hospital Douliu Branch
3. Summary:

   - According to the different severity of patients in each stage, dietitian assistance is still needed in diet management. By teaching dietary knowledge, such as protein and calories, personalized recommendations are made. If IT applications are required to combine with, it is recommended to test the patients under the age of 60 years old.
   - Patients often have more doubts about food choices, who are mainly unclear about what food can or cannot be eaten. If pictures or texts or even videos can be used to help these patients electronically, they can improve their knowledge and concepts of diet, so that patients can absorb them in the first time. Moreover, it can improve their willingness to learn, shorten the learning time, and improve medical effectiveness.
   - Controlling diet (e.g., phosphorus, potassium, sodium ion, and protein) is difficult for patients to judge whether food can or cannot be eaten and how much they should eat in daily life. Furthermore, they do not have a clear understanding of the food on the market, and the categories of food are quite diverse and complicated. Therefore, to increase the correctness and confidence of food selection, the method of inquiry can be used. Food information is presented in the form of health education graphics, labeling food nutritional information, such as phosphorus, potassium, sodium ions, protein, calories, portion size, and even further labeling food.

- There are different dietary restrictions in each stage. In the presentation of food information, if the information of foods containing high potassium and high phosphorus can be marked, such as using warning symbols or texts, the patients in each stage can clearly know which foods should be noted as inedible, having dietary suggestions. Moreover, patients can understand why they should not eat, how to choose, and how to better eat. In addition, if what other patients search for food, and which food is more commonly encountered and unclear can be known, it can help people better understand the cognition of food, and also quickly understand the first-hand information of what types of food people are inquiring today.
- The application of Web-AR can be combined with the health education manual. In health education, patients can use mobile phones to learn by themselves in advance, improve their willingness to learn, who can ask medical staff if they are unclear. Furthermore, they can also review the content of health education through the mobile phone when they forget any of them at home. It has a perfected care process from health education learning to self-care process.
- Web-AR is expected to show food information, including calories, portion size, and sugar. Such as a tablespoon of salt, the portion size of white rice, and the thickness of meat, the food itself can be presented more accurately. Thus, patients can understand the diet information in the first time and enhance the interest and user willingness from the interactive process.
- The information to be queried can make patients be clearer about the food content through the 3D presentation of the prototype food. It is mainly used in the tools of the health education teachers, and the instructions during the visit, which can help patients to understand the knowledge.
- Web-AR combined with lens scans external food, such as supermarket microwave food. Patients are informed of whether they can be eaten through the Web-AR presentation.

Interview with Patients with Chronic Kidney Disease

1. Case interview (patients).
2. Interviewee: The subjects of this experiment were 10 patients with chronic kidney disease over 18 years old. Current interview progress is as follows. A total of 10 patients had Stage 1–2 kidney disease.
3. Structured questionnaire: The daily health knowledge needs of patients with kidney disease were investigated through the questionnaire, including dietary knowledge, diet control, unclear sector of diet plan, searching willingness and tools, and daily inconvenience needs.
4. Summary:

   - To understand the problems faced by patients with kidney disease in daily life, and to search relevant knowledge through smartphones, including traditional Chinese medicine and health knowledge, there were a large level of dietary needs, including which foods should not be eaten, and the impact of foods with high blood potassium and phosphorus. These were the problems that patients usually encountered and wanted to find out. It was also learned that the willingness to search knowledge through mobile phones was quite high.

- Among them, the diet sector was the problem that patients often encountered in daily life, including food portion size, calories, and protein intake and calculation, food composition, diet and water control standards. The willingness of patients to understand health care knowledge (health education content) was high, mainly disease prevention, slow deterioration of kidney disease, and paying more attention to the principle of healthy diet.
- Health education inquiry platform must conform to the convenience, real-time, and correctness, which could better enhance the willingness to learn.

2.2 Interface Design Planning

In this study, according to the suggestions of patients with chronic kidney disease, food categories and items were planned to inquire, establishing health education content. A system was designed according to the suggestions of doctors, designing a functional system for image recognition and query, and assisting patients to take care of their own health.

System Structure. According to relevant studies, the characteristics of Web-AR had a positive impact on the learning situation and the improvement of learning motivation, achieving better learning results (Chuang, 2005). Therefore, geenee.ar platform was used in this study to develop Web-AR (presenting Web augmented reality on web pages) to develop image identification function, 3D model function, and practice with LINE chatbot interface. The food contents were inquired by clicking or typing in the LINE app, and the queried texts were compared with the Keywords in the database. Then the LINE chatbot system displayed the results in the user interface to present the content of Web-AR in the form of a web page. Patients were helped to increase the interaction and interest in the learning process through Web-AR learning experience, increasing the willingness and motivation of independent learning. Therefore, users could easily operate and self-learn dietary knowledge in daily life, as shown in Figs. 2 and 3. The presenting contents were based on doctor's advice. The food presentation information of Web-AR included calories, portion size, and sugar. The food itself could be presented more accurately, so that patients could understand the diet information in the first time, which was presented in the way of 3D model on the mobile phone.

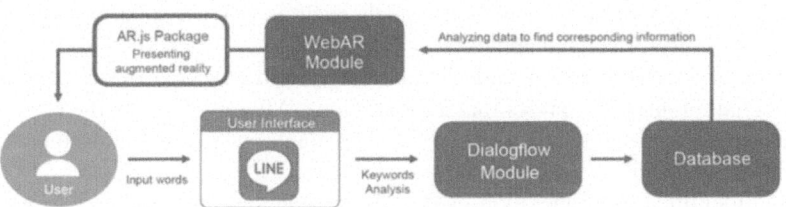

Fig. 2. System Structure

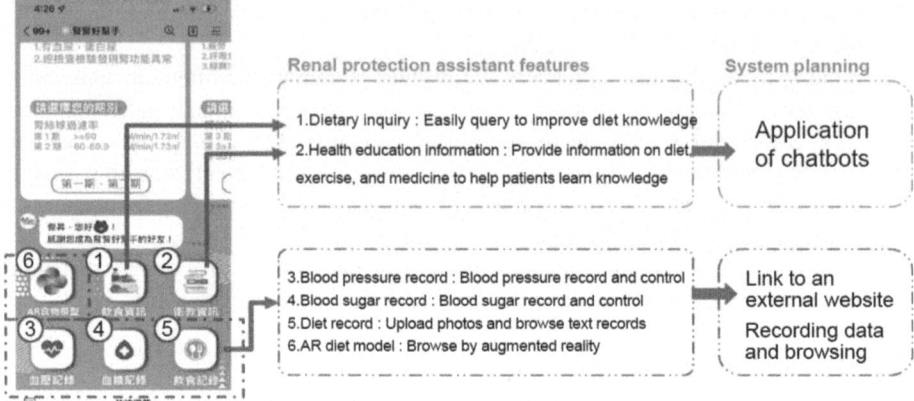

Fig. 3. User interface design

3   The Front-End System Functions Are Described as Follows

1. AR food model:

    This system was built according to the content of the interview. There are many doubts about food selection in patients' diet. They are mainly unclear of what kind of food can or cannot be eaten. Through the presentation of Web-AR, food can be simulated in the way of Web augmented reality, presenting the necessary reference information of food 3D appearance models, including portion size, calories, carbohydrates, and proteins. Thus, patients can absorb them in the first time, improving patients' willingness to learn, increasing the correctness and confidence of food selection, shortening the learning time, and improving medical effectiveness. For medical staffs who teach patients, 3D food models can also be presented through Web-AR, which can make patients be clearer about the food content. It can be applied to the tools of health education teachers, and instructions during the visit. In addition to helping patients deepen their understanding, making up for the limitations of space and types of physical health education models, it can also save medical costs and time costs. It is as shown in Fig. 4.

2. System structure: Through external website links, a Web-AR system was built in this system by AR guide model and image scanning code. Users can link to the web page through the LINE interface platform, and present the Web-AR of related foods, including the common virtual food models such as orange, salmon, egg, peanuts, pork, cauliflower, rice, and apple.

3. [AR guide model] Operation mode: The patient system is linked to a web page through LINE chatbot interface, presenting a camera lens. After clicking on the screen, a 3D virtual model is presented for the reference of patients and medical staff. It is as shown in Figs. 5, 6, and 7.

4. [Image identification] Operation mode: The patient system is linked to a web page through LINE chatbot interface. By clicking on the picture scanning to scan the relevant picture, the relevant 3D virtual model is presented for the reference of patients and medical staff. It is as shown in Fig. 8.

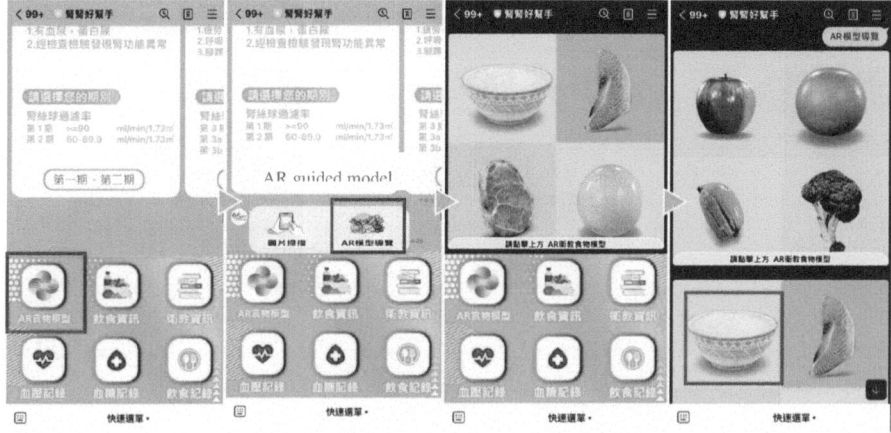

Fig. 4. Augmented reality guided model

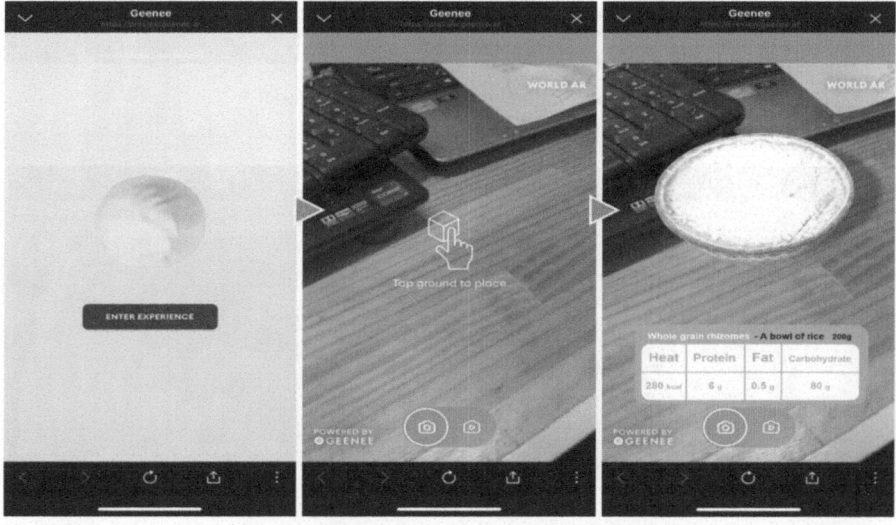

Fig. 5. Augmented reality guided model

1. Diet inquiry function:

According to the suggestions of medical staff, chronic kidney patients are very willing to search knowledge through mobile phones. Patients would like to search diet information through mobile phones, but due to the cumbersome network information, they cannot judge which food should or should not be eaten. The diet sector is a problem that patients frequently encounter in daily life, including food selection, protein intake and calculation, food composition, and diet control standards. In order to enable patients to inquire dietary knowledge in a short time and improve patients' diet problems, diet query function was developed in this study to help patients obtain

Fig. 6. Augmented reality guided model

Fig. 7. Augmented reality guided model

correct dietary knowledge and concepts by LINE chatbot which was implementing them in their daily life.

Fig. 8. Image recognition

2. Using mode: The system can perform Keywords analysis through the database when a user with chronic kidney disease enters a food name through the LINE chatbot. The analysis results can be presented in the dialogue window in the form of automatic reply. A user can judge whether to eat or not to eat according to the results, understanding the protein intake and calculation, food composition, and dietary control standards as a reference. It is as shown in Figs. 9, 10, and 11.

3. Presenting mode: Patients with chronic kidney disease are presented through the question-and-answer process of the chatbot, as shown in Fig. 8. Patients know whether the food can or cannot be eaten and explain the reason why it cannot be eaten or give relevant advice. It appears in red when potassium, sodium, and phosphorus ions values are too high, distinguishing safe and not recommended food. Also, it displays the nutritional composition and portion size of the food, such as calories, protein, carbohydrates and other values, so that patients can calculate and refer to. In addition to deepening the cognition of food, patients can also better understand what kind of food is suitable for their condition, achieving a vigilant effect. Moreover, for the Keywords after query, patients can browse the food queried in the past through hot word analysis to increase the cognition of food, as shown in Fig. 12.

1. Database Construction: The system establishes a database using food nutrient data organized by the Department of Health, Ministry of Health and Welfare, as shown in Fig. 7. The database is structured based on the nutritional values per 100 g of food, including calories, protein, phosphorus ions, sodium ions, potassium ions, carbohydrates, etc. Thresholds are set for high levels of phosphorus ions (>250 mg), sodium ions (>700 mg), and potassium ions (>300 mg), as well as for high biological value proteins and low biological value proteins, which serve as criteria for system identification. When the queried food exceeds the set thresholds, relevant suggestions are provided, and the content of these suggestions can be freely added, modified, or removed through the backend, as shown in Fig. 13.

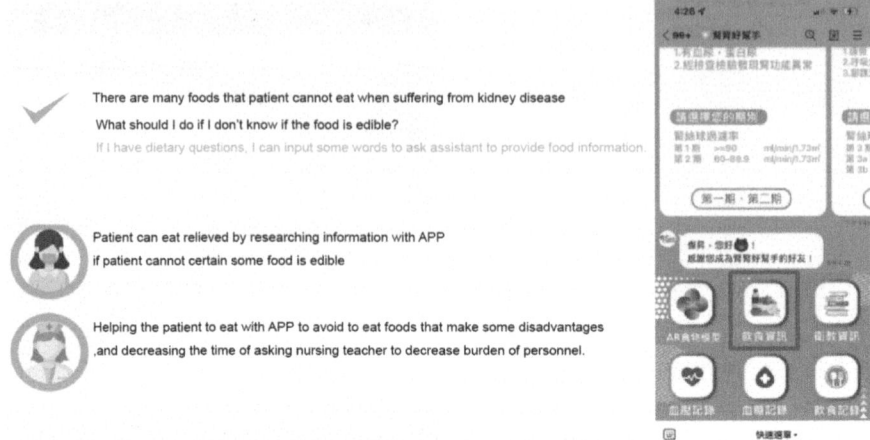

Fig. 9. Augmented reality guided model

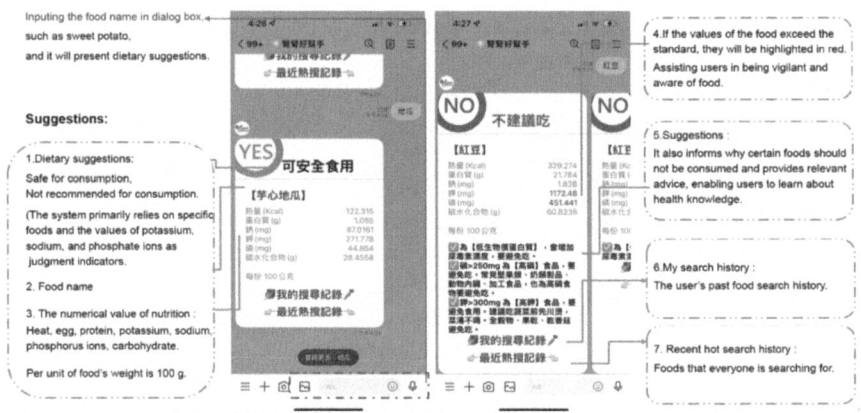

Fig. 10. Diet inquiry function

3.1 Research on Web-AR Interaction Mode

The results of the needs of patients with chronic kidney disease and the user experience of the system were comprehensively considered. The needs of service modes for patients with chronic kidney disease were explored to develop and establish innovative service types and service experiences, as shown in Fig. 14.

During the interaction between the Web-AR system and patients with chronic kidney disease, the subjects trusted the system, felt friendliness, kindness, care and concern, and followed the content provided by the system. They took actions according to the information suggestions, helping the middle-aged and elderly patients with self-health management. In terms of food, which foods should not be eaten, and the impact of high-potassium and phosphorus foods, these were the problems that patients usually encountered and wanted to search for and understand. However, limited by different

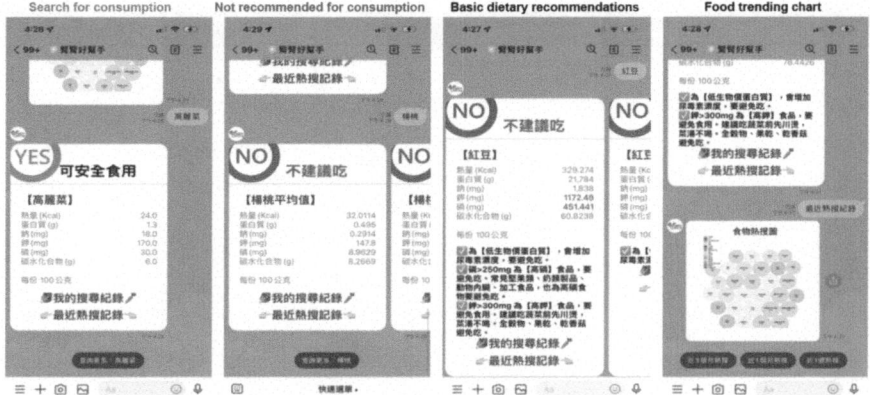

Fig. 11. Diet information presentation.

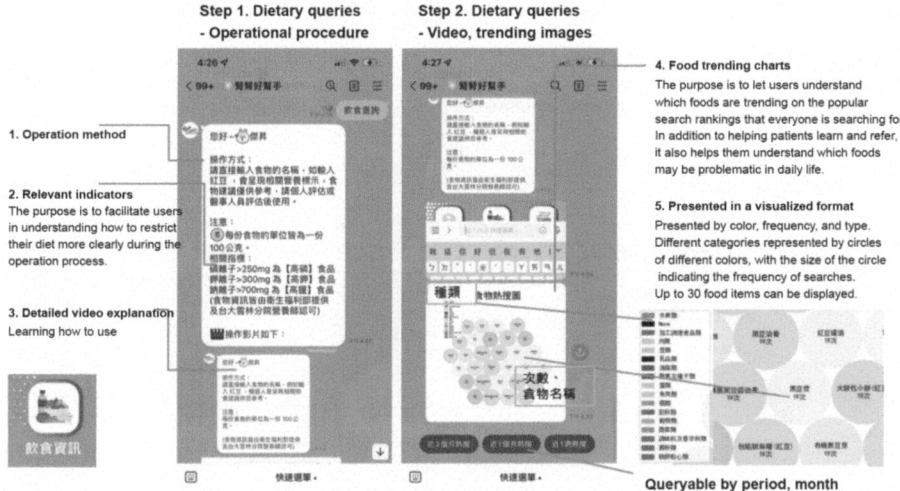

Fig. 12. Keywords Analysis

information sources, incomplete and trivial information was currently a problem that patients encountered in self-learning. Therefore, in the design of search system, real-time information sources should be considered. Convenience and correctness are the best ways to improve learning motivation and willingness. In addition, 3D appearance models of food, portion size, calories, protein, carbohydrates and other necessary reference information are presented, so that patients can absorb them in the first time, improving patients' learning willingness, and increasing their correctness and confidence in choosing food. Since the time is not limited, it can arrange by themselves to record blood pressure and provide medical information, so that users feel that the use of chatbot can bring health to the body, meeting the needs of users and increasing the willingness of users. In the operation process, the picture displays are clear and understandable, and

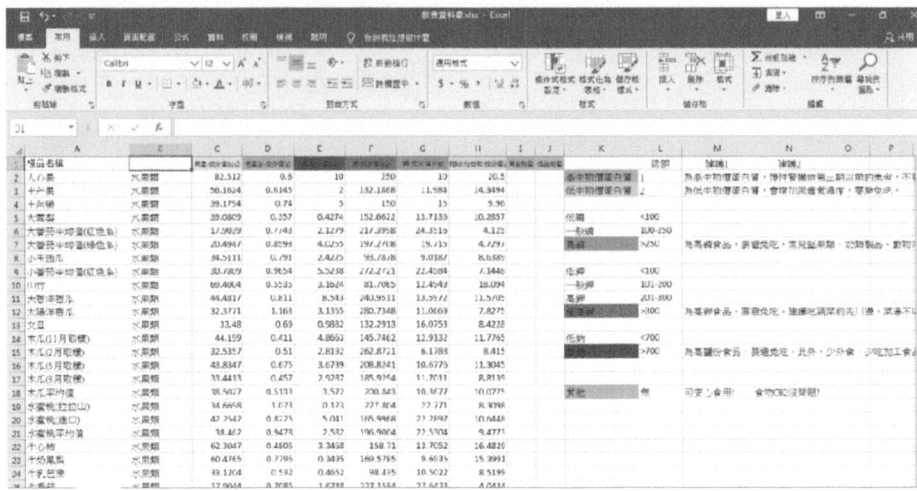

Fig. 13. Data base of system

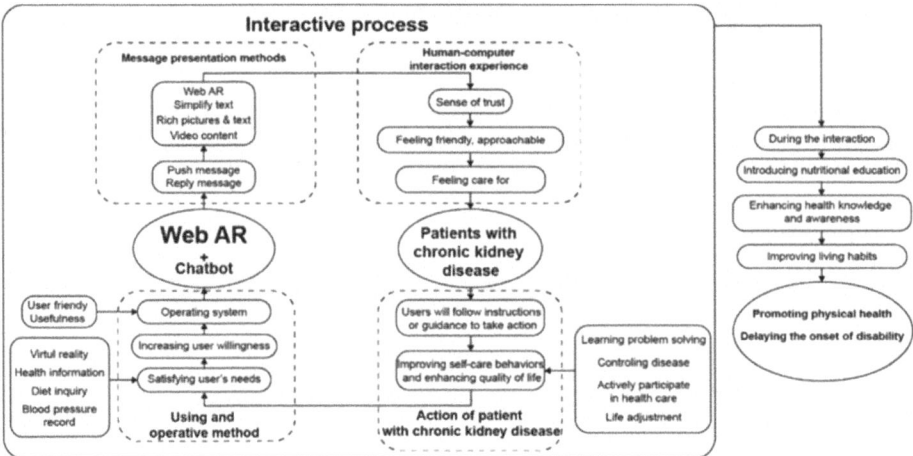

Fig. 14. Chatbot interaction mode

the operation mode is easy to achieve, in line with the principle of usability. Moreover, the push notification and reminder function is conducive to health of body and quality of life, in line with the principle of usefulness. While the chatbot transmits messages through the way of push notification and reply. The content needs to consider the text size of approximately 0.3 to 0.5 cm (12 pt to 14 pt), and the word limit must be considered, having the principle of key point and concise. The message needs to be presented with pictures, which can be enlarged, reduced, and adjusted during operation, or even explained in a short video. Thus, patients with chronic kidney disease can be attracted to watch in a limited time, and then the interactive feeling can be enhanced. In the interactive process, nutrition education can be introduced and implemented in daily life through the improvement of dietary knowledge. Appropriate foods are screened to cultivate good eating habits, in combination with exercise habits and drug control to improve life and rest, helping patients control the disease and maintain good health.

4   Research Results and Discussion

According to the survey, patients' willingness to inquire food information through smartphones combined with Web-AR is quite high. In addition to the six categories of food, the categories including traditional Chinese medicine, and health knowledge demand is also high, which food cannot eat, and the impact of high-potassium and phosphorus. These are the problems patients usually encounter and the sectors they would like to search and understand. However, limited by different information sources, and the incomplete and trivial information, they are the problems patients encounter in self-learning. Therefore, in the design of the search system, it is necessary to consider the real-time, convenience, and correctness of the information source, so as to better improve the learning motivation and willingness.

In addition, according to the doctor's advice, there are many doubts about food selection in patients' diet. Patients are mainly unclear what kind of food can or cannot be eaten. Through the presentation of Web-AR, the food can be simulated in the way of Web augmented reality, presenting the necessary reference information of food 3D appearance models with portion size, calories, protein and so on. Patients can absorb them in the first time, improving patients' willingness to learn, increasing the correctness and confidence of food selection, shortening the learning time, and improving medical effectiveness. It has different dietary restrictions in each stage. In the presentation of food information, for example, it can indicate which foods contain high potassium and high phosphorus, etc., such as warning symbols or words, so that patients in each stage can pay attention to which foods should not be eaten. With dietary suggestions, patients can understand why they should not eat, how to choose and how to eat better. In addition, the system design shows which foods are commonly searched for, it can help people better understand the cognition of food, and quickly understanding what types of first-hand information everyone is inquiring about today.

The Web-AR is also applied to the health education manual, which is different from the traditional health education book. It presents the health education content in the way of 3D models, increasing the interaction and learning novelty, and enhancing the willingness to learn. Patients ask the medical staff when there is no clarity, who can also review the content of health education through the mobile phone when they forget any of them at home. It has a perfected care process from health education learning to self-care process. For the medical staffs who teach patients, they can also present 3D food models through Web-AR, which can make patients be more clear about the food content. It can be applied to the tools of health education teachers, and instructions during the visit. In addition to helping patients deepen their understanding, it can also save medical costs and time costs.

While many patients have no concept of kidney organs, or unclear about the operation process of hemodialysis and peritoneal dialysis, these can also be presented through Web-AR, helping patients quickly understand them. The above functions are combined with the LINE chatbot, because the chatbot is not limited by any time and place. It simplifies the inquiry content in a streamlined way, improving efficiency and shortening the waiting time, and there is no need to install another app. Compared with other applications, the chatbot on the line platform can make users to operate in the most familiar interface. It can enable patients with chronic diseases to have a better quality of life and health.

5 Conclusion

WebAR technology is increasingly being used in the medical field, including the self-health management of patients with chronic kidney disease. This study was mainly based on the actual WebAR experience of patients with chronic kidney disease, through the combination of whether chatbot helped improve dietary knowledge of self-health management, and through the suggestions of respondents, to evaluate whether chatbot contributed to the effectiveness of dietary knowledge for patients. Also, the needs of chronic kidney disease patients for medical robot service mode were explored to develop and establish innovative service types and service experience. In terms of health knowledge, a week after patients experienced the chatbot, patients confirmed that the WebAR combined with the chatbot could help middle-aged and elderly patients with chronic kidney disease improve their dietary knowledge through nutrition education and related health education knowledge intervention. In the way of human-computer interaction, all patients could learn new health knowledge through this system. User experience feedback results showed that the application of WebAR provided patients with a new learning and interactive experience. Patients could in-depth understand their own diseases and related health knowledge through the virtual world, helping patients better manage their own conditions, reducing patients' discomfort and complications, and improving the quality of life. In the interaction process of WebAR, patients felt friendly, cordial, care and concern. WebAR technology can provide patients with a safe, comfortable and private learning environment. Compared with traditional health education methods, WebAR technology can better meet the learning needs and psychological needs of patients, so that patients can more actively participate in self-health management. In the self-health management of patients with chronic kidney disease, diet management is a very important link. Patients need to know which foods cannot be eaten, which foods are high in blood potassium and phosphorus, and the impacts of these foods on the body. However, when patients learn and understand the knowledge, they often encounter problems such as different information sources, incomplete information and triviality. These problems may reduce patients' motivation and willingness to learn, which in turn affects patients' self-health management. In addition, patients can trust the system because of the correctness of the information source, so that the trust level of use is high. The pictures are clearly displayed, which can be adjusted to the size of the text, in line with the principle of usability. By push notifying messages and replying to messages, it is considered to be effective, helpful, and in line with the principle of usefulness. Through the functions of health education information, diet information, diet record, blood glucose and blood pressure record, it helps to improve the awareness of self-care, among which health education information and diet information can better meet the needs of users, and thus improving the effectiveness of self-management. In the process of human-computer interaction, users can feel friendly. By talking in an anthropomorphic tone, patients can feel care and concern. Also, patients believe that it can help themselves to be healthier through the instructions and guidance of chatbot.

This study developed a system of WebAR combined with chatbot through system process construction, response presentation, emotional connection and interaction, and functional requirements, which was applied to the interactive process of patients with chronic kidney disease. Through the intervention of health education knowledge and nutrition education, it has been practically applied to daily life to achieve the service process and experience of self-health management of diet, so as to help patients maintain healthy body functions and promote healthy aging.

References

1. Annual Report of Health Promotion Administration. Daily Diet Guidebook, chrome-extension://efaidnbmnnnibpcajpcglclefindmkaj/ (2018). https://www.hpa.gov.tw/File/Attach/6712/File_6253.pdf
2. Chen, T.K., Knicely, D.H., Grams, M.E.: Chronic kidney disease diagnosis and management: a review. JAMA **322**(13), 1294–1304 (2019)
3. Logan, A.G., et al.: Effect on blood pressure of integrating a smartphone-based self-management system into the care of patients with advanced chronic kidney disease. J. Am. Soc. Hypertens. **10**(4, Supplement), e65 (2016)
4. Tuot, D.S., Boulware, L.E.: Telehealth applications to enhance CKD knowledge and awareness among patients and providers. Adv. Chronic Kidney Dis. **24**(1), 39–45 (2017)
5. Akraa, S., et al.: A smartphone-based point-of-care quantitative urinalysis device for chronic kidney disease patients. J. Netw. Comput. Appl. **115**, 59–69 (2018)
6. Diamantidis, C.J., Becker, S.: Health information technology (IT) to improve the care of patients with chronic kidney disease (CKD). BMC Nephrol. **15**, 7 (2014)
7. Calvillo-Arbizu, J., et al.: User-centred design for developing e-Health system for renal patients at home (AppNephro). Int. J. Med. Informatics **125**, 47–54 (2019)
8. Fakih El Khoury, C., Crutzen, R., Schols, J.M., Halfens, R.J., Karavetian, M.: Adequate management of phosphorus in patients undergoing hemodialysis using a dietary smartphone app: prospective pilot study. JMIR Format. Res. **5**(6), e17858 (2021)

Exploring the Resilience of Older Internal Migrants Through Immersive Technology

Jingjing Zhang[1] ⓘ, Xiaoxiao Wang[1] ⓘ, Huize Wan[1] ⓘ, Weiwei Zhang[2] ⓘ,
and Yuan Yao[1]([✉]) ⓘ

[1] School of Architecture and Design, Beijing Jiaotong University, Beijing, China
yuanyao@bjtu.edu.cn
[2] School of Digital Media and Design Arts, Beijing University of Posts and
Telecommunications, Beijing, China

Abstract. In HCI research on immigrants and aging, there's a focus on social supports, but less on older internal migrants' adaptability. We aim to identify the resilience sources in older adults and assist them in forging new emotional bonds with their past experiences. Conducted in Beijing, China, our study delves into the social adaptation challenges these individuals face, utilizing metadata surveys and in-depth semi-structured interviews with nine participants. We uncovered a significant resilience rooted in memories among the older internal migrant population. Furthermore, we emphasized the advantages of integrating memories with immersive VR technology and examined the prerequisites for deploying such memory-enhanced VR. Additionally, we introduced a novel VR reminiscence probe concept that bridges the past and present. This initiative seeks to stimulate dialogue on assisting older internal migrants in recalling their past, harnessing positive energy from VR immersive environments, and devising design strategies and methodologies to address the challenges confronting older internal migrants more effectively.

Keywords: Older Internal Migrants · VR · Resilience · Memory

1 Introduction

In recent years, the issue of social life adaptation and welfare support for new immigrants has gained attention in the field of HCI, encompassing various groups including international migrants, refugees, women, and youth. HCI is also actively providing support from multiple aspects such as design, technology, and culture [1–3] to help them adapt more quickly to new socio-cultural lifestyles. However, within the immigrant community, there is a growing segment of older internal migrants. Some of them have chosen to migrate to more livable cities upon retirement [4, 5] while others have passively followed their children to new cities. Despite being within the same country, different regions exhibit distinct living habits and cultural identities. Hence, we also consider the study of immigrants to better understand the challenges older internal migrants face. Most of these older adults possess autonomy and strong self-awareness, but they are

M. Antona et al. (Eds.): HCII 2024, LNCS 15379, pp. 290–303, 2025.
https://doi.org/10.1007/978-3-031-76818-7_20

forced to passively accept new lifestyles and social environments, facing passive social dilemmas [6]. HCI is concerned with the vulnerability of immigrants [7]. However, there is scant attention from HCI scholars to the adaptability issues of older internal migrants who relocate with their families.

When older individuals relocate to a new city to live with their children, it means temporarily giving up their familiar living environment and social circles. Upon arrival in the new city, they may face challenges in integrating into the new community in the short term, along with the potential difficulty of dealing with dialects, leading to social dilemmas. The altered lifestyle rhythms due to this migration significantly impact the lives of older adults (see Fig. 1).

In fact, society has been paying attention to the issue of older internal migrants for a long term and is committed to exploring the common social problems and immediate needs of older adults, and starting to provide functional service support and benefits from the host community level to support them in adapting to their new life [8, 9]. However, community institutions sometimes overlook their past cultural identities and social memories, ignoring the inequality between objective social support and subjective personal action. Some studies indicate that therapies involving cultural identity, memories, and group recollection can help new immigrant groups gain resilience [10], reduce feelings of alienation, and acquire a sense of unity from an individual subjective perspective [11, 12]. This prompts us to reflect that perhaps what older internal migrants need is to draw courage and strength for a new life from their 'past' selves by reconnecting with their past lives.

Fig. 1. Like migratory birds, some older internal migrants move from their familiar hometowns to unfamiliar living places for their children, embarking on a new round of dedication. Despite reuniting with their children, they still feel like outsiders.

Our work in this paper focuses on researching the cultural memories and resilience of older internal migrants. We use Beijing, China as the regional scenario for our study. Our preliminary investigation includes a meta-data survey (encompassing literature, case studies, and news) on the social adaptation challenges faced by these older internal migrants. We invited 9 participants for in-depth, semi-structured interviews and memory design disclosures. Building on our phased discoveries, we endeavored to develop a VR-integrated reminiscence design. This probe comprises a series of immersive, realistically recreated scenarios (including indoor, outdoor, and social settings where older adults engage), character roles (such as family, friends, and other social relations in community and medical environments), and guided questions. The probe is designed to help aging users with low technical backgrounds confront their social dilemmas by viewing 3D-recreated scenes. It aims to assist them in aligning their past cultural identities and social experiences with future life, rekindling their zest for life and resilience. Additionally, the study's outcomes provide HCI designers with insights into this vast and urgently needy social group.

2 Background and Related Work

2.1 Immigrant Care and Older Internal Migrants in HCI

Research on immigrant care and support in HCI is quite scattered [7]. Earlier work focused primarily on interactive technologies that promote communication and social interaction, such as communication interface design [13], the establishment of transnational communities [14], and chatbot design [1]. Subsequently, there emerged a focus on supporting cultural education, with projects like temporary language translation systems [15] and language learning systems [16]. In recent years, HCI has also paid attention to emotion support design to foster mental health and emotional recovery [3, 17–19]. Given the diverse multicultural backgrounds of immigrants, most research employs ethnographic studies [20]. Recently, participatory design has been increasingly used [21], allowing for detailed exploration within the design process to uncover effective strategies that support immigrant development.

For a long time, the fields of sociology and anthropology have focused on the issue of aging migration. Their research often starts from the reasons for migration [22, 23], extending to more macroscopic studies on the 'circulation of migrants' [4], patterns of living arrangements [9], and the adaptation and mechanisms of social welfare systems [8]. They also aim to advocate for the transformation of community services and the improvement of medical and welfare systems for older internal migrants [24]. These strategies are all aimed at helping older adults adapt to new urban lives at a social level. However, there is a notable gap in addressing the finer details of self-identity and cultural identity among older internal migrants [25]. This gap presents an opportunity for innovative collaborations and design approaches at the intersection of HCI and sociology.

2.2 VR for Older Adults

An increasing number of studies are focusing on the potential of VR design for older adults. Common applications include using VR technology in the daily lives of older adults, such as aiding in medical care and designing age-friendly systems [26–28], VR simulations for wayfinding [29], and stress relief [30]. They also develop immersive content mechanisms to enhance social connections among family and friends [31, 32]. Many studies also examine the impact of immersive digital tools on older adults, investigating whether they contribute to digital inclusion or exacerbate the digital divide [33, 34]. For example, social VR is utilized to challenge aging stereotypes and promote healthy aging [35]. Design of VR game difficulty levels tailored for older adults [36]. A wealth of previous research provides potential technical and design support for our subsequent studies.

2.3 Memory Design and Interactive Technology

In the HCI field, there is a substantial amount of work exploring how design and technology can effectively gather memories and support the recollection of older adults. This is achieved by employing a variety of mixed media, such as a combination of artifacts [37–40], photographs, audio recordings [41, 42], and multi-sensory experiences [43–45]. However, most of them focus on how to activate memories. We are more interested in finding the process of memory evocation and ways to enhance emotions through recollection [46]. For example, the memory-making design tool proposed by Dina Sabie and others advocates stimulating people's memories of people, places, relationships, events, activities, and other objects through the process of 'making' [47]. This approach to evoking memories inspires us to view recollection as an ongoing process rather than a result of our design. We aim to explore the sources of resilience in older adults during this process and support them in forming new emotional connections with their past lives.

3 About Older Internal Migration

To better understand the real difficulties and needs of older internal migrants, we undertook an internet-based meta-analysis focusing on this group. A significant number of older internal migrants encounter a variety of physical and mental challenges in their new living environments. The 2020 "China's Migrant Population Development Report" shows that our country's migrant population has entered a family migration, and there are nearly 18 million people in China, which is about twice the population of New York. Among the nearly 18 million older adults who moved with them, 43% made a special trip to take care of their younger generations, and 25% came to reunite with their children or take care of themselves in other places[1]. Some migrate voluntarily to move in with their children to reduce their burden, while others are influenced by their children's requests or the prospect of better medical facilities in larger cities. The report "Internet Social Support for New Urban Immigrants under the Context of New Urbanization"[2], focusing on urban residents over 60 in parts of Jiangsu, China, showed significant demand for information support among older internal migrants, at 61.1%. The need for emotional support and companionship was also notable, at 45%. Regarding the decision to migrate, 51.1% followed their children's suggestions, 33.0% decided independently, and 16.0% moved following recommendations from spouses or children.

Our metadata-based investigations have revealed that older internal migrants encounter numerous physical and mental challenges at their new residences. Many older internal migrants who relocate to live with their adult children in big cities say they have lost touch with old friends at home and are seen as unpaid nannies or housekeepers. Living away from home can significantly distress older internal migrants. One migrant shared, "Upon my initial move, I found myself isolated, knowing no one and without

---

[1] 2021 Along with the rural "old drifters" who have migrated to the city, it is a difficult journey to blend in with the city https://www.thepaper.cn/newsDetail_forward_15783744.

[2] 2021 "Old drifters", the physical and mental drift of the double predicament how to crack https://news.cctv.com/2021/01/14/ARTIQGT5cVLv6mrSFelfPVv5210114.shtml.

a place to stay, leaving me confined to my home. In contrast, back in my hometown, I often visited and chatted with relatives in my spare time." [48] This quote illustrates a key challenge: the initial lack of communication and integration in a new city. A major source of frustration for these migrants is the absence of a social network beyond their immediate family. Our observations indicate that many older individuals struggle to adapt to their new environment, often experiencing nostalgia for their hometowns[3]. Similarly, for older adults, it is also very difficult to bid farewell to their hometown life and adapt to the new daily life full of household chores before migration[4].

Currently, we believe that older internal migrants face numerous urgent social challenges and inconveniences. Their social dilemmas are not just due to a lack of acquaintances but also the anxiety from unfamiliar environments. Data surveys reveal that their issues mainly revolve around "difficulties in communication due to relocation," "alienation between generations," and "inadaptability to new customs." The reasons for these problems are closely related to the low ubiquity of today's digital technology, the fact that these groups do not have mature social relationships in new cities, are difficult to contact, and have difficulty in accurately and proactively discovering and describing their needs.

Based on the meta-analysis, we invited 9 older adults (female 4, male 5, mean age = 68.33 SD = 5.715) who had migrated to Beijing from other provinces in China with their children. With each participant, we conducted a simple 20-min semi-structured interview. These interviews, conducted from various perspectives, delved into their current living conditions, migration experiences, family member status, social life, daily routines, etc. The interviews took place in a relaxed setting, with researchers facilitating the process to minimize the interaction burden on the older participants. This older-focused and gradual approach was carefully planned to prevent any physiological or psychological distress.

Considering the positive role of Cognitive behavioral therapy [49], we prepared several 3D scene materials in advance to assist with the interviews. We used real-scene scanning software such as 3D Scanner to conduct model scanning, processing, and VR development of some indoor and outdoor environments such as "hutongs" and residential areas in Beijing. This was used as interview materials provided to participants during the interviews to help them understand VR technology and 3D scene scanning technology. This also facilitated further discussions with them about the potential of combining VR technology with reminiscence.

4 Insights

4.1 Current Living Conditions

In interviews, participants generally believed that they did not have too many worries about material life, but they continued to repeat the same numb life and work every day. They frequently mentioned the significant role of their cultural identity from their

---

[3] 2017 'Senior drifters' find big city life a lonely challenge https://europe.chinadaily.com.cn/china/2017-11/06/content_34177327.htm.

[4] 2020 The Lonely Lives of China's 'Elderly Drifters' https://www.sixthtone.com/news/1006341.

hometowns in their lives post-migration. This nostalgia often left them caught between the cultural identities of their hometown and their new residence. Many older adults have encountered a certain degree of social problems in the new environment. P6 spoke of preferring solitude after moving to the new city, taking up photography post-retirement, and believing in the quality, not quantity, of friendships. "I have only a few close friends. As you know, perhaps women's minds are also thoughtful, unlike most men who can easily get along with others. My acquaintances are mostly former colleagues, but I wouldn't call them friends." For those who are introverted or haven't established stable social connections in parks, the desire to find new friends or forms of entertainment through technological assistance is particularly strong. P8 said, "I don't have many friends here, I just wander around in the park without really meeting anyone. I'm not keen on participating in activities, just watching from the sidelines is good enough for me." But when we asked him if he was interested in having entertainment or social activities through the VR platform we built, he expressed his willingness to participate.

4.2 About Memories

When queried about their hometown memories, roughly one-third of the participants expressed missing friends and family there. As the research deepened, we also found that in addition to friends and colleagues of the same generation, older adults miss their parents more prominently. The emotional support provided by parents to the relocated older adults is an important part of the supply of emotional energy and is also their attachment to their hometown. Important carrier of memory. P4 shared, "In the past, I frequently visited my parents in my hometown. Since their passing, despite having siblings, my visits have diminished considerably, by almost a decade..." Migrants often reminisce about memories of their country, language, sounds, or smells, as well as interpersonal relationships [50]. The spatial separation caused by migration leads to inevitable regrets and helplessness among older internal migrants. This has become one of the most discussed topics in HCI technology's intervention in older adults' social interaction in recent years [31, 51].

On the other hand, around the location, the concept of "hometown" plays a significant role in the lives of immigrants [52]. Surprisingly, during the interviews, most older adults expressed that they actually do not remember and miss the environment of their hometown as much as the public spaces in their hometown. Compared with the houses that remind them of their lonely lives, they prefer open spaces such as doorsteps or yards where they can greet and chat with others. The nostalgia is higher. People turned to collective memories [53] because these memories not only reflected their past experiences but also provided them with a sense of direction, serving as both a mirror and a guiding light [50]. In their hometowns, many older adults lived alone or with their partners. During the interviews, p1 revealed in words how bored and lonely she felt when living alone in an empty home. She said, "Back in my hometown, I would just lie or sit upstairs all day. What's the point? I lived in a big courtyard, and I could see fields with fruits and vegetables growing. I could visit them every day, which is different from this city." P8 also mentioned the place he missed the most, saying, "I used to lie in the front yard sunbathing, one day after another, without much to do. In the afternoon, when I heard a group of people coming from afar, making noise and chatting, I would pack up and go to the courtyard to play cards with them. I often miss those days now." P8 described the mixed effects of recalling people, events, and scenes from the past. The courtyard in his hometown and the voices of his friends provided him with a sense of comfort, allowing him to piece together these mixed fragments and experience a moment of mental relaxation amidst vague memories.

Some participants spontaneously mentioned the enduring impact of their childhood in their hometown on their lives. The presence of their hometown is like a tangible memory probe, carrying with it the events, social relationships, and emotional responses that occurred there [54]. P7 said, "I really miss the carefree life of my youth when I could just take a bath in the river in front of my home and catch fish there. But now, that river has dried up." P7 described the contradiction between his cherished memories and the present reality. This change in the real environment makes childhood memories less evidence and fewer clues to trigger more memories. "The disappearance of the river still affects me. I wish I could see that river again…" Recreating changing scenes can help people draw strength from their memories. After we presented the VR and 3D scene reconstruction materials, the participants felt very excited. P7 said, "Sharing these memories with everyone, being able to see things that have disappeared, is beautiful and meaningful." In the context of the uncertain new migrant environment, older adults become newcomers, and they need their old life as a source of motivation to face a new life. At the same time, it provides immersive scenes for older adults to reconnect with their memories of the past and offers a potential channel.

4.3   About Immersive Scenarios and VR

Based on the interview results, most older adults gave a favorable evaluation of the potential role of immersive scenes, and are highly receptive to realistically restored three-dimensional memory scenes, which breaks the limitations of 2D photos and videos on mobile phones and transcends physical limitations. P7 stated, "It's like walking back in time." However, some participants also showed a high level of vigilance, expressing concerns about data privacy and property safety, as well as doubts about the feasibility of the technology. Some older adults felt that due to their age, they lacked the confidence to try new technologies, speculating that they might not fully understand and use VR equipment. Older adults were hesitant to try VR devices due to their unfamiliar appearance and complete visual enclosure.

Furthermore, through the initial exploration of user needs mentioned above, we noticed that most participants prefer VR scenes that are highly restored and realistic. VR is a promising and ecologically valid technique to simulate physical environments and examine landscape preferences and restorativeness. A substantial amount of evidence suggests that under certain conditions, natural simulations can support processes that promote health. More than 100 experimental reports indicate that pictures, videos, or immersive virtual environments with natural elements can enhance mood, improve executive cognitive functions, promote physiological stress recovery, or alleviate pain [55, 56].

4.4 About Resilience

At a time when they should be enjoying their old age, older internal migrants need to rebuild a new life in a new environment. Communication barriers from varied cultural backgrounds and lifestyle challenges due to different routines are distinct difficulties older internal migrants face, compared to other older adults. Seemingly trivial matters of daily life can slowly erode their self-esteem and confidence, like snowflakes. However, through brief interviews, we found that they could trigger energy in a moment of reminiscence, regaining the happiness and comfort of the past. This is not just about amplifying positive past emotions but using reminiscence to offset new life's emotional challenges, highlighting memory's restorative power as tacit knowledge. As older internal migrants, they may become lost in the difficulties of a new life, forgetting the meaning of their past lives. They need to be reminded that they also have the right and ability to live comfortably. Our goal is to mitigate the emotional stress that older internal migrants experience due to challenges in their new lives, thereby enhancing their opportunities to rediscover the beauty, blessings, freedom, and marvels of life.

5 Conceptual Design Combining the VR and Memory

Our study leverages the extensive and in-depth research of our predecessors, employing immersive technologies to help older internal migrants confront their past memories and current realities. This approach aims to empower them to overcome current challenges by drawing on the strength of authentic memories.

Encouraging older adults to share their memories is a commonly employed method in research involving senior users. By triggering recollections, they can disclose additional contextual information about their lives. Delivering this information to researchers in the form of textual scenes allows for a deeper understanding compared to traditional face-to-face questioning. Therefore, we propose a multi-party participatory reminiscence VR probe design concept. This approach utilizes real scene models as primary elements in immersive scenario maps, potentially aiding older adults in articulating their memories with greater clarity and depth than is possible through conventional face-to-face interviews. During the early development stages, designers will guide older adults in accurately reconstructing their memory worlds. Additionally, we advocate for incorporating insights from previous work on multimodal situational maps in reminiscence therapy into this design concept, such as integrating contextual maps with paper drawings [47], participatory mapping [57], and combinations of sound, smell, and images in contextual maps [58].

We propose that the reminiscence VR probe design concept should encompass four key elements: scenes, events, characters, and props (see Fig. 2). We found that changes in the living environment are the fundamental way to explore the life difficulties of older internal migrants. The parts involving reminiscence and scene recreation serve as powerful tools to manifest the impact of these changes [35]. For older internal migrants, changes in their living places have a significant impact. At the scene level, we assist users or other family members and friends to use mobile devices with depth cameras to scan the scenes of past and present memories or activities of the older internal migrants,

Fig. 2. VR reminiscence probe design: Enables simultaneous participation of older internal migrants and researchers in immersive scenarios for discussing, disclosing, defining, or editing memories.

and the designers will process and upload them. For unclear or potentially irrecoverable memory segments, as well as events and characters emerging from new social engagements encountered by older internal migrants, prior studies indicate that memory reinforcement can be achieved with methods like marking and annotation [59], and the use of virtual artifacts [60]. These techniques may aid older adults in memory sharing and social interaction. Consequently, we propose integrating props into the reminiscence VR probe design. Designers and researchers can provide simple stickers, models, and other materials in VR to assist older adults in disclosing their views and evaluations of past or current events and characters, reflecting on their past ways of facing life difficulties and stimulating emotional resilience. Additionally, we could gather more design suggestions to enhance the initiation of upcoming research effectively.

To develop a VR system accessible to older adults with limited tech experience, as well as stakeholders, designers, and researchers, we have identified several key criteria. These include multi-user support, quick scene model uploading, the integration of various props like images and text, and customizable basic interactive features. Given these requirements, we find the 3Dscanner mobile app to be highly suitable for scene scanning. Similarly, VR social platforms such as VRchat and VRreborn emerge as ideal for facilitating scene interactions.

Mobile device optical scanning technology enables quick scanning, saving, and sharing of any object or space as a 3D model. This can meet the probe's needs for efficient collection and uploading of scenes and has high model quality. It can visually restore the key memory scenes mentioned by the older adults, which greatly facilitates efficient communication with the older adults and facilitates the iteration of 3D scenes.

6   Reflections and Future Work

6.1   Objective Social Support is Not the Subjective Self-confidence of Older Adults

Our research, incorporating metadata surveys, interviews, and exploring VR reminiscence probe designs, has satisfyingly highlighted the societal support for older internal migrants. However, the survey uncovered that most of these older internal migrants maintain considerable autonomy and a strong self-awareness. Post-migration, their lives appear more like passive social choices influenced by family ties. Despite being independent social entities with the right to choose their cultural identity, many are involuntarily caught in the societal current, leading them to unfamiliar environments. Therefore, under the support of favorable objective social conditions, assisting older adults in re-establishing their self-identity at a subjective level such as building emotional confidence [61] and maintaining self-esteem [62] are worthwhile design directions to explore. Consequently, in the next phase of probe research, we will also pay attention to the potential emotional conflicts, social anxiety, and other issues disclosed by participants in their recollections, as a bridging contact point in design.

6.2 Aging of Memory and Customization of Memory

From interviews with older internal migrants, we have confirmed the effective impact of memories in fostering positive self-emotions. Regrettably, the negative effects of aging on episodic memory recall extend to diminished self-awareness [62, 63]. Therefore, efforts to support self-defining memories can be beneficial to the sense of self and confidence, by tapping into the sensorial richness of episodic memories underpinning them [44]. In our future participatory design of reminiscence VR probe, we plan to incorporate detailed disclosures from older adults, providing them with more tools and materials to strengthen and edit their memories.

7 Conclusion

Our study delves into the social standing of older internal migrants and examines how design and technology can efficiently collect memories and aid their recollection. This research builds on existing studies and incorporates user experiments. We conducted 20-min semi-structured interviews with nine older internal migrants in Beijing, discovering the crucial role of reminiscence in enhancing their resilience. Consequently, we developed a VR reminiscence scene to probe into the resilience sources among older internal migrants. This VR scene integrates immersive maps of real locations, characters, and events, facilitating an exploration of how older adults evoke memories. This technique not only boosts their readiness to share but also assists in the clearer articulation of their memories. Compared to conventional face-to-face interviews, this method reveals more profound information and significantly aids designers and researchers in comprehensively grasping the context of user statements. This enriches the design and research strategy, offering fresh insights for future inquiries into similar topics.

Subsequently, we created a VR probe to explore resilience in older adults by integrating immersive and realistic contextual elements such as maps, characters, and events, our goal was to comprehend the process of memory recall in older adults. This method encourages their willingness to share memories, facilitating clearer disclosure of recollections. The VR probe enables a more profound exploration compared to conventional face-to-face questioning. Additionally, it also enhances support for designers and researchers in comprehending users' contextual information, providing insights for future research design in the field.

References

1. Chen, Z., Lu, Y., Nieminen, M. P., Lucero, A.: Creating a chatbot for and with migrants: chatbot personality drives co-design activities. In Proceedings of the 2020 ACM Designing Interactive Systems Conference, pp. 219–230 (July 2020)

2. Hourcade, J.P., et al.: Child-computer interaction sig: designing for refugee children. In: Extended Abstracts of the 2019 CHI Conference on Human Factors in Computing Systems, pp. 1–4 (2019, May)

3. Tachtler, F., Talhouk, R., Michel, T., Slovak, P., & Fitzpatrick, G. (2021, May). Unaccompanied migrant youth and mental health technologies: A social-ecological approach to understanding and designing. In Proceedings of the 2021 CHI Conference on Human Factors in Computing Systems (pp. 1–19)

4. Bolzman, C., Fibbi, R., Vial, M.: What to do after retirement? Elderly migrants and the question of return. J. Ethn. Migr. Stud. 32(8), 1359–1375 (2006)

5. Krout, J.A.: Seasonal migration of the elderly. Gerontologist 23(3), 295–299 (1983)

6. White, P.: Migrant populations approaching old age: prospects in Europe. J. Ethn. Migr. Stud. 32(8), 1283–1300 (2006)

7. Sabie, D., et al.: Migration and mobility in HCI: rethinking boundaries, methods, and impact. In: Extended Abstracts of the 2021 CHI Conference on Human Factors in Computing Systems, pp. 1–6 (2021, May)

8. Livingston, G., Leavey, G., Kitchen, G., Manela, M., Sembhi, S., Katona, C.: Mental health of migrant elders–the Islington study. Br. J. Psychiatry 179(4), 361–366 (2001)

9. Schoenmakers, D., Lamkaddem, M., Suurmond, J.: The role of the social network in access to psychosocial services for migrant elderly—A qualitative study. Int. J. Environ. Res. Public Health 14(10), 1215 (2017)

10. Volkan, V.D.: Bloodlines: From ethnic pride to ethnic terrorism. (No Title) (1997)

11. Bhugra, D.: Migration, distress and cultural identity. Br. Med. Bull. 69(1), 129–141 (2004)

12. Kim, W.B.: Nostalgia, anxiety and hope: migration and ethnic identity of Chosonjok in China. Pac. Aff. 83(1), 95–114 (2010)

13. Wyche, S.P., Chetty, M.: " I want to imagine how that place looks" designing technologies to support connectivity between Africans living abroad and home. In: Proceedings of the SIGCHI Conference on Human Factors in Computing Systems, pp. 2755–2764 (April 2013)

14. Castro, L.A.: Connectedness: support to communities in diaspora via ICT. In: CHI'07 Extended Abstracts on Human Factors in Computing Systems, pp. 1629–1632 (2007, April)

15. Brown, D., Grinter, R.E.: Designing for transient use: a human-in-the-loop translation platform for refugees. In: Proceedings of the 2016 CHI Conference on Human Factors in Computing Systems, pp. 321–330 (2016, May)

16. Liaqat, A., Munteanu, C.: Towards a writing analytics framework for adult English language learners. In: Proceedings of the 8th International Conference on Learning Analytics and Knowledge, pp. 121–125 (March 2018)

17. Tachtler, F.: Designing for technology-enabled social-ecological resilience. In: 22nd International Conference on Human-Computer Interaction with Mobile Devices and Services, pp. 1–3 (2020, October)

18. Ayobi, A., et al.: Designing visual cards for digital mental health research with ethnic minorities. In: Proceedings of the 2021 ACM Designing Interactive Systems Conference, pp. 942–954 (2021, June)

19. Sien, S.W., Mohan, S., McGrenere, J.: Exploring design opportunities for supporting mental wellbeing among East Asian university students in Canada. In: Proceedings of the 2022 CHI Conference on Human Factors in Computing Systems , pp. 1–16 (April 2022)

20. Xu, T.B., et al.: Designing virtual environments for social engagement in older adults: a qualitative multi-site study. In: Proceedings of the 2023 CHI Conference on Human Factors in Computing Systems, pp. 1–15 (2023, April)

21. Duarte, A.M.B., Brendel, N., Degbelo, A., Kray, C.: Participatory design and participatory research: An HCI case study with young forced migrants. ACM Trans. Comput.-Hum. Interact. (TOCHI) 25(1), 1–39 (2018)

22. Chu, M., et al.: Improving the sense of city belonging among migrant elderly following family from an elderly service perspective: a cross-sectional study. BMC Public Health **22**(1), 2032 (2022)
23. Liu, Y., Sangthong, R., Ingviya, T., Wan, C.: Nothing like living with a family: a qualitative study of subjective well-being and its determinants among migrant and local elderly in Dongguan, China. Int. J. Environ. Res. Public Health **16**(23), 4874 (2019)
24. Wang, Q.: Health of the elderly migration population in China: benefit from individual and local socioeconomic status? Int. J. Environ. Res. Public Health **14**(4), 370 (2017)
25. Hall, S.: □ Cultural identity and diaspora. In: Colonial Discourse and Post-Colonial Theory, pp. 392–403. Routledge (2015)
26. Muñoz, D., Pedell, S., Sterling, L.: Evaluating engagement in technology-supported social interaction by people living with dementia in residential care. ACM Trans. Comput.-Hum. Interact. **29**(5), 1–31 (2022)
27. Zhao, W., Baker, S., Waycott, J.: Challenges of deploying VR in aged care: a two-phase exploration study. In: Proceedings of the 32nd Australian Conference on Human-Computer Interaction, pp. 87–98 (2020, December)
28. Franco dos Reis Alves, S., Uribe Quevedo, A., Chen, D., Morris, J., Radmard, S.: Leveraging simulation and virtual reality for a long-term care facility service robot during COVID-19. In: Proceedings of the 23rd Symposium on Virtual and Augmented Reality, pp. 187–191 (2021, October)
29. Lee, S.: Understanding wayfinding for the elderly using VR. In: Proceedings of the 9th ACM SIGGRAPH Conference on Virtual-Reality Continuum and its Applications in Industry, pp. 285–288 (2010, December)
30. Raja, A., Niforatos, E., Schneegass, C.: An Emotion-adaptive VR experience for recreational use in eldercare. In: Proceedings of Mensch und Computer 2023, pp. 354–358 (2023)
31. Wei, X., et al.: Bridging the generational gap: exploring how virtual reality supports remote communication between grandparents and grandchildren. In: Proceedings of the 2023 CHI Conference on Human Factors in Computing Systems, pp. 1–15 (2023, April)
32. Li, Z., Feng, L., Liang, C., Huang, Y., Fan, M.: Exploring the Opportunities of AR for Enriching Storytelling with Family Photos between Grandparents and Grandchildren. Proc. ACM Interact. Mob. Wearable Ubiquitous Technol. **7**(3), 1–26 (2023)
33. Chen, X., Östlund, B., Frennert, S.: Digital inclusion or digital divide for older immigrants? A scoping review. In: International conference on human-computer interaction, pp. 176–190. Cham: Springer International Publishing (2020, July). https://doi.org/10.1007/978-3-030-50232-4_13
34. Barsasella, D., et al.: Acceptability of virtual reality among older people: ordinal logistic regression study from Taiwan. In: Proceedings of the 6th International Conference on Bioinformatics Research and Applications, pp. 145–151 (2019, December)
35. Baker, S., Waycott, J., Carrasco, R., Hoang, T., Vetere, F.: Exploring the design of social VR experiences with older adults. In: Proceedings of the 2019 on Designing Interactive Systems Conference, pp. 303–315 (2019, June)
36. Kruse, L., Karaosmanoglu, S., Rings, S., Steinicke, F.: Evaluating difficulty adjustments in a VR exergame for younger and older adults: transferabilities and differences. In: Proceedings of the 2022 ACM Symposium on Spatial User Interaction, pp. 1–11 (2022, December)
37. Choi, K.Y., Shinsato, D., Zhang, S., Nakagaki, K., Ishii, H.: reMi: Translating ambient sounds of moment into tangible and shareable memories through animated paper. In: Adjunct Proceedings of the 31st Annual ACM Symposium on User Interface Software and Technology, pp. 84–86 (2018, October)
38. Dib, L., Petrelli, D., Whittaker, S.: Sonic souvenirs: exploring the paradoxes of recorded sound for family remembering. In: Proceedings of the 2010 ACM conference on Computer supported cooperative work, pp. 391–400 (2010, February)

39. West, D., Quigley, A., Kay, J.: MEMENTO: a digital-physical scrapbook for memory sharing. Pers. Ubiquit. Comput. **11**, 313–328 (2007)
40. Frohlich, D., Murphy, R.: The memory box. Pers. Technol. **4**, 238–240 (2000)
41. Niemantsverdriet, K., Versteeg, M.: Interactive jewellery as memory cue: Designing a sound locket for individual reminiscence. In: Proceedings of the TEI'16: Tenth International Conference on Tangible, Embedded, and Embodied Interaction , pp. 532–538 (2016, February)
42. Piper, A.M., Weibel, N., Hollan, J.D.: Designing audio-enhanced paper photos for older adult emotional wellbeing in communication therapy. Int. J. Hum. Comput. Stud. **72**(8–9), 629–639 (2014)
43. Zucco, G.M., Aiello, L., Turuani, L., Köster, E.: Odor-evoked autobiographical memories: age and gender differences along the life span. Chem. Senses **37**(2), 179–189 (2012)
44. Gayler, T., Sas, C., Kalnikaite, V.: "It took me back 25 years in one bound": self-generated flavor-based cues for self-defining memories in later life. Hum.-Comput. Interact. **38**(5–6), 417–458 (2023)
45. Mojet, J., Köster, E.: Flavor memory. In: Multisensory Flavor Perception, pp. 169–184. Woodhead Publishing (2016)
46. Bennett, P., et al.: TopoTiles: Storytelling in care homes with topographic tangibles. In: Proceedings of the 33rd Annual ACM Conference Extended Abstracts on Human Factors in Computing Systems, pp. 911–916 (2015, April)
47. Sabie, D., Sabie, S., Ahmed, S.I.: Memory through Design: Supporting Cultural Identity for Immigrants through a Paper-Based Home Drafting Tool. Association for Computing Machinery, New York, NY, USA, 1–16 (2020)
48. He, X., Zhang, F., Zhao, H., Li, J.: How migration in later life shapes their quality of life: a qualitative investigation of the well-being of the "drifting elderly" in China. Soc. Indic. Res. 1–25 (2020)
49. Castro, S.A., Infurna, F.J., Lemery-Chalfant, K., Waldron, V.R., Zautra, E.: Are daily well-being and emotional reactivity to stressors modifiable in midlife? Evidence from a randomized controlled trial of an online social intelligence training program. Prev. Sci. **24**(5), 841–851 (2023)
50. Falicov, C.J.: Working with transnational immigrants: expanding meanings of family, community, and culture. Fam. Process. **46**(2), 157–171 (2007)
51. Jiang, D., Fung, H.H., Lay, J.C., Ashe, M.C., Graf, P., Hoppmann, C.A.: Everyday solitude, affective experiences, and well-being in old age: the role of culture versus immigration. Aging Ment. Health **23**(9), 1095–1104 (2019)
52. Mowla, Q.A.: Memory association in place making: understanding an Urban space. Memory **9**, 52–54 (2004)
53. Halbwachs, M.: On Collective Memory. University of Chicago press (2020)
54. Downs, R.M., Tuan, Y.F.: Space and place: the perspective of experience. Geogr. Rev. **68**(3), 375 (1978)
55. Yuan, S., et al.: A virtual reality investigation of factors influencing landscape preferences: natural elements, emotions, and media creation. Landsc. Urban Plan. **230**, 104616 (2023)
56. Browning, M.H., Shipley, N., McAnirlin, O., Hartig, T., Dzhambov, A.M.: An actual natural setting improves mood better than its virtual counterpart: a meta-analysis of experimental data. Front. Psychol. **11**, 553684 (2020)
57. Huybrechts, L., Dreessen, K., Schepers, S.: Mapping design practices: on risk, hybridity and participation. In: Proceedings of the 12th Participatory Design Conference: Exploratory Papers, Workshop Descriptions, Industry Cases-Volume 2, pp. 29–32 (2012, August)
58. Pedell, S., Vetere, F.: Visualizing use context with picture scenarios in the design process. In: Proceedings of the 7th International Conference on Human Computer Interaction with Mobile Devices & Services, pp. 271–274 (2005, September)

59. Axtell, B., Saryazdi, R., Munteanu, C.: Design is worth a thousand words: The effect of digital interaction design on picture-prompted reminiscence. In: Proceedings of the 2022 CHI Conference on Human Factors in Computing Systems, pp. 1–12 (2022, April)
60. Lee, H.C., Cheng, Y.F., Cho, S.Y., Tang, H.H., Hsu, J., Chen, C.H.: Picgo: designing reminiscence and storytelling for the elderly with photo annotation. In: Proceedings of the 2014 Companion Publication on Designing Interactive Systems, pp. 9–12 (2014)
61. Chin Derix, E., Leong, T.W., Prior, J.: "It's the same conflict every time, on repeat." how digital technology use can contribute towards conflict in parents' relationships. In: Extended Abstracts of the 2021 CHI Conference on Human Factors in Computing Systems, pp. 1–6 (2021, May)
62. Sas, C.: Exploring self-defining memories in old age and their digital cues. In: Proceedings of the 2018 Designing Interactive Systems Conference, pp. 149–161 (2018, June)
63. El Haj, M., Gandolphe, M.C., Gallouj, K., Kapogiannis, D., Antoine, P.: From nose to memory: The involuntary nature of odor-evoked autobiographical memories in Alzheimer's disease. Chem. Senses **43**(1), 27–34 (2018)

Exploring Usability Disparities in Multi-touch Screen Interaction Among Older Adults and Younger Individuals

Tianmei Zhang[1]([✉]), Yong Wang[1], and Shida Guo[2]

[1] School of Architecture and Design, Harbin Institute of Technology, Harbin 150006, China
{zhangtianmei,wangyong77}@hit.edu.cn
[2] Academy of Art and Design, Tsinghua University, Beijing 100085, China
shida@mail.tsinghua.edu.cn

Abstract. Touch devices are widely integrated into various environments, including corporate settings and public information kiosks. The size of touch screen interface buttons significantly affects user interaction efficiency and accuracy. Current research predominantly focuses on button sizes for handheld and desktop devices, leaving a gap in studies on large touchscreen displays. To address this gap and improve user experience and operational efficiency, this study investigates nine button sizes on a 65-inch touchscreen tilted at a 90-degree angle to evaluate operational performance across different button sizes and spacing intervals. Twelve participants, stratified into two age groups (55 + and 25–55), completed tasks involving sequential button selection. Nine button sizes (10 mm to 50 mm) and four spacing intervals (25 to 100 pixels) were tested. Results showed a negative correlation between button size and response time for both age groups, with larger buttons yielding shorter response times. The optimal button size was 30 mm for younger participants and 40 mm for older participants. Accuracy rates were high ($>97\%$) across all button sizes, with larger buttons enhancing accuracy. These findings underscore the importance of age-specific design considerations in multi-touch interfaces to optimize usability for diverse user demographics.

Keywords: Multi-touch Screen · Usability disparities · Older Adults · Multi-touch interface design

1 Introduction

Touchscreens are increasingly applied in various scenarios due to their convenient operation and user-friendly interaction experience. They are prevalent in corporate environments, public information kiosks, and many other settings where diverse user demographics interact with technological interfaces. Among these user groups, younger and older individuals exhibit different patterns in utilizing and interacting with touchscreens, influenced by factors such as familiarity with technology, dexterity, and cognitive processing speed. This study investigates the usability disparities between older adults and younger individuals when engaging with touchscreens to better understand and address these differences.

M. Antona et al. (Eds.): HCII 2024, LNCS 15379, pp. 304–311, 2025.
https://doi.org/10.1007/978-3-031-76818-7_21

Numerous studies have investigated the optimal adaptation of button sizes for different touchscreen dimensions. Previous research has shown a positive correlation between button size and operational performance in freehand interaction contexts [1]. However, given the constraints of limited screen space, button size design should strike a balance between reasonable dimensions and usability to ensure effective interface functionality and information presentation. The ANSI/HFES 100–2007 standard recommends a minimum button size of 9.5 mm [2], while ISO 9241-9 suggests a range of 22–23 mm [3]. Despite these guidelines, there remains no universally standardized criterion for button size, particularly for large touchscreens, which necessitates further research.

Several studies have examined how older adults perform with different button sizes. Jin, Z. X. et al. (2007) found that healthy older adults performed optimally with a button size of 16.51 mm, while those with reduced finger flexibility required a larger button size of 19.05 mm [4]. Yu, N. et al. (2022) discovered that older users in home environments preferred icons with a size of 20 mm [5]. Furthermore, Chourasia, A.O. et al. (2013) observed that performance while standing was inferior to that while sitting when button size was 20 mm or less [6]. However, research on button size for different user groups on large touchscreen displays remains relatively scarce.

This study addresses a practical design requirement for a 65-inch touchscreen tilted at a 90-degree angle, catering to users of various age groups. It explores the effects of different button sizes on operational performance among older and younger users, with a particular focus on a specific human-computer interaction task involving the manipulation of drag-and-drop maps to access information about designated locations.

2 Experimental Method

2.1 Experimental Device

The experiment was conducted in a laboratory setting. Computer-generated experimental materials were utilized to control the experiment, and participants' responses were recorded.

The display used was an LCD touchscreen (size: 91*149 cm, resolution: 3840*2160 px, refresh rate: 60 Hz), with the screen tilted at a 90° angle (see Fig. 1). The interface display area measured 80*143.5 cm.

2.2 Experimental Variables and Design

Since the results of this study will be applied to scalable map design, two factors were considered:

- **Button size**, which had nine levels: 10 mm, 15 mm, 20 mm, 25 mm, 30 mm, 35 mm, 40 mm, 45 mm, and 50 mm.
- **Spacing between any two buttons**, which had four levels: 25, 50, 75, and 100 pixels. We believe there might be a trade-off between button size and the spacing between buttons.

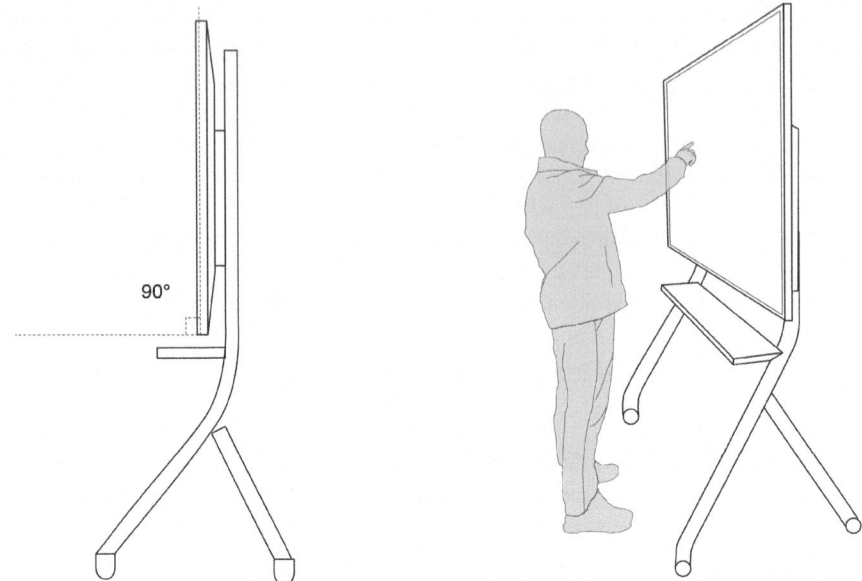

Fig. 1. Picture of experimental device

The dependent variables were the click accuracy rate and the right click time of the participants.

Control variables included lighting, display resolution, button display range, button color and shape, and others.

2.3 Participants

Twelve participants (6 female and 6 male) were selected in this experiment, stratified into two age groups: 5 participants (2 female and 3 male) aged 55 and above, and 7 participants (4 female and 3 male) aged 25 to 55.

All of the participants had no color blindness or color weakness, and their visual acuity or corrected visual acuity was above 5.0, all were right-handed.

2.4 Experimental Materials and Tasks

On the computer screen, a row of 9 buttons is presented at the top as stimuli. These buttons consist of 9-digit buttons, with their order randomized for each trial to prevent learning effects and ensure the reliability of the results.

In the middle of the screen is the testing area, which also comprises 9-digit buttons arranged in a 3 x 3 matrix from 1 to 9. This setup ensures a clear and consistent visual layout, allowing participants to focus solely on the task without being distracted by a changing interface.

Participants are instructed to sequentially point and select the button in the testing area that corresponds to the stimuli row displayed at the top. The size and spacing of the buttons in the testing area vary in each trial, which introduces a level of complexity and tests the adaptability of the participants to different interface designs. The reaction time and percentage of correct inputs for each button are automatically recorded by computer software, providing precise and objective data for analysis. Figure 2 illustrates a sample interface of the experimental task, demonstrating the arrangement of the stimuli and testing areas.

The task of the participants was to click the corresponding button as quickly as possible, in accordance with the numbers appearing at the top of the screen. This required both speed and accuracy, as the participants needed to match the stimuli with the correct button in the testing area. The varying button sizes and spacing tested their ability to adapt to different interface configurations, reflecting real-world scenarios where drag-and-drop maps interfaces can vary significantly.

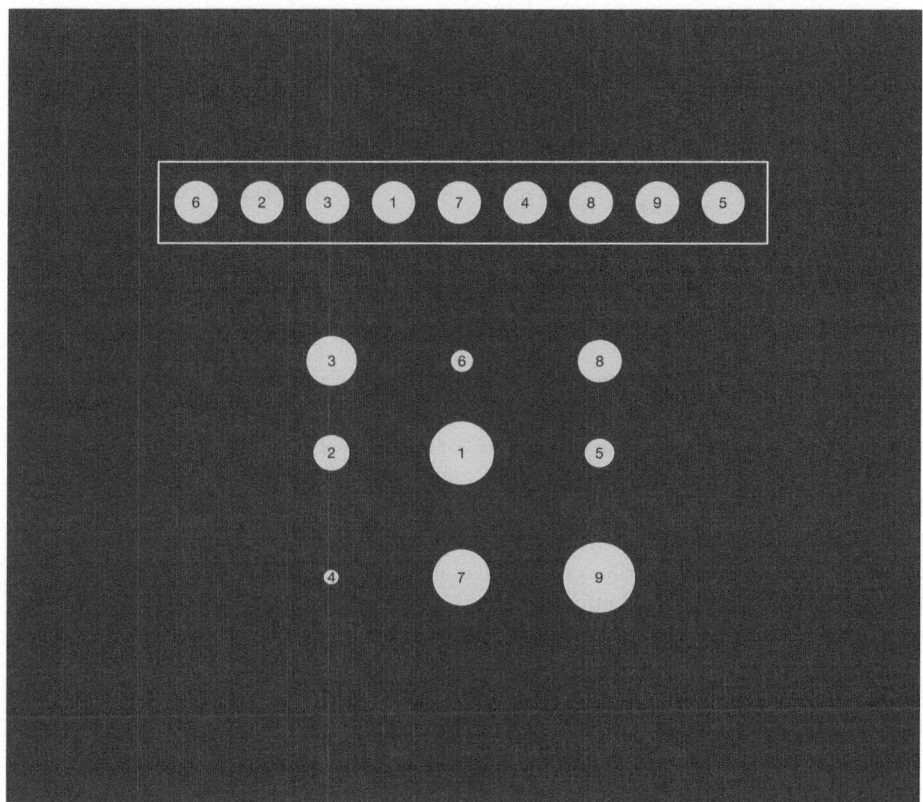

Fig. 2. Sample experimental task screen

2.5 Experiment Process

After entering the laboratory, the participants first adjusted their standing position to ensure their eye height was approximately 165 cm from the groundand their line of sight was around 65 cm.

During the experiment, participants used their right hand for all operations.

Before the formal experiment began, participants were informed of the experimental procedures and were given the option to stop at any time. After signing the informed consent form, the instructions were displayed in the middle of the screen, and participants filled in the required information according to the experimental guidelines. Under the guidance of the experimenter, participants then started practice experiments until they felt confident in their understanding of the tasks. The practice experiments were identical to the formal experimental procedures and were primarily used to help participants become familiar with the experimental setup and tasks.

In the formal experiment, participants completed 36 tasks according to the prompts displayed on the screen. After completing each set of tasks, they rested for three minutes to alleviate eye fatigue. They then continued to complete the next set of 36 tasks. This cycle of task completion and rest was repeated, resulting in a total of 10 sets of tasks.

At the conclusion of the experiment, each participant had completed a total of 360 tasks. The operation time for each task was limited to 10 s; if a task took longer than 10 s, it was automatically marked as a failure.

3 Results

3.1 Click Response Time for Different Button Sizes

The click response time for buttons of different sizes was analyzed. Experimental results reveal a negative correlation between response time and button size across both age groups. Specifically, larger button sizes are associated with shorter response times.

As illustrated in Fig. 3, response times ranged from 900 ms to 2600 ms. In general, the younger participant group exhibited superior response times compared to the older participant group. The maximum response time was observed for the 10 mm button size across all participants, regardless of age. Notably, for both age groups, a button size of 30 mm yielded significantly better response times compared to a button size of 25 mm, identifying 30 mm as a crucial design parameter for enhancing response time efficiency.

For the younger participant group, the differences in response times diminished progressively as the button size increased beyond 30 mm. This suggests that increasing the button size above 30 mm does not lead to substantial improvements in response time for younger users. Conversely, for the older participant group, the response time curve plateaued when the button size exceeded 40 mm. This indicates that enlarging the button size beyond 40 mm does not significantly enhance response time performance for older users.

The findings on the click response time for buttons of different sizes indicate that, for designing drag-and-drop maps on the target LCD touchscreen, the minimum button size for click operations should be no less than 30 mm. For designs intended for users across multiple age groups, maintaining a button size within the range of 30 mm to 40 mm is optimal.

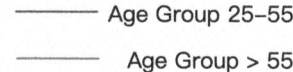

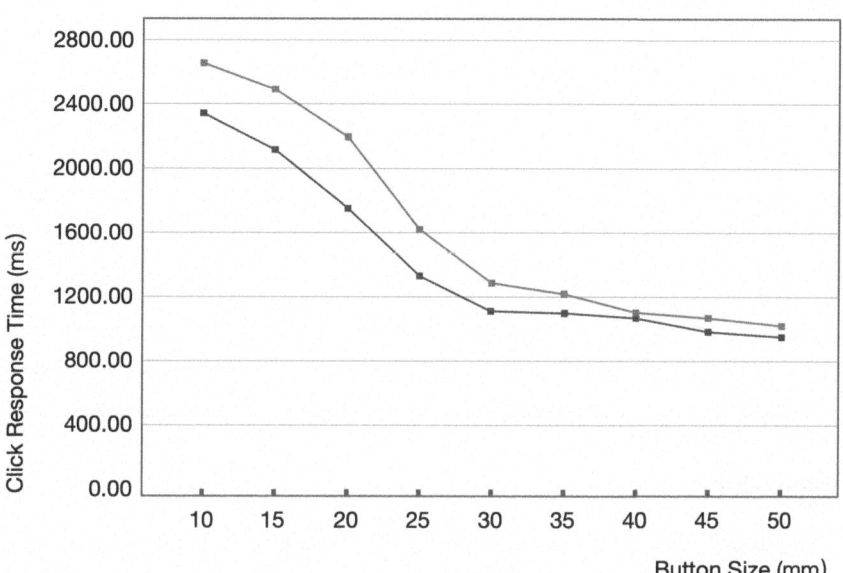

Fig. 3. Click response time for nine sizes of buttons

3.2 Click Accuracy for Different Button Sizes

The accuracy of clicking different button sizes was assessed. Results indicate that both age groups exhibited high accuracy rates (>97%) across all 9 button types tested. Moreover, larger button sizes were associated with higher accuracy rates.

The interaction between button spacing and button size demonstrated significant effects on user performance. Specifically, the percentage of correct inputs was lowest when the button size was smallest. As button size increased, the percentage of correct inputs showed a variable increase, stabilizing when the button size reached 35 mm. This suggests that increasing button size up to a certain threshold significantly enhances accuracy, beyond which additional increases provide diminishing returns.

Moreover, minimal button spacing resulted in the lowest percentage of correct inputs, indicating that closely spaced buttons hinder user accuracy. As both button size and spacing increased, input performance improved variably. Notably, when button spacing reached 75 and 100 pixels, the percentage of correct inputs remained almost constant. This indicates that there is an optimal range for button spacing that, once achieved, does not significantly benefit from further increases (Fig. 4).

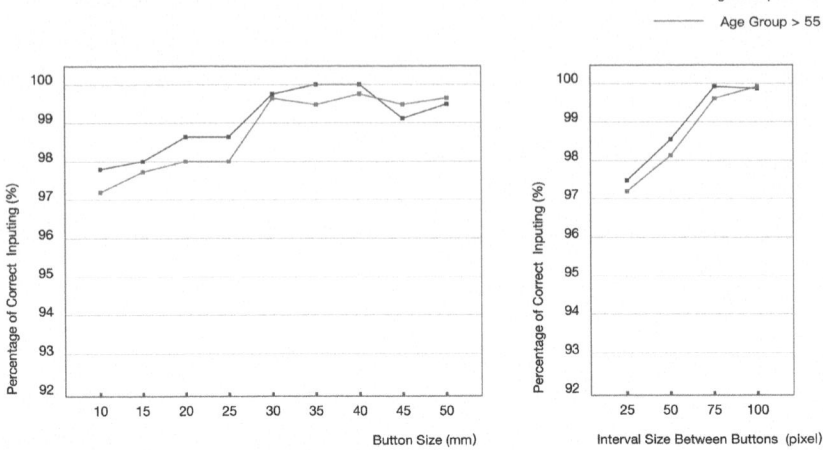

Fig. 4. Percentage of Correct Inputs Between Button Size and Interval Size

4   Discussion

The research underscores the critical importance of selecting appropriate button sizes to enhance user interaction efficiency on large touchscreens. The analysis of click response times revealed that smaller button sizes, particularly those below 30 mm, significantly increase response times and reduce overall user performance. This finding is pivotal for ensuring swift and accurate user interactions with touchscreen interfaces, especially in applications involving drag-and-drop maps.

For designs intended for multi-age groups, a button size between 30 mm and 40 mm strikes an optimal balance, catering to both younger and older users. Younger users exhibit optimal performance with a 30 mm button size, while older users benefit from slightly larger buttons, with 40 mm being the most effective. Thus, setting the button size within this range accommodates the varying needs of different age demographics, thereby enhancing usability and accessibility.

Furthermore, these findings highlight the necessity of carefully considering both button size and spacing in touchscreen interface design. For optimal user performance, particularly in tasks requiring precise interactions such as drag-and-drop maps, button sizes should be designed to be at least 35 mm. This size ensures that users can accurately select the correct input with minimal error.

Similarly, the optimal button spacing falls within the range of 75 to 100 pixels. Maintaining button spacing within this range maximizes user accuracy without necessitating excessive screen real estate. Designers should aim to balance button size and spacing to enhance usability while ensuring the interface remains efficient and visually uncluttered.

5   Conclusion

This study highlights the importance of button size and spacing in enhancing user interaction on large touchscreens. Findings indicate that button sizes below 30 mm significantly increase response times and reduce performance, while a size range of 30 mm to 40 mm optimally serves both younger and older users. Furthermore, button spacing between 75 and 100 pixels maximizes accuracy without excessive screen space usage.

For drag-and-drop map interface design, ensuring button sizes of at least 35 mm and maintaining optimal spacing is crucial for user accuracy and efficiency. These design suggestions will enhance usability and accessibility across diverse user groups, improving overall interaction with touchscreen interfaces.

In conclusion, the careful consideration of button size and spacing is essential for the development of effective touchscreen interfaces. Future research could further explore adaptive design strategies that dynamically adjust these parameters based on individual user needs and preferences, ensuring an even more personalized and efficient user interaction.

Acknowledgments. This study was funded by grant MH20231408.

Disclosure of Interests. Author has received research grants from Tianjin Northern Surveying and Mapping Co., Ltd.

References

1. Tao, D., Yuan, J., Shuang, L., Xingda, Q., Chen, X.: The effects of button characteristics on the usability of touch screen devices in input tasks. Ergonomics **022**(005), 1–6 (2016)
2. Human Factors and Ergonomics Society. American National Standard for Human Factors Engineering of Computer Workstations (ANSI/HFES Standard No. 100–2007); Human Factors & Ergonomics Society: Santa Monica, CA, USA (2007)
3. ISO 9241–9. Ergonomic requirements for office work with visual display terminals (VDTs) – Part 9: Requirements for non-keyboard input devices **2000**(2000), 54 (2000)
4. Jin, Z.X., Plocher, T., Kiff, L.: Touch screen user interfaces for older adults: button size and spacing. In: Proceedings of the International Conference on Universal Access in Human-computer Interaction, pp. 933–941 (2007)
5. Yu, N., Ouyang, Z., Wang, H., Tao, D., Jing, L.: The effects of smart home interface touch button design features on performance among young and senior users. Int. J. Environ. Res. Public Health **19**, 2391 (2022)
6. Chourasia, A.O., Wiegmann, D.A., Chen, K.B., Irwin, C.B., Sesto, M.E.: Effect of sitting or standing on touch screen performance and touch characteristics. Hum. Factors: J. Hum. Factors Ergon. Soc. **55**, 789–802 (2013)

Author Index

M. Antona et al. (Eds.): HCII 2024, LNCS 15379, pp. 313–314, 2025.
https://doi.org/10.1007/978-3-031-76818-7

GPSR Compliance

The European Union's (EU) General Product Safety Regulation (GPSR) is a set of rules that requires consumer products to be safe and our obligations to ensure this.

If you have any concerns about our products, you can contact us on ProductSafety@springernature.com

In case Publisher is established outside the EU, the EU authorized representative is:

Springer Nature Customer Service Center GmbH
Europaplatz 3
69115 Heidelberg, Germany

The manufacturer's authorised representative in the EU is Springer
Nature Customer Service Centre GmbH, Europaplatz 3, 69115 Heidelberg,
Germany. If you have any concerns regarding our products, please
contact ProductSafety@springernature.com

Printed and bound by CPI Group (UK) Ltd, Croydon, CR0 4YY

29/04/2026

02099532-0005